Complementary and Alternative Medicine for Psychologists

Complementary and Alternative Medicine for Psychologists

An Essential Resource

Jeffrey E. Barnett

Allison J. Shale

Gary Elkins

William Fisher

American Psychological Association

Washington, DC

Published by
American Psychological Association
750 First Street, NE
Washington, DC 20002
www.apa.org

To order
APA Order Department
P.O. Box 92984
Washington, DC 20090-2984
Tel: (800) 374-2721; Direct: (202) 336-5510
Fax: (202) 336-5502; TDD/TTY: (202) 336-6123
Online: www.apa.org/pubs/books
E-mail: order@apa.org

In the U.K., Europe, Africa, and the Middle East, copies may be ordered from
American Psychological Association
3 Henrietta Street
Covent Garden, London
WC2E 8LU England

Typeset in Goudy by Circle Graphics, Inc., Columbia, MD

Printer: Maple Press, York, PA
Cover Designer: Minker Design, Sarasota, FL

The opinions and statements published are the responsibility of the authors, and such opinions and statements do not necessarily represent the policies of the American Psychological Association.

Library of Congress Cataloging-in-Publication Data

Barnett, Jeffrey E., author.
  Complementary and alternative medicine for psychologists : an essential resource /
Jeffrey E. Barnett, Allison J. Shale, Gary Elkins, and William Fisher. — First edition.
     p. ; cm.
  Includes bibliographical references and index.
  ISBN 978-1-4338-1749-6 — ISBN 1-4338-1749-7
  I. Shale, Allison J., author. II. Elkins, Gary Ray, 1952- author. III. Fisher, William
(William I.), author. IV. American Psychological Association, issuing body. V. Title.
  [DNLM: 1. Mental Disorders—therapy. 2. Complementary Therapies—methods.
3. Complementary Therapies—psychology. WM 400]
  RC480.53
  616.8906—dc23
                              2014000557

British Library Cataloguing-in-Publication Data
A CIP record is available from the British Library.

Printed in the United States of America
First Edition

http://dx.doi.org/10.1037/14435-000

To my colleagues and friends—the faculty, students, and administrators at Loyola University Maryland: For providing me with such a supportive and stimulating environment in which to live and work.
—*Jeffrey E. Barnett*

To my parents and my husband: For all of the changes, moves, and adjustments in the past few years, I thank you three for remaining consistently supportive, encouraging, and loving.
—*Allison J. Shale*

To the students, postdoctoral fellows, and staff in the Mind–Body Medicine Research Laboratory at Baylor University.
—*Gary Elkins*

To my daughter, Isabel Fisher, my source of inspiration and greatest joy.
—*William Fisher*

CONTENTS

ACKNOWLEDGMENTS

The authors express their sincere appreciation to Susan Reynolds, senior acquisitions editor at American Psychological Association (APA) Books, for her initial interest in a handbook on complementary and alternative medicine for psychologists and for her encouragement and support in the early stages of development of this book. The initial support, feedback, and guidance received were invaluable. We also express deep appreciation to Judy Barnes, editorial manager at APA Books, for so thoughtfully and skillfully guiding us through the revision process, helping us to greatly improve on our initial submission. Both Susan and Judy played key roles in helping to bring out our best writing. We further express our appreciation to our outstanding production editor, Elizabeth Brace, whose guidance and support were invaluable. We also express our thanks to our copy editor, Elizabeth Sirimarco Budd, whose thoughtful feedback helped improve this book, and to our cover designer, Janet Minker of Minker Design, whose creativity is greatly appreciated.

Acknowledgment and gratitude are also expressed to the research team at the Mind–Body Medicine Research Laboratory at Baylor University for their contributions and recommendations, including Savanah Gosnell; Cassie

Kendrick, PsyD; Jim Sliwinski, MA; Aimee Johnson, MA; Kimberly Hickman, MSCP; Yimin Yu, MSCP; Nicholas Olendzki, MSCP; Juliette Bowers, MSCP; and Vicki Patterson, BA. Finally, we express our most sincere appreciation to Jeffrey Lating, PhD, and Matthew Kirkhart, PhD, for their thoughtful feedback on drafts of our early writing on complementary and alternative medicine as well as for their valuable encouragement and support.

Complementary and Alternative Medicine for Psychologists

INTRODUCTION

The aim of this book is to provide psychologists with a convenient and comprehensive guide to the field of complementary and alternative medicine (CAM), its domains and primary modalities, the ethics of integrating CAM into psychological practice, and a critical review of the quality of the current evidence for each commonly used modality. CAM comprises a group of diverse medical and health care systems, practices, and products that are not currently considered part of conventional medicine (P. M. Barnes, Powell-Griner, McFann, & Nahin, 2004). Defining CAM can be challenging because the field is broad and perpetually evolving; it includes diverse practices such as yoga, mindfulness meditation, acupuncture, and herbal therapies, as well as whole systems approaches such as traditional Chinese medicine. Furthermore, a distinction can be made between complementary medicine and alternative medicine. The National Institutes of Health's (NIH) National Center for Complementary and Alternative Medicine (NCCAM) defines *complementary*

http://dx.doi.org/10.1037/14435-001
Complementary and Alternative Medicine for Psychologists: An Essential Resource, by J. E. Barnett, A. J. Shale, G. Elkins, and W. Fisher

medicine as interventions used together with conventional treatment regimens, whereas *alternative medicine* consists of interventions that are used in place of conventional medical practice (NIH, 2011h).

There has been substantial interest in both complementary and alternative therapies among health care providers in recent years, and research into their potential efficacy has also been on the rise. The undaunted popularity, study, and development of CAM practice led to, in October 1991, the U.S. Congress passing legislation (Public Law 102-170) that provided funding to establish an office within the NIH to investigate and evaluate promising unconventional practices. Dr. Joseph Jacobs was appointed the first director of the Office of Alternative Medicine (OAM) in October 1992. In October 1998, Congress established NCCAM (Public Law 105-277), elevating the OAM to an NIH Center, and in 1999, NCCAM was made the 25th independent component of NIH. In 2012, the NCCAM appropriation was $128 million. The mission of NCCAM is to define, through rigorous scientific investigation, the usefulness and safety of complementary and alternative medicine interventions and their roles in improving health and health care (NIH, 2012j).

The use of both complementary and alternative therapies is increasing. They may be used by individuals on their own or as recommended by a health care provider. In addition, there has been greater recognition that many CAM modalities may be of potential benefit in the treatment of emotional and psychological concerns. As a result, it has become increasingly necessary and important for psychologists to be knowledgeable about the most frequently used forms of CAM to inform their patients and to potentially integrate CAM into clinical practice. Both adults and children may use CAM and it is important to understand the prevalence of its use when integrating CAM into psychological practice.

USE OF CAM AMONG U.S. ADULTS AND CHILDREN

The NCCAM and the National Center for Health Statistics (NCHS), part of the Centers for Disease Control and Prevention, released findings from the 2007 National Health Interview Survey (NHIS; P. M. Barnes, Bloom, & Nahin, 2008). The NHIS included questions on 36 types of CAM therapies commonly used in the United States—10 types of provider-based therapies, such as acupuncture and chiropractic, and 26 other therapies that do not require a provider, such as herbal supplements and meditation. The survey results, released in a National Health Statistics Report by NCHS, were based on data from more than 23,300 interviews with American adults and more than 9,400 interviews with adults on behalf of a child in their household. This survey was the second conducted by NCCAM, with the first done as part of the 2002 NHIS. Results of this survey revealed that in the United States, 38.3% of adults and 12% of children (approximately one in nine) were using some form of CAM (P. M. Barnes et al., 2008). This number represents a growing trend from a 2002 survey of CAM, which showed that 36% of U.S. adults had used CAM (P. M. Barnes et al., 2004; see Figure 1). Given that people are most likely to use a CAM therapy for treatment of some concern such as pain, anxiety, insomnia, or depression, the use of CAM among adults who seek medical or psychological consultation may be even higher (Astin, 1998).

The use of CAM cuts across ethnic and racial lines. CAM use by race and ethnicity ranges from more than 50% to approximately 24% (see Figure 2). It is likely that cultural factors and background contribute to the frequency and type of CAM therapy used. American Indians/Alaska Natives reported the highest use (50.3%), with White (43.1%) and Asian (39.9%) respondents also showing high rates of CAM use. Black and Hispanic respondents reported the lowest rate of CAM use (25.5% and 23.7%, respectively).

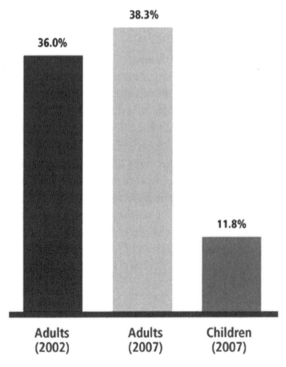

Figure 1. Complementary and alternative medicine use by U.S. adults (2002 and 2007) and children (2007). Data from Barnes, Bloom, and Nahin, 2008.

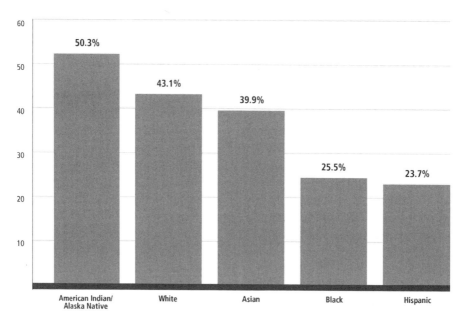

Figure 2. Complementary and alternative medicine use by race/ethnicity among adults—2007. Data from Barnes, Bloom, and Nahin, 2008.

Research has also examined the frequency with which various types of CAM modalities are used. The most commonly used CAM in 2007 (see Figure 3) was natural products (17.7%), followed by deep breathing (12.7%), meditation (9.4%), and chiropractic and osteopathic care (8.6%). Homeopathic treatments were reported as the least commonly used forms of CAM (1.8%). Consistent with results from the NHIS in 2002 (P. M. Barnes et al., 2004), CAM use was more prevalent among women, adults ages 30 to 69, adults with higher levels of education, adults who were not poor, adults living in the western United States, former smokers, and adults who were hospitalized in the past year (P. M. Barnes et al., 2008). Furthermore, in both the 2002 and 2007 samples, adults under age 70 were more likely to use alternative medical therapies compared with adults over age 70. Least likely to use CAM were uninsured adults (4.0%) or adults with private health insurance (3.9%; P. M. Barnes et al., 2008).

WHY PSYCHOLOGISTS NEED TO BE KNOWLEDGEABLE ABOUT CAM

Psychologists in clinical practice are especially well positioned to iden-tify and monitor their clients' use of CAM, to provide recommendations based on relevant research findings, and, where appropriate, to integrate

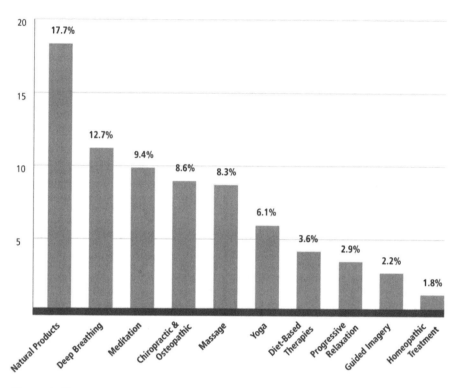

Figure 3. Ten most commonly used complementary and alternative medicine therapies among adults—2007. Data from Barnes, Bloom, and Nahin, 2008.

CAM therapies into treatment for particular symptoms or disorders. Many individuals use CAM modalities, and the use among individuals who seek psychotherapy may be even higher than in the general population. For example, a survey of 262 psychotherapy clients (Elkins, Marcus, Rajab, & Durgam, 2005) revealed that 64% of respondents reported using at least one CAM modality. The most frequently used CAM modalities were mind–body therapies (44%), followed by herbal therapies (34%), physical modalities (21%), spiritual modalities (17%), and special diet (14%). The respondents most often used CAM modalities for anxiety, depression, insomnia, or fatigue. However, only 34% reported that they had discussed their use of CAM with their psychotherapist (Elkins et al., 2005). There is reason to believe that many patients who seek psychotherapy may also use complementary and alternative therapies with or without the knowledge of their psychotherapists (Knaudt, Connor, Weisler, Churchill, & Davidson, 1999). These findings point to the importance of determining the interest and use of CAM therapies among clients who seek psychotherapy for problems such as anxiety or depression. Additionally, it has been suggested that CAM modalities can be used to enhance the effectiveness of standard psychological practice (Dittman, 2004).

Psychologists who are knowledgeable about CAM can make informed decisions about when it is appropriate to integrate a CAM modality into treatment as well as when referral to a CAM practitioner is indicated. As interest in CAM has increased, so has research into CAM interventions as they relate to psychological practice. Depression, anxiety, fatigue, insomnia, and chronic pain, concerns for which clients often seek psychotherapy, are among the most commonly cited reasons for the use of complementary and alternative therapies (Astin, 1998; Eisenberg et al., 1993). CAM modalities used to treat anxiety and depression range from acupuncture (Wang & Kain, 2001) and exercise (Martinsen, Hoffart, & Solberg, 1989) to herbals (Shelton et al., 2001) and mindfulness meditation (Miller, Fletcher, & Kabat-Zinn, 1995). In an epidemiological survey, Kessler et al. (2001) reported that 65.9% of respondents with self-defined anxiety attacks and 66.7% of respondents with self-defined severe depression used CAM therapies. A greater understanding of the role of CAM therapies as an adjunct to standard psychotherapy is needed because many clients who seek treatment in psychotherapy also use CAM therapies, and psychologists are often in a position both to advance knowledge in this area by conducting research or integrating these therapies into clinical practice.

INTEGRATION OF CAM INTO PSYCHOLOGICAL PRACTICE

Psychologists wishing to integrate CAM into clinical practice may find it helpful to include specific inquiries about CAM use in intake interviews and review of patients' health-related behaviors. The following are some standard questions to review CAM use.

We are interested in whether you are using any type of complementary and alternative medicine, such as herbs, massage, meditation, mind–body therapies, or acupuncture. Please answer the following questions:

- What are your primary concerns in seeking psychological care?
- Are you currently receiving any care from any complementary and alternative medicine practitioners?
- Are you taking any vitamins, minerals, herbs, or supplements? If yes, how much, how often, and for what concern? Are you benefiting? Are you experiencing any negative results or reactions?
- What previous experience have you had with any complementary and alternative therapy?
- Do you use any type of mind–body therapy or supplement to relax or cope with stress? If so, what do you use?

- Do you use any complementary and alternative therapy to help with your sleep, fatigue, pain, anxiety, depression, or any other concern? If yes, please explain.

Psychologists who advise patients about CAM use need to be aware of supporting or disconfirming research related to specific modalities. Patients may have questions about the expected benefits from CAM treatments as well as the associated risks, such as potential side effects. Clients may have questions regarding how many sessions are required for CAM modalities such as meditation, yoga, acupuncture, or biofeedback. Each chapter in this book provides specific recommendations for psychologists on a given modality, although when advising clients on any use of CAM, we recommend bearing the following general considerations in mind.

ADVISING PATIENTS ABOUT CAM

When advising clients about CAM use, it is important to consider and convey to clients the available information and research regarding efficacy, risks, benefits, and cost. A significant percentage of the population uses CAM, and Americans are spending a substantial amount of their discretionary income on these therapies. Of the $2.2 trillion in total health care spending in the United States in 2007, out-of-pocket spending on CAM equated $33.9 billion compared with $268.6 billion spent out-of-pocket on conventional medicine. Even if clients are insured, it is likely that their insurance does not cover most, if any, CAM therapies. As a result, most CAM treatments are paid for out of pocket (P. M. Barnes et al., 2008). CAM pricing can vary widely among practitioners because fees for most CAM providers are not regulated. It may be helpful for psychologists to advise their clients to ascertain the following: In terms of costs, what does the first appointment cost? What do follow-up appointments cost? Are there additional costs in terms of tests or supplements? Does the provider accept the client's insurance plan? Does the provider have a history of successful payment from the client's insurance provider? Who files the insurance claims? Is there any possibility of a payment plan or sliding scale?

ETHICAL IMPLICATIONS OF CAM

A host of ethical considerations are unique to CAM, sufficient that Chapter 3 in this book, "Ethical Issues and CAM in Mental Health Care Practice," is devoted to helping psychologists understand the issues involved.

The American Psychological Association (2010) "Ethical Principles of Psychologists and Code of Conduct" are particularly relevant in considering CAM research because there is inconclusive research and a lack of standardization in the training and certification of various CAM modalities. A complex issue inherent to CAM is whether psychologists can or should provide CAM therapies themselves. In some cases, with appropriate certification and training, it may be a useful addition to a psychotherapeutic repertoire; however, integration into psychological practice must be carefully considered because there are strong risks of conflicts of interest and violation of boundaries. For example, providing massage to a client, regardless of adequate licensure and certification, represents an inappropriate boundary violation, and we posit that it is unethical. As it is for the emerging field of telepsychology, the range of ethical considerations for CAM is extensive; readers are urged to consider the issues raised in the ethics chapter carefully before recommending a CAM product, referring a client to a CAM practitioner, or integrating CAM therapies into their own practice. Ethics issues and considerations are interwoven throughout the text.

HOW TO USE THIS BOOK

Complementary and Alternative Medicine for Psychologists: An Essential Resource provides readers the basic information they need to become familiar with CAM therapies, provides a critical review of current evidence for each commonly used CAM modality, and advises whether evidence currently supports recommendation. This text is a convenient resource that psychologists can use to familiarize themselves with the field of CAM as well as its domains and primary modalities. It also addresses key issues to consider when integrating CAM into psychological practice.

Chapters 1, 2, and 3 provide, respectively, the basics and fundamentals of CAM and its use, an analysis of ethics issues relevant to the use of CAM, and a general review of research on CAM, together with a discussion of how to thoughtfully interpret CAM research findings. We recommend reading these chapters first before delving into the more specific chapters that focus on individual CAM therapies.

Chapters 4 through 17 can each be read individually as needed or in order to learn about the essentials of CAM for psychologists. These chapters follow a standard format that includes an overview, definitions, a brief history, common uses, technique, mechanism of action, relevant research, contraindications and risks, tips for practitioners, and a discussion of integration with psychological practice. Additionally, information is provided on key resources, training, and certification needed to effectively practice the modality, areas in which the CAM modality is likely to be most effective, and what to look for in a CAM professional to whom one may refer a client.

We also included useful resources on how to educate oneself about specific CAM modalities. The chapters are organized within the broad categories of (a) mind–body therapies, (b) biologically based therapies, (c) manipulative and body-based therapies, and (d) energy medicine and whole medical systems, each of which are defined and explained in detail in Chapter 1, "Foundations of Complementary and Alternative Medicine." The CAM modalities included in this text were selected on the basis of frequency of use, availability of peer-reviewed literature, and relevance to psychological practice. Although no one resource can address every possible CAM modality or issue, this guidebook provides a reference on the major CAM modalities and provides a wide range of valuable information for practicing psychologists in their clinical work with their clients.

Throughout this book the words *patient* and *client* are used interchangeably because people who use CAM are referred to by both terms. The terms *modality* and *therapy* are also used interchangeably in the discussion of CAM treatments because they are also commonly referred to by both terms.

I

FOUNDATIONS

1

FOUNDATIONS OF COMPLEMENTARY AND ALTERNATIVE MEDICINE

The therapies that currently lie under the umbrella of complementary and alternative medicine (CAM) have a rich and varied history, with some therapies developed relatively recently and others dating back thousands of years. For example, the first written documentation of Traditional Chinese Medicine (TCM), a CAM categorized as a whole medical system (WMS), is in the *Huang Di nei jing* or *Yellow Emperor's Cannon of Internal Medicine*, dating from approximately 800 B.C.E. (Unschuld, 2003). It has been suggested that CAM practice, as an alternative form of treatment to conventional or orthodox medical practice and product of the time, began in the late 1700s; however, this practice was not described in the medical literature until the 1800s, when it was referred to as *irregular medicine*, reflecting that the first organized systems of care evolved in reaction to dissatisfaction with the confusion and often erroneous formulations of the orthodox medicine of the time (Whorton, 2006). Herbal therapies and hypnosis for treating psychological

http://dx.doi.org/10.1037/14435-002
Complementary and Alternative Medicine for Psychologists: An Essential Resource, by J. E. Barnett, A. J. Shale, G. Elkins, and W. Fisher

or physical problems were among the first popular CAM treatments of the late 1700s and early 1800s. Also, with the development of osteopathy, the practice of manual and manipulative therapy to facilitate the body's ability to heal itself began to emerge in the early 1870s. Although detailed information about the history and development of the individual modalities is discussed in the therapy chapters, it is apparent that the popularity, study, and development of CAM practices have increased exponentially since the late 20th century.

FOUNDATIONS

Because of its vast and diverse constituency, CAM has been classified using several different paradigms (Tataryn, 2002). Although there is some criticism of this categorical framework as lacking a robust typological system, the National Institutes of Health (NIH) National Center for Complementary and Alternative Medicine's (NCCAM) five-domain model serves as an excellent starting point for considering the breadth and scope of CAM and serves as the organizational schema for this handbook. The five-domain model includes: *mind–body medicine, biologically based practices, manipulative and body-based practices, energy medicine,* and *whole medical systems.*

MIND–BODY MEDICINE

The concept that the mind is important in health and illness dates back to ancient times. The role of the mind and its role in health and illness began to reenter Western health care in the 20th century, led by discoveries about pain control via the placebo effect and effects of stress on health (NIH, 2010). NCCAM defines *mind–body medicine* as comprising practices that focus on the interactions among the brain, mind, body, and behavior, with the use of the mind to promote health (NIH, 2008). Mind–body medicine also includes the ways in which emotional, mental, social, spiritual, experiential, and behavioral factors can directly affect health (NIH, 2010b). The 2007 National Health Interview Survey (NHIS) found that 19.2% of American adults and 4.3% of children ages 17 or younger had used at least one CAM mind–body therapy in the year before the survey (P. M. Barnes, Bloom, & Nahin, 2008). Examples of mind–body medicine include mindfulness meditation, hypnosis, tai chi, and yoga, although tai chi and yoga may also be considered part of TCM and Ayurveda, two examples of whole medical systems. Part II of this book, "Mind–Body Therapies," includes chapters on biofeedback, meditation, hypnosis, yoga, music therapy, and spirituality and prayer.

BIOLOGICALLY BASED PRACTICES

The CAM domain of biologically based practices includes, but is not limited to, the use of dietary supplements, including botanicals, animal-derived extracts, vitamins, minerals, dietary supplements or "herbals," fatty acids, amino acids, proteins, pre- and postbiotics, and regimens such as whole diets and the use of functional foods (NIH, 2007a)."Functional foods can be considered to be those whole, fortified, enriched or enhanced foods that provide health benefits beyond the provision of essential nutrients (e.g., vitamins and minerals), when they are consumed at efficacious levels as part of a varied diet on a regular basis" (Hasler, 2002, p. 3772). Examples of functional foods and their benefits include soy to lower cholesterol and reduce the risk of cardiovascular disease, and flaxseed and tomatoes to reduce the risk of certain cancers, among others (Hasler, 2014). The Office of Dietary Supplements (2011), part of the NIH, defines *botanicals* as plants or parts of plants valued for medicinal or therapeutic properties, flavor, scent, or a combination of these. Herbal products are a subset of botanicals. The regulation of supplement products and dietary ingredients is performed by the U.S. Food and Drug Administration (FDA) and differs from that concerning "conventional" foods and drug products (prescription and over the counter). Under the Dietary Supplement Health and Education Act of 1994, dietary supplement or dietary ingredient manufacturers are responsible for ensuring that their products are safe before marketing and that labeling is considered "truthful and not misleading." However, there are no specific requirements to demonstrate the efficacy and safety of these products (FDA, 2012), although there is some regulation of quality control of dietary supplements. In June 2007, a U.S. federal regulation (FDA Final Rule 21 CFR 111) was enacted that requires all domestic and foreign companies that manufacture, package, label, or distribute dietary supplements to comply with the Dietary Supplement Current Good Manufacturing Practices for quality control (FDA, 2012).

With many dietary supplements, such as herbal products, being marketed under the auspices of being "natural," there are some potentially fallacious notions that these products are more wholesome, have fewer side effects, and/ or are more environmentally friendly than conventional Western medications. Many herbal products are advertised as having psychotropic effects and are used by consumers to allay a vast assortment of symptoms, such as anxiety, insomnia, and depression. Psychologists must remain particularly cognizant of their use because some herbal agents have been shown to have deleterious effects when used in tandem with conventional pharmacological practice. For example, St. John's wort (*Hypericum perforatum*) has been used to treat mild to moderate depression, but it has been shown to be associated with potentially serious negative side effects when combined with some antidepressants (Clauson, Santamarina, & Rutledge, 2008). Perhaps of particular relevance to psychologists working with patients who are taking antidepressants, evidence suggests that St John's wort may have a pharmacodynamic interaction with selective serotonin reuptake inhibitors and serotonin receptor agonists, resulting in an increased risk of adverse reactions (Henderson, Yue, Bergquist, Gerden, & Arlett, 2002).

Herbal supplements are widely used for problems such as depression, anxiety, pain, and poor sleep. In addition, aromatherapy has been used for problems such as anxiety, stress, and coping with illness. Part III of this book, "Biologically Based Practices," covers herbals and aroma therapy.

MANIPULATIVE AND BODY-BASED PRACTICES

NCCAM defines *manipulative and body-based practices* as therapies that "focus primarily on the structures and systems of the body, including the bones and joints, soft tissues, and circulatory and lymphatic systems" (NIH, 2008, p. 1). The two most commonly used therapies from this domain are spinal manipulation and massage.

Spinal manipulation, the use of hands or a device to apply a controlled force to a joint of the spine, is practiced by chiropractors, osteopathic physicians, naturopathic physicians, physical therapists, and some medical doctors (NIH, 2008). It is commonly used for the treatment of low-back pain, for example, and the treatment goal of spinal manipulation is to relieve pain and improve physical functioning. In 2007, chiropractic care, the therapy most synonymous with spinal manipulation, was found to be used by more than 18 million U.S. adults (approximately 8%) and more than 2 million children (approximately 3%; P. M. Barnes et al., 2008).

Another body-based practice is *massage therapy*, a term that represents a number of different techniques, including Swedish massage, sports massage, deep-tissue massage, and trigger point massage, to name a few. Generally, massage involves manipulation of the muscles and soft tissues using the hands, fingers, forearms, elbows, or feet. People use massage for a variety of health-related purposes: to relieve pain, rehabilitate sports injuries, reduce stress, increase relaxation, address anxiety and depression, and aid general well-being (NIH, 2006). Although research into the efficacy of massage therapy is limited, a 2008 Cochrane review of 13 clinical trials suggested that massage may be particularly useful for problems such as chronic back pain (Furlan, Imamura, Dryden, & Irvin, 2008).

Similarly, movement therapies such as dance and exercise have been used for problems such as chronic pain and stress-related disorders. Part IV of this book, "Manipulative and Body-Based Therapies," addresses each of these: chiropractic care, massage therapy, and movement therapy.

ENERGY MEDICINE

In the United States in 2002, it was estimated that 1,080,000 adults ages 18 years and older used *energy medicine*, which functions under the belief that human beings are infused with a subtle form of energy (*qi* in TCM, *ki* in the Japanese Kampo system, *doshas* in Ayurvedic medicine, etc.). Results of the 2007 NHIS show that this number had increased to 1,216,000 adults and 161,000 children (P. M. Barnes et al., 2008). NCCAM suggests that energy medicine is a domain that encompasses *veritable* (measurable) and *putative* (yet to be measured) energy fields. Veritable energies are suggested to use mechanical vibrations (e.g., sound), and electromagnetic forces, including visible light, magnetism, monochromatic radiation (e.g., laser), and rays from other parts of the electromagnetic spectrum (NIH, 2007c). Putative energy fields (also referred to as *biofields*) have, to date, defied measurement by reproducible methods. Energy therapists report that they can work with this subtle energy, observe it directly, and use it to effect changes in the physical body and influence health (NIH, 2007c). Practitioners posit that illness results from a disturbance of these energies. One example of practices that involve putative energy fields is Reiki.

Reiki is a complex energy therapy that includes healing touch and mobilization of energy fields. The popularity of therapies that involve the use of so-called energy fields suggests that psychotherapy clients may believe in or may be employing some aspect of energy medicine, even if not a formal aspect of Reiki or healing touch. At the same time, it should be noted that energy medicine therapies are among the most controversial of CAM practices because of insufficient, inconclusive, or methodologically questionable research.

WHOLE MEDICAL SYSTEMS

WMS, another form of CAM, have evolved independently from or parallel to allopathic (conventional) medical practice (NIH, 2004). Many of these practices involve systems of medicine that originated in particular cultures, such as TCM, or India's Ayurvedic medicine (NIH, 2004). WMS have been developed by Native American, African, Middle Eastern, Tibetan, and Central and South American cultures. A comprehensive digest of WMS would require a separate book or series of books; therefore, this handbook provides information on the therapies that are considered most relevant to psychologists, emphasizing those most commonly used or about which the greatest amount of research has been published. Specifically, this section covers TCM and Ayurveda.

Dating back to 200 B.C.E., TCM is a complete system of healing that views the body as a delicate balance of two opposing and inseparable forces: *yin* and *yang* (NIH, 2004). *Yin* has been described as the cold, slow, or passive principle, whereas *yang* represents the hot, active, or excited principle. The TCM practitioner posits that health is achieved by maintaining the body in a balanced state, with disease occurring as a result of internal imbalance. According to TCM practitioners, internal imbalance leads to blockage in the flow of *qi* energy and of blood along pathways, called *meridians* (NIH, 2004). Three main components—herbs, acupuncture, and massage—are used to help unblock *qi* and blood in patients, with the goal of bringing the body back into harmony and wellness. Each of these components of TCM is addressed in its own chapter.

Ayurvedic medicine is an Indian healing system; *Ayurveda* means "the science of life" (NIH, 2004, para. 3). Ayurveda texts claim that the sages who developed India's original systems of meditation and yoga developed the foundations of this medical system. This system places equal emphasis on the body, mind, and spirit, striving to restore the innate harmony of the individual (NIH, 2004). The primary Ayurvedic treatments are diet, exercise, meditation, herbs, massage, sunlight exposure, and controlled breathing. In India, Ayurvedic treatments have been developed for specific diseases (e.g., diabetes, neurological disorders), but, in many clinical trials of these treatments, methodological deficits have compromised the reliability of the published results (NIH, 2004). Ayurveda is addressed in this book as a representative WMS.

EVALUATION OF CAM THERAPIES

Psychologists who (a) understand how CAM practice can be integrated with psychotherapeutic treatment, (b) recognize appropriate qualifications in existing CAM practitioners to whom they can make referrals, and (c) have an understanding of the best available CAM research will be empowered to better serve their clients. It has been suggested that practicing psychologists who are clinically competent in evaluating and using CAM possess sufficient knowledge to be able to share viable treatment options and alternatives with clients, are able to thoughtfully discuss their relative merits and limitations, adhere to ethical principles and standards, make referrals when indicated, and integrate patients' preferred CAM modality into treatment when doing so is supported by published results from well-designed studies (Barnett & Shale, 2012).

2

ETHICAL ISSUES AND CAM IN MENTAL HEALTH CARE PRACTICE

As a health care professional, it is each psychologist's responsibility to have a broad range of knowledge, including evidence that informs practice and awareness of treatment options that may be beneficial. Complementary and alternative medicine (CAM) therapies are emerging as important treatment options for some patients. However, although using CAM in psychological practice can benefit clients, there are cautions and potential ethical issues to be aware of. Whether incorporating CAM directly into their own practice or simply giving advice or providing referrals to CAM practitioners, psychologists must be aware of the American Psychological Association (APA) ethical principles and standards from the "Ethical Principles of Psychologists and Code of Conduct" (APA Ethics Code; APA, 2010).

Ethical *principles* provide a guide for psychologists; they are not enforceable and can be thought of as aspirational in nature. In contrast, ethical *standards* refer to an enforceable code that sets minimal requirements for

http://dx.doi.org/10.1037/14435-003
Complementary and Alternative Medicine for Psychologists: An Essential Resource, by J. E. Barnett, A. J. Shale, G. Elkins, and W. Fisher

clinicians. Standards and principles direct practice and should be considered throughout a psychologist's work. Both should be applied regarding the use of CAM if psychologists are to function at the most ethical level and ensure that clients receive the best care possible.

ETHICAL PRINCIPLES

Psychologists must consider the general principles from the APA Ethics Code in all of their professional roles and activities. Although as noted, these five principles are not enforceable standards, psychologists should use them to guide their ethical decision making while always working to uphold these aspirational principles (APA, 2010). These principles are listed in Table 2.1.

With regard to CAM, these general principles are particularly pertinent because there is inconclusive research in many of the areas with regard to efficacy and what symptoms are best treated with each modality as well as a lack of standardization in the training and certification of those who practice various CAM modalities. Psychologists should aim to ensure that clients receive the most comprehensive and appropriate care possible. To do so, they

TABLE 2.1
APA Ethical Principles

APA Ethics code: general principles	Meaning for CAM treatments
Beneficence and nonmaleficence	Involves not exposing clients to unnecessary or ineffective treatment while always keeping their best interest in mind
Fidelity and responsibility	Involves psychologists upholding their obligations, which can be clearly outlined through the use of an informed consent process
Integrity	Carried out in how psychologists present information on various CAM treatments and sharing information about them to include contraindications and any lack of clear support for their use
Justice	In the context of CAM, psychologists should exercise informed judgment and "take precautions to ensure that their potential biases, the boundaries of their competence, and the limitations of their expertise do not lead to or condone unjust practices" (APA, 2010, p. 3)
Respect for people's rights and dignity	Emphasizes maintaining privacy and confidentiality while also being aware of and respecting individual differences related to diversity; this focus on diversity should include each client's CAM use as well as his or her beliefs about CAM

must educate clients, assist them in making informed treatment decisions, offer treatment alternatives consistent with their clinical needs, coordinate their care with other professionals, and make needed referrals to competent CAM practitioners when in the client's best interest.

ETHICAL STANDARDS

When considering the ethical standards included in the APA Ethics Code (APA, 2010), it is important to recognize that the overarching goal should always be to avoid harm (Standard 3.04, Avoiding Harm). The Ethics Code specifically states that "psychologists take reasonable steps to avoid harming" clients while also working to "minimize harm where it is foreseeable and unavoidable" (p. 6). Avoiding harm, based on Principle A—Beneficence and Nonmaleficence, is something that underlies many other standards, including those related to informed consent and competence, such that they are in place to ensure the highest quality of care and overall protection of clients. Certain Ethics Code Standards are particularly relevant when dealing with CAM, and it is vital that practitioners are aware of their specific ethical obligations.

Competence

Rodolfa et al. (2005) stated that competence is "generally understood to mean that a professional is qualified, capable, and able to understand and do certain things in an appropriate and effective manner. Simply having knowledge or skill is insufficient for someone to be considered competent" (p. 348). How one implements one's knowledge and skills, and doing so in an ethical and culturally sensitive manner, are important elements of clinical competence.

Standard 2.01a, Boundaries of Competence, states that psychologists must "provide services, teach, and conduct research with populations and in areas only within the boundaries of their competence" (APA, 2010, p. 5). Many CAM treatments do not have standardized training programs, and thus competence may be difficult to attain; this also makes it difficult for others to assess or verify a practitioner's competency. Therefore, psychologists should "undertake relevant education, training, supervised experience, consultation, or study" if they are interested in incorporating a new area of treatment into their clinical repertoire (APA, 2010, p. 5). If there is not a standardized training protocol, the clinician must work to obtain whatever training is available while keeping up with relevant literature and training standards (Standard 2.01e, Boundaries of Competence; APA, 2010). This standard articulates that "in those emerging areas in which generally recognized standards for preparatory training do not yet exist, psychologists nevertheless take reasonable steps to ensure the competence of their work and to protect clients . . . from harm" (APA, 2010, p. 5). Many CAM modalities do have a formalized license, certification, or other credential that would provide psychologists with a means of demonstrating competence. As such, it behooves psychologists to become apprised of these certifying agencies, their training programs, and standards before incorporating a particular modality.

Regardless of the techniques or modalities used, Standard 2.04, Bases for Scientific and Professional Judgments, requires that psychologists use established ideas and principles as the basis of their work. When using CAM, psychologists should be familiar with the relevant literature on each modality's uses, efficacy, contraindications, potential side effects, and how they may interact with other treatments a client may be receiving. Psychologists must also work to understand "factors associated with age, gender, gender identity, race, ethnicity, culture, national origin, religion, sexual orientation, disability, language, or socioeconomic status" because they are "essential for effective implementation of their services or research" (APA, 2010, p. 5). Each client's individual background, relevant beliefs, and treatment preferences must be respected. One particular factor to be considered in evaluating the appropriateness of CAM is the client's cultural background. CAM has a multicultural context because for some clients, the use of CAM may be deeply ingrained in their beliefs and practices.

Also relevant to competence is being aware of all reasonably available treatment options and alternatives relevant to a client's treatment needs. Clients should be made aware of, and educated about, all reasonably available treatments that "might be used to treat their presenting problem [and] it is arguable that we must . . . apprise them of these possibilities, even when the treatments are outside the domain of the [particular] psychologist" (Bassman & Uellendahl, 2003, p. 268). Although this information should always be included in the informed consent process, it is particularly important with regard to CAM because it highlights each psychologist's responsibility to be knowledgeable in these areas, even if not choosing to use the modalities. At a minimum, psychologists should have sufficient knowledge about various CAM modalities so that they can provide clients with the information needed to make informed treatment decisions, regardless of the provider.

Psychologists should also keep in mind that competence is not a static phenomenon. As new information becomes available about the use and potential limitations of CAM modalities, psychologists will need to keep abreast of these developments. They can do this by participating in continuing education opportunities and ongoing professional development activities as well as keeping current with the rapidly evolving professional literature.

Thus, being aware of developing research is necessary for psychologists to provide the best possible care (Standard, 2.03, Maintaining Competence; APA, 2010).

Making referrals and having the resources to do so appropriately is an important ethical obligation. Standard 3.09, Cooperation With Other Professionals, further highlights the need for competence and knowledge, particularly if psychologists recognize that they are not capable of providing the necessary care to meet a client's treatment needs. Having a knowledge base regarding CAM will allow practitioners to appropriately and adequately discuss and coordinate their clients' ongoing treatment with colleagues who may be providing CAM treatment, whereas a lack of such knowledge may limit the quality of care. It is important to remember that when consulting, one must only disclose pertinent information to protect clients' privacy, keeping unrelated information confidential (Standard 4.06, Consultations; APA, 2010) unless the client specifically consents to the release of the information. Collaborative care may also include treating a client with CAM while simultaneously providing psychotherapy, which could at times lead to inappropriate multiple relationships.

Boundaries and Multiple Relationships

One set of ethical issues and dilemmas that may arise when using CAM in conjunction with psychotherapy has to do with boundaries and multiple relationships; psychologists must ask themselves if it is appropriate to be the provider of both services (Standard 3.05, Multiple Relationships; APA, 2010). In certain instances, such as using meditation or hypnosis, it will likely be fitting to introduce some of the techniques into traditional psychotherapy when appropriately trained and competent to do so. Being aware of boundaries and openly discussing levels of comfort with clients will help to ensure that they feel they are being respected and treated appropriately. Including them in the decision-making process and providing them with a variety of options through open discussion of potential risks and benefits will help avoid potential harm. However, the integration of some CAM modalities, such as massage therapy, into psychotherapy, even if the psychologist is a competent and credentialed massage therapist, raises greater boundary challenges and difficulties. Although massage therapy may be beneficial to some patients, it is not appropriate for a psychologist to provide massage treatment to his or her psychotherapy client. Incorporating massage into treatment results in boundary violations that are likely to be harmful to the psychotherapy relationship as well as being ethically and clinically contraindicated. Therefore, referral to a massage therapist would be most appropriate if this modality is recommended.

Multiple relationships and boundaries have been increasingly studied because although there are certain violations that are explicitly clear, such as having a sexual relationship with a client, other instances, such as those that may arise with CAM, may require special awareness because "regardless of psychologists' good intentions, they may often find themselves in situations with no easily discerned 'right answer'" (J. E. Barnett, Lazarus, Vasquez, Moorehead-Slaughter, & Johnson, 2007, p. 402). Numerous boundary issues, including the use of touch with clients, can present psychologists with ethical dilemmas in which a number of factors contribute to the decision of whether the action is an acceptable boundary crossing or an inappropriate and harmful boundary violation (D. Smith & Fitzpatrick, 1995). Examples include the client's mental health history and clinical needs, the client's beliefs and preferences, whether the client welcomes the action, the clinician's intent, the likely impact on the client, among others.

In addition to considering these factors, psychologists should use the APA Ethics Code and consult with colleagues regarding CAM practices when confronted with ethical dilemmas. If these initial steps do not provide the answers that a clinician is seeking, it is important to know what the next steps should be (J. E. Barnett, Behnke, Rosenthal, & Koocher, 2007). Many ethical decision-making models are available that can help in this process.

J. E. Barnett and Johnson (2008) developed a 10-step decision-making model:

1. Clearly define the dilemma that is faced.
2. Determine who will be impacted and how.
3. Consult the APA Ethics Code.
4. Refer to the necessary laws, regulations, and guidelines.
5. Allow for personal reflection on feelings and competency related to the issue at hand.
6. Consult with colleagues.
7. Develop alternative courses of action.
8. Consider all possible outcomes for all those involved.
9. Further consult with colleagues as well as ethics boards.
10. Make a decision and then monitor and alter the plan as necessary.

There are several other ethical decision-making models, with some being more focused on practice and others more closely considering moral decisions; however, no one model can solve all potential ethical dilemmas (J. E. Barnett, Behnke, et al., 2007). We recommend that psychologists refer to Cottone and Claus (2000), who comprehensively reviewed other available decision-making models.

Fees and Financial Arrangements

Should a situation arise in which it is appropriate to serve as both the CAM practitioner and the psychotherapist for a client, it is important to address payment, especially if additional services lead to increased fees. Standard 6.04a, Fees and Financial Arrangements, states that a payment agreement should be worked out "as early as is feasible" in the professional relationship (APA, 2010, p. 9). Psychologists' fees must be "consistent with law," and psychologists should be up-front and honest about the costs of services (p. 9). If it is possible that there will be limits to the services provided as a result of financial constraints, psychologists must promptly inform the client (Standard 6.04d, Fees and Financial Arrangements; APA, 2010).

In addition to changes in the client's personal finances, an example of financial constraints is the role of managed care and insurance. Psychologists should not assume that all CAM modalities are reimbursable expenses under a client's health insurance policy. Before beginning treatment, it is important to initiate a discussion with the client about which CAM modalities are indeed covered because clients who are not well-versed in insurance policies may assume that all practices are supported. It is best to first confirm which services will be covered, include this information in the client's informed consent discussions, and then create a treatment plan that is agreeable to the client based on their informed understanding of the situation and their options.

Informed Consent

Informed consent is an essential aspect of all therapeutic relationships. It should be viewed as an ongoing aspect of the therapeutic process, as opposed to something that is only addressed once at the start of treatment (J. E. Barnett, Wise, Johnson-Greene, & Bucky, 2007). Standard 3.10, Informed Consent, of the APA (2010) Ethics Code discusses what is needed to obtain consent. First, any written agreements or documents used should include information in language that is "reasonably understandable" to the client (APA, 2010, p. 6). Next, if a client is legally unable to give consent, due to age or impairment, psychologists must still explain the services, attempt to obtain assent, consider the client's interests, and obtain appropriate consent from a legal guardian or another person who is legally authorized to consent for the client (Standard 3.10b, Informed Consent; APA, 2010). If services are court mandated, the clinician must discuss their structure and format. Additionally, it is important to address any specific limits of confidentiality related to the nature of the treatment (Standard 3.10c; APA, 2010). Standard 3.10d indicates that consent and assent must always be appropriately documented.

The informed consent process is especially relevant when providing CAM services. Because of the complementary and alternative nature of these treatment modalities, clients must fully understand available options and alternatives, and their relative risks and benefits, before receiving any services. Thus, another aspect of informed consent that is of particular relevance is alternatives to treatment. If particular CAM modalities are known to be viable treatment options for the client's presenting problems, it is essential that psychologists discuss CAM, along with other clinically relevant treatments, in the options that clients may be interested in considering. Psychologists need to be knowledgeable in the areas that they are recommending so they can know when such treatments are appropriate. Also with CAM, it is important to highlight the expected duration of the treatment as well as any risks or drawbacks that may arise with participation. Clients must also be aware of their right to refuse or terminate treatment. Psychologists should be aware that cultural factors may affect the alternatives and options they suggest, as well as how that information may be most appropriately and effectively presented to their clients (J. E. Barnett, Wise, et al., 2007). In summary, it is valuable to remember that it is every psychologist's job to give clients adequate information so that they can make an independent, educated decision free from overt influence or coercion. When discussing CAM, as well as other treatment options, psychologists should provide enough information for clients to make an informed decision about participation. This information must be shared in a manner that the client can comprehend. As we have noted, informed consent is an ongoing process, so any time a substantive change is proposed to a client's treatment, the informed consent agreement should be updated, and the client's consent to the changes in treatment should be obtained (J. E. Barnett, Wise, et al., 2007).

An informed consent document must include specific information. First, when a particular treatment regimen is used in psychotherapy, it is necessary to explain the expectations and purposes associated with it. It is valuable to provide information regarding fees and billing as well as scheduling before beginning treatment so that clients are fully aware of the commitment needed to undertake treatment. Other areas that should be included in an informed consent document are alternatives to treatment as well as potential risks and benefits of any treatments. It is also necessary to ensure that beginning treatment is voluntary and that the client can terminate treatment at any point if he or she chooses to do so.

When eliciting informed consent at the beginning of treatment, psychologists should clearly explain the limits and maintenance of confidentiality and discuss the limits of confidentiality with the client (Standard 4.02a, b, Discussing the Limits of Confidentiality; APA, 2010). Furthermore, if the treatment involves using the Internet, telephone, or another form of electronic communication, clients must be told about the specific limits to confidentiality and privacy issues that may arise with these modalities (Standard 4.02c; APA, 2010). This is also relevant when consulting or collaborating with other professionals (e.g., consulting with colleagues) because only necessary and essential information should be disclosed (Standard 4.04, Minimizing Intrusions on Privacy; APA, 2010). It is important to have appropriate documentation, such as signed releases from clients, related to disclosing information to other professionals.

Advertising and Public Statements

As the field of CAM continues to grow, many professionals are considering ways to introduce different aspects of it into their practices. It is important that psychologists are aware of how they are portraying themselves to the public because not everyone is fully aware of what credentials are needed to practice specific CAM modalities. Standard 5.01b, Avoidance of False or Deceptive Statements, clearly delineates that psychologists cannot make "false, deceptive, or fraudulent statements" (APA, 2010, p. 8). It is vital that psychologists ensure that all advertising of services and public statements are accurate and that only factual and objective information is provided. For instance, if the psychologist is licensed, it is appropriate to state this in an advertisement by including the phrase *licensed psychologist*, or some similar phrase as authorized by one's licensing law, and listing a license number. However, subjective opinions or statements intended to take advantage of consumers' lack of sophistication about health professionals' credentials must be avoided. One should not advertise oneself as the "best" or a "premiere" psychologist, because these descriptions would be considered unethical and exploitative of the public. All statements about credentials and training must be made truthfully so that clients can make the most educated treatment choices possible. Psychologists who provide and advertise both psychological services and CAM modalities must specifically report their credentials in each. Listing that one is licensed but not specifying in what could potentially be misleading to the public. An appropriate example would be to advertise oneself as a licensed psychologist who is also credentialed through an organization such as the Biofeedback Certification International Alliance or the American Society of Clinical Hypnosis.

In areas of CAM practice for which no formal credential or certification exists, psychologists must also be truthful in their advertising and public statements. If there is no formal certification needed to practice a particular form of CAM, psychologists may still use the technique, but they cannot falsely claim specialization or expertise. If there are no conclusive data about the efficacy of a CAM treatment modality, psychologists may not make

statements about its effectiveness or imply the likelihood of certain anticipated results. Ultimately, psychologists should never imply expertise or specialization that they do not actually possess and should not promise particular
results, either explicitly or by implication.

Ethical Integration of CAM Into Psychological Practice

Psychologists should be aware that not all CAM modalities are com-
patible with all psychological treatments, and treatment decisions should
be based on the best available scientific data and each client's best interests.
Psychologists must also be aware that not all clients will openly share that
they have used or are using a CAM modality. As noted in the Introduction to
this volume, Elkins, Marcus, Rajab, and Durgam (2005) found that only 34%
of those they surveyed "had discussed their use of complementary or alternative therapy with their psychotherapist" (p. 232). Therefore, it is imperative
that psychologists ask appropriate and relevant questions related to CAM to
fully understand a client's treatment needs and to effectively develop the most
appropriate treatment plan for the client. Questions about the use of various
CAM modalities should be a part of every competent psychologist's intake
assessment with clients, regardless of presenting problems or referral source.
To fulfill this obligation, one must first have general knowledge of CAM
modalities and their appropriate and inappropriate uses and applications.

Practitioners also need to understand which methods should be used in
specific instances so that appropriate referrals and recommendations regarding treatment can be made, regardless of which techniques practitioners personally choose to use in their practice. Certain clients may want detailed
information about efficacy, common usage, and counter-indications when
choosing a method of treatment. Practitioners should be well acquainted with
this information as well as referral options available to clients. Regardless
of whether psychologists use the techniques themselves, they should make
sure they understand their uses and are knowledgeable about appropriate
community resources to which referrals can be made.

In summary, when considering using CAM, clinicians must consider
whether it is appropriate to provide treatment using a given CAM modality with a client, even if they are competent to do so. Specifically, one must
determine whether using the modality in treatment will have an impact
on the existing therapeutic relationship. Regardless of whether a clinician
is interested in integrating CAM into his or her practice, being aware of
ethical obligations is essential for successful practice. Clients may ask for
recommendations or information on a specific CAM modality, and being
knowledgeable is of the utmost importance to uphold the standard of care
that psychologists should strive for.

ADDITIONAL RESOURCES

1. APA Ethics Office. The APA Ethics Office works to promote the ethical practice of psychologists. Through their website, one can access the APA Ethics Code, file a formal complaint, access additional ethics resources, and obtain information about ethics consultations. The APA Ethics Office website can be accessed at http://www.apa.org/ethics

2. Barnett, J. E., & Johnson, W. B. (2008). *Ethics desk reference for psychologists*. Washington, DC: American Psychological Association. This book provides a practical review of the APA Ethics Code and offers specific guidance on how to apply it to a wide range of situations. Additionally, a comprehensive ethical decision-making model is provided, and the most likely areas of practice in which psychologists may face challenges and dilemmas are addressed.

3. IN-CAM. An online resource provided by the Canadian Interdisciplinary Network for Complementary & Alternative Medicine Research that provides a list of journals and databases relevant to CAM. It also provides information on CAM-related continuing education events and other training opportunities. Available at http://www.incamresearch.ca/index.php?id=27

4. Knapp, S. J., & VandeCreek, L. D. (2012). *Practical ethics for psychologists: A positive approach* (2nd ed.). Washington, DC: American Psychological Association. This book provides a comprehensive review of ethics for psychologists from the approach of aspirational ethics—a focus on ethics from the perspective of being guided by a commitment to the highest ideals of our profession rather than by seeking the minimum needed to avoid difficulties. They apply this approach to a wide range of contemporary challenges psychologists face.

5. Nagy, T. E. (2005). *Ethics in plain English: An illustrative casebook for psychologists* (2nd ed.). Washington, DC: American Psychological Association. This book also reviews the ethical standards that make up the APA Ethics Code but does so by providing various cases and vignettes. Each chapter is devoted to a different standard and provides vignettes as well as critical thinking questions that alert the reader to various ethical considerations. Additionally, each vignette has a "thumbs-up" or a "thumbs-down" to help alert the reader as to whether the situation was handled in an exemplary manner.

3

CAM RESEARCH

Research in complementary and alternative medicine (CAM) is unique because, unlike conventional medical science, in which treatments are formulated and researched before implementation, CAM research typically occurs after what is sometimes a long history of practice. As CAM research progresses and positive results from adequately powered, well-designed studies are replicated, the techniques under investigation may become generally accepted practice. With CAM increasingly being found effective in adjunctive and palliative care, integration with conventional medicine is on the rise. Acceptance of CAM is evident in the growing number of medical schools that are incorporating CAM into their curricula. In a survey of 125 U.S. medical schools, 75 offered students some form of education on CAM (Wetzel, Eisenberg, & Kaptchuk, 1998). In the United Kingdom, 18 of 31 surveyed medical schools incorporated CAM in their curricula

http://dx.doi.org/10.1037/14435-004
Complementary and Alternative Medicine for Psychologists: An Essential Resource, by J. E. Barnett, A. J. Shale, G. Elkins, and W. Fisher

(K. R. Smith, 2011), and Canada has begun a national initiative to incorporate CAM in undergraduate education (Verhoef & Brundin-Mather, 2007). Survey results suggest that a majority of respondents in Austria, Germany, and Switzerland also endorse the integration of CAM into the medical system (Brinkhaus et al., 2011).

The amount of published research in CAM is growing exponentially. A rudimentary search of the Web of Knowledge database (Thompson-Reuters; http://wokinfo.com), using the term *complementary and alternative medicine* revealed more than 6,000 articles. Given that this database inquiry does not include search terms for published clinical trials, it clearly indicates a growing trend. The expansion of funding of CAM research by the National Center for Complementary and Alternative Medicine (NCCAM) and other funding agencies indicates that research in this field is likely to continue to expand (see Figure 3.1). Since NCCAM's inception, grants and awards have totaled more than $1 billion, with NCCAM requesting an appropriation of $127,930,000 for fiscal year 2013. Furthermore, NCCAM has identified the management of chronic pain as an area of urgent public health need and is slated to support a growing portfolio of studies on the use of nonpharmacological interventions for the management of chronic pain.

METHODOLOGICAL CHALLENGES

The scope and volume of research that has been performed and is ongoing is remarkable. However, ubiquitous methodological challenges can obscure and obfuscate findings. These challenges include (a) a paucity

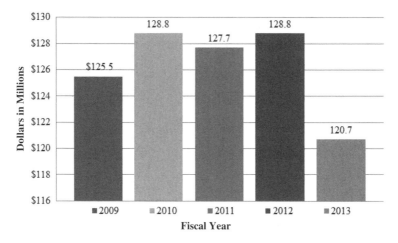

Figure 3.1. Funding levels by fiscal year. Data from National Institutes of Health, National Center for Complementary and Alternative Medicine, 2014.

of randomized controlled trials, (b) potential investigator and publisher bias, and (c) use of unconventional or unproven theories in some CAM research.

Paucity of Randomized Controlled Trials

A common critique of CAM has been the paucity of foundational research reporting strong effects from rigorous randomized, controlled trials. Although irrefutable, this critique may be unfair because several (e.g., Ayurveda) modalities arose before the development of modern scientific approaches.

Another major obstacle for CAM researchers is the issue of control. Randomized, blinded, and controlled trials are the gold standard in psychological and medical research; however, for a variety of reasons, this can be a particularly difficult if not impossible design when studying CAM modalities. For instance, creating a sham condition for comparison is often difficult and controversial. Acupuncture has had the challenge of creating a sham condition for the insertion of acupuncture needles into the skin, for example. Studies have tried various methods of creating this sham condition, from "placebo needles" that act like a stage dagger, with a blunt, collapsing tip that does not penetrate the skin (Lund & Lundeberg, 2006) to sham acupuncture controls in which needles were inserted deliberately at "wrong" points or points that violate traditional acupuncture theories of point locations (Moffet, 2009). This has been difficult because, for example, placebo needles were posited to stimulate acupressure, which may have a greater effect than other placebos (Kaptchuk et al., 2006). Additionally, sham conditions for treatments such as massage are extremely difficult to conceptualize. Without the ability to adequately control or blind to condition, CAM researchers are faced with a substantially greater burden of proof for their findings than would a study of a pharmacological treatment regimen, in which researchers could easily adopt the gold standard methodology.

Potential Investigator Bias

A pervasive issue unique to CAM research is that many investigators are publishing in the area in which they are the practitioners and often the champions of that specific modality. Many of the published studies read as if conducted to provide support for a chosen specialty, rather than to provide a rigorous scientific investigation of its effects. Although this is not always the case, there are often sweeping claims for efficacy on the basis of results from underpowered, inadequately controlled trials. Globally, this is an area of opportunity for CAM researchers, particularly those who use more controversial modalities. Another critique lies in the fact that claims of efficacy from published trials are most often published in CAM-oriented journals. This is not always the investigators' choice; it is not unheard of for conventional medical journals to return manuscripts unread before the peer-review process because of substantial negative bias regarding CAM among many in the conventional medical community. This bias, however, is on the wane, with integrative medicine gaining popularity and an increasing number of medical schools now offering CAM education as part of their curriculum. Bias aside, however, CAM theories do not always fit well with traditional medical therapies.

Unconventional or Unproven Theories

Another difficulty for CAM researchers is that some modalities operate from a theory that does not yet have a corollary in conventional theory, medical, or psychological practice. For example, *Vatha*, *Pitta*, and *Kapha* are Ayurvedic *doshas*, or subtle energies that have not been isolated, quantified, or objectively defined in such a way that yields valid and reliable measurement, preventing their use as outcomes in conventional research. Thus, Ayurvedic interventions that focus on *doshas* could only be measured in terms of health outcomes, but *doshas* as a mechanism of action cannot be evaluated. In the absence of a logical underlying mechanism of action, it has been suggested that CAM requires a higher level of proof at the clinical trial level (Jacobs & Gundling, 2009).

EVALUATING PUBLISHED RESEARCH

Assessing Treatment Efficacy

It can be a daunting task to take the body of literature on a given subject and determine whether the evidence presented is adequate for adoption of CAM in one's practice or referral of a client to a trained CAM practitioner. In 1993, the American Psychological Association (APA) convened a task force to consider how to define empirically validated treatments, and it established guidelines for determining whether the research evidence in support of particular treatments is adequate to warrant their recommendation (Chambless et al., 1993). In its final report, the task force suggested two categories for determining treatment efficacy: *well-established treatments* and *probably efficacious treatments*. They suggested that treatments that had not been established and did not yet qualify as probably efficacious should be considered *experimental treatments*. The criteria for well-established treatments were admittedly arbitrary, having at least two good group design studies, conducted by different investigators, demonstrating efficacy by being superior to pill or psychological placebo or another treatment or equivalent to an already established treatment in studies with adequate statistical power. Also, if a large series of single case design studies that have used good experimental designs and compared an intervention with another treatment demonstrates efficacy, the intervention could be considered a well-established treatment. Additionally, to assign this grade, the studies must have been conducted with treatment manuals, and the characteristics of the client samples must have been clearly specified. To be considered a probably efficacious treatment, there must be two studies showing the treatment as more effective than a waitlist control, two studies otherwise meeting the criteria for well-established treatments but conducted by the same investigator, at least two good studies demonstrating effectiveness but flawed by heterogeneity of the client sample, or a small series of single case design studies using good experimental designs.

In 2005, another APA task force issued a report that defined *evidence-based practice in psychology* (EBPP) as the "integration of the best available research with clinical expertise in the context of patient characteristics, culture, and preferences" (APA Presidential Task Force, 2006, p. 1). This report is particularly important when considering CAM research because it emphasizes the need for researchers and practitioners to join together to ensure that the research available on psychological practice is both clinically relevant and valid, yet it also cautions psychologists against making the assumption that interventions that have not yet been studied in controlled trials are ineffective. It is particularly noteworthy to consider that the task force identified a central goal of EBPP as maximizing patient choice among effective alternative interventions.

A number of methods are used to qualify published research. Weighing the level of evidence of an empirical investigation follows a typical hierarchy that is generally well respected across scientific fields. Systematic reviews of randomized controlled trials (e.g., the well-known Cochrane Reviews, conducted by the Cochrane Collaboration; see http://www.cochrane.org/cochrane-reviews) are always preferred because they are considered the highest form of evidence for gauging an empirical question, with expert opinion or editorials considered the lowest. Randomized controlled trials are the gold standard research methodology, and replication of these trials showing good effect sizes are considered persuasive. Although case reports are considered weak forms of evidence, they may still be considered because they are important in alerting us to potential rare harms or benefits of an effective treatment (Vandenbroucke, 2001). Although use of a system or grading level based on this typical hierarchy is preferable to having no justification for selecting research reports to support recommendation of treatment or further study, Glasziou et al. (2004) suggested that different types of questions require different types of evidence.

Method of Research Selection and Evaluation

The research literature used in this book was retrieved using a strategy that included a multiple database search using keyword searches of EBSCO MEDLINE, PsycARTICLES, PsycCRITIQUES, Psychology and Behavioral Sciences Collection, PsycINFO, Health Source: Nursing/Academic Edition, Google Scholar, and PubMed. Additional literature was extracted from the bibliography of representative studies, systematic reviews, and meta-analyses. Meta-analyses, systematic reviews, or well-designed and powered randomized, controlled trials were specifically sought out and included. Literature was selected on the basis of relevance to psychologists and their patients; therefore, the literature presented in this book is not to be considered a comprehensive review of all the literature for each CAM modality presented. Genetic or purely medical studies not considered contributive to the understanding of integrated care are not included in this book (e.g., CAM therapy solely aimed at reducing low-density lipoprotein cholesterol).

To provide psychologists with an at-a-glance reference to gauge the quality of the evidence and make patient-care decisions based on that evidence, it was decided that the two category system mentioned earlier (Chambless et al., 1993) was inadequate as a grading rubric for CAM. Several biomedical evidence-level systems were considered for this text because their criteria were more comprehensive and less ambiguous; however, as Glasziou et al. (2004) pointed out, there are three major disadvantages to the level system. First, they suggested that the definitions of the levels vary within hierarchies so that Level 2 will mean different things to different readers. Additionally, novel or hybrid research designs are not accommodated in these hierarchies. Lastly, hierarchies can lead to anomalous rankings.

A 2002 review from the Agency for Healthcare Research and Quality, an agency within the U.S. Department of Health and Human Services, identified 20 systems to evaluate systematic reviews, 49 for randomized controlled trials, 19 for observational studies, 18 for diagnostic test studies, and 40 for a body of evidence (West et al., 2002). It was determined that many grading systems are not well designed for clinical recommendations because they are either too focused on individual studies or are overly complex. Many grading systems use a rigid hierarchy of evidence (randomized controlled trials,

TABLE 3.1
Criteria for Rating Quality of Evidence of CAM Therapies

A	High quality	Further research is unlikely to change our confidence in the estimate of effect.
B	Moderate quality	Further research may have an important impact on our confidence in the estimate of effect and may change that estimate.
C	Low quality	Further research is likely to have an important impact on our confidence in the estimate of effect and is likely to change that estimate.

cohort, case–control, case series) that is simplistic and misunderstands the meaning of evidence.

The model employed to evaluate evidence in this book is the GRADE system (Guyatt et al., 2008). The Grading of Recommendations Assessment, Development, and Evaluation (GRADE) Working Group is an international collaboration of professionals who are interested in addressing the shortcomings of current grading systems in health care. The aim of the GRADE Working Group is the development of a common, sensible approach to grading quality of evidence and strength of recommendation. The GRADE system is increasingly being adopted globally and is currently in use by the Cochrane Collaboration. The GRADE system uses a rubric that ultimately classifies three levels of quality of evidence and provides two categories of recommendations, as shown in Table 3.1.

GRADING LEVELS FOR RECOMMENDATIONS
FOR CAM PRACTICES

The GRADE system offers two grades of recommendation: *strong* and *weak*. The system does not have a category for treatment modalities that are specifically contraindicated, which would be useful for the purposes of this book. We therefore added the category of *not recommended* as per the definition from the Oncology Nursing Society's Putting Evidence Into Practice guidelines (Gobel, Beck, & O'Leary, 2006). Table 3.2 lists the system of recommendation we use here.

To provide psychologists with a means of quickly estimating the quality of the evidence and recommendations for each CAM modality, each chapter in this volume includes a table that lists the relevant studies, symptoms treated, populations sampled, and an evaluation and recommendation using the GRADE criteria. This is illustrated in Table 3.3 with the

TABLE 3.2
System of Recommendation

1	Strong recommendation	The desirable effects of an intervention clearly outweigh the undesirable effects.
2	Weak recommendation	The desirable effects of an intervention do not clearly outweigh the undesirable effects. Low-quality evidence or methodological deficits makes weak recommendation mandatory.
NR	Not recommended	Interventions for which lack of effectiveness or harmfulness has been demonstrated by strong evidence from rigorously conducted studies, meta-analyses, or systematic reviews, or interventions for which the costs, burden, or harm associated with the intervention exceed anticipated benefit.

example of research in dance therapy as a CAM intervention. The table lists (a) symptoms for which research on dance therapy has been applied; (b) representative studies; (c) a sample description, such as populations and patients studied; (d) grading levels for quality of evidence and level of recommendation; and (e) an overall evaluation and statement regarding strength of recommendation or that the intervention is not recommended for treatment of the symptom based upon the grading of quality of evidence.

UNDERSTANDING CAM RESEARCH

It is imperative that mental health practitioners seek out and use the best available research in their consideration of CAM modalities. Doing so is consistent with the foundations of *evidence-based practice* defined as "the integration of best available research with clinical expertise in the context of patient characteristics, culture, and preferences" (APA Presidential Task Force, 2006, p. 1). However, particularly for CAM modalities, there are areas in which the existing research may be limited to case studies or poorly controlled trials, and longitudinal studies may be lacking. This should be acknowledged and considered whether incorporating CAM therapies into one's own practice or referring clients to another practitioner. However, it should also be acknowledged that the absence of high-quality, well-designed, and adequately powered trials is not evidence of inefficacy; rather, it indicates an unanswered empirical question. As discussed earlier in this chapter, the use of gold standard methodology may be impossible or impractical in research on CAM modalities. It is conceptually useful to

TABLE 3.3
Example Summary Table

Symptom	Studies[a]	Sample	GRADE[b]	Evaluation
Anxiety	2 randomized controlled pilots, 1 non-randomized controlled pilot, 1 controlled clinical trial, 1 uncontrolled pre–post trial	Undergraduate students; graduate students; trade students; psychiatric patients	1B	Strong recommendation, moderate-quality evidence
Body image	2 controlled pilots, 1 controlled clinical trial, 1 nonrandomized trial	Obese women with emotional eating; hospitalized patients with schizophrenia; adults with severe mental retardation; children with mental retardation	2B	Weak recommendation, moderate-quality evidence
Depression	3 randomized clinical trials, 1 controlled pilot	Female adolescents; men and women aged 21–66; depressed adolescents; depressed psychiatric patients	1B	Strong recommendation, moderate-quality evidence
Fatigue	1 controlled clinical trial	Breast cancer patients	2B	Weak recommendation, moderate-quality evidence
Psychological distress	1 RCT, 1 exercise controlled pilot	Adolescent girls (mean age 16); obese women with emotional eating	2B	Weak recommendation, moderate-quality evidence
Quality of life	1 controlled clinical trial	Breast cancer patients	2B	Weak recommendation, moderate-quality evidence

Note. RCT = randomized controlled trial; GRADE = Grading of Recommendations, Assessment, Development and Evaluation.
[a]Citations available in text or references. Studies are representative; table should not be considered a comprehensive review of all available literature.
[b]Data from the Grade Working Group. Available at http://www.gradeworkinggroup.org/intro.htm.

think of CAM research as a journey from practice to science. In that vein, when discussing CAM research with clients, it may be beneficial to explain where the research currently is in that journey, rather than attempt to offer putative results. Thus, it is vital that both CAM researchers and those who read the literature become cognizant of efficacious research methodology to better design and evaluate the level of evidence for a given therapeutic modality.

II

MIND–BODY THERAPIES

4

BIOFEEDBACK

Biofeedback involves using electrical equipment to monitor a client's internal physiological state so that he or she can learn to manipulate internal events through the *feedback* of monitored information (Basmajian, 1989). By using a biofeedback device, clients can learn to adjust their mental processes to control internal functions such as temperature, blood pressure, muscle tension, or heart rate. Biofeedback is noninvasive and often involves being "attached by surface electrodes to equipment that is linked to a computer that transforms and records psychological responses" (Turk, Swanson, & Tunks, 2008, p. 219). This recorded information is then conveyed through either visual or auditory signals that clients can monitor so that they can learn to better understand, and eventually control, those responses (Turk et al., 2008).

http://dx.doi.org/10.1037/14435-005
Complementary and Alternative Medicine for Psychologists: An Essential Resource, by J. E. Barnett, A. J. Shale, G. Elkins, and W. Fisher

TABLE 4.1
Biofeedback Modalities

Modality	Method
Electromyography feedback (EMG)	Uses surface electrodes to detect and measure muscle contractions
Electrodermal biofeedback (EDG)	Uses surface electrodes to detect changes in skin conductance and potential
Electroencephalography (EEG)	Uses precious metal electrodes on various scalp sites to measure postsynaptic potentials
Heart rate variability (HRV); blood volume pulse feedback	Uses a photoplethysmograph (or other methods) to measure variation in the beat-to-beat interval between heartbeats, usually through a finger digit
Thermal biofeedback Peripheral skin temperature feedback	Uses surface electrodes to detect temperature at desired area of the body

DEFINITIONS

There are various types of biofeedback modalities, with the four most common being electromyography (EMG), which monitors muscle tension; thermal biofeedback, which monitors skin temperature; neurofeedback or electroencephalography (EEG), which monitors and records brainwaves (Ehrlich, 2009); and heart-rate variability (HRV), which monitors heart rate (see Table 4.1). With all of these modalities, it is important to recognize that biofeedback serves as only one aspect of a client's comprehensive mind–body approach to treatment.

HISTORY

The field of biofeedback began in the 1950s, blending disciplines such as psychophysiology, behavioral medicine, and conditioning of the autonomic nervous system (Schwartz & Andrasik, 2003). At that time, the term *biofeedback* was used to "describe laboratory procedures then being used to train experimental research participants to alter brain activity, blood pressure, heart rate, and other bodily functions that normally are not controlled voluntarily" (Runck, 1983, para. 6). At present, research is beginning to reveal the positive impact that biofeedback can have on a variety of physiological symptoms.

Four previously distinct areas of research were combined to form what is now labeled biofeedback: (a) work exploring operant conditioning of the heart, (b) research studying the galvanic skin response, (c) studies with cura-rized animals, and (d) feedback control of the alpha rhythm of the human EEG (Blanchard & Epstein, 1978). The idea that people learn through consequences is known as *instrumental conditioning* or *operant conditioning*. In other words, people are likely to repeat an action if there is a positive response and are less likely to repeat an action if there is a negative response (Schwartz & Andrasik, 2003). Previously, it was thought that aspects of the autonomic nervous system, such as heart rate, galvanic skin response, and blood pressure, occurred automatically and could not be affected by reinforcement principles (Blanchard & Epstein, 1978; Schwartz & Andrasik, 2003); only aspects of the central nervous system were thought to respond to this type of reinforce-ment. Recent biofeedback studies are beginning to challenge this notion, however (Schwartz & Andrasik, 2003).

Three researchers have been credited with the development of bio-feedback: Joe Kamiya, John Basmajian, and Neal Miller. In 1958, Kamiya became interested in determining whether people could differentiate between alpha and beta brainwave states (D. Moss, 2002). Working with his first participant, Richard Bach, Kamiya noted that when using EEG feedback, Bach was able to differentiate between the states with 65% accuracy on the first day of study and 100% accuracy by the fourth day (Livergood, 2011). Kamiya hypothesized that feedback from the EEGs allowed Bach to voluntarily produce either alpha and beta brainwave states (D. Moss, 2002). Simultaneously, Basmajian was doing research on the ability of participants to control skeletal muscles. Similar to Kamiya, his results indicated that, with the help of informative feedback, most participants could learn to "single out motor units and control their iso-lated contractions" (Basmajian, 1963, p. 440). Miller's work with animals echoed the results of Kamiya and Basmajian as he discovered that the animals were able to control internal processes such as heart rate through conditioning (D. Moss, 2002). Lastly, cybernetics greatly affected the field of biofeedback by providing the framework of a cybernetic model, which focuses on "sources, transfer, and flow of information" (Hatch, Fisher, & Rugh, 1987, p. 134). Cybernetics also emphasizes the idea that being able to understand feedback is what allows people to learn, another cor-nerstone in the current biofeedback field (Schwartz & Andrasik, 2003). The framework established by these researchers set the foundation for all future biofeedback research.

With these advances in research, the Biofeedback Research Society, now known as the Association for Applied Psychophysiology and Biofeedback (AAPB), was founded in 1969 as a nonprofit organization with a goal of promoting "a new understanding of biofeedback and advance the methods used in this practice" (AAPB, 2008a, para. 1). Information on membership to this organization and others is included in the section "Integration With Psychological Practice."

COMMON USES

Biofeedback is most prevalently used with cases in which there is a strong physical component that can be mediated through psychological means, such as chronic pain, fibromyalgia, and migraines. However, research has recently revealed therapeutic benefits of biofeedback for depression, anxiety, and substance abuse, among other disorders. The efficacy of the different biofeedback modalities varies from weak to substantial across different populations and symptoms. Choosing which modality to use is dependent on the client's health and his or her overall treatment objectives. For instance, muscle tension or backache may be most appropriately treated using EMG biofeedback, whereas neurological disorders may call for the use of EEG biofeedback. For more information on the different biofeedback modalities as well as the relevant research, refer to Tables 4.1 and 4.2.

TECHNIQUE

In a typical biofeedback training session, the client is connected to electronic sensors that provide immediate, real-time feedback based on various biological functions, such as temperature, heart rate, and brainwave activity. Clients are informed of changes in these processes so that they can be conscious of the psychological or physiological symptoms related to their inner state. Ultimately, "the presentation of this information—often in conjunction with changes in thinking, emotions, and behavior—supports desired physiological changes. Over time, these changes can endure without continued use of an instrument" (Biofeedback Certification International Alliance [BCIA] Board of Directors, 2011a, para. 4). Typically, patients undergo weekly sessions over an extended period of time. The specific number of sessions can vary greatly based on the client, his or her symptoms, and the biofeedback modality. For instance, "treatment of headache, incontinence, and Raynaud's disease requires at least 10 weekly sessions and some follow-up sessions as health improves. Conditions like high blood pressure, however, usually require 20 weekly biofeedback sessions before you see improvement" (Ehrlich, 2009, para. 5).

The client–clinician relationship may also have an impact on the efficacy of biofeedback treatment. There is still debate in the field over the role

TABLE 4.2
Biofeedback Research Summary Table

Symptom	Studies[a]	Sample	GRADE[b]	Evaluation
TTHs	2 meta-analyses	Any adult with migraines or TTH	1A	Strong recommendation, moderate-quality evidence
Migraines	1 RCT, 1 pre–post study	Children aged 8–14 with TTH	2C	Weak recommendation, weak-quality evidence
Fibromyalgia	1 RCT, 1 pilot study	Adults with fibromyalgia	2C	Weak recommendation, weak-quality evidence
Phantom limb pain	1 pilot study, 1 case report	Adults with amputations	2C	Weak recommendation, weak-quality evidence
Raynaud's disease	7 RCTs	Majority adult female	1B	Strong recommendation, moderate quality of evidence
Depression	2 pilot studies	Adult population	2C	Weak recommendation, weak-quality evidence
Anxiety	2 RCTs	Test anxiety in college student population	2B	Weak recommendation, moderate-quality evidence
	1 RCT	PTSD in Vietnam Veterans	2C	Weak recommendation, weak-quality evidence
	3 RCTs	Performance Anxiety	1B	Strong recommendation, moderate-quality evidence
Substance abuse	1 RCT, 1 pre–post test	Substance abuse population	2B	Weak recommendation, moderate-quality evidence
ADHD	1 meta-analysis	Children with ADHD	1B	Strong recommendation, moderate-quality of evidence

Note. ADHD = attention deficit/hyperactivity disorder; RCT = randomized controlled trial; TTH = tension-type headaches; GRADE = Grading of Recommendations, Assessment, Development and Evaluation.
[a]Citations available in text or references. Studies are representative; table should not be considered a comprehensive review of all available literature.
[b]Data from the Grade Working Group. Available at http://www.gradeworkinggroup.org/intro.htm.

that psychologists should play in the biofeedback therapy process. Some believe that psychologists should be present for the entire duration of the treatment session, but others feel they should be completely absent from the process (Schwartz & Andrasik, 2003). Ultimately, a clinician's role in his or her client's treatment should be cooperatively determined with the client, keeping the client's best interests in mind. As with any form of therapy, therapist absences should always be a planned part of a client's treatment program, and all relevant precautions and appropriate guidelines should be explained to the client before the treatment process (Schwartz & Andrasik, 2003).

MECHANISM OF ACTION

Currently no established mechanism of action adequately explains the process of biofeedback. However, the theory behind this modality lies in operant conditioning—the idea that behavior can be modified by consequences. When clients are made consciously aware of an internal, physiological event (a consequence), they are able to alter their mental processes (behavior) in a way that achieves the desired result. Other studies have shown that relaxing during biofeedback can have an impact on the overall process (Turk et al., 2008). Many people who report benefiting from biofeedback also report that their conditions are influenced by stress. Thus, one possible explanation could be that biofeedback is treating some of the client's physiological manifestations of stress, such as blood pressure and heart rate, which then decreases the client's comorbid presenting psychological symptoms (Ehrlich, 2009). In summary, biofeedback allows the client to gain greater conscious regulation of various physiological processes through education and conditioning. The exact mechanism of action may be unknown, but the role of a skilled clinician is undoubtedly beneficial in guiding clients through the biofeedback therapy process.

RELEVANT RESEARCH

Over the years, the effects of biofeedback have been examined in relation to headaches, pain, blood pressure, and cardiac issues, among others (Harden et al., 2005; Hawkins & Hart, 2003; Nestoriuc, Martin, Rief, & Andrasik, 2008; Swanson et al., 2009). There appears to be increasing interest in biofeedback, which may be attributed to its clinical efficacy and lack of negative side effects (Ehrlich, 2009). Biofeedback allows clients to gain a sense of control over their symptoms, and this perceived control can have an impact on "emotions, work activity, relationships, and other areas of life" (D. Moss, 2002, p. 136). Currently, biofeedback is the least used among the mind–body therapies, which include hypnosis, meditation, yoga, and qigong (P. M. Barnes, Bloom, & Nahin, 2008). However, it is one that is most accepted by physicians, which may reflect a need for greater collaboration and training among physicians and psychologists (P. M. Barnes et al., 2008).

Table 4.2 provides an evaluation of the scope and quality of the research, as well as author recommendations based on the available evidence.

Tension-Type Headaches

There is an abundance of evidence in the literature supporting the efficacy of biofeedback modalities for the treatment of tension-type headaches (TTH). A meta-analysis by Nestoriuc, Rief, and Martin (2008) reviewed the effectiveness of various modalities of biofeedback on TTH across 53 studies. Although the meta-analysis is predominated by studies using EMG biofeedback, it also includes studies that used other modalities such as peripheral skin temperature feedback (TEMP), galvanic skin response biofeedback, and EEG feedback. The results from the meta-analysis reveal a "robust treatment effect of medium-to-large magnitude" (Nestoriuc & Martin, 2007, p. 125) for biofeedback compared with placebo and relaxation therapies. Although there is strong support in the literature for biofeedback treatment efficacy in the adult population, the evidence for its efficacy in children is much less established. At this time, there exists one pre–post treatment study that looked at the effects of TEMP feedback on TTH for children between 8 and 14 years of age. In this study, the authors implemented four TEMP feedback sessions and were able to demonstrate clinically significant reductions in one of three aspects of pain: intensity, duration, or frequency. A 6-month follow-up revealed that four of the five subjects were headache-free. Although these results are impressive, the lack of randomization and control and the small sample size indicate that investigations into biofeedback treatment for children with TTH are still in their nascent stage.

Migraines

Similar to the TTH literature, there is also an abundance of evidence suggesting that biofeedback modalities are efficacious in the treatment of migraine symptoms. A meta-analysis by Nestoriuc, Martin, et al. (2008) looked at the effects of various biofeedback modalities on migraine symptoms across 55 studies. The results demonstrated strong evidence for the efficacy of biofeedback for migraine as measured by symptom reduction of more than half a standard deviation compared with control group therapies (Nestoriuc, Martin, et al., 2008). Additionally, treatment efficacy levels for groups assigned to the biofeedback treatment were at least equal to those for groups assigned to psychological placebo, relaxation, and pharmacotherapy conditions. Although multiple biofeedback modalities were used, blood volume pulse feedback yielded the numerically highest effect size of all examined modalities. However, future studies are needed to establish the statistical reliability of the superiority of this specific modality. Chambless and Ollendick (2001) arrived at similar results in their comprehensive review of empirically supported psychological interventions; they found that both EMG and thermal biofeedback, in conjunction with relaxation training, are more efficacious than waitlist control in the treatment of migraines. Together these analyses provide strong evidence for the efficacy of biofeedback therapies in the treatment of migraine symptoms.

Chronic Pain

In their comprehensive review of empirically supported psychological interventions, Chambless and Ollendick (2001) found that EMG biofeedback, as treatment for heterogeneous chronic pain, was more efficacious than control group treatments. These results are echoed by the meta-analysis of Morley, Eccleston, and Williams (1999), which found that, across 25 random controlled trials, treatments based on cognitive-behavioral therapy (including behavioral therapy and biofeedback) produced significant changes in positive outcome measures compared with control groups. Outcome measures in this study included pain experience, mood and affect, and cognitive coping and appraisal, among others. The effect size matched those found in similar meta-analyses in the field (Morley et al., 1999). However, the lack of specificity for biofeedback as a separate modality of treatment and the lack of distinction between types of chronic pain limit the degree to which the results may be generalized for the use of biofeedback on chronic pain. Nonetheless, taken together, the evidence suggests that biofeedback may be an efficacious alternative treatment for symptoms of chronic pain.

Fibromyalgia

Currently, there is a relatively small body of literature on the efficacy of biofeedback modalities for the treatment of fibromyalgia syndrome (FMS). Babu, Mathew, Danda, and Prakash (2007) conducted a randomized controlled trial using EMG feedback to treat symptoms of FMS. The authors found that across 30 patients randomly assigned to EMG feedback or sham feedback therapy, EMG feedback was able to significantly reduce the pain and number of tender points compared with the control sham feedback. Although these results are notable, the small sample size is a weakness of the study.

At this point, there exists a single pilot study on the effectiveness of HRV biofeedback for the treatment of FMS. Hassett et al. (2007) studied 12 female patients over the course of 10 sessions of HRV feedback and found a clinically significant improvement in their overall functioning and symptoms of depression. However, only some of the patients demonstrated significant improvement in pain and a trending improvement in sleep. Although the results are promising, the lack of improvement across all patients and its small sample size are limitations of the study. Future investigations are necessary to solidify the efficacy of HRV as a treatment for FMS.

Phantom Limb Pain

Currently, there is not a large body of literature that demonstrates robust evidence for the treatment of phantom limb pain (PLP). Harden et al. (2005) performed a pilot study in which they looked at the effect of thermal biofeedback on pain. After seven thermal biofeedback sessions across 4 to 6 weeks, the results demonstrated a significant decrease in daily reported pain, as measured by self-report and visual analogue scales. Although these results are encouraging, the lack of randomization and control and the small sample size are limitations of the study.

A case study by Belleggia and Birbaumer (2001) looked at the effect that the combination of thermal biofeedback and EMG feedback had on a patient with extreme PLP after amputation of the right upper limb. The results revealed a complete elimination of PLP after six sessions of EMG biofeedback followed by temperature training. Although this result is encouraging, the small sample size and lack of control comparison are factors that should be taken into account when considering the efficacy of this treatment modality in the broader context of treating PLP.

Raynaud's Disease

Raynaud's Disease (or "syndrome") is a condition that causes some areas of the body to experience excessively reduced blood flow in response to cold or emotional stress, causing pain and discoloration of the fingers or toes. A literature review by Karavidas, Tsai, Yucha, McGrady, and Lehrer (2006) cites seven randomized controlled trials in the realm of thermal biofeedback for Raynaud's disease (Freedman, Ianni, & Wenig, 1983; Freedman, Sabharwal, Ianni, Desai, Wenig, & Mayes, 1988; Guglielini, Roberts, & Patterson, 1982; Jacobson, Manschreck, & Silverberg, 1979; Keefe, Surwit, & Pilon, 1980; Raynaud's Treatment Study Investigators, 2000; Surwit, Pilon, & Fenton, 1978). Most of the studies featured predominantly female participants, and the results indicated the efficacy of TEMP biofeedback for symptoms of Raynaud's disease. A good example of these studies can be found in Keefe, Surwit, and Pilon (1980). The authors reported on 21 female participants who met criteria for Raynaud's disease. Participants were randomly assigned to autogenic training, relaxation, or thermal biofeedback training. Evaluation was based on self-reports of vasospastic attacks as well as cold stress tests in which the participants were exposed to cold temperatures and asked to keep their hands warm. All participants showed a statistically significant improvement in their ability to maintain warmth in their hands.

Depression

In a preliminary study on the effects of biofeedback on depression, Karavidas et al. (2007) studied eight participants over 10 sessions using an HRV protocol. Subjects ranged in age from 25 to 58 in a nonrandomized pilot study. The results revealed a significant reduction in depression, although the authors noted that the study's small sample size and lack of control may be limitations in generalizing these results to other populations of depressed patients.

Hammond (2005) studied the effects of neurofeedback on eight patients with depression. Participants received approximately 10 hours of neurofeedback training on alpha and theta brainwaves. The results of the study revealed an improvement across all cases. However, the lack of effect size and specific findings decrease the generalizability of this biofeedback treatment modality to depression but may inform further research in this area.

Posttraumatic Stress Disorder

Currently, there is a relatively small body of literature on the effect that biofeedback has on posttraumatic stress disorder (PTSD). Peniston and Kulkosky (1991) examined the effect that neurofeedback may have on PTSD symptoms across 29 Vietnam War veterans who met criteria for PTSD. Participants were asked to reduce their medication in a safe way whenever possible throughout the study. Veterans were randomly assigned to either the traditional medical control group or the biofeedback group. Participants each attended 30 biofeedback sessions, each lasting 30 minutes. The results demonstrated a reduction in symptoms of PTSD and a decreased need for medication for the biofeedback participants. Although these results are promising, further research is needed to strengthen the validity of biofeedback treatment for PTSD.

Performance Anxiety

Biofeedback has been used to study performance anxiety in a variety of contexts, including sports and music. Paul and Garg (2012) studied the effect of HRV treatment on performance anxiety reduction for basketball players. The authors randomly sorted 30 participants into three groups: no treatment, control treatment, and biofeedback treatment. Outcome measures included ratings of anxiety symptoms and dribbling, shooting, and passing results for performance. The results revealed that after 10 sessions of biofeedback of 20 minutes per day, the participants in the biofeedback group displayed a significant reduction in anxiety and significantly improved performance in shooting and passing as compared with participants in the other two groups. Thurber, Boderhamer-Davis, Johnson, Chesky, and Chandler (2010) studied 14 college-age music performers using HRV. Participants were randomized into either an HRV biofeedback treatment group or no treatment control group. Biofeedback treatment involved four or five sessions, with each session ranging from 30 to 50 minutes. Results showed a significant reduction in performance anxiety for the treatment group compared with the control group. These results are echoed in a study by Wells, Outhred, Heathers, Quintana, and Kemp (2012) in which the researchers examined the effect of HRV biofeedback on performance anxiety. The authors randomly sorted 46 musicians into three groups: biofeedback and slow breathing, slow breathing only, and no treatment. Outcome measures included standardized measures of anxiety. The results revealed that participants with high anxiety were able to reduce their anxiety with slow breathing and biofeedback compared with the other treatment modalities. Together, these studies provide encouraging evidence for biofeedback as an effective treatment for performance anxiety, although further studies are needed to solidify the validity of this modality.

Substance Abuse

Several studies have examined the effects of biofeedback on the reduction of substance abuse symptoms. Two of these studies used a modification of the Peniston protocol (Peniston & Kulkosky 1989) called the Scott Kaiser modification, a neurofeedback modality that gives feedback on alpha-theta brainwaves. One randomized controlled study randomized 120 participants with various substance dependencies between a standard care control consisting of daily group therapy and a biofeedback treatment group; there was also a non–substance dependent group that received biofeedback training (Peniston & Kulkosky 1989, 1990). Results demonstrated that participants in the biofeedback treatment groups stayed in treatment for longer periods of time and had greater abstinence rates compared with participants in the control group. Another study used the Peniston Protocol (Burkett, Cummins, Dickson, & Skolnick, 2005) and randomized 178 participants with diagnosed cocaine addictions to either neurofeedback therapy or no-treatment control. After treatment, the authors reported a 51% relapse rate in the treatment group compared with the 70% relapse rate in the control group, a statistically significant difference. Together these findings suggest that biofeedback treatment may be a promising addition in the treatment of substance abuse therapies.

Attention-Deficit/Hyperactivity Disorder

A meta-analysis by Arns, de Ridder, Strehl, Breteler, and Coenen (2009) reviewed the effects of neurofeedback on treating attention-deficit/hyperactivity disorder (ADHD) symptoms, specifically, inattention, hyperactivity, and impulsivity. The authors reviewed the following modalities of neurofeedback: slow cortical potentials, sensorimotor EMG potentials, and theta-beta waves. Studies included had both wait-list and active control groups in randomized trials. Results of the meta-analysis showed significant improvements in inattention and impulsivity and a significant but moderate effect on hyperactivity for participants who received biofeedback therapy. These results strongly indicate that neurofeedback techniques can be beneficial in working with children with ADHD. The research in this area is still new to the field and may be worth exploring in the future.

CONTRAINDICATIONS AND RISKS

On the whole, biofeedback is considered a safe method of treatment because it is noninvasive and no chemicals or foreign substances are introduced to the body. However, as with other CAM modalities, there are situations in which biofeedback is not recommended. For instance, clients with active psychosis or other "major mental health disorders" may not be able to achieve desired results with biofeedback because it requires concentration and focus, which may be difficult for clients in these populations (Mayo Clinic, 2013). Additionally, biofeedback may cause complications with patients who require strict blood glucose control, with medications such as insulin. By enhancing the body's use of glucose, biofeedback therapy may potentially lower blood glucose levels for up to 4 hours after a session. As such, "it is a good idea to check blood glucose levels frequently following biofeedback" (Dinsmoor, 2006, para. 10). Some of the sensors used in biofeedback modalities could affect the functioning of pacemakers or other internal devices, so it is important to ensure that clients have spoken with their physicians before beginning treatment. Biofeedback can be used in conjunction with other forms of medical and psychological treatment. However, it is vital to note that although "biofeedback can be used in combination with conventional medical treatment for illnesses such as cancer and diabetes, it should not replace those treatments" (Thomas, 2011, para. 7).

A variety of factors should be considered before using biofeedback, including but not limited to "age, mental retardation, psychotic disorders, the presence of life-threatening medical disorders, and personality disorders" (D. Moss, 2002, p. 144). Additionally, a client's ability to "understand and accept the goal of self-regulation" should also be assessed along with other factors that may have an impact on his or her ability to focus and learn the necessary techniques (D. Moss, 2002, p. 144). In the end, "the most common contraindication for biofeedback treatment . . . is a closed mind" because clients may begin treatment with doubts or a lack of interest in the technique (D. Moss, 2002, p. 144), which may reduce its efficacy. Therefore, positive expectations and an emphasis on the power that people can have over their symptoms may be helpful in encouraging clients to attempt biofeedback.

Despite the noninvasive nature of the biofeedback therapeutic modality, the clinician should be aware of the potential for negative reactions to this modality. For example, some clients beginning biofeedback training may feel anxious because "the unfamiliarity of inward quieting can be frightening" (D. Moss, 2002, p. 143). Being aware of a client's emotional and psychological state, attending to those accordingly, and recognizing when to pause treatment are essential for the client's overall safety and well-being.

TIPS FOR PRACTITIONERS

- The most common uses for biofeedback modalities include migraines, TTH, chronic pain, and Raynaud's disease.
- Biofeedback is a part of an evolving treatment for disorders such as depression, ADHD, and PTSD, among others.
- Most insurance companies do not reimburse for biofeedback therapy.
- Biofeedback is usually used as an adjunct to other psychological or medical services for psychiatric disorders.
- Some states require certification before a clinician is allowed to practice biofeedback. It is important to check with your state for the appropriate guidelines.

INTEGRATION WITH PSYCHOLOGICAL PRACTICE

As with many growing areas of CAM, there are specific trainings that psychologists can take advantage of to better acquaint themselves with biofeedback. Although certification is not required to practice biofeedback in all states, it is possible to obtain board certification through the BCIA. The BCIA, formally known as the Biofeedback Certification Institute of America, was established in 1981 in an attempt standardize the procedures for certification. The BCIA is "recognized as the certification body for the clinical practice of biofeedback by both the Association of Applied Psychophysiology & Biofeedback (AAPB) and the International Society for Neurofeedback and Research (ISNR)" (BCIA, 2011b, para. 7). There are three levels of certification through the BCIA: General, EEG, and Pelvic Muscle Dysfunction (BCIA, 2011a). Information about their application process can be found at http://bcia.org/i4a/pages/index.cfm?pageid=3636.

Other professional organizations are also open to psychologists interested in biofeedback. In the AAPB, there are many levels of membership: regular member, associate member, friend of the AAPB, supporting member, retired member, hardship member, various levels of student member, corresponding member, corporate member, and corporate clinical member (AAPB, 2008b). Regular members are those who are "engaged in the scientific and professional advancement of applied psychophysiology and biofeedback or related fields" and currently hold advanced degrees from appropriately accredited institutions (AAPB, 2008b, para. 20). The membership application for AAPB can be downloaded at http://www.resourcenter.net/images/aapb/files/MembershipApp.pdf. The ISNR is another resource, the mission of which is "to promote excellence in clinical practice, educational applications, and research in applied neuroscience in order to better understand and enhance brain function" (International Society for Neurofeedback and Research, 2011, para. 1). Within the organization, its objectives are to help others through the use of neurofeedback gain better understanding of the workings of the brain, promote research, and disseminate information to the public regarding neurofeedback. Membership opportunities are available online at http://www.isnr.org/isnrlist.cfm#Apps.

ADDITIONAL RESOURCES

1. Association for Applied Psychophysiology and Biofeedback— As discussed earlier in this chapter, the AAPB is a nonprofit organization that works to promote and advance the field of biofeedback. Its website provides information on certification, how to get involved in local chapters, training, news, and events. The AAPB website can be accessed at http://www.aapb.org.
2. Biofeedback Certification International Alliance (BCIA)— The BCIA is a nonprofit organization that offers board certification in biofeedback. There is information for practitioners (how to apply for certification) as well as for consumers (what are the different areas of biofeedback) available on the BCIA website. Additional information on the BCIA can be accessed at http://www.bcia.org.

a. The BCIA has a directory of Board Certified Practitioners and Mentors. It is an international search tool that can be found at http://www.resourcenter.net/Scripts/4Disapi6.dll/4DCGI/resctr/search.html?

3. Biofeedback Network—This website has a list with links to various state and international biofeedback societies. It can be accessed at http://www.biofeedback.net/biofeedback associations.html.

4. For psychologists interested in learning about, and possibly purchasing, biofeedback devices, equipment, and supplies, there are a number of online resources available. We do not endorse any particular companies or products. One can find many companies in addition to those listed by searching for key words such as *biofeedback devices*. Examples include the following:

a. The Stens Corporation—This company offers a full range of biofeedback products, training opportunities in biofeedback, and information about the various types of biofeedback. Its website may be accessed at http://www.stens-biofeedback.com.

b. Allied Products Biofeedback Instrument Corporation—This company offers a wide range of biofeedback and neurofeedback devices, equipment, and related supplies. Its website may be accessed at http://www.biof.com/index.asp.

c. Thought Technology, Ltd.—This company sells a wide range of biofeedback, neurofeedback, and muscle rehabilitation devices, equipment, and supplies. It also offers online courses for professionals, general information in biofeedback, and an introduction to stress control on their website. This website may be accessed at http://www.thoughttechnology.com.

5

MEDITATION

Meditation is a mind–body practice with roots in many spiritual and religious traditions, including, but not limited to, Christianity, Hinduism, and Buddhism. As one might expect given the diversity of these religious practices, *meditation* in the traditional sense refers not to a single, well-defined practice but to a multiplicity of contemplative practices, each with a unique procedural practice, set of goals, and presumed benefits. Meditation is a widely used form of complementary and alternative medicine in the United States today, and according to one survey, nearly 10% of Americans used meditation in 2007 (P. M. Barnes, Bloom, & Nahin, 2008).

In recent years, in the process of adapting meditation to the rigor of increasing scientific inquiry, the practice has become more standardized and more carefully defined, but it is important to remain aware that *meditation* remains an umbrella term for a number of clinical, secular, and religious practices. That being said, the focus of this chapter is on meditation used in

http://dx.doi.org/10.1037/14435-006
Complementary and Alternative Medicine for Psychologists: An Essential Resource, by J. E. Barnett, A. J. Shale, G. Elkins, and W. Fisher

modern psychological research and clinical practice, the bulk of which is a secularized iteration of Buddhist or Vedic meditation.

Meditation is most commonly integrated as one tool in a larger therapeutic context. In fact, even in the spiritual traditions from whence meditation practice is drawn, it is only one part of a rich spiritual tapestry. Mindfulness meditation is considered an important element in so-called third-wave cognitive-behavioral therapies, such as mindfulness-based stress reduction (MBSR), mindfulness-based cognitive therapy (MBCT), acceptance and commitment therapy (ACT), and dialectical behavioral therapy. Even in these mindfulness-based or mindfulness-influenced therapies, meditation is only one of many tools and techniques used by clinicians in achieving their overall goals. As such, the outcome of a CAM approach involving meditation will depend not only on determining which patients and symptoms are most likely to respond to its use but also on the clinician learning how to effectively integrate that intervention into the overall structure and goals of treatment.

DEFINITIONS

Two commonly studied forms of meditation are mindfulness meditation and transcendental meditation. *Mindfulness meditation* is commonly defined as paying attention in a particular way—with intention, in the present moment, and nonjudgmentally (Kabat-Zinn, 1994). Because the important part of mindfulness meditation is the meditator's state of mind rather than a specific posture or procedure, it can take many forms, including sitting and focusing on the sensations of breathing or walking slowly and paying attention to the sensations of locomotion. Although mindfulness meditation or *formal practice* usually refers to a discrete and well-defined period of practice, mindfulness can also be integrated into routine activities, such as washing the dishes, taking a shower, eating, or walking. This integration of a mindful state of mind into daily life is often called *informal practice* and is often encouraged to reinforce the psychological gains from formal practice.

Transcendental meditation is a concentrative form of meditation that teaches the participant to focus on a repeated sound, word, or phrase, often referred to as a *mantra*. With the goal being to achieve a state of relaxed awareness, this helps the individual to free his or her conscious mind of distractions (National Institutes of Health [NIH], 2010a). By engaging in this practice, the participant is described by the Transcendental Meditation Program as being able to achieve "a state of pure awareness, also known as transcendental consciousness," in which he or she experiences deep rest and relaxation (Transcendental Meditation Program, 2010c, para. 2). According to practitioners, transcendental meditation also "allows the mind to simply, naturally and effortlessly transcend thinking and to experience a deep state of restfully alert consciousness" (Transcendental Meditation Program, 2010c, para. 6). States of mind such as transcendental consciousness are not well described in the scientific literature, nor were procedural instructions for transcendental meditation exercises found in our literature search. It may be beneficial, if the psychologist does not have the appropriate training and expertise in this modality, to refer clients to an expert in transcendental meditation if they are expected to benefit from the technique.

There are several other forms of meditation that have received some scientific scrutiny, such as *metta* (also called *loving kindness meditation*; see Hofmann, Grossman, & Hinton, 2011) or *vipassana* (also called *insight meditation*, see Cahn, Delorme, & Polich, 2013; Perelman et al., 2012). Use of these other forms in psychotherapy continues but to date the evidence accumulated is not sufficient to warrant review.

HISTORY

Initially, researchers studied the characteristics of experienced meditators, observing their ability to regulate and control aspects of functioning previously considered involuntary. Examples include the ability to alter heart rate, blood pressure, brainwaves, and the production of cortisol and other stress hormones (Baer, 2006). One of the first researchers of meditation in the United States was a Harvard cardiologist, Herbert Benson, who founded the Mind/Body Medical Institute at Massachusetts General Hospital. In his seminal work, *The Relaxation Response*, Benson (1975) studied the effects of stress on patients with various conditions such as high blood pressure, heart disease, and other stress-related ailments. Benson explored and documented the ameliorative effects of meditation on patients and described the state achieved by meditators as the *relaxation response*. He found that the relaxation response could be achieved in all individuals who practiced meditation regardless of the type of meditation used, religious belief or affiliation, or level of experience with its practice.

This work led to the development of the MBSR program at the University of Massachusetts Medical Center, opened in 1979, which incorporated mindfulness-based meditation with conventional medical care (Kabat-Zinn, 2003b; Kabat-Zinn, 2005). The success of MBSR led to the development of other mindfulness-based therapy programs, many of which have adopted a similar, 8-week group structure, such as MBCT, and mindfulness-based relapse prevention. The secular, empirically focused approach of these programs has had a large impact on the greater acceptance of mindfulness interventions into the mainstream of Western medicine.

COMMON USES

Meditation has been demonstrated to have far-ranging effects on emotional functioning, health, and stress reduction. Specific benefits include reductions in anxiety, depression, stress, pain, insomnia, physical and emotional symptoms of a wide range of chronic medical conditions, and the promotion of overall wellness (Chiesa & Serretti, 2009; Grossman, Niemann, Schmidt, & Walach, 2004; NIH, 2010a; Powers, Vörding, & Emmelkamp, 2009; Veehof, Oskam, Schreurs, & Bohlmeijer, 2011).

A number of meta-analyses have found MBSR to be an effective treatment intervention for promoting wellness, reducing stress and its effects, and improving general quality of life as well as emotional and interpersonal functioning (e.g., Grossman et al., 2004; Ledesma & Kumano, 2009). Additionally, Goldin and Gross (2010) found that individuals who participated in MBSR demonstrated significant reductions in anxiety and depression, along with increased feelings of self-esteem and increased attention and focus.

TECHNIQUE

An example of mindfulness meditation involves focusing on the in and out of one's breath without evaluating thoughts or experiences that arise during this process. By focusing attention fully on what is being experienced, without evaluation or judgment, the individual can learn to do the same with his or her thoughts, feelings, and other aspects of experience in daily life "with greater balance and acceptance" (NIH, 2010a, para. 10). As Field (2008) described it, a primary goal of mindfulness meditation is assisting the individual to become more accepting of all that is experienced.

To meditate, "a person focuses attention on his or her breathing, or on repeating a word, phrase or sound in order to suspend the stream of thoughts that normally occupies the conscious mind" (Mayo Clinic, 2010, p. 103). By focusing one's attention in this way, individuals who meditate can experience a state of calmness and feelings of inner peace that are associated with specific physiologic changes that are relevant to relaxation and are inimical to stress.

MECHANISM OF ACTION

A number of theories exist about how meditation might work, based on a growing body of research into its underlying mechanisms. Shapiro, Carlson, Astin, and Freedman (2006) suggested that intentionally attending to experience with openness and a nonjudgmental attitude leads to a significant shift in perspective, which they term *reperceiving*; this in turn leads to change and a positive outcome (Shapiro et al., 2006). These changes were posited to occur in conjunction with positive changes in self-regulation; values clarification; cognitive, emotional, and behavioral flexibility and exposure, and all factors were theorized to affect each other in a mutually interdependent relationship. Carmody, Baer, Lykins, and Olendzki (2009) tested this theory using a large ($n = 309$) sample size and found that mindfulness and reperceiving were highly correlated constructs, yet when taken together, they led to positive outcomes, partially mediated by Shapiro et al.'s four factors of self-regulation, values clarification, flexibility, and exposure.

Also, a number of studies indicate that various forms of meditation may have their effects through their effects on the autonomic nervous system. Meditation practice appears to decrease stress, blood pressure, and resting heart rate and to increase alpha and theta brainwave activity associated with relaxation. Evidence is beginning to converge, suggesting that these changes are made through alterations in the function of the sympathetic and parasympathetic nervous systems (NIH, 2010a). For instance, research by Lazar et al. (2000) using functional magnetic resonance imaging (fMRI) found that during meditation, increased activity in sites associated with attention and control of the autonomic nervous system could be observed in the brain. Other studies have found that meditation results in functional changes in the prefrontal cortex, anterior cingulate cortex, and cerebral cortex—changes that may have beneficial effects on attention and executive function (Chiesa & Serretti, 2010; Orme-Johnson, Schneider, Son, Nidich, & Cho, 2006).

There is substantial evidence that mindfulness practice also results in permanent structural changes in the brain. The most reliable changes were found in an increased gray matter concentration in the posterior cingulate cortex, temporoparietal junction, and cerebellum of MBSR participants. These areas of the brain are involved in learning, memory, emotional regulation, self-referential processing, and perspective-taking (Ben-Eliyahu, 2003; Hölzel et al., 2011; Kiecolt-Glaser, McGuire, Robles, & Glaser, 2002) and are described by Hölzel et al. (2011) as regions of the brain "involved in learning and memory processes, emotion regulation, self-referential processing, and perspective taking" (p. 36). In one study of MBSR, fMRI research found reduced amygdala activity as well as increase activity in areas of the brain associated with attentional deployment (Goldin & Gross, 2010). Together these structural and functional changes may be responsible for the beneficial effects of MBSR, including greater emotional regulation and decreased anxiety, as well as its utility in treating chronic pain.

Studies have also demonstrated that over time, transcendental meditation results in changes in the thalamus, prefrontal cortex, and the anterior cingulate cortex (Orme-Johnson et al., 2006). The moderating effect of transcendental meditation on pain may be due to reduced thalamic activity in the brain, theoretically leading to reduced affective and motivational responses to pain (Orme-Johnson et al., 2006). Zen meditation appears to have the same effect on pain, and functional changes in the prefrontal cortex, amygdala, and hippocampus were associated with a reduced executive, evaluative, and emotional responses for pain; in essence allowing for a reduction in suffering even when pain is present (Grant, Courtemanche, & Rainville, 2011).

RELEVANT RESEARCH

MBSR (Kabat-Zinn, 1982, 1990) has been extensively studied and shown to have positive effects on anxiety, depression, and a wide range of stress-related disorders and other health conditions (Carmody & Baer, 2009), including substance abuse, chronic pain, and eating disorders (Hölzel et al., 2011); it has also been shown to promote general psychological health and well-being (Carmody & Baer, 2008). Research into transcendental meditation suggests that it can be used to treat cardiovascular symptoms and hypertension, and there have also been studies investigating its potential utility in reducing pain, stress, anxiety, depression, insomnia, the rate of medical care utilization and hospitalization, and substance abuse and to improve attention, focus, creativity, and academic functioning, for example (Alexander, Langer, Newman, Chandler, & Davies, 1989; Alexander, Robinson, & Rainforth, 1994; Orme-Johnson & Walton, 1998; Rainforth et al., 2007; So & Orme-Johnson, 2001; Transcendental Meditation Program, 2010b; Walton, Schneider, & Nidich, 2004). MBSR has been found to bring about reductions in emotional reactivity and ruminative thinking (Goldin & Gross, 2010); reductions in anxiety, depression, and stress-related difficulties (Bishop, 2002); to enhance behavioral self-regulation (Lykins & Baer, 2009); and to increase immune functioning (Fang et al., 2010). Table 5.1 provides an evaluation of the scope and quality of the research along with author recommendations based on the available evidence.

Anxiety and Stress

In a meta-analysis including diverse clinical populations, Veehof, Oskam, Schreurs, and Bohlmeijer (2011) reported a significant impact of MBSR on symptoms of anxiety and stress. The reported effect size varied from small to medium, depending on whether a more restrictive, better controlled study criterion or a more inclusive criterion was used. Notably, Grossman et al.'s (2004) meta-analytic review reported a large effect size for MBSR but included pre–post interventions as well as randomized controlled trials. Powers et al. (2009)

TABLE 5.1
Meditation Summary Table

Symptom	Studies[a]	Sample	GRADE[b]	Evaluation
Anxiety	5 meta-analyses, 1 RCT	Clinical outpatient, nonclinical outpatient, cancer patients	1B	Strong recommendation, moderate-quality evidence
Depression	4 meta-analyses, 2 RCTs	Clinical outpatient, nonclinical outpatient, cancer patients, clinical outpatients with multiple depressive relapses	2B	Weak recommendation, moderate-quality evidence
Chronic pain	4 meta-analyses	Clinical outpatient, nonclinical outpatient, cancer patients	2B	Weak recommendation, moderate-quality evidence
Hypertension	1 meta-analysis	Prehypertensive and hypertensive patients	2B	Weak recommendation, moderate-quality evidence

Note. RCT = randomized controlled trial; GRADE = Grading of Recommendations, Assessment, Development and Evaluation.
[a]Citations available in text or references. Studies are representative; table should not be considered a comprehensive review of all available literature.
[b]Data from the Grade Working Group. Available at http://www.gradeworkinggroup.org/intro.html.

did a meta-analysis on ACT specifically and found that it performed equally as well as established treatments such as cognitive behavioral therapy but did not outperform them by a significant margin. In a randomized controlled trial comparing MBSR versus cognitive behavioral group therapy (CBGT) for social anxiety disorder, participants improved in both groups, but measures of social anxiety were significantly lower in clients who had received CBGT compared with MBSR (Koszycki, Benger, Shlik, & Bradwejn, 2007).

With regard to the effects of MBSR on healthy individuals, Chiesa and Serretti (2009) conducted a meta-analysis of all relevant studies published before 2008. They found that healthy individuals who participate in MBSR treatment experienced a significant reduction in their level of stress overall. Additionally, MBSR was found to reduce anxiety and ruminative thinking as well as increase empathy and self-compassion compared with relaxation.

There is comparatively less evidence for the use of transcendental meditation in treating anxiety disorders, although the one meta-analysis we found suggests that transcendental meditation may have a large effect compared with other relaxation techniques, including progressive muscle relaxation and electromyography biofeedback (Eppley, Abrams, & Shear, 1989). The large effect size reported by this study indicates that transcendental meditation may hold promise for the treatment of anxiety disorders, but further research is warranted.

Depression

Overall, the meta-analyses in the previous section reported significant effect sizes for mindfulness approaches ranging from small (Powers et al., 2007; Veehof et al., 2011) to large (Grossman et al., 2004). The results for depression and anxiety are often reported in tandem within the same research studies because the most commonly studied mindfulness programs either have a standard curriculum applicable to a wide variety of psychological illnesses (e.g., MBSR) or are easily adapted to target whichever condition is most germane to treatment (e.g., ACT). A noteworthy new application of mindfulness, MBCT, has been developed specifically for patients with two or more depressive relapses (Ma & Teasdale, 2004; Teasdale, Segal, Williams, Ridgeway, Soulsby, & Lau, 2000). The initial findings were that MBCT was more effective for those who have had multiple relapses, although a follow-up study by Manicavasagar, Parker, and Perich (2011) found MBCT to be equally as effective as CBGT in relieving depression regardless of previous relapses; in fact, although there was no significant difference between treatments, CBGT was shown to be more effective in treating multiple-relapse patients than patients with few relapses. There were no such differences in the MBCT group. Although MBCT only has initial support thus far, it is developing into a promising alternative to cognitive behavioral therapy in the treatment of depression.

Pain Management

MBSR was initially developed to treat chronic pain that was previously resistant to treatment by conventional means. The meta-analyses in the previous two sections generally reported small effect sizes for pain (Powers et al., 2007; Veehof et al., 2011), with the notable exception being the Grossman et al. (2004) study, which reported a large effect size. Although the bulk of evidence appears to point toward a small effect size, it is debatable whether a subjective decrease in pain is the most appropriate measure of the efficacy of mindfulness approaches because they generally do not aim to reduce pain. Instead, the primary aim of mindfulness-based approaches is to change the degree of subjective distress and bother *caused* by pain. This is an important distinction for practitioners and clients to be aware of because it is a departure from the typical treatment approach.

Although most empirical evidence is based around 8 or more weeks of treatment, one-time interventions with inexperienced meditators have also been shown to demonstrate a significant reduction in experienced pain (Zeidan, Gordon, Merchant, & Goolkasian, 2010). Thus, one may experience many of the positive effects of mindfulness meditation over a short period of time.

Hypertension

A meta-analysis of 17 randomized controlled trials of transcendental meditation, involving 960 participants, studied its effects on blood pressure in hypertensive patients compared with biofeedback, relaxation-assisted biofeedback, progressive muscle relaxation, stress management training, and control group conditions. The results indicate that transcendental meditation was the only approach to demonstrate statistically and clinically significant reductions in blood pressure (Rainforth et al., 2007). Paul-Labrador and colleagues (2006) examined the effectiveness of transcendental meditation on the metabolic syndrome, a component of coronary heart disease. They found that patients with coronary heart disease who participated in a 16-week transcendental meditation program had "significant reductions in blood pressure and significant increases in insulin resistance components of the metabolic syndrome as well as cardiac autonomic nervous system tone" (p. 1218) compared with patients placed in a control group condition.

Transcendental meditation has also been studied for it effects on longevity. In a retrospective study of two randomized controlled trials of transcendental meditation, Schneider and colleagues (2005) found that meditators experienced reduced stress and blood pressure that were associated with "significantly lower mortality rates when compared with other behavioral interventions and usual care" (p. 1063). Significant reductions in mortality risk from all causes of death (23%) and from cardiovascular disease (30%) were found.

Although most research has focused on the effects of mindfulness meditation after 8 weeks or more of practice, there have also been studies using novice meditators and a brief meditation protocol. For example, brief mindfulness meditation has been shown to bring about significant reductions in one's perceived level of stress as well as in the extent of one's symptoms of negative mood (Lane, Seskevich, & Peiper, 2007).

CONTRAINDICATIONS AND RISKS

Meditation in all of its forms is generally found to be safe. In a systematic review of 82 studies that involved 958 individuals, Arias, Steinberg, Banga, and Trestman (2006) found "no adverse events" among the participants (p. 817). These authors did not find any contraindications or side effects from participating in meditation regardless of presenting problems (e.g., depression, anxiety, and premenstrual symptoms). Instead, they found that meditation had positive effects for many subjects. Although meditation has been shown to be effective in reducing a number of mental health–related symptoms, it should not be viewed as a panacea. The National Center for Complementary and Alternative Medicine (NCCAM; NIH, 2010a) reported that meditation is generally safe for most individuals. Although it may be effectively integrated into or used in addition to ongoing psychotherapy, it may not be appropriate for all mental health difficulties. NCCAM cautions that individuals with certain psychiatric disorders may not be appropriate for participation in meditation. For example, patients with psychotic disorders or the tendency to dissociate may not be suitable for meditative practices. As such, an overreliance on meditation as a treatment modality might prove harmful to some clients if a more effective and empirically supported treatment is delayed or withheld in favor of meditation. Additionally, some individuals with physical limitations may not be able to maintain the particular postures or movements involved in some forms of meditation.

In summary, no controlled studies have reported adverse effects from participation in meditation, whereas numerous studies over a number of years have highlighted the general effectiveness and safety of this modality as an independent practice, an adjunct to psychotherapy, and a component of ongoing psychotherapy.

TIPS FOR PRACTITIONERS

- There is substantial evidence that mindfulness meditation may be beneficial in treating anxiety, stress, depression, pain, and hypertension.
- The concept of mindfulness includes many psychological constructs that may seem familiar to clinical practitioners, such as focus and "being in the present moment," but it also includes several unfamiliar concepts as well, such as the focus on changing a client's relationship with experience rather than the experience itself.
- Practitioners with limited experience with mindfulness meditation are encouraged to seek additional training and supervision before initiating a mindfulness-based therapy with a patient or integrating mindfulness into traditional psychotherapy practice.
- To date, few negative effects or health care risks have been found to be associated with meditation practices; however, informed consent should be obtained before providing meditation interventions.

INTEGRATION WITH PSYCHOLOGICAL PRACTICE

Meditation in its various forms can be easily integrated into ongoing psychotherapy, both as a component of the psychotherapy offered by the psychologist or as an adjunct to psychotherapy. It can be a helpful aspect of treatment for clients suffering from anxiety, depression, insomnia, stress, pain, high blood pressure, cardiovascular disorders, and other chronic health conditions and thus may be relevant for many psychotherapy clients. Appropriately trained psychologists may integrate meditation into treatment sessions or may assign its use as homework assignments. However, it is important that clients be appropriately trained in their use of meditation. It is recommended that meditation first be practiced with the psychologist before assigning it as a homework activity unless it is to be practiced under the supervision of another trained meditation instructor.

A number of forms of psychotherapy already integrate elements of meditation. Several incorporate a focus on mindfulness, an essential feature of Kabat-Zinn's (1982, 1990) MBSR. MBCT (Segal, Williams, & Teasdale, 2002) integrates this focus with the principles and techniques of cognitive behavioral therapy. Results of research indicate that it is highly effective in the treatment of depression and in preventing relapses for those who have previously experienced depression (Chiesa & Serretti, 2010). A focus on mindfulness is also incorporated into dialectical behavior therapy (Linehan, 1993) and in ACT (Hayes, Strosahl, & Wilson, 1999). No licensure is offered for practitioners who provide meditation instruction and training, but certification is available in transcendental meditation (Transcendental Meditation Program, 2010c) and for MBSR (Kabat-Zinn, 2003b). Psychologists seeking to make referrals to meditation for their clients should ensure that meditation instructors have appropriate training and that they are open to working collaboratively with mental health professionals. Psychologists who plan to offer meditation training to their clients directly should first seek appropriate training. Additionally, psychologists incorporating meditation into the psychotherapy treatments that they provide should likely be practicing meditation themselves on an ongoing basis (Kabat-Zinn, 2003a).

With clients who are already practicing meditation when they begin psychotherapy, psychologists may wish to discuss the role of meditation in their lives, for example, how they may or may not be integrating the underlying principles and teachings of the form of meditation used into their lives. Those who are not already practicing meditation may benefit from hearing how this may be done and possibly how it might be integrated into psychotherapy. For example, many clients will find the integration of Buddhist teachings of relevance to their lives and consistent with psychotherapy treatment goals. Similarly, principles of mindfulness may prove helpful to clients in enhancing quality of life overall and stress reduction when integrated into psychotherapy. In fact, some authors have advocated for the integration of meditation principles and practices into all psychotherapies because of their overall value and general benefit. Avila and Nummela (1977) recommended that meditation "should become one of the basic tools of the helping professions" (p. 842). Their research found that regular practice of transcendental meditation results in increased tolerance, decreased anger and hostility, stronger and more positive feelings for those around them, reduced fear and anxiety, greater assertiveness, and improvements in self-esteem—qualities that should be consistent with the goals of psychotherapy in general and of value and benefit for most psychotherapy clients.

ADDITIONAL RESOURCES

1. The Transcendental Meditation Program—Official website of the Transcendental Meditation Program founded by Maharishi Mahesh Yogi. This site contains information on what transcendental meditation is, a review of research on this technique, training opportunities, and other resources. This site may be accessed at http://www.tm.org.

2. Insight Meditation Society—This organization offers training and retreat programs in insight meditation, a type of mindfulness meditation rooted in the teachings of Buddha. The Insight Meditation Society is a 501(c)3 religious nonprofit organization that has been in existence for more than 35 years. The society's website may be accessed at http://www.dharma.org/index.html.

3. Meditation Resources—From the Insight Meditation Society, this site provides links to audio resources, training programs, and meditation centers and communities around the world. These resources may be found online at http://www.dharma.org/ims.

4. National Center for Complementary and Alternative Medicine (NCCAM)—NCCAM provides a compilation of resources relevant to meditation on its website. Resources include audio and video presentations about meditation, summaries of relevant research, continuing education activities, clinical practice guidelines, and information for consumers. The meditation section of the NCCAM website may be accessed at http://nccam.nih.gov/health/meditation.

6

HYPNOSIS

Hypnosis, also known as *hypnotherapy*, is a mind–body therapy in which a patient is provided suggestions for relaxation, mental imagery, an altered state of consciousness, and improvement in symptoms. Scientific investigation and the clinical practice of hypnosis date back more than 220 years, and enthusiasm for the technique remains strong. Hypnosis may be of particular interest to psychologists because this complementary and alternative medicine modality is one that can be and has been integrated successfully into mental health practice.

DEFINITIONS

Although there are various definitions of hypnosis, the Division of Psychological Hypnosis of the American Psychological Association stated that "when using hypnosis, one person (the subject) is guided by another (the

http://dx.doi.org/10.1037/14435-007
Complementary and Alternative Medicine for Psychologists: An Essential Resource, by J. E. Barnett, A. J. Shale, G. Elkins, and W. Fisher

hypnotist) to respond to suggestions for changes in subjective experience, alterations in perception, sensation, emotion, thought or behavior" (Green, Barabasz, Barrett, & Montgomery, 2005, p. 263). Individuals can also learn self-hypnosis, the act of administering hypnotic procedures on one's own (Green et al., 2005).

HISTORY

The term *hypnosis* was first used in 1891 by Dr. James Braid (Crasilneck & Hall, 1985); however, the process of hypnosis involves techniques that have been used for thousands of years. The use of suggestive therapies dates back to Egypt more than 4,000 years ago and to Greece and Rome more than 2,000 years ago (Gravitz & Gerton, 1984). The modern history of hypnosis began in the late 18th century with the work of Franz Anton Mesmer (Sarbin & Coe, 1972), a physician who completed his medical degree at the University of Vienna in 1766 and is generally considered to be the "father of modern hypnosis" (Oster, 2006, p. 26). Mesmer originally proposed that "the body responded to various planetary gravitational forces, which he termed animal magnetism" (Riskin & Frankel, 1994, p. 602). He believed that he could manipulate these forces, leading to improved health, by passing magnets over his patient's bodies and providing suggestions for healing. Later on, however, Mesmer realized that he did not need magnets; providing suggestions alone was sufficient to achieve the desired therapeutic benefit (Elkins, 2013).

Additionally, Braid's work sparked the interest of Jean Martin Charcot, a French neurologist who treated patients with hysteria and believed that hypnosis was reflective of neurological fragility (Lynn & Kirsch, 2006). Charcot's work later influenced Josef Breuer and Sigmund Freud, who used hypnosis as a treatment for hysteria (Kroger, 1977) and, in 1880, as part of the treatment in the well-known case of Anna O. However, Freud eventually deserted the practice of hypnosis in favor of his methods of free association, and because he came to see the practice of hypnosis as "unreliable" (Cheek, 1994, p. 14), interest in hypnosis again declined.

It was not until World Wars I and II that hypnosis again became more prevalent. At that time, interest in hypnosis increased and was used to treat war neuroses and acute pain (Cheek, 1994). As a result, there was an increased interest in hypnosis among health care professionals, leading to the publication of *Hypnosis and Suggestibility: An Experimental Approach* by American psychologist Clark Hull in 1933. Also in 1933, Ernest Hilgard, another American psychologist, began his study of hypnosis at Stanford University, founding the Laboratory of Hypnosis Research, and, along with Andre Weitzenhoffer, developed the first standardized measure of hypnotizability, the Stanford Hypnotic

Susceptibility Scales (Weitzenhoffer & Hilgard, 1959). This scale was designed to evaluate the degree to which a person experiences hypnosis or hypnotic suggestions. The development of standardized tests of hypnotic susceptibility was critical in the advancement of hypnosis research because scientists were finally able to evaluate the phenomena demonstrated by practitioners of earlier eras.

Milton Erickson developed many of the modern techniques of clinical hypnosis. In the early 1920s, while he was a medical student, Erickson was mentored by Clark Hull and developed an intense interest in hypnosis and psychiatry. Erickson is credited with introducing a wide range of innovative methods of hypnotic suggestion (Zeig, 1985) and influencing the current practice of hypnosis as well as psychotherapy in general (Yapko, 2003). With the approach of the mid-20th century, hypnosis use increased and training became more prevalent, and thus came the founding of a number of professional organizations.

COMMON USES

The uses of hypnotherapy are broad, spanning the fields of mental health and medicine. Hypnosis has been used to address headaches (e.g., Ezra, Gotkine, Goldman, Adahan, & Ben-Hur, 2012), symptoms associated with irritable bowel syndrome (Palsson, Turner, Johnson, Burnett, & Whitehead, 2002), chronic pain (Jensen et al., 2009a; Jensen et al., 2009b), and acute and procedural pain (Lang et al., 2006). It has also been used as an aid in weight loss (Kirsch, 1996), smoking cessation (Elkins, Marcus, Bates, Rajab, & Cook, 2006), and cancer care (Redd, Andresen, & Minagawa, 1982; Richardson et al., 2007). Emerging areas include wound healing of bone fractures (Ginandes & Rosenthal, 1999), treatment of symptoms associated with Parkinson's disease (Elkins, Sliwinski, Bowers, & Encarnacion, 2013), treatment of hot flashes among postmenopausal women, and breast cancer survivors (Elkins et al., 2008; Elkins, Sliwinski, Bowers, & Encarnacion, 2013).

TECHNIQUE

Hypnosis generally comprises two primary components (Nash & Barnier, 2008): first, a hypnotic induction, and second, suggestions directed toward a specific goal, such as relaxation or symptom alteration. During the induction, the hypnotherapy practitioner provides suggestions to a patient for focused attention, relaxation, and concentration on particular sensations or imaginative experiences (Green et al., 2005). In general, this induction is viewed as a process that leads the patient into an altered state of consciousness in which he or she can receive additional suggestions directed toward a therapeutic goal. These suggestions are intended to produce what is considered the second component of hypnosis—the product or outcomes of a hypnotherapeutic intervention.

An initial consultation is usually conducted before initiating a hypnotic induction. The consultation includes providing the patient with information about hypnosis, debunking any myths (e.g., the idea that hypnosis represents "mind control"), setting realistic expectations, and identifying specific goals for hypnotherapy (Elkins, 2013). The number of sessions depends on the patient's response to the hypnotherapy intervention; however, treatment typically ranges from five to 20 sessions, with each lasting approximately 45 to 60 minutes. In some cases, the clinician may assess the patient's level of hypnotizability using a standard scale such as the Stanford Hypnotic Susceptibility Scale (Weitzenhoffer & Hilgard, 1959) or a brief scale (e.g., the Elkins Hypnotizability Scale; Elkins, 2013). The techniques used by practitioners of hypnosis vary according to clinician preference, session goals, and the overall goals of the intervention. Examples of hypnotic induction transcripts can be found at http://www.springerpub.com/product/9780826199393.

MECHANISM OF ACTION

The exact mechanism of action underlying the effects of hypnosis is not yet fully known; however, it is generally believed that patients who have more positive expectations (Kirsch, 1991) and are more highly hypnotizable (Lynn & Shindler, 2002) are likely to benefit the most. Hypnosis may operate by increasing relaxation (Brown & Fromm, 1987) and through suggestions for alternation in sensations (Lynn, Kirsch, Barabasz, Cardena, & Patterson, 2000). For example, research has demonstrated increased heart rate variability (Yüksel, Ozcan, & Dane, 2013) and alterations in cerebral blood flow (Uslu et al., 2012) following a hypnotic induction. Additionally, through the use of neuroimaging technology, such as functional magnetic resonance imagery and positron emission tomography, researchers have demonstrated significant differences in cerebral blood flow during hypnosis of low and high hypnotizable persons (Crawford, Gur, Skolnick, Gur, & Benson, 1993). Some neuroimaging studies suggest a mostly prefrontal cortex involvement (Crawford et al., 1993), whereas others show a much wider area of cortical activation during hypnosis (Maquet et al., 1999; Rainville, Hofbauer, Bushnell, Duncan, & Price, 2002; Rainville et al., 1999). Additionally, hypnosis has been shown to alleviate anxiety (Snow et al., 2012) and have a beneficial effect on the individual's experience of stress, burnout, and well-being (Cardeña, Svensson, & Hejdström, 2013). Thus, although the study of the exact mechanism of action of hypnosis is still ongoing, it is likely that hypnosis represents a complex interaction of autonomic, neurological, and psychological indices.

RELEVANT RESEARCH

This selective review is not designed to be comprehensive; rather, we outline research that is (a) considered relevant to psychology practice and (b) related to hypnosis practices that are commonly employed. A brief overview of each category of study is provided, along with some representative studies. Table 6.1 provides an evaluation of the scope and quality of the research as well as author recommendations based on the available evidence.

Acute and Procedural Pain

Hypnosis has significant effects in reducing acute and procedural pain, reduces the use of self-administered analgesics (Lang, Joyce, Spiegel, Hamilton, & Lee, 1996), and shows comparable results to pharmacotherapy for procedural anxiety (Everett, Patterson, Burns, Montgomery, & Heimbach, 1993). Clinical hypnosis has shown significant effects in the treatment of acute and procedural pain in gynecological procedures (Marc et al., 2007), renal procedures (Lang et al., 2000), bone marrow aspiration (Liossi & Hatira, 1999), burn wounds (Askay, Patterson, Jensen, & Sharar, 2007; Patterson, Wiechman, Jensen, & Sharar, 2006), angioplasty (Weinstein & Au, 1991), surgery (Faymonville et al., 1997), adult oncology (Lang et al., 2008; Montgomery et al., 2007), pediatric oncology (Liossi, White, & Hatira, 2009), and mixed medical procedures.

An illustrative study of the kind of work conducted in this area is a randomized controlled trial of a brief hypnosis intervention aiming to control side effects associated with breast cancer surgery (Montgomery et al., 2007). In this trial, 200 patients who were scheduled to undergo excisional breast biopsy or lumpectomy procedures were randomized, unblinded, to a 15-minute hypnosis session group or a nondirective empathic listening attention control group (Montgomery et al., 2007). The scripted hypnosis intervention included a relaxation-based induction, including imagery for muscle relaxation, suggestions for pleasant visual imagery, suggestions to experience relaxation and peace, specific symptom-focused suggestions (i.e., to experience reduced pain, nausea, and fatigue), a deepening procedure, and

TABLE 6.1
Hypnosis Summary Table

Symptom	Studies[a]	Sample	GRADE[b]	Evaluation
Acute and procedural pain	3 RCTs, 2 comparative studies, 2 uncontrolled pre–post studies, 1 prospective study, 1 case series, 1 pilot	Patients undergoing gynecological procedures, renal procedures, bone marrow aspiration, burn wounds, angioplasty, surgery, adult oncology, pediatric oncology and mixed medical procedures	1B	Strong recommendation, moderate-quality evidence
Chronic pain	1 meta-analysis, 2 RCTs, 4 uncontrolled trials, 4 comparative studies, 1 pilot	Back pain, osteoarthritis, sickle cell disease, temporomandibular disorder, fibromyalgia, multiple sclerosis, noncardiac chest pain, idiopathic orofacial pain, disability-related pain, recurrent abdominal pain, chronic widespread pain	1B	Strong recommendation, moderate-quality evidence
Headaches	1 systematic review, 1 randomized waitlist-controlled study, 1 uncontrolled trial, 2 comparative studies, 1 longitudinal cohort study	Female adolescents; men and women ages 21–66; mildly depressed adolescents; depressed psychiatric patients	2B	Weak recommendation, moderate-quality evidence
Smoking cessation	2 meta-analyses, 1 RCTs, 1 prospective study, 1 uncontrolled trial	Adult smokers who desired to quit	2B	Weak recommendation, moderate-quality evidence
Weight loss	3 meta-analyses, 1 RCT, 2 uncontrolled studies	Adults interested in weight loss, women ages 20–65, at least 20% overweight	2C	Weak recommendation, low-quality evidence
IBS	1 meta-analysis, 6 RCTs, 8 uncontrolled trials	Patients diagnosed with IBS	1A	Strong recommendation, high-quality evidence
Chemotherapy side effects	1 meta-analysis, 1 systematic review, 2 RCTs, 1 prospective study	Cancer patients (adults and pediatric) undergoing chemotherapy	1B	Strong recommendation, moderate-quality evidence

Note. IBS = irritable bowel syndrome; RCT = randomized controlled trial; GRADE = Grading of Recommendations, Assessment, Development and Evaluation.
[a]Citations available in text or references. Studies are representative; table should not be considered a comprehensive review of all available literature.
[b]Data from the Grade Working Group. Available at http://www.gradeworkinggroup.org/intro.htm.

instruction for how patients could use hypnosis on their own after the session. The attention control procedure involved matched time and supportive and empathic comments according to a standardized procedure. Results revealed that perioperative anesthesia use of lidocaine was significantly reduced in the hypnosis group compared with the control group. Postsurgical outcomes on patient symptoms using a 0–100 visual analog scale revealed significant reductions compared with control in pain intensity, pain unpleasantness, nausea, fatigue, and overall discomfort.

Chronic Pain

Substantial empirical evidence also supports the use of hypnotic analgesia to reduce pain and its associated costs. Hypnosis has been investigated for the treatment of back pain (Jensen et al., 2009a), osteoarthritis (Gay, Philippot, & Luminet, 2002), sickle cell disease (Dinges et al., 1997), temporomandibular disorder (Abrahamsen et al., 2010), fibromyalgia (Bernardy, Fuber, Klose, & Hauser, 2011), multiple sclerosis (Jensen et al., 2009b), noncardiac chest pain (H. Jones, Cooper, Miller, Brooks, & Whorwell, 2006), idiopathic orofacial pain (Abrahamsen, Baad-Hansen, & Svensson, 2008), disability-related pain (Jensen et al., 2008), recurrent abdominal pain (Galili, Shaoul, & Mogilner, 2009), and chronic-widespread pain (Grøndahl & Rosvold, 2008).

For example, in a study of 37 adults with spinal cord injury and chronic pain, 10 sessions of hypnosis was compared with an equal number of electromyography (EMG) biofeedback relaxation training sessions via random assignment to determine their relative efficacy in relieving symptoms (Jensen et al., 2009a). Participants were largely male (76%) and Caucasian (95%), and most were experiencing spinal cord injury or neuropathic pain. The hypnotic intervention included five specific suggestions for analgesia or comfort/relaxation: decreased pain, deep relaxation, hypnotic anesthesia, decreased unpleasantness, and sensory substitution. The EMG biofeedback condition used a laptop computer–based biofeedback module and program. Participants in both conditions were provided audio recordings for home use. Participants in both sessions reported statistically significant decreases in pain intensity scores. Overall, the authors concluded that hypnosis and biofeedback show a similar immediate effect on pain intensity and that hypnosis was at least as effective as (and possibly more effective than) biofeedback for reducing daily average pain.

Headaches

Research suggests that hypnosis may reduce the frequency, duration, and severity of headaches (for a review, see Hammond, 2007). Therapist-delivered hypnotherapy (Melis, Rooimans, Spierings, & Hoogduin, 1991), group hypnosis (Emmerson & Trexler, 1999), self-hypnosis (Olness, MacDonald, & Uden, 1987), and cognitive self-hypnosis (ter Kuile, Spinhoven, Linssen, & van Houwelingen, 1996) have each been investigated in the treatment of chronic tension headaches, chronic recurrent headaches, and migraines in adults as well as children (Kohen, 2010). Despite positive results, however, it has been suggested that hypnotic treatments for headaches do not differ significantly from autogenic or relaxation training treatments (Patterson & Jensen, 2003).

Smoking Cessation

Every year, approximately half of the 51 million smokers in North America try to quit for at least 1 day (Tahiri, Mottillo, Joseph, Pilote, & Eisenberg, 2012). In 2005, 13% of smokers trying to quit underwent hypnotherapy, and 40% of smokers who wished to quit reported an interest in trying hypnotherapy (Sood, Ebbert, Sood, & Stevens, 2006). Research into hypnosis for smoking cessation has reported a wide range of cessation rates, from as high as 80% (Elkins & Rajab, 2004) to as low as 22% (Lambe, Osier, & Franks, 1986). A recent meta-analysis suggested that hypnosis may be effective and recommends hypnotherapy for those patients who seek an alternative to pharmacologic interventions (Tahiri et al., 2012). However, a 2010 Cochrane Review of randomized controlled trials reported that hypnotherapy may be no more effective than rapid smoking cessation or psychological treatment (J. Barnes et al., 2010). The variability in effects has been attributed to the differences in the intensity of the intervention. Studies of hypnosis for smoking cessation of minimal duration (i.e., consisting of only one or two group sessions) have generally reported lower cessation rates, whereas more intensive hypnotherapy (i.e., five or more individual sessions) has led to much greater cessation rates (Elkins & Perfect, 2008). Holroyd (1980) identified intensive approaches to hypnosis as including individualized hypnotic suggestions, individualized counseling with follow-up, and an intense interpersonal relationship.

For example, a prospective pilot trial of intensive hypnotherapy for smoking cessation was conducted in which 20 English-speaking participants ages 18 years or older who smoked 10 or more cigarettes a day and were interested in quitting were randomized to either receive intensive hypnotherapy for smoking cessation or to a waiting-list control group (Elkins et al., 2006). The control group received self-help material from the National Cancer Institute (Glynn & Manley, 1993), and these individuals were encouraged to set a date to quit smoking. Assessments of smoking cessation were completed after 8, 12, and 26 weeks. The results showed that at 26-week follow-up, the rate of smoking cessation was 40%, as confirmed by expired carbon monoxide values. This reported rate is comparable with or higher than that achieved through pharmacological or nonhypnotic behavioral interventions.

Weight Loss

Given the obesity epidemic in the United States, it is not surprising that hypnosis has been investigated as a means for losing weight. Although one uncontrolled study was published in 1959 (Winkelstein, 1959) and another uncontrolled study of hypnosis for weight reduction in nurses was published in 1961 (Glover, 1961), the majority of the research in this area was performed in the late 1970s and 1980s, with little recent work. Hypnotic treatment procedures including direct suggestions (both positive and negative), imagery, ego-enhancing suggestions, self-hypnosis, and group hypnosis have all been investigated. Although there is some contention over effect sizes as evidenced by meta-analysis (Kirsch, Montgomery, & Sapirstein, 1995), meta-analytic reappraisal (Allison & Faith, 1996), and meta-reanalysis (Kirsch, 1996), hypnosis, and in particular, hypnosis as an adjunct to a cognitive behavioral intervention, appears to be of benefit to patients who seek weight reduction.

In a randomized waitlist control group study of hypnosis treatment using audiotapes and hypnosis treatment without the audiotapes for weight loss treatment, 60 women ages 20 to 65 who were at least 20% overweight were recruited (Cochrane & Friesen, 1986). The hypnosis interventions used were group hypnosis, therapeutic stories, and metaphors designed for ego enhancement along with individual hypnosis to facilitate the identification of unconscious weight-related issues. The two hypnosis groups (with and without audiotapes) were not significantly different from one another, averaging 6.53- and 8.00-pound losses (for hypnosis plus audio recording and hypnosis alone, respectively) and 17.82- and 17.12-pound losses at 6-months compared with a 1.5-pound increase at 1 month and a .50-pound decrease at 6 months in the waitlist control. The authors suggested that the results of this study support the use of hypnotherapy as a treatment for obesity; however, further study is warranted.

Irritable Bowel Syndrome

Irritable bowel syndrome (IBS) has been defined as a functional gastrointestinal disorder characterized by abdominal pain, distension, and an altered bowel habit for which no cause can be found (Whorwell, Prior, & Faragher, 1984). According to the American Society of Colon and Rectal Surgeons

(2013), IBS may affect more than 15% of the general population and may include symptoms of diarrhea, constipation, abdominal cramps, fullness or bloating, abnormal stool consistency, passage of mucous, urgency, or a feeling of incomplete bowel movements. Hypnosis has been particularly well researched in this area and has met efficacy guidelines of the Clinical Psychology Division of the American Psychological Association as being both efficacious and specific (Tan, Hammond, & Gurrala, 2005). In a review by Tan et al. (2005), 14 published studies (six controlled, eight uncontrolled, $N = 644$) were evaluated for efficacy. The authors concluded that hypnosis consistently produces significant results and improves the cardinal symptoms of IBS in the majority of patients, as well as having a positive effect on noncolonic symptoms.

Forbes, MacAuley, and Chiotakakou-Faliakou (2000) completed a study of hypnotherapy in the treatment of IBS in which 37 women were randomized to a 12-week study involving six sessions of individual hypnotherapy or a 30-minute audio recording of background information about IBS and suggested means to reduce life stresses. The hypnotherapy regime involved a gut-directed approach, which involves an induction of trance via fixation, followed by deepening strategies, and reinforced by hand levitation. Patients randomized to hypnosis received sessions at 2-week intervals, with each appointment lasting 30 minutes, including 15 minutes in hypnosis. Audiotapes of the third session were made for between-appointment use at home. The results showed that hypnotherapy recipients had clinically significant improvements that were superior to audiotape, although both approaches appeared valuable in resistant IBS. The results of this study, and those several systematic reviews weighing the results of numerous other studies, provide a clear picture of hypnosis as a safe and effective treatment option for patients with IBS.

Chemotherapy Side Effects

Clinical hypnosis has been well researched in oncology. In the mid-1990s, the Technology Assessment Panel of the National Institutes of Health (1996) published a report indicating conclusive evidence for the use of clinical hypnosis in alleviating chronic pain associated with cancer. Additionally, hypnosis has also been shown to be associated with relief of anticipatory nausea (Zeltzer, Dolgin, LeBaron, & LeBaron, 1991) and chemotherapy-related vomiting (Richardson et al., 2007) and to reduce the need for antiemetic medication during chemotherapy treatment (Jacknow, Tschann, Link, & Boyce, 1994). A 2006 meta-analysis of hypnosis for nausea and vomiting in cancer chemotherapy found that hypnotic treatment provided a large effect size when compared with treatment as usual and that hypnosis was at least as large as that of cognitive–behavioral therapy and that hypnosis could be a clinically valuable intervention for anticipatory and chemotherapy-induced nausea and vomiting in children with cancer (Richardson et al., 2007).

In a two-armed randomized controlled trial of hypnosis for alleviating chemotherapy-related nausea and vomiting and reducing antiemetic medication use, Jacknow and colleagues (1994) recruited 20 newly diagnosed pediatric cancer patients undergoing chemotherapy. In this study, participants were randomized to a hypnosis group or attention control. The results of the study indicated that the hypnosis group used significantly less antiemetic medication than the control group, and anticipatory nausea was significantly less in the hypnosis group 1 to 2 months postdischarge. This study, in keeping with the other studies in this area, provides support for the efficacy of hypnosis in treating chemotherapy-related side effects. Psychologists are urged to consider this option when speaking to their clients about palliative options to cancer care.

CONTRAINDICATIONS AND RISKS

It does not appear that hypnosis itself is harmful; in fact, it is generally safe and relatively easy to use. MacHovec (1988, 2012) published an assessment of the various risks and side effects associated with hypnosis. He determined that side effects were relatively rare and were most often related to either a lack of competence on the part of the hypnotherapist or psychopathology on the part of the patient. Through his review, he discovered a wide variety of rare complications, including but not limited to headaches, stiffness, nausea, memory impairment, anxiety, brief feelings of confusion, irritability, and depression. There is the risk that painful memories could be brought to the forefront during hypnosis, but discussing these issues, should they arise, can help the client deal with any potential problems. Additionally, recognizing the possibility of having a false memory is something that should be discussed (Pearson, Rademaker, & Tong, 2011). For these reasons, practitioners should undergo sufficient training before offering hypnotherapy to their patients, and patients should be provided with sufficient information to give their informed consent regarding the use of hypnosis as part of their treatment.

TIPS FOR PRACTITIONERS

- Hypnosis is commonly used for chronic pain reduction, anxiety and stress management, and the treatment of tension and migraine headaches.

- Emerging areas of hypnosis use include the treatment of menopausal symptoms, including hot flashes; IBS; acute and procedural pain; and chemotherapy side effects.
- Practitioners should only use hypnosis within their areas of competence and should seek appropriate training before offering hypnotherapy.
- Research on hypnosis for smoking cessation and weight loss has yielded mixed findings, and better results may be obtained when a more intensive approach to hypnosis is used or when hypnosis is used as an adjunct to cognitive–behavioral therapy.

INTEGRATION WITH PSYCHOLOGICAL PRACTICE

When incorporating hypnosis into psychological practice, psychologists must ensure that they are competent with the technique or make an appropriate referral. Despite the growth of training organizations, there is currently no standard certification for becoming a hypnotist or hypnotherapist. Fortunately, however, the American Society of Clinical Hypnosis (ASCH) Certification program is gaining greater credibility (Elkins & Hammond, 1998; Hammond & Elkins, 1994). This program is unique in that it requires that members be licensed health care professionals. Within the program, there are two levels of certification: entry level and advanced level. At the entry level, the practitioner earns certification and must meet the following standards (ASCH, 2010, para. 1):

- Hold at least a master's degree in a health care discipline considered appropriate by the Society
- Membership in a professional society consistent with degree
- Licensure or certification from the state or province in which you practice
- Minimum of 40 hours of ASCH-approved workshop training (20 hours each of beginning and intermediate workshops)
- Minimum of 2 years of independent practice using clinical hypnosis
- Minimum of 20 hours of individualized training and consultation with an ASCH-approved consultant
- An advanced consultant holds ASCH advanced level certification, which recognizes individuals who have obtained advanced training in clinical hypnosis and who have extensive experience using hypnosis within their professional practices. This certification requires a minimum of 60 additional hours of ASCH-approved workshop training, a minimum of 5 years

of independent practice using clinical hypnosis, and a minimum of 5 years of membership in ASCH, SCEH, or equivalent. Those certified are qualified to provide individualized training and consultation for those seeking certification.

The standards of training in clinical hypnosis (Elkins & Hammond, 1998; Hammond & Elkins, 1994) provide a basis for training and integration of hypnosis into psychological practice. Also, if using hypnosis, there are various ethical considerations to be aware of. First, one must always remember that the goal is to help, and not to hurt, so if for some reason hypnosis does not appear to be appropriate for a particular patient or situation, one should not use it. As stated earlier, it is most important to never go beyond one's range of expertise or competence (Elkins, 2013) and to receive sufficient training and certification before integrating hypnosis into psychological practice.

ADDITIONAL RESOURCES

1. American Society of Clinical Hypnosis (ASCH)—This website provides links to information about certification, workshops, and referrals, making it a website that can be referenced by both clinicians and clients. The ASCH is the largest organization for health care professionals who use hypnosis in their practices in the United States. The ASCH homepage is http://www.asch.net.

2. The Society for Clinical and Experimental Hypnosis (SCEH)—The SCEH is an international organization that aims to "educate health care professionals, academicians, researchers, students and the general public about the nature and ethical uses of hypnosis and related phenomena" (see http://www.linkedin.com/company/society-for-clinical-and-experimental-hypnosis, 2011, para. 4). It can be accessed at http://www.sceh.us.

3. Society of Psychological Hypnosis, American Psychological Association Division 30—This division of the American Psychological Association is focused on educating the public and advancing research in the field of hypnosis. The organization publishes *Psychological Hypnosis: A Bulletin of Division 30* three times a year. Their website has information on ethics, education, and membership and can be found at http://www.apa.org/divisions/div30/homepage.html.

4. The International Society of Hypnosis (ISH)—The ISH, formerly known as the International Society for Clinical and

Experimental Hypnosis (ISCEH), is another international organization for hypnosis. The ISH has a newsletter and holds a congress every three years for the international exchange of information and research among those practicing hypnosis. The ISH website is http://www.ishhypnosis.org.

5. *International Journal of Clinical and Experimental Hypnosis* (IJCEH)—IJCEH is the official publication of the SCEH, the ISH, and APA Division 30, and it has been in publication for more than 50 years. The IJCEH may be accessed online at http://www.ijceh.com.

6. Rhue, J. W., Lynn, S. J., & Kirsch, I. (Eds.). (2010). *Handbook of clinical hypnosis* (2nd ed.). Arlington, VA: American Psychiatric Association Publishing. This handbook provides information on the history of hypnosis, the theories behind hypnosis, various general hypnotic techniques, and specific techniques that can be used to treat a variety of presenting problems. The book also provides a section that highlights some concerns within hypnosis, such as training issues and cultural considerations.

7

YOGA

According to the 2007 National Health Interview Survey (NHIS), yoga is one of the 10 most frequently used complementary and alternative medicine (CAM) modalities in the United States, with more than 13 million adults having participated in yoga in the preceding year (National Institutes of Health [NIH], 2011i). The NHIS also found that between 2002 and 2007, the number of adults participating in yoga increased by approximately 3 million. Furthermore, the NHIS reported that 1.5 million children practiced yoga in the preceding year (NIH, 2011i). A 2004 survey of users of mind–body practices found that 3.4% of Americans reported practicing yoga in the past year (Wolsko, Eisenberg, Davis, & Phillips, 2004), and another survey conducted at the same time found that 7.5% of Americans had used yoga at least once in their lifetime, both for the promotion of general wellness and the treatment of specific health concerns (Saper, Eisenberg, Davis, Culpepper, & Phillips, 2004).

http://dx.doi.org/10.1037/14435-008
Complementary and Alternative Medicine for Psychologists: An Essential Resource, by J. E. Barnett, A. J. Shale, G. Elkins, and W. Fisher

DEFINITIONS

Yoga is a form of mind–body medicine that has been practiced to promote health and wellness, physical fitness, and relaxation for approximately 5,000 years (NIH, 2011i, para. 6). The National Center for Complementary and Alternative Medicine (NCCAM) reported that the word *yoga* comes from the Sanskrit word *yuj*, which means "yoke or union" and that "it is believed that this describes the union between the mind and the body" (NIH, 2011i, para. 6). Khalsa, Shorter, Cope, Wyshak, and Sklar (2009) described yoga as "a holistic system of mind–body practices for mental and physical health [that] incorporates multiple techniques including meditation, breathing exercises, sustained concentration, and physical postures that develop strength and flexibility." (p. 279).

HISTORY

The first known text on yoga, *The Yoga Sutras*, was written in India by Patanjali around 200 BCE. The *sutras* are known as the eight foundations or limbs of yoga. These sutras serve as the basis for the many schools of yoga in use today. A brief description of each sutra is provided in Table 7.1.

Historically, the goals of yoga were to promote discipline and attitudes that would lead to spiritual enlightenment (NIH, 2011i), and the "union" was seen as a union between individual consciousness and cosmic consciousness (Sanatansociety.org, 2010). Today the goals and objectives of yoga are described as being to "unite body, mind, and spirit, or, in its more spiritual forms, the individual and the universe" (Duke Center for Integrative Medicine [DCIM], 2006, p. 476). Yoga's goals are achieved through physical postures,

TABLE 7.1
The Eight Yoga Sutras

Sutra	Description
Yama	Engaging in moral behavior while refraining from vice.
Niyama	Practicing healthy habits. Being tolerant and observant.
Asana	Practicing different physical postures.
Pranayama	Focused breathing exercises.
Pratyahara	Preparation for meditation. Sensory withdrawal and detachment.
Dharana	Deep concentration. Focusing on a single object for a set of time.
Dhyana	Contemplation or meditation, being able to focus on one thing, or nothing, indefinitely.
Samadhi	Achieving higher consciousness. Losing one's sense of being an individual entity and entering a state of supreme bliss.

Note. Adapted from *The Duke Encyclopedia of New Medicine: Conventional & Alternative Medicine for All Ages* (p. 478), by the Duke Center for Integrative Medicine, copyright 2006. Reprinted with permission.

meditation, breathing exercises, and living one's life based on yoga's philosophy and approach to life that "includes a healthy lifestyle, good moral habits, and a search for higher consciousness" (DCIM, 2006, p. 476).

COMMON USES

Yoga is reported to provide benefits for a wide range of health conditions, including stress and anxiety, depression, hypertension, heart disease, low back pain, headaches, attention-deficit/hyperactivity disorder, diabetes, asthma, epilepsy, multiple sclerosis, cancer, and cancer treatment–related symptoms (Wolsko et al., 2004). As with all CAM modalities, a careful review of the available scientific literature and consultation with the client's physician are advised before recommending yoga as part of the treatment for any of these conditions. More generally, yoga is used as a form of self-care to promote general health and wellness because it is reported to increase strength, flexibility, and overall fitness and to promote relaxation and a general sense of well-being (NIH, 2011i).

TECHNIQUE

A wide range of yoga schools or traditions exist today that have developed over the centuries. Different schools place various emphases on each of the eight sutras, with some schools opting to practice only the sutras they find most important or relevant. The two most commonly cited schools of yoga in the research literature are *Hatha yoga* and *Iyengar yoga*. Therefore, a detailed description of these two traditions is provided. Despite the frequency with which these two schools of yoga appear within the research literature, many other schools of yoga are increasing in popularity, and it is possible that psychologists may treat patients with an interest in these various schools. Furthermore, many of the research studies now in publication have used mixed yoga techniques that draw from separate elements of the various schools. Therefore, these alternative schools are also briefly described in this chapter.

The most popular and widely practiced form of yoga in the United States is Hatha yoga (Field, 2008). Hatha yoga was first described in the 15th century in India by Yogi Svatmarama in his commentary, the *Hatha Yoga Pradipika* (DCIM, 2006). An English translation of the original *Hatha Yoga Pradipika* is available online at http://www.yogavidya.com/Yoga/HathaYogaPradipika. pdf. Hatha yoga emphasizes three sutras: asana, pranayama, and dhyana (Pilkington, Kirkwood, Rampes, & Richardson, 2005). Goals of Hatha yoga include bringing about relaxation, developing inner meditation techniques, achieving harmony of the mind and body, increasing strength, and opening channels for the flow of consciousness, which are referred to as *nadis* (DCIM, 2006; Sanatansociety.org, 2010).

Iyengar yoga was developed by Yogacharya B. K. S. Iyengar, who founded his yoga institute in 1975 (Bksiyengar.com, 2011). Iyengar yoga emphasizes the practice of a series of specific asanas along with pranayama. Meditation, or yoga nidra, is often considered the final element of Iyengar yoga. It has been described as a trancelike state of relaxation that lies somewhere between wakefulness and sleep. More than 200 asanas are practiced, along with 14 types of breath control and breathing exercises. A number of variations of each asana exist and range in difficulty from basic to complex (Iyengar-yoga.com, 2011). When completing asanas, Iyengar yoga emphasizes correct body alignment and allows for practitioners to use various props to assist them in achieving proper form. These props include "wooden blocks, chairs, blankets and belts that help one adjust or support oneself in the different postures so that one can work in a range of motion that is safe and effective" (Iyengar-yoga.com, 2011, para. 2). Aside from the use of props, Iyengar yoga is thought to be different from other forms of yoga because of the sequence of, and amount of time spent in, each posture and exercise (Iyengar-yoga.com, 2011).

Ananda yoga is a trademarked form of yoga developed from Hatha yoga that integrates the uses of asanas, pranayama, and dhyana, with a focus on yogic philosophy and asana affirmations as well as the use of energization exercises (Anandayoga.org, 2011). The energization exercises comprise 39 energy-control techniques that are designed to help practitioners increase their focus and control their own life force (Anandayoga.org, 2011, para. 5). The main goal of Ananda yoga is described as the integration and harmony of the physical, mental, and spiritual aspects of one's being and the raising of one's level of consciousness.

> Each yoga posture is paired with its own affirmation, which one practices while in the asana. The affirmation is designed to reinforce the asana's natural effect on one's state of consciousness, bringing the mind actively and directly into one's practice. (Anandayoga.org, 2011, para. 6)

Another branch of Hatha yoga is *Anusara yoga*, which was developed in 1997 by John Friend (Anusarayoga.com, 2011). Anusara yoga focuses on the Shiva-Shakti tantric philosophy of the intrinsic goodness of beings, creatures, and things, as well as the trademarked Universal Principles of Alignment, which are a set of asanas that are practiced based on Anusara yoga's particular philosophy. The goals of Anusara yoga are to promote a spiritually uplifting philosophy, a strong sense of community that encourages acceptance and love, and a celebration of the good in all things. It is reported that Anusara yoga is practiced by hundreds of thousands of individuals on every continent and in more than 70 countries (Anusarayoga.com, 2011).

Ashtanga yoga, or eight-limbed yoga, is a system of yoga that is based on all eight yoga sutras. Ashtanga yoga places an emphasis on maintaining an internal focus while engaging in a system of simultaneous movement and breathing. Practitioners are instructed to take one breath while completing each movement (Ashtanga.com, 2011). A system of long, even breathing, moving through a series of postures, and completing a series of gazing points in an effort to focus the mind, are practiced according to Ashtanga principles. Specific goals of Ashtanga yoga include purifying the nervous system, improving circulation, increasing control of the mind, removing impurities from the body, promoting general health, and increasing flexibility and strength (Ashtanga.com, 2011).

Bikram yoga, or hot yoga, is a form of Hatha yoga that focuses on practicing 26 specific postures in a room heated to 105° Fahrenheit. This is a form of yoga that has become increasingly popular in the United States in recent years (DCIM, 2006). The use of a heated room is designed to warm the body, thus making it more flexible, and to promote the practice of the 26 postures as well as to flush out impurities as the participant perspires (Bikramyoga.com, 2011a). The practice of the 26 postures in this manner is designed to "systematically work every part of the body, to give all internal organs, all the veins, all the ligaments, and all the muscles everything they need to maintain optimum health and maximum function" (Bikramyoga.com, 2011a, para. 2).

Kundalini yoga is a form of yoga that emphasizes awareness and awakening; the word *kundalini* means "awareness." Kundalini yoga incorporates the use of specific asanas and pranayama, as well as meditative chanting (mantra). It focuses on "moving energy through seven energy centers, or chakras, which enables kundalini, the life force at the base of the spine, to rise up through the body" (DCIM, 2006, p. 478). Kundalini yoga is described as a particularly spiritual form of yoga that seeks to promote the awakening of inner consciousness. Its goals are also described as promoting physical health and well-being along with "emotional balance, mental clarity, stress relief, and personal transformation" (Yogayoga.com, 2011, para. 2).

Bhakti yoga is a form of yoga that has a primarily spiritual focus. The word *bhakti* means "to be attached to God" (Sivananda, 2011). Bhakti yoga is also known as *devotional yoga* (DCIM, 2006) and emphasizes a focus on the existence of a divine being (DCIM, 2006). By practicing Bhakti yoga, one may progress through a series of steps: faith, attraction, adoration, suppression of mundane desires, single-mindedness and satisfaction, attachment, and supreme love toward God (Sivananda, 2011). The ultimate goal of Bhakti yoga is oneness with God, which results in a state of spiritual oneness and divine illumination. This state of spiritual oneness and divine illumination reportedly results in the presence of knowledge and wisdom, feelings of calmness and peace, and the absence of negative emotional states such as anxiety, fear, worry, anger, jealousy, hatred, and other similar emotions.

MECHANISM OF ACTION

Although the underlying mechanisms of action of yoga are not yet fully understood, a number of researchers have found support for several theories related to the actions that bring about yoga's positive effects and benefits. Although some of these theories offer a general perspective on why yoga promotes mental and physical health, other theories are narrower in focus and provide suggestions for why yoga may be able to alleviate the severity of particular symptoms or disorders.

With regard to a more global explanation of why practicing yoga improves mental and physical health, various researchers have found evidence indicating that yoga may be able to alter brain chemistry. For example, results from a study conducted by Streeter et al. (2010) suggested that the regular practice of yoga can lead to a significant increase in circulating levels of thalamic gamma-aminobutyric acid, which has been associated with improvements in mood and anxiety (Esterlis et al., 2009). Furthermore, Riley (2003) reported that the practice of yoga can result in enhanced control of the autonomic nervous system. This finding is in line with the results of a study by Lee, Mancuso, and Charlson (2004), which found that participants who practiced yoga experienced significantly smaller increases in circulating cortisol levels, as well as other biochemical markers, when subjected to stress.

Many individuals who participate in yoga do so in classes and groups. Therefore, it is possible that many of the beneficial effects attributed to yoga could be the result of being a member of a group and in turn having the opportunity to receive emotional support from other group members (Lee, Mancuso, & Charlson, 2004). Several studies have indicated that increased social support results in better health outcomes (e.g., Ashida & Heaney, 2008; Wang, Xiong, Levkoff, & Yu, 2010).

RELEVANT RESEARCH

The number of studies investigating the clinical utility of yoga has increased greatly since the turn of the 20th century. Multiple randomized controlled trials (RCTs) have been conducted to assess yoga's potential benefits for the treatment of depression, anxiety, pain, schizophrenia, and symptoms related to the treatment of breast cancer. Additionally, a small number of RCTs have investigated whether yoga can be used to improve quality of life and interpersonal relationships, decrease eating disorder symptoms, improve memory performance, and decrease the number of psychosomatic symptoms reported by women with various menstrual disorders. A representative sample of these RCTs follows. Table 7.2 provides an evaluation of the scope and quality of the research and provides author recommendations based on the available evidence.

Depression and Anxiety

A number of studies have attempted to determine whether yoga can improve mood and psychological well-being in mildly distressed individuals. For example, Michalsen et al. (2012) randomized 72 women to an intervention group that received twelve 90-minute Iyengar yoga sessions over the course of 12 weeks, to a separate intervention group that received twenty-four 90-minute Iyengar yoga sessions over the course of 12 weeks, or to a wait-list control group. Yoga classes were delivered either once or twice weekly depending on group assignment.

Results indicated that participants assigned to either of the two yoga interventions reported significantly greater improvements in distress levels following treatment than did participants assigned to the control condition. When the results of both intervention groups were pooled, improvement in perceived stress, depression, pain, and well-being was seen between participants receiving yoga and those assigned to the wait-list control group. In a related study, Javnbakht, Hejazi Kenari, and Ghasemi (2009) randomly assigned 65 women with mild depression and anxiety to either a 2-month yoga intervention or a wait-list control group. Participants assigned to the experimental group were asked to attend two 90-minute Iyengar yoga classes each week for 8 weeks.

Results indicated that depression scores did not significantly improve in either the experimental or control group after treatment. However, anxiety improved significantly for participants receiving yoga but not for those who were assigned to the wait-list control condition. In another study (Woolery, Myers, Sternlieb, & Zeltzer, 2004), 28 young adults with mild depression were randomly assigned to either a 5-week Iyengar yoga intervention or a wait-list control group. Yoga classes where conducted twice per week and lasted for approximately 1 hour. Results indicated that depression and anxiety were significantly improved after treatment for participants assigned to the yoga intervention. Furthermore, postintervention depression and anxiety scores were significantly lower for participants in the experimental condition compared with participants in the control condition after 5 weeks. Consistent with the results reported by Javnbakht et al. (2009), changes in anxiety were

TABLE 7.2
Yoga Summary Table

Symptom	Studies[a]	Sample	GRADE[b]	Evaluation
Depression	4 RCTs	Adults taking medication for depression; young adults with mild depression; women reporting moderate distress	2B	Weak recommendation, moderate-quality evidence
Anxiety	4 RCTs	Adults taking medication for depression; young adults with mild depression; women reporting moderate distress	2B	Weak recommendation, moderate-quality evidence
Pain	3 RCTs	Female fibromyalgia patients; adults with frequent migraines; adults with back pain	1A	Strong recommendation, high-quality evidence
Schizophrenia	1 meta-analysis, 1 systematic review, 2 RCTs, 1 within-subjects pilot study	Clinically stable adult inpatients	2C	Weak recommendation, low-quality evidence
Memory	1 RCT	Adult males in the Brazilian military	2B	Weak recommendation, moderate-quality evidence
Coping skills	2 RCTs	Breast cancer patients, pregnant women	1B	Strong recommendation, moderate-quality evidence
Eating disorders	1 RCT	Young adults and adolescents	2B	Weak recommendation, moderate-quality evidence

Note. RCT = randomized controlled trial; GRADE = Grading of Recommendations, Assessment, Development and Evaluation.
[a]Citations available in text or references. Studies are representative; table should not be considered a comprehensive review of all available literature.
[b]Data from the Grade Working Group. Available at http://www.gradeworkinggroup.org/intro.htm.

not significantly related to changes in depression. Furthermore, improvements were not dependent on interest or motivation levels or on expectations for improvement, thus suggesting that the benefits of yoga were likely not due entirely to a placebo effect.

Pain

Yoga's effects on pain and various pain-related conditions have also been assessed. For example, Carson et al. (2010) conducted an RCT assessing the effects of an 8-week yoga training program for women with fibromyalgia. Patients in the treatment condition ($n = 22$) practiced gentle poses, meditation, breathing exercises, and yoga-based coping, whereas those assigned to the control group received standard treatment for fibromyalgia ($n = 28$). Yoga sessions lasted for 2 hours and were delivered once per week by a certified yoga instructor according to the guidelines of a standardized treatment manual. Results indicated that participants assigned to the yoga condition reported significantly greater improvements in fibromyalgia symptoms than did control participants. Those receiving yoga reported significantly greater improvements in pain, fatigue, stiffness, depression, anxiety, memory, vigor, emotional distress, tenderness, and balance. Participants who were assigned to the yoga condition also reported significant improvements in coping across a number of domains including pain catastrophizing, engagement, problem solving, positive reappraisal, use of religion, self-isolation, disengagement, acceptance, and relaxation.

John, Sharma, Sharma, and Kankane (2007) investigated the effects of 3 months of yoga therapy versus self-care for the treatment of migraine headaches. Seventy-two participants were randomized to a mixed yoga intervention or a standard care control group. Yoga sessions lasted for 1 hour and were held 5 days per week. Participants in the standard care condition were educated on the causes of migraines, how to avoiding triggering factors, proper diet, and proper medication use. Interventions lasted 3 months. Patients receiving yoga reported significant reductions in the frequency, intensity, and duration of migraines. Conversely, participants receiving standard care reported an increase in pain intensity and frequency following treatment. Furthermore, participants in the yoga condition reported significantly lower levels of anxiety and depression following treatment compared with control participants. These results provide initial support for the utility of yoga for treating migraines.

Finally, in a study conducted by Tekur, Nagarathna, Chametcha, Hankey, and Nagendra (2012), 80 inpatients with chronic low back pain were randomized to either a 7-day yoga intervention program or a physical therapy control group. Participants assigned to the yoga intervention spent 1 hour each day receiving a lecture on yogic lifestyle, which was followed by 1 hour of pranayama and then 1 additional hour of asanas specifically designed to reduce back pain. Meanwhile, control participants attended daily 1-hour lectures on leading a healthy lifestyle, which was followed by 1 hour of nonyogic breathing and an additional hour of physical therapy. Results indicated that participants in both groups reported significant improvements in self-reported pain and depression, with participants in the yoga group reporting significantly greater improvements than participants receiving physical therapy. Furthermore, only participants assigned to the yoga intervention reported significant improvements in anxiety.

Breast Cancer

A considerable amount of research has been conducted to determine whether yoga can help improve psychological well-being in breast cancer survivors. For example, Raghavendra et al. (2007) randomized 62 women with Stage II and Stage III breast cancer who were receiving chemotherapy to either a mixed yoga intervention or a supportive therapy control group.

Mean differences between groups indicated that yoga was significantly more effective than supportive counseling at reducing anxiety and depression. Participants receiving yoga also experienced significant declines in rates of anticipatory nausea and vomiting, as well as the actual severity and frequency of nausea after chemotherapy. Furthermore, systemic and organ toxicity rates were also significantly lower for patients receiving yoga compared with those who received supportive therapy.

In a similar study (Banerjee et al., 2007), 58 women with Stage II or III breast cancer who were being treated with radiotherapy were randomized to either a 6-week integrative yoga program or 6 weeks of supportive therapy. Results indicated that anxiety and depression were significantly reduced for participants randomized to the yoga intervention. Anxiety and depression increased in participants receiving supportive therapy, and between-group differences were significant. Furthermore, although radiotherapy had caused a significant amount of DNA damage to all patients regardless of group assignment, the extent of damage was significantly less severe for participants who had been randomized to the yoga condition.

A follow-up to the Banerjee et al. (2007) study was conducted by Vadiraja et al. (2009). During this study, 75 women with Stage II or III breast cancer who were undergoing 6 weeks of radiotherapy were assigned to either a yoga intervention or a supportive counseling control group. Similar to the Banerjee et al. (2007) study, results indicated that patients receiving yoga reported significantly greater improvements in anxiety, depression, and perceived stress levels compared with participants receiving supportive therapy (Vadiraja et al., 2009). Furthermore, participants receiving yoga had significantly lower morning stress hormone (cortisol) levels compared with control participants. Collectively, these results suggest that yoga may be effective in helping breast cancer patients manage psychological distress during treatment and may also lead to better health outcomes.

Schizophrenia

Recently, researchers have begun to assess whether yoga may be beneficial to patients diagnosed with schizophrenia. In a study conducted by Vancampfort et al. (2011), 40 participants who had been diagnosed with schizophrenia or schizoaffective disorder were asked to participate in a repeated-measures experiment in which all patients completed one 30-minute session of Hatha yoga, a 20-minute cycling session, and a 20-minute control session, during which time participants were asked to sit quietly in a room and read. Results indicated that participants' psychological stress and state anxiety levels decreased significantly after participating in yoga and cycling classes. Also, participants reported significant improvements in well-being after the yoga and cycling session but not after the control condition. No significant differences in effectiveness were seen between the yoga and cycling conditions.

In a study conducted by Visceglia and Lewis (2011), 18 patients with schizophrenia were randomized to a yoga intervention group or a wait-list control group. Participants receiving yoga reported significantly greater improvements in the severity of positive symptoms, negative symptoms, general psychopathology, anergia (abnormally low energy), thought disturbance, activation, paranoia and belligerence, and depression. Significant postintervention between-group differences were also seen in regard to self-reported physical health and psychological well-being but not for social relationships.

Finally, in an RCT conducted by Varambally et al. (2012), 95 schizophrenic outpatients were assigned to a yoga condition, an exercise condition, or a wait-list control group. Participants assigned to the yoga group attended twenty-five 45-minute yoga sessions over the course of 1 month. Patients in both the yoga and exercise conditions reported significant improvements in self-reported social and occupational functioning. Also, significant improvements in self-reported positive and negative symptoms were reported only by participants who had received yoga. An odds ratio analysis suggested that participants who received yoga were 5 times more likely to report significant improvements in negative symptoms compared with participants assigned to the exercise or wait-list conditions (Varambally et al., 2012).

It is worth noting that a systematic review of the literature, conducted by Vancampfort et al. (2012), was only able to identify three RCTs that had assessed the clinical utility of yoga for treating schizophrenia. The review concluded that yoga used in combination with standard psychopharmacological therapy is effective in reducing both positive and negative symptoms of schizophrenia as well as general psychopathology. However, in a follow-up systematic review and meta-analysis that included five RCTs, Cramer, Lauche, Klose, Langhorst, and Dobos (2013) concluded that yoga was no more effective than usual care at reducing both the positive and negative symptoms of schizophrenia as well as cognitive function and was only moderately more effective at improving quality of life. Furthermore, yoga was found to be no more effective than exercise at improving symptom profiles across the board. Cramer et al. pointed out several flaws in the currently available literature, including bias in interpreting and reporting results, the lack of a standardized method of treatment, failure to control for the effects of antipsychotic medication, and a failure to report adherence rates.

Mixed RCTs

Although the bulk of the literature on yoga therapy has been conducted with the populations mentioned in this section, several researchers have also begun to examine whether yoga may be beneficial to participants suffering from other ailments as well. Therefore, the remainder of this section highlights some of the better-designed studies conducted within these other populations.

An RCT investigating the effects of yoga on memory has been conducted by Rocha et al. (2012). Thirty-six male members of the Brazilian army were randomly assigned to an experimental group that completed two 60-minute yoga classes per week in addition to two 60-minute standard physical exercise classes each week, or to a control group that attended four 60-minute exercise classes each week. The intervention lasted 6 months. Results indicated that members of the army who had participated in the yoga classes performed significantly better than control participants on word-recognition tasks designed to measure both short- and long-term memory. However, only long-term memory scores showed a significant improvement from baseline. Additional testing also revealed that depression, anxiety, and self-reported stress decreased significantly over the course of treatment for participants receiving yoga, whereas improvements were not seen in the control group. Furthermore, morning cortisol levels decreased significantly in the yoga group, whereas a significant increase was seen in the control group. Together, these results suggest that long-term yoga therapy may be highly effective at relieving stress and improving cognitive performance.

An additional study has produced evidence indicating that 6 months of yoga may help to reduce psychosomatic symptoms in women with various menstrual disorders (Rani, Tiwari, Singh, Agrawal, & Srivastava, 2011). In this study, 150 premenopausal women were randomized to either a yoga nidra intervention or a standard-care control group. In addition to receiving medication, participants in the yoga nidra group were asked to attend 35-minute yoga sessions 5 days each week. All classes were taught by the same yoga instructor, who had been selected by an expert panel. Results indicated that participants assigned to the yoga group reported significantly greater improvements in pain, gastrointestinal discomfort, cardiovascular symptoms, and urogenital symptoms.

In a study investigating the beneficial effects of yoga on quality of life and interpersonal relationship needs satisfaction, Rakhshani et al. (2010) randomized 111 pregnant women to a 4-month yoga intervention or a standard antenatal control group. Participants assigned to the yoga condition attended three 1-hour yoga sessions each week that included a standardized set of asanas deemed safe to practice during pregnancy as well as pranayama, and meditation. Control participants took part in three 1-hour exercise sessions that included simple stretches. Results indicated that women who had participated in the yoga classes experienced significantly greater improvements in quality of life within the domains of general health, physical health, psychological health, and social relationships than did participants assigned to the control condition. Additionally, participants who received yoga reported significant improvements in the rates with which they wanted and received feelings of inclusion, control, and affection within interpersonal relationships. These results suggest that yoga may help women improve skills necessary for coping with stress during pregnancy.

Yoga has also been studied as an adjunctive treatment for adolescents and young adults with eating disorders (Carei, Fyfe-Johnson, Breuner, & Brown, 2010). During this study, 53 participants between the ages of 10 and 21 years (93% female) were randomly assigned to either an 8-week yoga plus standard-care treatment intervention or a standard-care only control group. Yoga sessions were held twice a week for 1 hour and were led by certified Viniyoga instructors.

Results indicated that participant scores on the Eating Disorder Examination (EDE; Cooper & Fairburn, 1987) improved significantly from baseline to end point regardless of group assignment. All participants also reported significant improvements in depression, state and trait anxiety, and food preoccupation, with between-group differences failing to reach significance. These results do not provide strong support for the clinical utility of yoga for treating the symptoms of eating disorders.

CONTRAINDICATIONS AND RISKS

In general, yoga is safe and appropriate for a wide range of individuals, including those of varying ages, genders, and fitness levels, as well as for pregnant women. However, certain forms of yoga may be inappropriate for individuals with recent injuries or certain chronic health conditions (DCIM, 2006), and not all forms of yoga are suitable for all people. The NCCAM reported that yoga is generally safe and well tolerated when practiced appropriately; however, they added that

> people with certain medical conditions should not use some yoga practices. For example, people with disc disease of the spine, extremely high or low blood pressure, glaucoma, retinal detachment, fragile or atherosclerotic arteries, a risk of blood clots, ear problems, severe osteoporosis, or cervical spondylitis should avoid some inverted poses. Bikram yoga and other more strenuous forms of yoga should be practiced with caution by pregnant women and should be practiced only with the approval of the participant's physician. (NIH, 2011i, para. 2)

For those who practice Bikram yoga, it is not uncommon to report dizziness, nausea, and lightheadedness after initial classes. It is reported that participants may need to acclimate themselves to the high temperature, profuse perspiration, and physical exertion involved. Additionally, failure to be appropriately hydrate before, during, and after Bikram yoga may contribute to these uncomfortable feelings (Bikramyoga.com, 2011b). It is also recommended that those with degenerative disc diseases such as herniated or ruptured discs should not engage in bending motions that add pressure on these discs or that would add to nerve impingement. However, competent yoga instructors may be able to guide participants in proper bending techniques that will not result in further injury (Bikramyoga. com, 2011b).

Individuals with certain heart, lung, or breathing difficulties, such as asthma and other pulmonary conditions, may need to exercise caution in the practice of some advanced breathing techniques. There are reports of participants experiencing breathing and pulmonary difficulties as a result of practicing these techniques (DCIM, 2006). Clients with these health concerns should specifically be cleared by their physicians before attempting yoga. Field (2008) cautioned against Bikram yoga for individuals with high blood pressure and cardiac conditions because of the high temperature involved and its strenuous nature.

As with other forms of CAM, it is important that yoga not be used as a substitute for standard medical care. Clients who experience arthritis, joint pain, or back problems should not view yoga as a cure-all for these conditions. Clients need to be aware that yoga has the potential to exacerbate some health conditions if not practiced appropriately. Even with physician clearance, it is important to slowly begin the practice of yoga and to not push oneself too quickly to perform more advanced positions and poses.

TIPS FOR PRACTITIONERS

- Patients should receive medical clearance from a physician before practicing yoga.
- Pranayama can be dangerous for patients with certain breathing disorders.
- Training credentials differ drastically depending on the school or form of yoga.
- Yoga can be contraindicated for some patients with certain heart conditions or pain disorders.
- Yoga may be of benefit in reducing pain, anxiety, and depression as well as improving general well-being.

INTEGRATION WITH PSYCHOLOGICAL PRACTICE

Yoga may be appropriately integrated into psychological practice for many clients. An important first step for psychologists is to educate themselves on the many forms of yoga available, the specific practices involved, and their relative likely benefits, drawbacks, and contraindications. Depending on each client's presenting problems, current level of physical functioning, and desired goals and objectives, different forms of yoga may be of possible relevance and benefit. Furthermore, for many clients, yoga should be introduced as a behavior for general health promotion and enhancement, rather than as a form of "treatment" for psychological disorders. That said, clients experiencing stress-related difficulties, lifestyle issues, and a range of presenting problems may benefit from yoga.

Psychologists who are knowledgeable about yoga and their clients' needs may appropriately recommend yoga as an adjunct to ongoing psychotherapy. The psychologist can review relevant research findings about yoga's potential benefits and possible limitations with clients and can help ensure that clients have realistic expectations about the practice of yoga. Topics for discussion include a review of the various schools of yoga, the amount of time and effort involved, how yoga principles and philosophy can be integrated into daily life, the possible benefits of practicing yoga over time, and potential risks and limitations.

It is possible that in addition to being practitioners of yoga, some psychologists may also be certified yoga instructors in selected forms or schools of yoga. Accordingly, these psychologists may teach or lead yoga classes in addition to their practice of psychology. This raises several possible ethical issues and concerns that should be addressed with careful forethought by these psychologists. The first issue involves the psychologist personally integrating the practice of yoga into a client's ongoing psychotherapy sessions. Although it may be appropriate to integrate some of the philosophical underpinnings of yoga and breathing exercises into the psychotherapy process, what is less clear is how one would integrate the practice of yoga postures or poses into psychotherapy. The integration of many of yoga's philosophies may be seen as similar to and consistent with mindfulness approaches to psychotherapy and the integration of breathing exercises is likely seen as consistent with some forms of relaxation training. Thus, there is support for these approaches. Psychologists should be cautious about integrating actual postures and poses into psychotherapy before finding empirical support for doing so in the relevant literature. Furthermore, differentiating between where the practice of yoga ends and psychotherapy begins may be confusing for some clients. Accordingly, if yoga is integrated into ongoing treatment sessions by a psychologist, such issues should be thoughtfully addressed in the informed consent process to help ensure the client's understanding of the services to be provided and their relative role, benefits, and risks.

When considering making referrals for patients to particular yoga programs or for making general yoga-related recommendations, it is important to be aware of competence and credentialing issues for yoga instructors. There is no licensing process for yoga instructors, but various schools of yoga have their own training and certification programs. Psychologists should view yoga certification with caution because some yoga training programs may last only 2 days, whereas others can take up to 2 years to complete. Thus, when seeing that an individual is a certified yoga instructor in a particular form of yoga, it is important to consider which organization conferred the certification and what standards had to be met by the practitioner to receive it.

Beyond certification provided by individual training programs and schools, nonprofit groups exist that keep registries of yoga instructors and training programs that meet minimum standards for education and training. For example, the International Yoga Registry (http://internationalyogaregistry.org) lists only those instructors and training programs that meet the minimum standards in techniques, teaching methodology, anatomy and physiology, psychology and spirituality, philosophy, ethics, and lifestyle and practical teaching. Specific numbers of contact hours and the demonstration of certain knowledge and skill levels in each of these areas must be demonstrated to achieve registry listing. It is essential that psychologists confirm a yoga instructor's or training program's credentials and understand what those credentials mean before making referrals and recommendations. Doing so will help maximize the chances of instruction by a competent, knowledgeable, and skilled teacher.

ADDITIONAL RESOURCES

1. The Yoga Resource Center—This website provides detailed information about the various forms of yoga, explains the benefits of practice, offers articles about yoga, provides information about how to practice yoga at the office, includes a helpful question-and-answer section on yoga and its practice, offers a blog, and provides a comprehensive directory that includes listings of yoga training programs, centers, festivals, retreats, teachers, resources and supplies, publications, and resources. The Yoga Resource Center can be accessed at http://www.A2zYoga.com.

2. My Yoga Resource—This website provides links to information on the various types of yoga, information on yoga poses and different types of yoga for different populations (e.g., pregnant women), videos and books, equipment, and product reviews. The website may be accessed at http://www.MyYogaResource.com.

3. National Center for Complementary and Alternative Medicine (NCCAM)—Part of the National Institutes of Health, NCCAM provides a wealth of information on all forms of CAM, including yoga. Its website offers information on what yoga is, a review of research findings on yoga, a listing of areas of health in which yoga is currently being studied, information on training and certification in yoga, and tips for those considering beginning the practice. The yoga section of the NCCAM website may be accessed at http://nccam.nih.gov/health/yoga/introduction.htm.

4. The International Yoga Registry—This nonprofit organization provides a registry of yoga instructors and training programs internationally that meet required criteria for education, knowledge, supervised experience, and competence. It is a

credentialing agency, and each level of credential clearly identifies the level of education, supervised experience, and training involved. The International Yoga Registry may be accessed at http://internationalyogaregistry.org.

5. Yoga Movement—This online resource provides information about yoga, listings of yoga centers and events, books and other yoga-related resources and supplies, and links to other yoga-related sites. This site may be accessed at: http://www.Yogamovement.com.

6. Yoga Point—The official website of Yoga Vidya Gurukul (University). It provides information on yoga training, yoga teacher training, yoga types and history, yoga poses, detailed information on a wide range of pranayama (breathing techniques), cleansing techniques, and meditations, as well as yoga lifestyle information and recommendations. This website may be accessed at http://www.YogaPoint.com.

8

MUSIC THERAPY

Music has been used for thousands of years to promote emotional expression, social interaction, and symptom relief in individuals. Historically, music therapy dates back to ancient Greek philosophers who believed that music could be both physically and spiritually healing (American Cancer Society [ACS], 2011). The ancient Chinese medical reference *Yellow Emperor's Classics of Internal Medicine* mentioned the use of music for treatment (Ni, 1995), and ancient Indian treatises, such as *Samaveda*, discussed the therapeutic utility of music (Katz, 2000). Music—creating music, singing, and chanting, for example—has been used as part of healing rituals for thousands of years. Music therapy can be provided in either an individual or group setting, and participants do not require any music experience or expertise. The goals of music therapy do not focus on musical talent, ability, or performance quality but on musical expression, the exploration of emotions and reactions to different passages of music, and emotional expression.

http://dx.doi.org/10.1037/14435-009
Complementary and Alternative Medicine for Psychologists: An Essential Resource, by J. E. Barnett, A. J. Shale, G. Elkins, and W. Fisher

DEFINITIONS

Music therapy is difficult to define because of its various forms as well as the fact that it is not a single, isolated disciple with clearly defined, unchanging boundaries (Bruscia, 1998). However, the American Music Therapy Association suggests that "Music Therapy is the clinical and evidence-based use of music interventions to accomplish individualized goals within a therapeutic relationship by a credentialed professional who has completed an approved music therapy program" (2011b, para. 1). This does not serve as a universal definition, however, because multiple definitions exist with varying cultural conceptualizations. Bruscia (1998) proposed a working definition that defines music therapy as "a systematic process wherein the therapist helps the client to promote health, using music experiences and the relationships that develop through them as dynamic forces of change" (p. 20).

HISTORY

Music therapy became a recognized profession after World War II when musicians played for wounded veterans in Veterans Administration hospitals (D. Holmes, 2012). Upon observing patients demonstrate physical and emotional improvement after listening to performances by volunteer musicians, hospitals began hiring musicians for this purpose. In the United States, music therapy gained popularity and played a central role in the recovery of Congresswomen Gabrielle Giffords, who, as a result of being shot in an assassination attempt, suffered severe damage to the left hemisphere of her brain. Her injury left her unable to speak, but after receiving music therapy, she was capable of singing phrases in songs. As her treatment progressed, Giffords was eventually able to articulate with the natural rhythm of speech (D. Holmes, 2012).

According to the American Music Therapy Association (AMTA; 2011a), there are currently more than 70 accredited music therapy education and training programs in the United States. In 1950, the National Association for Music Therapy was established to help promote and advance the growing field and profession of music therapy, and then in 1971, the American Association for Music Therapy was created. Realizing their overlapping goals and objectives, these two organizations merged in 1998, resulting in the formation of the AMTA (2011a). The national credentialing agency for music therapy, the Certification Board for Music Therapists (CBMT), reports that at present there are more than 5,000 individuals who have earned the credential music therapist—board certified (MT-BC; CBMT, 2011). To earn this credential and professional standing, one needs to have graduated from an AMTA-approved program in music therapy, which includes music therapy coursework and an internship experience in music therapy. AMTA defined music therapy as a practice that uses "music interventions to accomplish individualized goals within a therapeutic relationship by a credentialed professional who has completed an approved music therapy program" (AMTA, 2011b, para. 1).

COMMON USES

Music is now used in a variety of medical settings. The ACS (2011) reported that music therapy can be used in conjunction with conventional treatments to help alleviate or reduce the pain, anxiety, and nausea that are often experienced by patients undergoing chemotherapy. Furthermore, music therapy may have a range of beneficial effects, including lowering of blood pressure, heart rate, and respiration rate; reduction of pain; reduction of anxiety postsurgery and in patients in the intensive care unit; reduction of emotional distress in patients undergoing radiation treatment; reduction of anxiety associated with surgery and short-term postsurgical pain; and decreased pain and emotional distress in hospice patients (ACS, 2011). In modern health care, music has often been used in specialized domains such as psychiatry, neurology, intensive care, gastroenterology, and coronary care, as well as surgery and general geriatric care (Guétin et al., 2012).

TECHNIQUE

According to the participation of the patients, music therapy can be either passive or active (see Table 8.1 for various approaches to music therapy). During active improvisation, which can be spontaneous or instructional, a music therapist may guide patients in playing an instrument, singing, or writing lyrics or a whole song. In passive music therapy, the patient is asked to listen to music or specific sounds that can be reproduced from a recording; active approaches involve music therapy directly played by the therapist

TABLE 8.1
Approach to Music Therapy

Criteria	Variations of music therapy	
Participant involvement	Active	Passive
Method of music delivery	Live	Recorded
Duration of intervention	Single session	Multisession
Music therapy methods	Improvised	Instructional
Participant setting	Individual	Group

and/or patient. In the United States, passive or combined music therapy approaches are the most prevalent modalities, whereas active approaches used more widely in Europe. Music therapy is delivered over a range of time periods from a few weeks to several years. Frequency of treatment also varies from daily to weekly to monthly sessions. People may participate in music therapy in groups or individually; they may drop in on an open group (e.g., in a psychiatric ward setting) or be referred to and assessed by a music therapist before being placed in individual treatment or a closed group.

MECHANISM OF ACTION

The underlying mechanism of action of music therapy is unknown. One hypothesis that attempts to explain the therapeutic effects of music is based on increased neuroplasticity, which is considered to be one of the crucial mechanisms behind changes in memory performance. It is also posited that music acts as distractor diverting an individual's attention away from a noxious stimulus (Nilsson, 2008). Studies using functional magnetic resonance imaging, positron emission tomography, electroencephalography, and magneto-encephalography have shown that perception and responses to music use many of the same areas and neural networks in the brain that also support language and motor function (D. Holmes, 2012). Ellis and Thayer (2010) proposed that music has an impact on the autonomic nervous system and described their neurovisceral integration model, which includes the interactions between the central and autonomic nervous systems, resulting in physiologic, emotional, and cognitive effects. Additional research on the underlying mechanisms of music therapy is clearly needed so that it may be better understood.

RELEVANT RESEARCH

Music therapy has been widely used in a number of clinical settings; however, empirical research has only recently been conducted. In general, the findings have been positive, with demonstrated benefits to various patient groups (Biley, 2000; Evans, 2002). Table 8.2 provides an evaluation of the scope and quality of the research and provides author recommendations based on the available evidence.

Chemotherapy Side Effects

Oncology patients experience a multitude of physical and psychological symptoms (e.g., fatigue, depression, anxiety) as they undergo chemotherapy

TABLE 8.2
Music Therapy Summary Table

Symptom	Studies[a]	Sample	GRADE[b]	Evaluation
Chemotherapy	1 RCT, 1 experimental and cross-sectional study	Outpatient chemotherapy patients; cancer patients experiencing chemotherapy-induced nausea and vomiting	2B	Weak recommendation, moderate-quality evidence
Depression	1 meta-analysis; 1 Cochrane Review; 11 RCTs	Older adults, depressed adults, working-age adults, dementia patients	2A	Weak recommendation, high-quality evidence
PTSD	1 exploratory RCT; 2 uncontrolled studies	Patients with PTSD not responding to cognitive behavioral therapy	2B	Weak recommendation, moderate-quality evidence
Chronic pain	1 systematic review of 42 RCTs; 1 single-blind RCT	Patients suffering from pain before or after surgery; patients with lumbar pain; fibromyalgia; inflammatory disease	2B	Weak recommendation, moderate-quality evidence
Dementia	4 uncontrolled studies	Dementia patients; nursing care patients	2C	Weak recommendation, low-quality evidence
Schizophrenia	1 controlled trial; 1 RCT; 1 quantitative study	Patients admitted for an acute psychotic episode; hospitalized psychiatric patients experiencing anxiety	2B	Weak recommendation, moderate-quality evidence

Note. PTSD = posttraumatic stress disorder; RCT = randomized controlled trial; GRADE = Grading of Recommendations, Assessment, Development and Evaluation.
[a]Citations available in text or references. Studies are representative; table should not be considered a comprehensive review of all available literature.
[b]Data from the Grade Working Group. Available at http://www.gradeworkinggroup.org/intro.htm.

(Jacobsen et al., 1999; Pelletier, 2004; Williams et al., 2006). Research has linked anxiety to the incidence of pretherapy and posttherapy nausea and vomiting. Because of this link, it is critical for patients to develop skills for managing negative emotional responses and distress. Recently, music interventions have shown promise in decreasing psychological distress during cancer treatment (Clark et al., 2006). Music-assisted relaxation is effective in decreasing arousal for individuals under stress (Pelletier, 2004). Therefore, cancer-related pain, discomfort, and psychological distress may be reduced with music listening, guided imagery, and relaxation.

A randomized controlled trial (RCT) was conducted in an outpatient chemotherapy clinic operated by a university medical center in Taiwan (Lin, Hsieh, Hsu, Fetzer, & Hsu, 2011). In this trial, 98 oncology patients were randomly assigned to receive a 60-minute session of music therapy, a 30-minute verbal-guided relaxation session, or a standard-care control condition. This study showed positive results for both music and verbal relaxation therapy in the reduction of chemotherapy-induced anxiety. Specifically, patients with high state anxiety receiving chemotherapy obtain the most benefit from music or verbal relaxation. Follow-up data were not reported; therefore, the long-term effects of the intervention are not known. Also, although music therapy provided positive benefits in reducing anxiety in this study, it was not superior to verbal relaxation. Replication is necessary to control for therapist engagement, which may provide additional support for music therapy use as an adjunct in the treatment of chemotherapy-related anxiety.

In a related study, an experimental and cross-sectional design was implemented to determine the effects of music therapy and visual imagery on chemotherapy-induced anxiety, nausea, and vomiting. This study was conducted on a single sample group with a pretest–posttest, repeated-measures design. Karagozoglu, Tekyasar, and Yilmaz (2013) identified 40 patients who had experienced nausea and vomiting within a 24-hour period after the first course of chemotherapy. Participants received a combination of music therapy and guided visual imagery, comprising five nature paintings for the guided visual imagery with a researcher-prepared music CD for each painting that included 60 minutes of soft, serene instrumental Turkish music. During the third chemotherapy cycle, patients were assigned to receive the music and visual imagery intervention. Before receiving chemotherapy, patients selected the painting that most appealed to them and gave them a sense of peace and calmness. During the chemotherapy session, the painting was placed near the patients, and they were instructed to imagine that they were in the place the painting depicted while listening to the recorded CD. After chemotherapy, participants completed measures of anxiety and nausea and emesis. The results showed a significant reduction in anxiety levels for patients who received music and guided visual imagery. Additionally, the music therapy and visual imagery intervention significantly reduced the severity and duration of chemotherapy-induced nausea. Results showed that 40% of the patients did not have anticipatory nausea, and 55% of the patients did not have anticipatory vomiting during the third chemotherapy cycle in which music therapy and guided visual imagery were implemented. Although this study showed positive results of a music therapy and visual imagery intervention on chemotherapy-induced anxiety, nausea, and vomiting, there was no control condition; follow-up studies are necessary to determine the long-term effects and optimal dose and confirm whether music therapy is better than standard care.

Depression

In a recent Cochrane Review, five studies were identified that tested music therapy in the treatment of depression in RCTs. Four of the trials reported greater reduction in symptoms of depression among those randomized to music therapy than among those in standard-care conditions (Maratos, Gold, Wang, & Crawford, 2009). One randomized trial did not yield significant results and reported no significant change in mental state for music therapy compared with standard care. Dropout rates from music therapy conditions appeared to be low in all studies, suggesting that music interventions are well received by participants. Overall, these reviews comprised good-quality RCTs using music interventions for alleviation of depression. However, the lack of clear randomization methods and the small sample sizes in the studies hindered firm conclusions. As the authors of the Cochrane Review acknowledged, the heterogeneity of the studies, the differences in research design, and the diverse outcome measures of depression also posed major challenges in conducting a meta-analysis. The music-listening interventions were diverse in nature, without a clear, standardized intervention duration or frequency and in terms of the types of music used. Hence, more studies comparing these factors could be conducted to better understand the effects of such factors on depression.

Most studies fail to investigate the efficacy of different types of music in alleviating depression symptoms. Maratos, Gold, Wang, and Crawford (2009), however, did compare the difference between rock and classical music and found that both types of music were efficacious in reducing postpartum depression. There is evidence to suggest that music interventions, regardless of music type, could potentially reduce depressive symptoms; however, further research is necessary before a specific type of music can be recommended.

In a representative study, music therapy combined with standard care was compared with standard care alone for the treatment of depression in adults (Erkkilä et al., 2011). The researchers randomized 79 participants with a diagnosis of depression based on criterion classification of the 10th revision of the

International Classification of Diseases to receive individualized music therapy plus standard care (20 biweekly sessions) or standard care only. During music sessions, the therapist and client played identical instruments. Results showed that participants who received music therapy plus standard care showed greater improvements in depression symptoms and anxiety symptoms at 3-month follow-up compared with those receiving standard care only. However, although there was significant benefit at the end of treatment, these positive results did not persist at 6-month follow-up. The results from these early studies of music therapy in the treatment of depression are encouraging, but additional studies with improved methodology, larger sample sizes to adequately power effect size estimates, and improved controls are necessary.

Posttraumatic Stress Disorder

Music therapy might be uniquely and broadly suited to the treatment of posttraumatic stress disorder (PTSD) because research has shown that music engages people in a context that is perceived as safe and enjoyable and is universal to all cultures (Pavlicevic, 1997). To date, a small number of studies have examined the use of music therapy to treat adult PTSD patients, finding that it leads to improvements in PTSD symptoms, but small sample sizes and poor methodology dictate that these studies can only be considered preliminary (Bensimon, Amir, & Wolf, 2008).

Recently, however, Carr et al. (2012) assessed whether group music therapy was feasible for patients who did not respond to cognitive behavioral therapy (CBT) and whether it had an effect on PTSD symptoms and depression. In this exploratory RCT, 17 patients with significant PTSD symptoms were randomly assigned to a music intervention or to a control group after completion of a CBT intervention. The treatment group received 10 weeks of group music therapy after which exit interviews were conducted. The results showed that patients receiving the music therapy experienced a significant reduction in the severity of PTSD symptoms and a marginally significant reduction in depression at 10 weeks from baseline compared with the control group. On the basis of these initial results, group music therapy appears to be a potentially feasible and effective treatment for PTSD. However, because of the small sample size and lack of blinding, additional research is required to support these findings.

Chronic Pain

Research suggests that when music is perceived as pleasant to the patient, it is likely to contribute to a reduction in overall pain (Västjäll, Larsson, & Kleiner, 2002). It has also been suggested that the analgesic effect of music may be due to neurophysiological effects specific to pain, with music acting on the sensory, cognitive, affective, and behavioral components. In a review of 51 studies, Cepeda, Carr, Lau, and Alvarez (2006) found that patients who participated in music therapy experienced significant reductions in pain intensity and had a significantly decreased need for opioid treatments for their pain. Nilsson (2008) conducted a review of 42 RCTs of the effects of music therapy on anxiety and pain before, during, and immediately after surgery. The results of this review were mixed, finding significant reductions of symptoms of anxiety and pain for the patients in half of the studies reviewed.

A recent single-blind RCT assessed the efficacy of a music intervention to aid in the management of chronic pain (Guetin et al., 2012). The study included 87 patients presenting with lumbar pain, fibromyalgia, inflammatory disease, or neurological disease. During hospitalization, patients who were assigned to receive the music intervention ($n = 43$) received at least two daily sessions of music listening in addition to standard care between Days 1 and 10. During these sessions, the patients were lying down in their rooms with their eyes closed under minimum lighting so that they felt at ease. The music was played to them through earphones. Patients assigned to the control condition received only standard care ($n = 43$). Results found that participants who received the music intervention showed a significant reduction in pain compared with control. Additionally, music intervention contributed to significantly reducing anxiety and depression as well as the consumption of anxiolytic agents. These results show the promising results of music intervention for the management of chronic pain, anxiety, and depression. However, there was no long-term follow-up and a lack of blinding. Furthermore, reliance on self-report measures limits generalization. Taken together, the studies to date suggest that music therapy may be beneficial in reducing chronic pain, anxiety, and depression; however, additional research is needed before recommending music therapy as a treatment intervention for patients with these symptoms (Cepeda et al., 2006).

Dementia

Music therapy has been used and studied as a component of a comprehensive psychoeducational intervention for patients with mild to moderate dementia (Fischer-Terworth & Probst, 2011). Music therapy was paired with cognitive-behavioral interventions to improve patients' communication, their interactions with the world around them, and their improved resilience in response to their social environment. Although the usual anticipated pattern of cognitive decline was observed in patients receiving standard care, for patients participating in the music therapy and cognitive-behavioral interventions, there was a significant reduction in anxiety, depression, and behavioral agitation. Additionally, patients in the intervention demonstrated significant improvements in communication, social interaction, and emotional regulation compared with those who did not receive the music therapy intervention. Fischer-Terworth (2010) also found that music therapy paired with cognitive behavioral therapy that focused on the structuring of schedules and activities, led to significant decreases in apathy and significant increases in social engagement in dementia patients.

P. Han and colleagues (2010) studied the effects of a music therapy program on disruptive behaviors and depression associated with dementia. They found that participation in a music therapy and activity program resulted in a significant decrease in both disruptive behaviors and depression in the population studied, whereas patients in the waitlist control group demonstrated increases in symptoms in both of these areas of functioning. Similarly, Raglio and colleagues (2010) studied the effects of music therapy on disruptive behaviors in elderly patients with dementia. Patients received three 30-minute music therapy sessions per week for 4 consecutive weeks, and control participants received treatment as usual with no music therapy intervention. They found that music therapy treatment with older adults suffering from dementia resulted in a significant reduction in disruptive behaviors as well as in delusions, agitation, and apathy.

Schizophrenia

Recent investigations have studied the effects of music therapy as an adjunct to pharmacological therapy during an acute psychotic episode. Quantitative evidence indicates that music therapy has the potential to lessen severe emotional and behavioral disturbances, improve symptoms such as thought disorder and severe mood disturbance, and increase communication and social interaction in patients with schizophrenia (Gold, Solli, Krüger, & Lie, 2009; Hayashi et al. 2002). A recent quasi-randomized study performed analysis on 60 participants assigned to either a music intervention or a wait-list control group to determine the effects of music therapy on patients having acute psychotic episodes (Morgan, Bartrop, Telfer, & Tennant, 2011). The treatment group received four individual sessions of active music therapy (improvisation or song writing), whereas the control group received four sessions sitting with the therapist and listening to a prerecorded CD that played relaxing nature sounds. All sessions occurred over a 2-week period with each session lasting from 10 to 30 minutes in length. Results of the study demonstrated significant changes in self-reported psychotic symptoms in the treatment group compared with the control group. However, there were no significant differences detected between the treatment and control groups in depression and anxiety. This study did not show positive results of a music intervention as an adjunctive treatment for acute psychosis.

In a related study, 24 participants were randomized to receive a music intervention aimed at reducing anxiety in hospitalized psychiatric patients (Yang et al., 2012). Patients in the experimental group received music therapy in a therapy room at a set time for 30 minutes each morning for 11 days. Results of the study showed that participants who received music therapy had lower self-reported anxiety than control participants immediately after the music therapy and at 1-week follow-up, indicating that they were experiencing significantly less anxiety. Music therapy may be useful as potential adjunct treatment for anxiety in hospitalized psychiatric patients; however, additional research is necessary to determine optimal dose and duration.

CONTRAINDICATIONS AND RISKS

One review of the music therapy literature found music therapy to have positive effects or to be neutral, with no negative effects reported (Wakim, Smith, & Guinn, 2010). However, it is important for psychologists and their clients to keep in mind that music therapy alone is not an accepted treatment for any medical condition or disorder. Instead, music therapy is intended to be used as an adjunctive treatment. Thus, at this time, music therapy should be considered a complementary medicine, not an alternative one. When administered by a qualified music professional, this modality has been found to be generally safe, and no significant side effects have been reported (Geffen, 2011).

TIPS FOR PRACTITIONERS

- Music therapy may be of benefit in reducing pain, anxiety, and depression as well as for improving general well-being.
- Psychologists who use music therapy should become well acquainted with the relevant literature.
- There are various forms of music therapy and several options for how it is applied (i.e., active vs. passive) that may be integrated with other forms of treatment.
- When music therapy is considered, psychologists should advise their patients on the relevant empirical research and refer them to a certified music therapist.

INTEGRATION WITH PSYCHOLOGICAL PRACTICE

In practice, health care professionals may wish to encourage some patients to listen to music because it is a safe, simple, and inexpensive method of improving quality of life; however, further research is warranted to establish the efficacy of music therapy. Although the range of uses of music therapy that have been demonstrated to be effective are not all applicable to the work of practicing psychologists, some of these may be relevant for psychologists practicing in medical settings. Medical and health psychologists may find the use of music therapy to be beneficial as an adjunct treatment for a variety of patients. As was highlighted in the review of relevant research on music therapy, music interventions may be useful in the management of pain, with oncology patients, and with dementia patients. Although music therapy may not be integrated into ongoing psychotherapy given the time constraints of the typical therapeutic milieu, psychologists working in medical settings and nursing homes may be uniquely qualified to assess these patients' needs. Many of these patients may display symptoms of depression, anxiety, agitation, pain, and emotional or social withdrawal—symptoms that may be amenable to psychological interventions as well as to music therapy interventions. Additionally, psychologists working with patients to help prepare them for, or recover from, surgery or a range of medical procedures may find the integration of music therapy into ongoing treatment to be efficacious.

Music therapy may be beneficial as an adjunct to outpatient psychotherapy for clients who suffer from chronic pain, anxiety, or PTSD. It is, however, important that psychologists be well acquainted with the relevant literature. Furthermore, psychologists will need to be familiar with the training and qualifications needed for the practice of music therapy. Unless a psychologist is also a certified music therapist, it is appropriate to refer the client to a trained and credentialed music therapist to provide music therapy as an adjunct to the psychological interventions provided by the psychologist and any medical interventions provided by the client's physician.

Psychologists can also assist clients in deciding whether music therapy is an appropriate intervention for them. By reviewing the relevant findings from the research literature with clients, psychologists can assist them in making informed decisions about available treatment options and alternatives.

ADDITIONAL RESOURCES

1. American Music Therapy Association (AMTA)—The national professional association for music therapists. AMTA's website (http://musictherapy.org) provides a range of resources relevant

to music therapy for both professionals and the public. Resources include articles on music therapy, information on conferences, and music therapy–related products. Additionally, the AMTA provides a referral service for finding qualified music therapists in one's local area and can be contacted by e-mail for this purpose at findMT@musictherapy.org.

2. Davis, W., Gfeller, K., & Thaut, M. (1999). *An introduction to music therapy: Theory and practice* (3rd ed.). Boston, MA: McGraw-Hill—This comprehensive text provides an excellent review of the history of and recent developments in music therapy. It also reviews recent research findings, discusses the relevant ethical issues, and explains the music therapy treatment process. This book is published by the AMTA and is available online at http://musictherapy.org.

3. MacDonald, R., Kreutz, G., & Mitchell, L. (Eds.). (2012). *Music, health, and wellbeing.* New York, NY: Oxford University Press—This book brings together research from music psychology, therapy, public health, and medicine, to explore the relationship between music, health and wellbeing. It presents a range of chapters from internationally recognized experts, resulting in a comprehensive, multidisciplinary, and pluralistic account of recent advances and applications in both clinical and nonclinical practice and research.

4. The Boyer College of Music and Dance at Temple University—The Boyer College website is an excellent resource for descriptions of what music therapy is, for whom and which difficulties it may be helpful, and the types of music therapy experiences available for clients, as well as for explanations of what clients may actually experience and do in music therapy. The information provided on this site may serve as an excellent introduction to music therapy for psychotherapy clients wanting to learn more about it. The relevant section of the Boyer College website may be accessed at http://www.temple.edu/musictherapy/home/program/faq.htm#a.

5. The Certification Board for Music Therapists (CBMT)—The national credentialing organization for music therapists. CBMT's website provides information on the certification and recertification processes including examinations and continuing education requirements, the CBMT Code of Professional Practice, and a searchable database of certified music therapists. The CBMT website may be accessed at http://www.cbmt.org.

9

SPIRITUALITY AND PRAYER

Many people employ prayer and spirituality to better their health and wellbeing. Survey research has indicated that 82% believe in the healing power of personal prayer, furthermore, 94% of patients admitted to hospitals believe that spiritual health is as important as physical health, and 77% believe that health care providers should consider patients' spiritual needs as a part of their medical care (King & Bushwick, 1994). A 1998 study, conducted to determine the prevalence of CAM use in the United States, found that prayer was the fifth most frequently used treatment among all CAM therapies assessed (Astin, 1998). Additionally, the same study found that 35% of participants reported using prayer to address health-related problems. Prayer is central to the value and philosophic systems of numerous individuals across various faiths and cultures. A recent national survey of critical care nurses determined that 73% integrated prayer into their practices, 81% had recommended it to patients, and 79% had been requested by patients and their

http://dx.doi.org/10.1037/14435-010
Complementary and Alternative Medicine for Psychologists: An Essential Resource, by J. E. Barnett, A. J. Shale, G. Elkins, and W. Fisher

families to pray on their behalf (Tracy et al., 2005). It is estimated that 95% of Americans believe in God or a "greater power" (J. Jones & Saad, 2011) and 77% believe God can intervene to cure those with a serious illness (Kaplan, 1996). It is apparent that prayer is widely used by patients in health care settings and should be studied and better understood (Masters & Speilman, 2007). A substantial body of research has been devoted to examining the relationship of spirituality, religion and health, with sufficient research regularly published to warrant stand-alone, topical, peer-reviewed, professional journals. The *Journal of Religion and Health*, for example, was founded in 1964 and is an international interdisciplinary journal which publishes original peer-reviewed articles that deal with mental and physical health in relation to religion and spirituality of all kinds.

DEFINITIONS

Spirituality is a broad term used to classify approaches involving the intentional influence of one or more persons on another living system without using known physical means of intervention (Benor, 1990). *Prayer* is also a broad term, and there are a number of types of prayer (Masters & Speilman, 2007). Prevailing conceptualizations are typically reliant on theological and scientific frameworks; however, comparisons are difficult because of multiple taxonomies and problems with construct validity. Foster (1992) categorized prayer under three general dimensions: inward prayers (seeking self-transformation), upward prayers (seeking intimacy with the divine), and outward prayers (seeking connections with others). Foster suggested that each of these broad categories can be further dissembled into seven specific types of prayer for a total of 21 prayer types. Although based on Christian conceptualizations of prayer, Foster's model provides a framework for empirical study of prayer types within various cultures. Several other researchers have identified various types of prayer that may be linked to health and well-being (Breslin & Lewis, 2008; Laird et al., 2004; Poloma & Pendleton, 1991).

HISTORY

Since the beginning of recorded history, all cultures throughout the world have developed systems of religion and spirituality. The early religions of ancient Egypt and Greece have given way to relatively more recent religions such as Christianity, Judaism, Hinduism, Islam, and Buddhism.

Within each culture, some form of spirituality and prayer has served as the institutionalized means of seeking assistance from a supreme being or beings perceived as powerful enough to alter nature, health, and disease. Different religions hold different beliefs about a supreme being. Given the scope of religion and prayer, this chapter focuses solely on the scientific study of prayer pertaining to health.

Prayer is the oldest and most widespread intervention used with the intention of alleviating illness and promoting increased quality of life (P. M. Barnes, Powell-Griner, McFann, & Nahin, 2004; McCaffrey, Eisenberg, & Legedza, 2004). The scientific study of prayer can trace its origins back to the work of Sir Francis Galton (1872), who concluded in his pioneering study that prayer had no efficacy. Regardless of that negative initial study, research in the area has slowly developed over the years. Over the past two decades, there has been an increase in the scientific study of prayer and its effects on health (Koenig, McCullough, & Larson, 2000).

COMMON USES

Spirituality and prayer are used for many purposes, ranging from coping with illness and improving general health to facilitating the grieving process after loss (Eisenberg et al., 1998). Also, for many patients, prayer is commonly used to cope with stressful events and for stress reduction. Pain reduction is another common use of prayer. In a study of 157 hospitalized adults with moderate to high pain levels, prayer was second only to pain medications (76% vs. 82%) as the most common self-reported means of controlling pain (McNeill, Sherwood, Starck, & Thompson, 1998). Furthermore, several types of prayer have been associated with lower levels of distress and greater well-being (e.g., Ladd & Spilka, 2006). Additionally, prayer is often used as a coping mechanism for those with cancer or other terminal illness (e.g., Levine, Aviv, Yoo, Ewing, & Au, 2009).

TECHNIQUE

Prayer has many forms and can be practiced in many ways; it may be silent, spoken aloud, sung, or chanted. Additionally, it can be performed alone in any setting, or it can be done in groups, such as in a church, mosque, synagogue, or temple. Regular attendance at a place of worship may involve prayer that focuses on oneself (called *supplication*) or on others (called *intercessory prayer*). In this setting, the entire congregation may be asked to pray for a sick person or the person's family. Some religions set aside certain times of day and days of the week for prayer. Standard prayers written by religious leaders are often memorized and repeated in private sessions and in groups.

Prayer is also practiced individually and in informal groups, without a specific religion or denomination and on no particular schedule. Prayers often ask a higher being for help, understanding, wisdom, or strength in dealing with life's problems.

Spirituality also can be practiced with or without a formal religion. Meditation, 12-step work (as practiced in Alcoholics Anonymous and similar groups), and seeking meaning in life all involve spirituality. Even simple practices such as silent observation, listening, or gratitude, can become part of an open-ended spirituality that can infuse everyday life. Some people express their spirituality by spending time with nature, doing creative work, or serving others. Furthermore, many medical institutions and practitioners include spirituality and prayer as important components of healing. In addition, hospitals have chapels and contracts with ministers, rabbis, clerics, and voluntary organizations to serve their patients' spiritual needs.

MECHANISM OF ACTION

The mechanisms through which spirituality and prayer may work are unknown; however, the underlying mechanisms have been the topic of some scientific study. Involvement in religious activities such as church attendance can provide increased social support and positive interactions and discourage unhealthy behaviors such as smoking and excessive alcohol use (Koenig, McCullough, & Larson, 2000). In this regard, religious involvement is associated with fewer hospitalizations and shorter hospital stays because of the social support and improved health behaviors in provides (Koenig, McCullough, & Larson, 2000).

Another proposed mechanism of action related to prayer is the relaxation response; prayer may elicit the lowering of blood pressure and other factors heightened by stress (Benson et al., 2006). There is some evidence to suggest that prayer may provide beneficial physiological responses such as decreased heart rate, decreased episodes of angina in cardiology patients, and increased immune function (Benson, 1984; Meisenhelder & Chandler, 2000). Also, a mind–body–spirit connection has been proposed as a potential mechanism. When prayer uplifts or calms, it inhibits the release of cortisol and other stress-related hormones, thus reducing the negative impact of stress on the immune system and promoting healing (Center for Spirituality and Healing, 2009).

Finally, the placebo response has been proposed to explain the benefits of prayer. It may be that a change in cognitive expectancies and beliefs following prayer may lead to improved health. In any case, it can be confidently stated that the mechanism of action that fully explains the benefits seen through prayer have yet to be determined. There is a paucity of physiological and neuroimaging studies involving the use of prayer. Although there is no clear answer as to how prayer, spirituality, and religion affect one's health and well-being, it is likely that with continued research in the area, it will be possible to eventually gain further understanding as to how and why they work.

RELEVANT RESEARCH

Despite several reviews that examined the research on the positive effects of prayer (e.g., Benor, 1990; Sicher, Targ, Moore, & Smith, 1998; Targ, 1997), there is continuing debate regarding the efficacy of spirituality and prayer as health interventions (Rosa, Rosa, Sarner, & Barrett, 1998; Sloan, Bagiella, & Powell, 1999). Some scientists and researchers do not believe that the efficacy of spirituality and prayer is something that can be empirically tested because it "resembles a nonscientific, almost mystical perspective" (Chapman, 1996, p. 41). Despite this view, a significant amount of research on prayer and spirituality has examined its utility in treatment and the impact it has on people with specific symptoms and ailments, such as addiction, depression, and chronic pain (Cook, 2004; Poyser, 2004). Table 9.1 provides an evaluation of the scope and quality of the research and provides author recommendations based on the available evidence.

Cardiac Care and Intercessory Prayer

Several studies have investigated the effect of intercessory prayer on recovery from cardiac surgery. The findings are mixed, and it is not yet known if intercessory prayer improves outcomes for cardiac patients. However, several studies have involved large samples and used double-blind research designs. In a double-blind, randomized controlled study, Benson et al. (2006) examined whether remote intercessory prayer influenced recovery after coronary artery bypass graft surgery and whether the uncertainty of being prayed for was associated with better outcome measures. The sample consisted of 1,802 patients in six U.S. hospitals. Study participants were randomized into three groups: 604 were prayed for after being informed that they may or may not be prayed for, 597 were not prayed for after also being informed that they may or may not be prayed for, and 601 were prayed for after being informed that they would be prayed for. The first name and last initial of the last name and anonymous site code for patients assigned to Groups 1 and 3 were placed on a prayer list for 14 consecutive days, starting the night before each patient's scheduled surgery. Intercessors from three Catholic groups and one Protestant group provided prayer throughout the trial. The primary outcome assessed was the presence of any complication within 30 days of surgery,

TABLE 9.1
Summary Table for Spirituality and Prayer

Symptom	Studies[a]	Sample	GRADE[b]	Evaluation
Cardiac care	2 blinded RCTs	Patients received coronary artery bypass graft surgery; patients in the coronary care unit	2A	Weak recommendation, high-quality evidence
Oncology	1 triple blinded randomized trial; 1 randomized blinded study	Pediatric oncology patients with leukemia; patients with various types of cancer	2B	Weak recommendation, moderate-quality evidence
Depression and anxiety	1 systematic review of 13 trials; 1 meta-analysis; 1 RCT	Patients who met the *DSM–IV* criteria for depressive disorder; psychiatric inpatients with major depressive disorder	2A	Weak recommendation, high-quality evidence
Chronic pain	1 survey study	Patients reporting chronic pain	2C	Weak recommendation, low-quality evidence
Alcohol addiction	1 randomized, double-blind, pilot study; 1 survey study	Patients entering treatment for alcohol abuse or dependence	2C	Weak recommendation, weak-quality evidence

Note. DSM–IV = Diagnostic and Statistical Manual of Mental Disorders (4th ed.); RCT = randomized controlled trial; GRADE = Grading of Recommendations, Assessment, Development and Evaluation.
[a]Citations available in text or references. Studies are representative; table should not be considered a comprehensive review of all available literature.
[b]Data from the Grade Working Group. Available at http://www.gradeworkinggroup.org/intro.htm.

and data were collected by blinded nursing staff. Results of the study showed that in the two groups that did not know for certain whether they were being prayed for, complications occurred in 52% of patients who had received prayer and in 51% of those who did not receive intercessory prayer. In contrast, complications occurred in a significantly larger percentage of patients (59%) who knew for certain that they were being prayed for. However, major events and 30-day mortality events show no significant differences between groups. In conclusion, this showed that remote intercessory prayer did not improve outcomes after coronary artery bypass graft surgery. This finding was surprising as it was both counter-intuitive and inconsistent with the expected outcome that prayer would be beneficial. While the reason for the findings in this particular study remains elusive, it is possible that the participants who received intercessory prayer actually suffered from more serious illness than those in the control group in spite of careful attention to randomization. In any case, this points to the challenging nature of clinical studies of prayer in health care.

In contrast to this, Harris and colleagues (1999) found that intercessory prayer may reduce medical complications among cardiac patients. In their blinded randomized controlled trial with 990 coronary care unit patients, the researchers randomly assigned each participant to an experimental condition in which a group of Christian intercessors prayed for them or to a control condition. Results of the study showed participants who had been assigned to receive intercessory prayer showed fewer complications than participants in the control condition. However, no significant difference was found between groups for length of cardiac care unit or hospital stay.

Although its effect on recovery from cardiac surgery is inconclusive, intercessory prayer may have other benefits that have not yet been fully explored. In this regard, it should be noted that a Cochrane Review (Roberts, Ahmed, Hall, & Davison, 2009) and others (Abbot, 2000; Astin, Harkness, & Ernst, 2000) concluded that further scientific investigation into the possible effects of intercessory prayer is warranted.

Oncology

In prayer studies involving oncology patients, religiosity and spiritual well-being appear to correlate with positive mood, hope, and quality of life (Fehring, Miller, & Shaw, 1997; Mickley, Soeken, & Belcher, 1992; Schnoll, Harlow, & Brower, 2000). Results of a questionnaire survey of 1,000 oncology patients showed that patients with expressed faith identified fewer psychosocial needs than those patients without faith (Soothill et al., 2002). One of the first studies to assess the efficacy of prayer in oncology patients was conducted with children with leukemia (Collipp, 1969). This was a triple-blind study in which physicians treating these leukemic children supplied the name, age, date of diagnosis, and date of mortality. The only explanation to these physicians was that the study would evaluate the responses of the children and their family to their disease. At monthly intervals, parents of the children and each child's physician would complete questionnaires regarding whether the adjustment of the child was better, unchanged, or worse. The names of 10 leukemia patients were randomly selected and sent to 10 families in a Protestant church to pray for the pediatric oncology patients, but they were not informed of the study. Results of the study demonstrated that after 15 months of prayer, of the 10 leukemia patients assigned to the prayer condition, seven remained alive. Of the eight children assigned to the control group, only two remained alive. However, because of the small sample size, the results are difficult to discern and are not generalizable. This study did support the possibility of efficacy and provided support for further study.

More recently, a randomized, blinded study of intercessory prayer was conducted with oncology patients (Olver & Dutney, 2012). The researchers hypothesized that the most likely measurable impact of intercessory prayer was improvement in spiritual well-being, which was the primary outcome in this study. Results of the study demonstrated that the participants receiving intercessory prayer showed significantly greater improvements over time in spiritual well-being compared with the control group. Furthermore, the study found a similar result for emotional well-being and functional well-being. As hypothesized, this study indicated that the addition of intercessory prayer to standard medical care for cancer is associated with a small but significant improvement in spiritual well-being. Further research is warranted because research indicated that spiritual well-being has an impact on various parameters of quality of life (J. G. Smith & Fisher, 2000).

Depression and Anxiety

Several studies have investigated the use of prayer as a coping mechanism for dealing with depression and anxiety. The evidence is mixed (Koenig, 2009). For instance, a systematic review of 23 trials involving 2,774 participants evaluated the efficacy of any form of "distant healing" (i.e., intercessory prayer) for any medical condition showed that 13 trials yielded significant treatment effects, nine trials showed no effect, and one study showed a negative effect of prayer (Astin et al., 2000). Additionally, a meta-analysis of 14 studies of distant prayer for healing suggested no treatment efficacy (Masters, Speilman, & Goodson, 2006).

Boelens, Reeves, Replogle, and Koenig (2009) investigated the effects of direct person-to-person prayer on depression, anxiety, positive emotions, and salivary cortisol levels. Eligible participants who met the criteria for *Diagnostic and Statistical Manual of Mental Disorders* (4th ed.; American Psychiatric Association, 1994) depressive disorder with symptoms of anxiety were randomized into a prayer intervention group or a control group. Participants assigned to the prayer intervention completed a series of weekly sessions for 6 weeks. The control group received no prayer intervention or any other intervention; however, control group participants were eligible to cross over to receive the prayer intervention at the end of the study. Results showed that participants who received the prayer intervention had significant improvements in depression and anxiety scores as measured by the Hamilton Depression and Anxiety Rating Scales (Hamilton, 1959, 1960). Additionally, participants assigned to the prayer condition had significant increases in daily spiritual experiences and optimism as determined by the Life Orientation Test (Scheier & Carver, 1985). However, no significant differences were found in cortisol levels between pre- and postprayer conditions. Participants maintained significant improvements for at least 1 month after the final prayer session. A recent follow-up study reassessed participants with the same measures 1 year later (Boelens, Reeves, Replogle, & Koenig, 2012), finding that participants who had received the prayer intervention showed significantly less depression and anxiety and more optimism than participants did at baseline. These studies suggest that direct person-to-person prayer may be a useful adjunctive treatment in addition to standard medical care for patients with depression and anxiety; however, further replication is necessary before recommendation.

Chronic Pain

In a 2008 study, 118 patients with chronic pain completed online questionnaires to investigate the relationship between chronic pain and praying (Andersson, 2008). Participants suffered from various forms of chronic pain, with the majority of pain represented with chronic low back pain and neck pain. All participants completed a three-item subscale measuring prayer as a coping strategy that was derived from the Coping Strategies Questionnaire (Rosenstiel & Keefe, 1983). The questionnaire was adapted to refer to "a higher power" instead of "God." The participants' pain was assessed by the Multidimensional Pain Inventory (Kerns, Turk, & Rudy, 1985) and the Pain and Impairment Relationship Scale (Riley, Ahern, & Follick, 1988). Additionally, anxiety and depression were measured via the Hospital Anxiety Depression Scale (Zigmond & Snaith, 1983).

Results revealed significant correlations between praying and pain interference and impairment. Furthermore, praying was also associated with anxiety and depression scores. Prayer predicted depression scores at follow-up, and follow-up prayer was predicted by pain interference at the baseline assessment. Higher levels of distress were associated with more praying both concurrently and prospectively. Further research is needed and a randomized controlled trial is necessary if the relationship between prayer and the management of chronic pain is to be more fully understood.

Alcohol Addiction

The treatment of psychoactive substance abuse disorders is one of the few areas of allopathic medicine in which spirituality is considered relevant to clinical outcomes (Miller, 1990; Miller & Kurtz, 1994). Religious involvement has been found to correlate with less risk of substance abuse problems (Kendler, Gardner, & Prescott, 1997; Moore, 1990). However, it is active involvement rather than mere attendance in spirituality-based programs such as Alcoholics Anonymous that has been shown to be helpful in recovery from alcohol problems (S. Carroll, 1993; Montgomery, Miller, & Tonigan, 1995). A literature review by Cook (2004) identified that 36% of the 265 articles regarding the relationship between addiction and spirituality pertained to the use of prayer as a potential treatment for alcohol addiction. The literature suggests that spirituality may be a potential point of reference for the treatment of addiction because people with addiction report a general lack of purpose or direction in their lives. Researchers hypothesize that spirituality may be the necessary initial step toward meeting that need (Piderman, Schneekloth, Pankratz, Maloney, & Altchuler, 2007).

The role of intercessory prayer in treatment for alcohol dependence has also been investigated. Walker, Tonigan, Miller, Corner, and Kahlich (1997) conducted a randomized, double-blind pilot study to determine the efficacy of intercessory prayer on patients entering treatment for alcohol abuse or dependence. In addition to standard care, 40 participants who were admitted to a public substance abuse treatment facility who gave informed consent were randomized to receive or not receive intercessory prayer by outside volunteers. Results of the study found no significant difference between the prayer intervention and nonintervention groups on alcohol consumption. Compared with a normative group of patients treated at the same facility, participants who had received the prayer intervention experienced a delay in drinking reduction. Those who had reported at baseline that a family member or friend was praying for them were found to be drinking significantly more at 6 months than those who reported not being aware of anyone praying for them. However, greater frequency of prayer was associated with less drinking, but results from daily logs showed significance only at Months 2 and 3. Intercessory prayer did not demonstrate positive results under these study conditions. Further research must be conducted before prayer may be recommended as an adjunctive treatment for alcohol addiction.

CONTRAINDICATIONS AND RISKS

When incorporating spirituality and religion into psychotherapy, it is important that psychologists do not attempt to impose their own beliefs or values on their clients. This type of imposition can occur if the psychotherapist tries to "preach, teach, or otherwise persuade clients that their own particular religious and spiritual ideology, denomination, cause, or worldview is the most correct, worthwhile, moral, or healthy" (Richards & Bergin, 1997, p. 154). This is especially relevant because many professionals who want to integrate spirituality and religion into psychology may "come from an active and involved religious tradition" (Plante, 2007, p. 898). Therefore, it is possible that although psychologists may be knowledgeable with regard to their own beliefs and traditions, they may be "rather uninformed about issues related to other faith traditions" (Plante, 2007, p. 898). Recognizing this potential weakness is important, and monitoring for personal biases is essential for adequate and ethical treatment.

Another common potential pitfall is related to competence; many people may assume that being a practicing member of a particular faith or religious group makes them competent to integrate spirituality and religion into psychotherapy. It is important for psychologists to recognize the difference between a clinician who integrates religion and spirituality into the psychotherapy he or she provides versus attempting to serve as a member of the clergy by offering "pastoral care, spiritual direction, or theological consultation if they are not competent to do so" (Plante, 2007, p. 899). Also, it is important to keep in mind that the American Psychological Association (APA) Ethics Code (APA, 2010) requires psychologists to be tolerant and respectful of others' beliefs, but it does not ask psychologists to be "complacent or condone destructive thoughts, feelings, and behaviors, most especially when they result in significant physical or mental harm, abuse, or neglect" (Plante, 2007, p. 899). Therefore, the APA Ethics Code requires that psychologists protect others from undue harm, and it is important to take the necessary steps if it becomes apparent that clients or others are in danger because of their religious or spiritual beliefs. For example, Plante (2007) described a situation in which a client suggested withholding medical care from a child diagnosed with diabetes as a result of the client's personal beliefs. In this situation, if the clinician is unable to resolve this with the client through psychotherapy, the likely step would be to file a report with Child Protective Services because the clinician is legally mandated to report this instance of neglect, even though it is founded in religious beliefs.

INTEGRATION WITH PSYCHOLOGICAL PRACTICE

Spiritual and religious issues may have an impact on a patient's emotional and psychological distress or may provide an important source of strength and support. However, unless there is an inquiry by the psychologist, these issues may be overlooked (Plante, 2009). It is therefore recommended that consideration be given for a spiritual and religious assessment to be included in the initial assessment of every psychotherapy patient. In addition to gathering information about patients' religious and spiritual history and current practices, it may be important to directly ask about spiritual and religious issues that may be of relevance to their mental health difficulties and concerns and to ask if they are interested in addressing these issues in psychotherapy or would prefer a referral to a member of the clergy. Although some patients will be pleased to discuss these issues in psychotherapy, others may not believe that their religious issues are relevant for discussion with psychologists in psychotherapy and may prefer that such issues must be saved for discussion with members of the clergy (Hathaway, Scott, & Garver, 2004).

For those patients who wish to address these issues in psychotherapy, it is important to discuss all elements of this decision, including the specific techniques to be integrated into treatment, in the informed consent process. Spiritual assessment is a three-stage process: the initial spiritual assessment, the extensive spiritual assessment, and the implicit spiritual assessment. The initial assessment, while traditionally covering a client's history, should also address the importance of spirituality in the client's life, religious affiliation if there is one, and the relevance of spirituality to the problem as well as the solution (Pargament & Krumrie, 2009). The aim of the extensive assessment is to "gain more detailed information about clients' spiritual beliefs, practices, and experiences and the role that each places in their clinical problems or the solutions to them" (Pargament & Krumrie, 2009, p. 101). Therefore, this phase of the assessment is more of an opportunity for the client to share his or her spiritual story as opposed to a structured interview. Last is the implicit assessment that is a time for the clinician to listen for underlying spiritual themes. Additionally, it may be beneficial to ask "questions that open the door for discussion about a broad range of spiritual experiences" (Pargament & Krumrie, 2009, p. 111).

Once the assessment has been completed, a variety of techniques can be used when seeking to utilize spirituality and prayer in psychotherapy. Spirituality may be integrated into psychotherapy through techniques such as prayer, spiritual journaling, reading scripture, and forgiveness techniques (Richards & Potts, 1995). One must always be assessing the appropriateness of using these techniques in sessions, and client feedback is extremely important. Psychologists must also be constantly aware of their own beliefs and ensure that their work is in the best of interest of the client as opposed to preaching about a specific religion or set of beliefs. This is a topic that can be discussed during clients' intake; their current practices may suffice for incorporating spirituality and religion into the process of creating change in their lives. The use of spirituality and religion may be particularly pertinent to those with addictions as well as those grieving or those who have recently suffered some sort of loss. These tools may help them understand the meaning of certain life situations.

One practice that is often avoided is praying together in session because at times it may "take the therapeutic relationship and turn it into something akin to spiritual direction" (West, 2000, p. 102). In other instances, however, it may be helpful to assign passages of scripture as a form of homework (West, 2000). Another technique that can be effective is relaxation or religious imagery (Propst, 1996). Additionally, encouraging forgiveness can be a valuable tool to use with spiritually minded clients (West, 2000). Forgiveness allows clients to let go of "what can be presumed to be predictable human tendencies to respond to injury and injustice with resentment, blame, envy, bitterness, vengefulness, spite, or grudge bearing" (Lansky, 2009, p. 374). West (2000) suggested that it may also be beneficial to use religious bibliotherapy, which can involve suggestions for "clients to read and study such texts outside of sessions," or to have the psychotherapist quote sacred writings (p. 105). This can be difficult to use appropriately and should be included only after fully assessing the client's comfort and compatibility with this technique and only when the clinician is competent to use these strategies.

It should also be noted that spirituality and religion are not factors that have to be incorporated into each clinician's work, and it is important to be aware of appropriate ways to make referrals. At times, it may be appropriate to make a referral to the clergy, so it is valuable to take the time to form relationships with members of the local clergy to be able to consult with them as well as to make referrals when necessary. At times, it may also be valuable to consult with a member of the clergy to learn about a particular faith that a patient may be discussing. This is especially important when a client is describing religious beliefs or practices that the psychologist is unfamiliar with and that may not be appropriate or widely accepted.

Ultimately, it is essential that patients feel "that it is okay to talk about their religious and spiritual beliefs and concerns and that when they do" share, their clinician will work to understand and empathize with them (Richards & Bergin, 1997, p. 138). La Torre (2002) noted that whether or not we choose to incorporate religion and spirituality into psychotherapy, "our attitudes and beliefs, experience with religion, and view of the world come with us when we enter a therapeutic session," so it is important to be aware of them as well as their implications (p. 109).

ADDITIONAL RESOURCES

1. The Association for Spirituality and Psychotherapy (ASP)— The ASP, originally known as the Center for Spirituality and Psychotherapy, is an international organization that is committed to gaining greater understanding of the relationship between spirituality and psychotherapy. The ASP puts out a semiannual publication titled *Psychospiritual Dialogue*. Its website can be found at http://asphealing.org.

2. The American Association of Pastoral Counselors (AAPC)—The AAPC offers a wide range of events, conferences, and meetings that focus on the incorporation of spirituality and religion into psychotherapy. A list of their upcoming events can be found at http://www.aapc.org/content/conferences-meetings-and-events.

3. American Psychological Association Society for the Psychology of Religion and Spirituality (APA Division 36)—Division 36 is a nonsectarian branch of the APA that works to further research into understanding how and when religion and/or spirituality can be incorporated in psychotherapy. Division 36 produces a quarterly publication titled *Psychology of Religion and Spirituality* and hosts an annual conference on topics relevant to the psychology or religion and spirituality. Its homepage can be accessed at http://www.division36.org.

4. Directory of Pastoral Counselors—Although it is not required to be a pastoral counselor to incorporate spirituality and religion into more traditional psychotherapy, some clients may want to work with someone who is explicitly trained in this area. The AAPC provides a practitioner locator tool that can be accessed at http://www.aapc.org/content/find-counselor.

10

ACUPUNCTURE

Acupuncture is a traditional treatment that has been used for thousands of years involving the stimulation of certain points on the human body. However, despite the reported use of acupuncture over centuries, research on the efficacy of acupuncture began in earnest in the 1970s. Acupuncture is widely used both as a standalone treatment and as a complementary treatment in conjunction with more conventional forms of health care. Data from the 2007 National Health Interview Survey indicate that approximately 3.1 million adults and 150,000 children in the United States had an acupuncture treatment in the preceding year (P. M. Barnes, Bloom, & Nahin, 2008). Additionally, results indicated that acupuncture use by adults in the United States increased from 2.1 million to 3.1 million between 2001 and 2006 (P. M. Barnes et al., 2008). Burke, Upchurch, Dye, and Chyu (2006) reported that the typical acupuncture treatment tends to span between 2 and 4 sessions. The most frequent complaint addressed by acupuncture is lower back pain (Burke et al., 2006).

http://dx.doi.org/10.1037/14435-011
Complementary and Alternative Medicine for Psychologists: An Essential Resource, by J. E. Barnett, A. J. Shale, G. Elkins, and W. Fisher

Current research on acupuncture includes its effects on chronic low-back pain, joint pain, and headaches as well as a variety of other health concerns.

DEFINITIONS

The word *acupuncture* has its roots in the Latin words *acus*, which means "needle," and *punctura*, which means "perforation" or "prick" (Duke Center for Integrative Medicine [DCIM], 2006). The technique requires specific areas on the body to be excited, typically through "penetrating the skin with thin, solid, metallic needles that are manipulated by the hands or by electrical stimulation" (National Institutes of Health [NIH], 2011b, para. 3). The specific location of the needle placement and the depth of placement, as well as how long the needles are left in place and how they are moved or stimulated are essential elements of skill needed by the acupuncture practitioner. The acupuncture needles are inserted "at specific points on the body to stimulate or balance the flow of life energy, called *qi* in Oriental philosophy" (DCIM, 2006, p. 464). *Qi* "is said to flow along 14 channels called *meridians*; the needling is targeted to about 360 specific *acupoints* along these channels" (DCIM, 2006, p. 464). Yet some sources report that there may actually be up to 20 meridians and more than 2,000 acupoints (NIH, 2011b). The number, placement, and stimulation of the needles are also thought to bring about different effects for a wide range of conditions and ailments (Ergil & Ergil, 2010).

In Oriental philosophy, "the body is seen as a delicate balance of two opposing and inseparable forces: yin and yang" (NIH, 2011b, para. 4). It believed that for a person to experience health, these two opposing forces must be in balance. When they are out of balance, different disease states may be experienced. On the basis of the symptoms being experienced and knowledge of the meridians and the acupoints, acupuncture practitioners can help the individual obtain harmony, thereby improving health. The National Center for Complementary and Alternative Medicine (NIH, 2011b) stated that the imbalance between yin and yang "leads to blockage in the flow of *qi*," which is believed to be "the vital energy or life force proposed to regulate a person's spiritual, emotional, mental, and physical health" (para. 4). These blockages in the flow of *qi* occur along the meridians. When placed at appropriate points on the body, the acupuncture needles can help unblock the meridians and help to bring yin and yang back into balance, allowing the individual to achieve a healthy state. In acupuncture, yin and yang are represented by the body and the needle; the body is large, soft, and full of life (yin), whereas the needle is small, hard, and artificial (yang; Ergil & Ergil, 2010).

HISTORY

It has been reported that acupuncture was present in ancient China more than 5,000 years ago. A 5,200-year-old mummified body was recovered from a glacier in the Alps that "had tattoos that corresponded to specific acupuncture points that relate to ailments of the joints and stomach" (DCIM, 2006, p. 464). *The Yellow Emperor's Classic of Internal Medicine*, which dates from approximately 100 BCE clearly articulates the concepts of meridians and qi. This book is reported to be a compilation of wisdom passed down over centuries. It was followed by *The Great Compendium of Acupuncture and Moxibustion*, which was published during the Ming dynasty (1368–1644), and which has been described as the basis for modern acupuncture (White & Ernst, 2004). Furthermore, White and Ernst (2004) explained clear descriptions of the full set of 365 points that represent openings to the channels through which needles could be inserted to modify the flow of *qi* energy.

Acupuncture spread from China to Japan and Korea in the 6th century, followed by Vietnam between the 8th and 10th centuries. It reached Europe in the 16th century, brought by Jesuit missionaries returning from Asia (White & Ernst, 2004). Acupuncture first received widespread attention in the United States when James Reston, a journalist, was in China providing coverage in preparation for President Richard Nixon's arrival. Mr. Reston became ill and underwent an emergency appendectomy at a hospital in China, and acupuncture was used to assist with pain during his postoperative period. He chronicled these events in the *New York Times*, bringing information on acupuncture to a wide audience in the United States (Reston, 1971). However, acupuncture did not receive any widespread acceptance in the United States until the publication of the NIH's Consensus Statement on Acupuncture (NIH Consensus Panel, 1997). Although this statement pointed out that, at the time, research findings on the effectiveness of acupuncture were difficult to interpret because of the design and size of most available research, it did state that acupuncture was found to be effective for postoperative pain, fibromyalgia, menstrual cramps, and side effects of chemotherapy such as nausea (Marwick, 1997; NIH Consensus Panel, 1997).

COMMON USES

Acupuncture is the most widely used form of Traditional Chinese Medicine (TCM) in the United States today (Sherman et al., 2005). A number of other types or schools of acupuncture are also practiced, and these include Japanese, Korean, Vietnamese, and French-based schools of acupuncture as well as the

Worsley Five Elements school of acupuncture (L. L. Barnes, 2005). Other less widely used and related forms of treatment include auricular acupuncture, moxibustion, and electroacupuncture. Acupuncture is widely used in the treatment of lower back pain, and it is reported that up to 34% of treatments provided by acupuncture professionals address this concern, followed by other musculoskeletal and pain-related difficulties including joint pain, neck pain, headache, and migraines (Burke, Upchurch, Dye, & Chyu, 2006). Acupuncture is also frequently used to treat allergies, arthritis, fibromyalgia, anxiety, and depression. Additionally, it has been used as a form of anesthesia, for general pain management, in oncology treatment for pain control and to address nausea secondary to chemotherapy, in substance abuse and addictions treatment, and in HIV treatment (Bier, Wilson, Studt, & Shakleton, 2002; Burke et al., 2006; Sherman et al., 2005). Acupuncture has also been used in infertility treatment, to treat stoke, and as the primary form of anesthesia for childbirth (DCIM, 2006).

MECHANISM OF ACTION

J. S. Han and Terenius (1982) proposed a neurological model to explain acupuncture's effects, citing evidence that "acupuncture needles stimulate nerve endings and alter brain function, particularly the intrinsic pain inhibitory mechanisms" (White & Ernst, 2004, p. 663). K. J. Cheng (2009) proposed that traditional acupuncture points have neuroanatomical significance such that acupuncture can result in intramuscular stimulation and nerve stimulation. Furthermore, functional magnetic resonance imaging data provide evidence of acupuncture stimulation at specific traditional acupuncture points relaying changes in the corresponding places in the brain. For example, Dhond, Kettner, and Napadow (2007) shared data on acupuncture stimulation of vision-related traditional acupuncture points resulting in activation of vision-related centers in the occipital cortex. Acupuncture may promote the release of various types of neurotransmitters, including opioid peptides (J. S. Han & Terenius, 1982). Additionally, through the use of neuroimaging and genomics scientists have been able to document changes in the brain's pain centers in response to acupuncture to include molecular changes in the nervous and immune systems (Complementary and Alternative Medicine, 2011).

Some research suggests that acupuncture modifies how individuals perceive pain and how pain is processed in the brain (Complementary and Alternative Medicine, 2011). Other research (e.g., Napadow et al., 2007) has documented changes in the hypothalamus and amygdala in response to acupuncture for carpal tunnel syndrome. Additional research is warranted to fully understand the underlying mechanisms.

TECHNIQUE

Trained acupuncturists know the location and function of each meridian and each acupoint. Twelve of the meridians have relevance to specific organ systems, six of which are classified as yin and six of which are classified as yang. Each of the yin channels is paired with a yang channel exhibiting their physiological connection to one another. The meridians connect all parts of the body and allow *qi*, blood, and body fluids to move freely throughout the body. However, when these channels become blocked, an imbalance is created, and this is what is believed to cause ill health (Ergil & Ergil, 2010). The points or *holes* are the places along the meridians where "we can touch the Qi, blood and spirit of the patient" (Ergil & Ergil, 2010, p. 413). It is in these points that acupuncturists strategically place needles. These points have been standardized; however, some acupuncturists prefer their own methods and base the location of the needle placement predominantly on patient response and the presence of *qi*.

An acupuncturist can identify the channel that is blocked by noting the specific symptoms. This is based on the belief that when different channels are blocked, they cause specific physiological symptoms and signs. It is also possible for these symptoms to reflect not only a blockage in the channel but a pathology originating in the organ with which the channel is associated. By understanding the problem in the flow of *qi*, acupuncturists can direct the needle in the same or opposing orientation of the *qi* flow to increase or decrease the flow. The most common needle is a filiform needle with a handle about 1 inch long and a shaft between 1 and 1.5 inches long. However, there is no standard length, diameter, or configuration, and they can vary widely between practitioners (Ergil & Ergil, 2010). Treatment duration varies according to the method used but typically lasts between 20 to 40 minutes; in some cases, however, the needles are removed quickly or remain in the person for more than a day (Synovitz & Larson, 2012).

RELEVANT RESEARCH

Since 1970, more than 756 randomized controlled trials (RCTs) on acupuncture have been conducted (Ergil & Ergil, 2010). Acupuncture is currently used in the treatment of a large variety of health problems; however, according to a Cochrane Review, it has only been established as effective in the treatment of pelvic and back pain during pregnancy, lower back pain, headaches, postoperative nausea and vomiting, chemotherapy-induced nausea and vomiting, neck disorders and bedwetting (Synovitz & Larson, 2012, p. 106). It is notable that the Cochrane Review also found evidence of substantial placebo effects in acupuncture treatment (Synovitz & Larson, 2012). Table 10.1 provides an evaluation of the scope and quality of the research and author recommendations based on the available evidence.

Anxiety

Anxiety is often associated with problems that are frequently treated with acupuncture, such as pain, nausea, drug or nicotine addiction, and depression (Rainone, 2000). In a systematic review, Pilkington, Kirkwood, Rampes, Cummings, and Richardson (2007) sought to evaluate the evidence on the efficacy of acupuncture for the treatment of anxiety and anxiety disorders by systematically reviewing the relevant research. Studies in the review had to include participants with anxiety or an anxiety disorder (adults or children) who were treated with acupuncture, either traditional or a Western medical approach. Twelve studies were identified: four RCTs and two non-RCTs in patients with generalized anxiety disorder or anxiety neurosis and six RCTs with patients suffering from situational anxiety. Results from these studies demonstrate initial positive findings for situational and generalized anxiety; however, interpretation is difficult given the lack of standardization and lack of reporting of methodology details.

One well-designed RCT investigated the use of acupuncture to treat generalized anxiety (Eich, Agelink, Lehmann, Lemmer, & Kliesser, 2000). Patients diagnosed with minor depression or generalized anxiety disorder were randomly assigned to receive either body acupuncture at five points or sham acupuncture for 10 sessions. All treatments were delivered by an experienced TCM practitioner. Results showed that patients receiving acupuncture showed a significantly larger clinical improvement than patients receiving sham acupuncture after 10 sessions. However, this improvement was not seen after only five sessions of acupuncture. Additionally, there was a significant number of responders in the acupuncture group compared with the sham group (60% vs. 21.4%). Of the patients diagnosed with generalized anxiety disorders, four patients assigned to the acupuncture group and eight in the sham group withdrew due to pain and restlessness. Because of the small number of participants suffering from a generalized anxiety disorder, it is necessary to conduct an adequately powered trial comparing acupuncture to sham acupuncture to determine its efficacy for patients with anxiety disorders. There is currently insufficient evidence to support acupuncture in the treatment of anxiety disorders before additional high-quality, RCTs are conducted.

TABLE 10.1
Summary Table for Acupuncture

Symptom	Studies[a]	Sample	GRADE[b]	Evaluation
Anxiety	1 systematic review; 10 RCTs, 2 non-RCTs	Adults and children with generalized anxiety disorder or anxiety neurosis, situational anxiety	2B	Weak recommendation, moderate-quality evidence
Depression	1 meta-analysis; 2 RCTs	Older adults, depressed adults, working age adults, dementia patients	2C	Weak recommendation, low-quality evidence
Chronic low-back pain	1 Cochrane Review; 3 RCTs	Patients with a history of chronic low-back pain for a mean of 8 years	2B	Weak recommendation, moderate-quality evidence
Cancer-related pain	1 systematic review; 3 single-blind RCTs	Patients with chronic peripheral or central neuropathic pain related to cancer	2B	Weak recommendation, moderate-quality evidence
Cancer-related fatigue	1 single-blind pilot study; 1 RCT	Oncology patients suffering from fatigue	2C	Weak recommendation, low-quality evidence
Insomnia	1 systematic review; 46 randomized trials	Patients reporting insomnia or poor sleep quality	2B	Weak recommendation, moderate-quality evidence
Migraines and headaches	1 systematic review; 16 RCT	Patients suffering from chronic headaches and acute migraines	2B	Weak recommendation, moderate-quality evidence
Schizophrenia	1 systematic review; 13 RCTs	Hospitalized psychiatric patients experiencing auditory hallucinations or other positive symptoms	2B	Weak recommendation, moderate-quality evidence

Note. RCT = randomized controlled trial; GRADE = Grading of Recommendations, Assessment, Development and Evaluation.
[a]Citations available in text or references. Studies are representative; table should not be considered a comprehensive review of all available literature.
[b]Data from the Grade Working Group. Available at http://www.gradeworkinggroup.org/intro.htm.

Depression

Acupuncture has been studied to determine its efficacy in individuals with depression. Zhang, Yang, and Zhong (2009) conducted a double-blind RCT comparing the effects of verum acupuncture plus a low dose of fluoxetine to sham acupuncture plus the recommended dose of fluoxetine. They found no significant difference in depression scores between groups. However, the secondary outcomes measuring anxiety and side effects caused by fluoxetine decreased more in the verum acupuncture group than the sham group. These findings suggest that although acupuncture should not be the primary treatment for depression, it may be beneficial in reducing anxiety problems and side effects from medications (Zhang, Yang, & Zhong, 2009).

Similar results have been found in additional studies; however, the evidence determining the efficacy of acupuncture for depression remains inconclusive. C. A. Smith, Hay, and MacPherson (2010) completed a review and meta-analysis of 30 studies ($N = 2,812$) investigating the effects of acupuncture on depression. The authors revealed a number of methodological challenges in the literature: (a) The majority of the trials were found to have a high bias risk, (b) inadequate sequence generation reporting, (c) inadequate report of allocation concealment, (d) inadequate or absent blinding, and (e) outcome measures not clearly defined. Additional inconsistency between trials arises because some authors believe the effects of acupuncture to be a placebo effect that acts as a confounding variable in nonblinded trials; however, many of the studies were not adequately reported, and the level of bias can only be estimated. There is also a lack of consistency across trials in aspects of the study such as patient population, inclusion criteria, exclusion criteria, and acupuncture methodology. Unfortunately, there is no standardized protocol for acupuncture; therefore, multiple studies vary in the duration and frequency of treatment, duration of trial, and number and depth of needles used and treatment protocol (standardized versus individualized). The methodological inconsistencies and flaws dictate that results must be viewed cautiously. Nonetheless, the aggregate results of the meta-analysis indicate that acupuncture is as efficacious as medications for depression; however, the majority of studies showed no benefit to using acupuncture in conjunction with medication.

Results from trials comparing electroacupuncture with manual acupuncture showed no significant difference between the methods in the treatment of depression (C. A. Smith, Hay, et al., 2010). There was also no significant difference found between these two methods and laser acupuncture. In the studies comparing acupuncture with a wait-list control or sham acupuncture, the findings did not support acupuncture as a significantly more beneficial treatment than either control. The authors concluded that acupuncture cannot currently be recommended as a treatment for depression. Additional studies with blinding, properly reported methods, and strict inclusion, exclusion, and outcome criteria are necessary to determine the efficacy of acupuncture in treating depression (C. A. Smith, Hay, et al., 2010).

Chronic Low-Back Pain

A number of clinical trials have sought to determine the efficacy of acupuncture as a potential treatment for chronic low-back pain. A meta-analysis was conducted involving 6,359 patients with chronic low-back pain (Yuan et al., 2008). Results showed that real acupuncture treatments were no more effective than sham acupuncture treatments. However, the evidence remains inconclusive. A subsequent Cochrane Review meta-analysis suggested that real acupuncture and sham acupuncture were more effective than no treatment (Rubinstein et al., 2010). Additionally, acupuncture has shown positive results as a useful supplement to other conventional therapy for low-back pain.

In a large study, 1,162 patients with a history of chronic low-back pain for a mean of 8 years were randomly assigned to receive real acupuncture, sham acupuncture, or conventional therapy (Haake et al., 2007). Conventional therapy was defined as a combination of drug, physical therapy, and exercise. The real acupuncture treatments consisted of needle insertions at standardized acupuncture points plus additional points chosen by a trained practitioner. Brief manual manipulation was used to stimulate the needles after insertion. Sham acupuncture consisted of insertion of needles at non-acupuncture points without stimulation. The primary outcome consisted of a treatment response defined as either a 33% improvement in the Von Korff Chronic Pain Grade Scale (Von Korff, Ormel, Keefe, & Dworkin, 1992) or 12% improvement on the Hannover Functional Ability Questionnaire (Kohlmann & Raspe, 1996). At 6 months, results revealed that there was no significant difference between response rates with real acupuncture (47.6%) compared with a 44.2% response rate with sham acupuncture. However, both real and sham acupuncture were significantly better than the 27% response rate in conventional therapy. The evidence of the most recent well-powered clinical trials for acupuncture for low-back pain suggests that sham acupuncture is as effective as real acupuncture (Wittet al., 2009). It is recommended that all patients with chronic or recurrent low-back pain undergo a careful diagnostic evaluation before selecting a course of therapy such as acupuncture.

Cancer-Related Pain

It has been suggested that acupuncture may have a role in pain management in oncology patients. Forty percent of individuals with early or intermediate-stage cancer and 90% with advanced cancer suffer from severe pain (Laird, Colvin, & Fallon 2008). Recently, Paley, Johnson, Tashani, and Bagnall (2011) conducted a Cochrane Review to evaluate the efficacy of acupuncture for relief of cancer-related pain in adults. The review identified RCTs that included 204 participants in total (Alimi et al., 2003; Chen, Guo, & Wu, 2008; Dang & Yang, 1998). One of the RCTs randomly assigned 90 participants with chronic peripheral or central neuropathic pain related to cancer to one of three groups: auricular acupuncture using semipermanent needles; sham auricular acupuncture; and noninvasive auricular "seeds," a noninvasive technique using small adhesive metal beads on the outer ear, administered at nonacupuncture points (Alimi et al., 2003). Each group received two courses of treatment with needles or seeds left in situ. Results of the study showed a significant decrease in pain intensity of 36% from baseline at 2 months in the acupuncture group as measured by a visual analog scale. In contrast, the placebo acupuncture decreased by only 2%. Furthermore, pain scores were lower in the true acupuncture group than either of the two other groups. Participants in the true acupuncture group had significantly lower pain scores at 2 months than either placebo acupuncture or the group that had noninvasive auricular seeds. Although the studies reported positive results for oncology patients receiving acupuncture, these results must be viewed with caution because of methodological limitations such as small sample size, poor reporting, and inadequate analysis. Currently there is insufficient evidence to determine whether acupuncture may be a potential treatment for cancer-related pain.

Cancer-Related Fatigue

It is estimated that 50% to 90% of all oncology patients experience fatigue (Campos, Hassan, Riechelmann, & Del Giglio, 2011). Initial pilot studies have shown promising results for the relief of cancer-related fatigue with 40% or greater improvement in fatigue scores (Vickers, Straus, Fearon, & Cassileth, 2004). However, most of the initial studies are limited by small sample size and lack of generalizability.

A recent single-center randomized, sham-controlled study was conducted to evaluate whether acupuncture treatment reduced fatigue in patients whose fatigue had persisted after the completion of chemotherapy (Deng et al., 2013). Patients were randomly assigned receive six standardized treatment sessions of true or sham acupuncture over 6 weeks. The sham acupuncture was performed exactly as the true acupuncture, with the exception of the use of sham needles and that points that were millimeters off the meridians and away from the points used in true acupuncture. The sham needles were blunt-tipped needles that move up inside their handle when pressed against the skin. All patients were informed that they would receive either true or sham acupuncture and that the two methods would look and feel similar. Results showed that participant scores on the Brief Fatigue Inventory declined by about 1 point between baseline and follow-up for both groups. Furthermore, there were no significant differences between the true and sham acupuncture on measures of fatigue and anxiety. Patients in the sham acupuncture group crossed over to receive true acupuncture at Week 7. Results of this RCT showed that true acupuncture did not reduce postchemotherapy chronic fatigue more than sham acupuncture. The authors concluded that acupuncture as provided in this study is unlikely to be a viable option in the management of postchemo- therapy chronic fatigue (Deng et al., 2013).

Insomnia

Cao, Pan, Li, and Liu (2009) conducted a systematic review to evaluate the beneficial and harmful effects of acupuncture for the treatment of insomnia in RCTs. The review identified 46 randomized trials involving 3,811 patients. The methodological quality of the evidence was evaluated as fair in terms of randomization, blinding, and intention-to-treat analysis. In studies comparing acupuncture with no treatment, results showed that acupuncture was signifi- cantly better than no treatment on improving sleep quality (Tang, 2007; Tsay, Cho, & Chen, 2004). Three studies evaluated real versus sham acupuncture and revealed that real acupuncture was more effective than sham acupuncture for the treatment of insomnia (M. L. Chen, Lin, Wu, & Lin, 1999; Y. S. Kim, Lee, & Jung, 2004; Tsay, Rong, & Lin, 2003). To date, 26 studies have com- pared acupuncture with Western medications for patients suffering from insom- nia. The results of these trials are inconclusive. Although most of these studies show positive results for the treatment of insomnia, one meta-analysis reported no difference between acupuncture and drugs on improving self-reported sleep duration (Huang et al., 2009; Xuan, Guo, Wang, & Wu, 2007).

A representative, pilot, randomized controlled study sought to deter- mine the effects of intradermal acupuncture on insomnia patients after stroke (Y. S. Kim et al., 2004). Thirty patients with persistent insomnia and who were hospitalized at a stroke center were assigned to a real transdermal acu- puncture group or a sham acupuncture group. Results showed significant improvement on three insomnia-related scales. On the basis of the systematic reviews and meta-analyses, the majority of the studies showed that compared with no treatment, sham acupuncture, or medications, acupuncture was sig- nificantly better on improving outcome measures in sleep quality and dura- tion. However, many of the trials have methodological flaws, including small sample size, inadequate follow-up, and inadequate reporting of randomization and blinding. Furthermore, there may be a language bias because 43 of the

46 trials were published in Chinese, and three were published in English but conducted in Taiwan and Korea (Cao et al., 2009). Larger, well-designed RCTs are necessary to determine if acupuncture may be a potential treatment for insomnia.

Migraines and Headaches

The efficacy of acupuncture for headaches has been explored. L. P. Wang and colleagues (2011) conducted a multicenter, single-blinded RCT to investigate the efficacy of acupuncture for the treatment of acute migraine attacks. The effects of verum acupuncture ($n = 75$) were compared with sham acupuncture ($n = 75$) using 11-point visual analog scales for pain. After screening, 162 participants were selected to be screened for the study, and of those, 150 were randomized to receive either a single verum or sham acupuncture treatment. Results showed that the verum acupuncture was found to reduce pain significantly more than the sham acupuncture. Also, the number of those in the verum acupuncture group who required acute medications was reduced compared with the number of those requiring it in the sham acupuncture group.

Zhao, Guo, Wang, and Yan (2011) performed a systematic review of 16 RCTs ($N = 1,535$) on acupuncture for the treatment of neurovascular headaches. This review indicated that acupuncture therapy was significantly more effective than Western medicine therapy, and comprehensive acupuncture therapy (acupuncture therapy plus other therapies such as points inspection, scalp acupuncture, or auricular acupuncture) was significantly more effective than acupuncture therapy. The studies reviewed contained several methodological flaws, however, including small sample sizes, poor reliability, and high risk of bias. To make more informed conclusions about the efficacy of acupuncture in treating headaches, further research is required.

Sham Acupuncture

There is a growing body of literature suggesting that the therapeutic effects of acupuncture are contributed by placebo. To test this hypothesis, Moffet (2009) performed a systematic review of 38 clinical trials comparing acupuncture with sham acupuncture. The studies included treatments of migraine, chronic sinusitis, knee osteoarthritis, irritable bowel, ulcerative colitis, overactive bladder, and fibromyalgia. Twenty-two of the studies reviewed found no significant difference in outcomes, and 13 of those 22 studies concluded that sham acupuncture was as efficacious as acupuncture. Deng et al. (2013) conducted a randomized, blinded trial comparing sham acupuncture with true acupuncture in the treatment of postchemotherapy chronic fatigue. The participants received weekly treatment for 6 weeks. One hundred and one patients were randomized, and 74 were analyzed (sham $n = 40$; true $n = 34$) using the Brief Fatigue Inventory (BFI; Mendoza et al., 1999) as the primary outcome. The study found no significant differences in fatigue between the sham and true acupuncture groups.

Schizophrenia

Acupuncture has been used as adjunctive treatment of schizophrenia for symptoms of auditory hallucinations. M. S. Lee, Shin, Ronan, and Ernst (2009) sought to critically review the evidence from RCTs to determine the effectiveness of acupuncture in relieving positive symptoms of schizophrenia. The systematic review included all studies using acupuncture as the sole treatment or as an adjunct to other treatments. Results identified 13 RCTs, all of which originated in China. One RCT reported significant results using electroacupuncture plus drug therapy for improving auditory hallucinations and positive symptoms compared with sham electroacupunture plus drug therapy. Additionally, four RCTs showed significant effects of acupuncture for response rate compared with antipsychotic drugs. Seven RCTs showed significant effects of acupuncture plus antipsychotic drug therapy for response rate compared with antipsychotic drug therapy. Although acupuncture shows promising results, the total number of RCT included have low methodologic quality, making it difficult to interpret. Because all the studies were conducted in China, the generalizability of the results is limited and need to be replicated across cultures (M. S. Lee et al., 2009).

An RCT was conducted to determine the efficacy of electroacupuncture compared with sham acupuncture for the treatment of auditory hallucinations in patients with schizophrenia (J. Cheng et al., 2009). Sixty patients with schizophrenia who are partially responsive or nonresponsive to risperidone were randomized to receive either real electroacupuncture group or sham electroacupuncture. All participants completed a 4-week baseline evaluation, and the risperidone run-in phase was followed by 6 weeks of real acupuncture treatment or sham electroacupuncture. Results showed patients receiving the real acupuncture condition experienced greater improvement in the Psychotic Symptom Rating Scales Auditory Hallucination (Kay, Opler, & Fiszbein, 1987) subscale than the sham at Weeks 4 and 6. There were no significant between-group differences in side effects. Although the study shows initial positive results for acupunctures as a potential adjunctive treatment for auditory hallucinations and positive symptoms for patients with schizophrenia, further research is necessary.

CONTRAINDICATIONS AND RISKS

Thomas et al. (2005) found acupuncture to be safe, cost-effective, and without any significant side effects in the treatment of chronic low-back pain in a primary care setting. They report it to be more effective than conventional treatments and without many of the side effects that may come with conventional medical treatments. Furthermore, Kaptchuk (2002), in reviewing 25 systematic reviews and meta-analyses of the use of acupuncture for a wide range of conditions, found it to be safe when properly provided by a skilled acupuncture practitioner. Lao (1996) stressed the importance of acupuncture being provided by a skilled acupuncture professional that follows appropriate sterile technique. The book *Clean Needle Technique Manual for Acupuncturists: Guidelines and Standards for the Clean and Safe Practice of Acupuncture* (available at http://www.nationalacupuncturefoundation. org) incorporates Centers for Disease Control and Prevention and Occupational Safety and Health Administration guidelines and procedures for minimizing the risks of infection and disease transmission. Practitioners who do not carefully follow these guidelines can cause infection and other side effects for patients.

Standard acupuncture procedures involve the use of sterile single-use needles that are appropriately disposed of after each treatment. The U.S. Food and Drug Administration regulates the production of acupuncture needles, requiring them to be sterile, nontoxic, and labeled for single use only (NIH, 2011a). The needles must be placed and manipulated according to standardized procedures. Failure to do so can result in skin irritation, soreness, or even pain. Pain and soreness may also result from patient movement during acupuncture treatment, unskilled or inappropriate needle manipulation by the practitioner, or as a result of the use of defective, bent, or broken needles (Lao, 1996). Acupuncture needles should come in sealed packaging and should be opened at the time of use. Acupuncture sites on the patient's body should be cleaned or disinfected before the acupuncture needles being inserted as a step to help minimize infection (NIH, 2011a).

Lao (1996) highlighted that acupuncture may not be appropriate for all individuals. For instance, women who are pregnant may not be appropriate recipients of acupuncture in the lumbar-sacral and abdominal regions. Although reports of adverse effects of acupuncture are small in number, some of these adverse effects are serious, such as hepatitis and pneumothorax (International Encyclopedia of Rehabilitation, 2010). How acupuncture treatment might affect the pregnant woman and her fetus are not currently understood sufficiently to warrant the potential risks involved. Additionally, great care is recommended in the placement of acupuncture needles in areas close to vital organs. Ernst and White (2001) reported that some patients can experience soreness and pain at needle placement locations, but this may be related to that depth of needle placement and the length of time that the needles are left in place. Acupuncture should only be provided by an appropriately trained professional who possesses relevant licensure and certification credentials that demonstrate the possession of the requisite knowledge and skills to provide acupuncture treatments safely and effectively.

TIPS FOR PRACTITIONERS

- Advise patients to ask if the individual who is responsible for administering acupuncture treatment has the proper licenses and credentials.
- Acupuncture should not be used in place of conventional care.
- Practitioners should be knowledgeable about the empirical evidence on the effectiveness of acupuncture before making any recommendations.
- Patients should be well informed on the potential risks and side effects.

INTEGRATION WITH PSYCHOLOGICAL PRACTICE

As can be seen from both historical evidence and recent research, acupuncture is used to treat a wide range of conditions as either a standalone treatment (alternative treatment) or as an aspect of ongoing conventional health care (adjunctive treatment). Acupuncture can easily be integrated into ongoing psychotherapy for many clients. However, acupuncture is not necessarily effective for every condition or ailment. Psychologists should carefully consider the available scientific literature before encouraging clients to seek out acupuncture.

Acupuncture should only be provided by an appropriately credentialed professional. When considering referring a client for acupuncture treatment, it is important to first assess the acupuncture professional's training and credentials. A first step is to ascertain whether acupuncture is a licensed profession regulated by law in your state or province. If it is, one should only refer to licensed acupuncture professionals. If licensure is not required in your jurisdiction, it is important to confirm certification by an appropriate credentialing agency and the possession of a master's degree in acupuncture from an accredited school or training program (see Additional Resources). Beyond being certified or licensed, it is recommended that board-certified acupuncture providers be used to ensure the highest possible competence and expertise.

Numerous acupuncture training schools exist in the United States. Each may have a different focus, such as TCM or Korean, Japanese, or one of the other schools of acupuncture. Individuals who undergo this training may be holistic health care providers who integrate acupuncture and other traditional forms of assessment and treatment into a more holistic health care and health promotion approach. For example, TCM practitioners may integrate the use of acupuncture, herbal remedies, and other aspects of TCM in a patient's treatment. Acupuncture professionals may also be trained only in the provision of acupuncture. Additionally, medical acupuncturists are physicians who possess training and certification in acupuncture and integrate the use of acupuncture into their medical practice.

When considering making a referral for acupuncture treatment, it is important to first discuss this methodology thoroughly with your client. Review the research on acupuncture treatment that is relevant to the client's specific ailment or treatment needs. Additionally, the relative risks and benefits of acupuncture treatment, of other reasonably available treatment options, and of no treatment should be reviewed and discussed. After doing so, if the client desires a referral, the psychologist can assist in the referral process based on knowledge of licensure, certification, board certification, and training requirements in their state or jurisdiction.

Once a referral is made, with the client's verbal and written consent, it is important to communicate with the acupuncture professional to ensure that the psychological treatment and acupuncture treatment are coordinated and not working at cross purposes. Interestingly, although Burke et al. (2006) found that approximately 26% of all referrals to acupuncture professionals come from conventional medical professionals, Sherman et al. (2005) found that acupuncture professionals rarely communicate with medical professionals who are treating the same patient for the same ailment or condition. Thus, psychologists should actively work to ensure good communication and coordinated collaborative care with acupuncture professionals providing treatment to their clients.

Psychologists may seek out the additional training needed to become licensed acupuncture professionals, just as physicians who practice medical acupuncture do. However, this dual licensure and training presents ethical challenges and dilemmas for psychologists that are not present for physicians. The issue of touch by psychologists is important, and with it arises concern with the distinction between boundary crossing and boundary violation. The very nature of the psychotherapy relationship makes it inappropriate to have a client disrobe, even if to participate in a legitimate treatment. Additionally, many psychology licensure laws clearly state that psychologists may not provide any treatment that pierces the skin. Such an action is typically considered part of the practice of medicine, not a part of providing psychological services.

ADDITIONAL RESOURCES

1. American Academy of Medical Acupuncture (AAMA)—This is a professional organization for physician acupuncturists who are committed to holistic, integrated health care. AAMA members follow the AAMA Code of Ethics. The AAMA offers continuing education and training opportunities, disseminates research results through its journal, and promotes the ethical practice of acupuncture by its members. The AAMA's website may be accessed at http://www.medicalacupuncture.org.
2. The Accreditation Commission for Acupuncture and Oriental Medicine (ACAOM)—This is the national accrediting agency for master's degree and master's-level certificate programs in acupuncture. It is recognized by the U.S. Department of Education and is an excellent resource for assessing the training of an acupuncture practitioner. The ACAOM website may be accessed at http://www.acaom.org/index.htm.
3. National Certification Commission for Acupuncture and Oriental Medicine (NCCAOM)—NCCAOM is a private, voluntary certification organization that conducts examinations to provide national certification in acupuncture and Oriental medicine. Certified professionals are required to adhere to standards of professional conduct disseminated by NCCAOM. The NCCAOM website may be accessed at http://www.nccaom.org/about/index.html.
4. Acupuncture.com: State Laws—Many states require professionals to be certified or licensed to practice acupuncture in their jurisdiction. This website provides information on licensure and certification in each state and includes links to relevant statutes in states that regulate acupuncture. This website may be accessed at http://www.acupuncture.com/statelaws/statelaw.htm.
5. Acupuncture Schools—A comprehensive listing of acupuncture schools that are accredited by the Accreditation Commission for Acupuncture and Oriental Medicine (ACAOM). Links are provided for every ACAOM-accredited program and every program that is a candidate for ACAOM accreditation

in North America. This listing may be accessed at http://acupuncturetoday.com/schools.

6. National Acupuncture Foundation (NAF)—NAF has as its goals the promotion of acupuncture as a profession and its integration into Western medicine. It offers publications, encourages research and scholarship, and educates the public about acupuncture and TCM. This book integrates the most recent Centers for Disease Control and Occupational Safety and Health Administration standards relevant to the practice of acupuncture. This resource may be accessed at http://www.nationalacupuncturefoundation.org.

III

BIOLOGICALLY BASED PRACTICES

11

HERBALS AND BIOLOGICALLY BASED PRACTICES

In complementary and alternative medicine (CAM), the domain of herbals and biologically based practices is especially broad, and it includes, but is not limited to, botanicals, animal-derived extracts, vitamins, minerals, fatty acids, amino acids, proteins, prebiotics, probiotics, whole diets, and functional foods (National Institutes of Health [NIH], 2007a). These products are widely marketed and readily available to consumers, often sold as *dietary supplements*. Dietary supplements are widely used in the United States. P. M. Barnes, Bloom, and Nahin (2008) found that in 2007, 17.7% of American adults had used a dietary supplement (other than vitamins and minerals) in the past 12 months, making this the second most widely used form of CAM after spirituality and prayer. They found that 37.4% of their sample used fish oil/omega 3, 19.9% used glucosamine, 19.8% used echinacea, 15.9% used flaxseed oil or pills, and 14.1% used ginseng. When all forms of dietary supplements to include vitamins and minerals are considered, more than 52% of Americans

http://dx.doi.org/10.1037/14435-012
Complementary and Alternative Medicine for Psychologists: An Essential Resource, by J. E. Barnett, A. J. Shale, G. Elkins, and W. Fisher

reported using at least one type of supplement in the past 30 days, with multi-vitamin use reported by 35% of those surveyed, followed by vitamins E and C, calcium, and B-complex vitamins, with each of these being taken by at least 5% of those surveyed in the past month (Radimer et al., 2004). Additionally, these authors found that most supplement users were taking them on a daily basis for more than 2 years and that more than half of those surveyed took more than one supplement each day. Some dietary supplements are used to promote general health and wellness, whereas others are used in an attempt to prevent or treat specific ailments or conditions. Psychologists are urged to take particular note of their patients' use of these biologically based practices because many patients may have taken or may currently take these supplements to alleviate or prevent symptoms that are salient to their psychotherapeutic care.

Because these agents are not regulated the same manner as are other drug products, psychologists and their patients are urged to be well-informed of the identity, purity, strength, composition, and possible contraindications associated with the agents. The U.S. Food and Drug Administration (FDA) is the governing body that regulates dietary supplements. On June 22, 2007, the FDA announced a final rule establishing current good manufacturing practice requirements (CGMPs) for dietary supplements sold in the United States (FDA, 2013). These CGMPs apply to all domestic and foreign companies that manufacture, package, label, or hold dietary supplements, including those involved with the activities of testing, quality control, packaging and labeling, and distributing them in the United States. Although these new regulations provide quality standards in the manufacture of these agents, as well as labeling to ensure identity, purity, strength, and composition, they do not address the safety of the ingredients or their effects on health when proper manufacturing techniques are used. Responsibility for the safe and proper use of these agents ultimately falls to the consumer.

DEFINITIONS

Because a broad spectrum of agents and practices comprise biologically based practices, we have provided a table to provide a basic overview of some of the constituent agents with examples (see Table 11.1). NIH's Office of Dietary Supplements (ODS; 2011) defined a dietary supplement as follows:

> a product (other than tobacco) that is intended to supplement the diet; contains one or more dietary ingredients (including vitamins; minerals; herbs or other botanicals; amino acids; and other substances) or their constituents; is intended to be taken by mouth as a pill, capsule, tablet, or liquid; and is labeled on the front panel as being a dietary supplement. (para. 1)

TABLE 11.1

Biologically Based Practices: Definitions and Examples

Agent	Definition	Example	Example of CAM use*
Amino acids	These biologically important organic compounds are made from amine and carboxylic acid functional groups and serve as the building blocks of protein.	L-arginine	Senile dementia, erectile dysfunction
Animal-derived extracts	These extracts are derived from animal tissues or organs for use in various products.	Fish oil, powdered bovine or shark cartilage	Bovine cartilage for brain cancer
Botanicals (herbs)	These plant or plant parts are used to make medicine, aromatics, or oils and may consist of a leaf, flower, stem, seed, root, fruit, bark, or any other plant part.	St. John's wort, fenugreek, Asian ginseng, valerian	St. John's wort for depression
Fatty acids	A carboxylic acid with a long aliphatic tail, which is either saturated or unsaturated. Fatty acids are important sources of fuel, yielding large quantities of adenosine triphosphate. Many cell types can use either glucose or fatty acids for this purpose. In particular, heart and skeletal muscle prefer fatty acids.	Omega-3	ADHD
Functional foods	Functional foods are components of the usual diet that may have biologically active components that provide health benefits beyond basic nutrition.	Polyphenols, phytoestrogens, fish oils, carotenoid	Phytoestrogens for menopausal symptoms

(continues)

Agent	Definition	Example	Example of CAM use*
Prebiotics	A prebiotic is a nondigestible food ingredient that promotes the growth of beneficial micro-organisms in the intestines.	Raw chicory root, raw Jerusalem artichoke	Reduction of pathogens
Probiotics	Probiotics are live microorganisms (e.g., bacteria) that are either the same as or similar to microorganisms found naturally in the human body and may be beneficial to health. Also referred to as good bacteria or helpful bacteria.	*Lactobacillus rhamnosus*	Irritable bowel syndrome
Proteins	Proteins are highly varied organic molecules constituting a large portion of the mass of every life form. They are necessary in the diet of all animals and other nonphoto-synthesizing organisms and are composed of 20 or more amino acids linked in a genetically controlled linear sequence into one or more long polypeptide chains.	Soy protein	Cardiovascular disease, breast cancer, menopause-related symptoms, and bone loss
Vitamins and minerals	Vitamins and minerals are substances that the human body requires to grow and develop normally.	Vitamins A, C, D, E, and K; thiamine; calcium; phosphorus; zinc; etc.	Complementary approach to flu and colds, antioxidant, cancer prevention
Whole diets	Whole diets are rules or guidelines surrounding the consumption of food and/or drink.	Atkins Diet, macrobiotic diets, Ornish diet, Pritikin Diet, South Beach Diet, vegetarian diets, etc.	Weight control, eating disorders

Note. *Data present only the purported use for an exemplar agent, not efficacy.

HISTORY

Dietary supplements have an extensive history of use for medicinal purposes. The discovery of a Neanderthal body in 1960 revealed that a man living 60,000 years ago used several medicinal herbs: Seven of the eight species of plants found at the burial site are used for medicinal purposes today (Freeman & Lawlis, 2001). Examination of the personal effects found on the 5,300-year-old mummified remains of a man found in the Oetztal Alps in 1991 revealed that he used natural (botanical) laxatives and antibiotics (Capasso, 1998). Since the dawn of civilization, native plants have supplied medicinal compounds (Griggs & Van der Zee, 1997). Of the 10 top-selling herbal dietary supplements sold today, seven were used by various Native American societies (Borchers, Keen, Stern, & Gershwin, 2000). Conventional Western pharmacy has its roots in Greek and Roman herbal remedies that were used for generations (Sigerist, 1987). Roughly 25% of modern prescription drugs are of plant origin, and an even greater percentage is based on synthetic or semisynthetic ingredients originally isolated from plants (Levetin & McMahon, 1996). For example, a chemical found in Indian snakeroot is the active component in the prescription drug reserpine, used to treat mild to moderate hypertension, schizophrenia, and some symptoms of poor circulation (Cox & Balick, 1994).

Although Western medicine has strayed from herbalism, 75%–90% of the rural population in the rest of the world still relies on herbal medicine as their only health care (Levetin & McMahon, 1996). Interest in and use of dietary supplements has expanded enormously in the past two decades, with approximately one quarter of all U.S. adults reporting use of an herb to treat a medical illness within the previous year (Bent, 2008; Bent & Ko, 2004). In light of growing popularity and in response to a U.S. congressional mandate, the ODS initiated the Botanical Research Centers Program in 1999, in partnership with the National Center for Complementary and Alternative Medicine (NCCAM), to promote "collaborative, integrated, interdisciplinary study of botanicals, particularly those found as ingredients in dietary supplements, and to conduct research of high potential for being translated into practical benefits for human health" (ODS, 2013, para. 2.).

COMMON USES

People use biologically based practices for numerous reasons. It has been suggested, for example, that they may be used to provide a sense of control over one's health, which may be of relevance to the fact that many people who use these remedies have chronic or incurable diseases (e.g., diabetes, arthritis, cancer, AIDS; Winslow & Kroll, 1998). There is a growing societal trend toward "natural" or "green" products in general, and this trend is evident in the practice of herbal medicine. Qualitative research into the uses of herbal medicines performed in the United Kingdom suggested that people found herbal remedies to be safe, natural, and gentle (Herbal Medicines Advisory Committee, 2008). A UK national survey found

> immediate associations with herbal medicines included such words as "safe," "natural," "non-addictive" and "pure." It is clear that the phrase itself gives both users and non-users a sense of reassurance and safety, as most feel that natural products do not pose any danger. Many participants also felt that herbal medicines work gently and slowly in comparison with conventional medicines, and that they are less powerful. A number of users also suggested that the long history of human use of herbal medicines is evidence of their safety. (Herbal Medicines Advisory Committee, 2008, p. 9)

The perception that natural plant products are healthier than manufactured medicine may have some unintentional support in the lay press given that conventional medications are advertised and their adverse effects reported (as required by law) at a much higher rate than any report of herbal toxicity (Winslow & Kroll, 1998).

TECHNIQUE

The methods of preparation and application of biologically based practices are as varied as the agents themselves. In practice, one can use a botanical agent (or combination of agents) in a decoction (concentrated tea or soup), taken orally in a capsule, pill or tablet, applied topically via a paste, gel or salve, taken as a suppository, inhaled in a vapor, consumed with food, or consumed as food (as in the case of functional foods or specialized diets). It is advisable when discussing CAM use with patients to ascertain the method of delivery to derive an accurate estimate of dose. Unless the agent is consumed in a capsule or pill form, for which FDA regulation now dictates that the exact amount and purity of the agents is provided on the packaging, ascertaining how much of the agent is being used can be difficult.

MECHANISM OF ACTION

A wide range of mechanisms of action have been reported across the range of biologically based practices due to the significant differences between these many substances. Although the mechanism of action of every known agent far exceeds the scope of this chapter, several representative examples are provided to illustrate some of the reported biological mechanisms.

Black currant seed oil is reported to reduce inflammation in disorders, such as rheumatoid arthritis, by causing a reduction in "the secretion of the inflammatory cytokines IL-1beta and TNF-alpha via redirection of eicosanoid metabolism although the possibility cannot be excluded that the PUFAs [polyunsaturated fatty acids] may be altering cytokine release directly through an effect on monocyte membranes" (Watson, Byars, McGill, & Kelman, 1993, p. 1055).

Dietary supplements containing bitter orange (*Citrus aurantium*) have been found to stimulate the cardiovascular system, including significant increases in blood pressure and heart rate. These cardiovascular effects are reported to be similar to the effects of ephedra, a botanical agent with a long history of use in Traditional Chinese Medicine (TCM) but banned from sale in the United States by the FDA, citing little evidence of ephedra's effectiveness except for short-term weight loss and increased risk of heart problems and stroke outweighing any benefits (Haller, Benowitz, & Jacob, 2005).

SAMe (S-adenosylmethionine) is a naturally occurring modified amino acid in the human body. Individuals with reduced levels of these amino acids have been found to exhibit symptoms of depression. Therefore, it is hypothesized that dietary supplements containing SAMe will be effective in alleviating symptoms of depression (Mischoulon & Fava, 2002). Additionally, a deficiency of omega-3 fatty acids has also been found to be associated with symptoms of depression and possibly with a number of other mental health disorders, including schizophrenia (Mischoulon & Fava, 2000). It is therefore hypothesized based on the available evidence that dietary supplements high in omega-3 fatty acids would help alleviate symptoms of depression and schizophrenia (Schachter, Kourad, Merali, Lumb, Tran, & Miguelez, 2005).

Omega-3 fatty acids are thought to alter the metabolism of lipoproteins, modulate the metabolism of nitric oxide, and have direct effects on myocardial tissues to stabilize membranes and prolong the relative refractory period (Mechanick et al., 2005).

Many botanical dietary supplements are reported to be converted into biologically reactive intermediates (BSIs) when metabolized on ingestion (Dietz & Bolton, 2011). This process may result in the formation of either stable BSIs that may have chemoprotective effects, such as curcumin from turmeric and Z-ligustilide from dang gui, or, for some botanical dietary supplements, in the formation of BSIs that produce toxicity, such as sassafras oil. Additionally, a number of botanical dietary supplements are reported to convert into "BSIs of intermediate reactivity" (Dietz & Bolton, 2011, p. 72), which may produce either chemoprotective or toxic effects depending on the dose of the particular supplement and the individual's metabolic processes. Examples of this later group include kava, black cohosh, and pennyroyal oil.

RELEVANT RESEARCH

Research on dietary supplements has involved basic and clinical research, including ethnobotanical investigations, analytical research, methodology research, bioavailability, pharmacokinetic, and pharmacodynamic studies (NIH, 2007a). The vast majority of the research in this area is clinical (Phase II) for all types of dietary supplements. There are some challenges in ascertaining the efficacy of these agents because methodological flaws are common in the literature, including insufficient sample size, poor design, a lack of preliminary dosing data, lack of blinding, and failure to incorporate objective or standardized outcomes measures (NIH, 2007a). Additional challenges include the lack of data on the absorption, disposition, metabolism, and excretion of the agents. Furthermore, research is confounded by a lack of consistent and reliable botanical products, making the standardization of clinical trials extremely difficult. Also, because some botanicals are blends of multiple agents, the determination and isolation of their putative active ingredient(s) may be difficult or impossible. Similarly, the study of probiotics is challenged as little empirical attention has been directed at the viability, type, titer, stability of enteric protection of the product.

There are more than 20,000 herbal and related products used in the United States (Winslow & Kroll, 1998); thus, a complete review of all of the biologically based practices is impossible. This review of the literature examines studies and reviews involving the top 10 most commonly used agents based on the data taken from the 2002 and 2007 surveys of CAM use by adults in the United States (see Figures 11.1 and 11.2; P. M. Barnes et al., 2008; P. M. Barnes, Powell-Griner, McFann, & Nahin, 2004) as well as agents that were specifically investigated for the treatment of symptoms most likely to be relevant to psychology practice, specifically those of pain, depression, and anxiety. Probiotics, although an interesting new line of inquiry, are not reviewed in detail within this chapter because their use is still in the early stages of scientific inquiry (for additional information on probiotics, see Kopp-Hoolihan, 2001). Table 11.2 provides an evaluation of the scope and quality of the research and provides author recommendations based on the available evidence.

Chamomile

Chamomile (*Matricaria recutita; Chamomilla recutita*) is a flowering plant, the tops of which have been widely used in children and adults for thousands

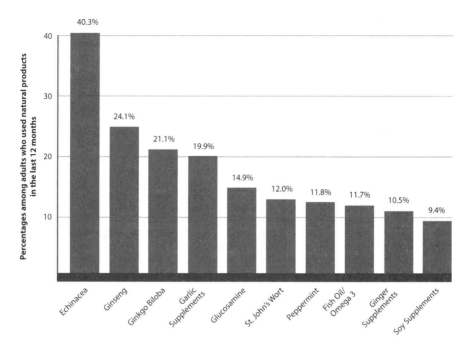

Figure 11.1. Ten most common natural products among adults, 2002. Data from Barnes, Powell-Griner, McFann, and Nahin, 2004.

of years for a variety of health conditions including sleeplessness, anxiety, upset stomach, skin conditions, and mouth ulcers (NIH, 2007b). The flowering tops of the chamomile plant are used to make teas, liquid extracts, capsules, tablets, creams, ointments, and mouth rinse. There are reports of allergic reactions, including skin rashes, throat swelling, shortness of breath, and anaphylaxis, although people are more likely to experience allergic reactions to chamomile if they are allergic to related plants in the daisy family (e.g., ragweed, marigolds, daisies; NIH, 2007b). According to NCCAM, chamomile has not been well studied in people, so there is little evidence to support its use for any condition, although early studies point to chamomile's possible benefits for certain skin conditions, mouth ulcers, upset stomach, diarrhea in children, and colic in infants (NIH, 2007b). NCCAM-funded research has examined the use of chamomile in generalized anxiety disorder (GAD) in a randomized, double-blind, placebo-controlled trial of oral chamomile extract therapy. In this study, 57 outpatients with mild to moderate GAD were randomized to receive capsulated pharmaceutical grade German chamomile or an identical appearing placebo capsule (Amsterdam et al., 2009). The findings in this study were significant reductions in anxiety scores (as measured by the Hamilton Anxiety Rating scale) versus placebo. The

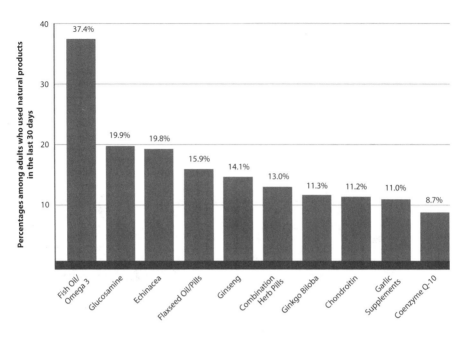

Figure 11.2. Ten most common natural products among adults, 2007. Data from Barnes, Bloom, and Nahin, 2008.

authors concluded that chamomile may have a modest anxiolytic effect in patients with mild to moderate GAD.

Chondroitin

Chondroitin sulfate is a complex carbohydrate that helps cartilage retain water. Chondroitin was first extracted and purified in the 1960s (Mayo Clinic, 2011). It is currently manufactured from natural sources (shark and beef cartilage or bovine trachea) or by synthetic means and is sold in capsules. Chondroitin is considered likely to be safe, although there have been reports of upset stomach, diarrhea, and constipation (Bourgeois et al., 1998). The consensus of expert and industry opinions supports the use of chondroitin and its common partner agent, glucosamine, for improving symptoms and stopping (or possibly reversing) the degenerative process of osteoarthritis (Mayo Clinic, 2011).

Coenzyme Q10

Coenzyme Q10 (CoQ10) is a substance that is found in almost every cell in the body and is defined as a crucial component of the oxidative

TABLE 11.2
Herbals and Biologically Based Practices Summary Table

Modality/symptom	Studies[a]	Sample	GRADE[b]	Evaluation
Chamomile/anxiety	1 randomized placebo-controlled trial	57 outpatients with mild to moderate GAD	2C	Weak recommendation, weak-quality evidence
Coenzyme Q10/migraine	1 double-blind placebo-controlled trial	42 adult migraine patients	2C	Weak recommendation, weak-quality evidence
Omega-3/ADHD	10 RCTs	Children diagnosed with ADHD	2B	Weak recommendation, moderate-quality evidence
Ginger/nausea	1 double-blind multi-center controlled trial	744 adult chemotherapy patients	2B	Weak recommendation, moderate-quality evidence
Gingko biloba/Alzheimer's	9 RCTs	Patients with Alzheimer's disease	2C	Weak recommendation, weak-quality evidence
Gingko biloba/cognitive impairment secondary to electroconvulsive treatment for depression	1 randomized, placebo-controlled trial	81 patients with major depression undergoing electroconvulsive treatment	2C	Weak recommendation, weak-quality evidence
Ginseng/cancer-related fatigue	1 randomized, double-blind, placebo-controlled trial	299 adults with cancer	2C	Weak recommendation, weak-quality evidence
Kava/anxiety	12 RCTs	Adults with GAD, adults with self-reported anxiety	NR	Not recommended for use
Peppermint/IBS	1 randomized, double-blind, placebo-controlled trial	90 outpatient adults with IBS	2C	Weak recommendation, weak-quality evidence

(continues)

TABLE 11.2
Herbals and Biologically Based Practices Summary Table (Continued)

Modality/symptom	Studies[a]	Sample	GRADE[b]	Evaluation
Peppermint/tension headache	2 randomized, controlled, double-blind, crossover trials	32 adult subjects with tension headaches, 41 adult subjects with tension headaches	1B	Strong recommendation, weak-quality evidence
Soy/menopausal symptoms	11 RCTs	Women in menopause, breast-cancer survivors	2C	Weak recommendation, moderate-quality evidence
St. John's wort/ depression	2 meta-analyses: 37 trials and 29 trials	Depressed adults, adults with major depressive disorder	2A	Weak recommendation, high-quality evidence

Note. ADHD = attention-deficit/hyperactivity disorder; GAD = generalized anxiety disorder; IBS = irritable bowel syndrome; NR = not recommended; GRADE = Grading of Recommendations, Assessment, Development and Evaluation.
[a]Citations available in text or references. Studies are representative; table should not be considered a comprehensive review of all available literature.
[b]Data from the GRADE Working Group. Available at http://www.gradeworkinggroup.org/intro.htm.

phosphorylation process in mitochondria, which converts the energy in carbohydrates and fatty acids into adenosine triphosphate to drive cellular machinery and synthesis (Crane, 2001). CoQ10 has been studied as a dietary supplement taken orally in capsule form, although one study used intravenous dosing. There have been few reported side effects; however, the Mayo Clinic reported that it may lower blood pressure, and one case has been reported of a patient experiencing low platelet count (Mayo Clinic, 2012). CoQ10 has been studied for its use in treating numerous conditions (e.g., hypertension, diabetes, tinnitus), with mixed results. Notably, in a phase II, placebo-controlled multicenter clinical trial, CoQ10 was found to slow the disease progression in patients with early-stage Parkinson's disease (Shults et al., 2002). In another study that may be of particular interest to psychologists, the efficacy of CoQ10 in migraine prophylaxis was explored. In this double-blind, placebo-controlled trial, CoQ10 was superior to placebo for migraine attack frequency (47% of the CoQ10 achieving 50% reductions vs. 14% in placebo), headache days, and days with nausea in the third treatment month (Sandor et al., 2005).

Echinacea

There are nine species of echinacea, an herbaceous flowering plant in the daisy family, all of which are native to the United States and southern Canada. The most commonly used species is *Echinacea purpurea*. Echinacea has been traditionally used for colds, flu, and other infections (NIH, 2012b). Both the above-ground parts of the plant and roots of echinacea are used dried to make teas or squeezed fresh for juice, extracts, or preparations for external use. This agent has been studied in the treatment of upper respiratory tract infections (e.g., the common cold). NCCAM-supported research over two studies has not found benefit from echinacea, either as *Echinacea purpurea* fresh-pressed juice for treating colds in children or as an unrefined mixture of *Echinacea angustifolia* root and *Echinacea purpurea* root and herb in adults (NIH, 2012b). NCCAM-supported research continues in the treatment of upper respiratory infections but also for its potential effects on the immune system. Side effects from echinacea are rare; however, some people report experiencing allergic reactions. People are more likely to be allergic if they are allergic to other plants in the daisy family.

Fish Oil/Omega-3

The research literature on fish oil and its abundant constituent, the fatty acid omega-3, is vast. Fish oil can be obtained from eating fish (fish especially rich in omega-3 include mackerel, tuna, salmon, sturgeon, mullet, bluefish, anchovy, sardines, herring, trout, and menhaden) or by taking supplements. Fish oil has been used for a wide range of conditions related to the heart and blood system. According to the U.S. National Library of Medicine's Natural Medicines Comprehensive Database (NIH, 2013b), people report using fish oil to lower blood pressure or triglyceride levels, to prevent heart disease or stroke, for dry eyes, for glaucoma, to prevent painful menstruation, for breast pain, diabetes, asthma, and movement disorders, as well as to help with depression, psychosis, attention-deficit/hyperactivity disorder (ADHD), and Alzheimer's disease.

There have been few reported side effects of fish oil and omega-3 supplements, although omega-3 supplements may interact with drugs that affect blood clotting (NIH, 2012k). Omega-3 has been well studied in heart disease, but the findings have been inconsistent, and two combined analyses of the results did not find convincing evidence that omega-3 protects against heart disease (NIH, 2012k). NCCAM reports that there is some evidence that omega-3 is modestly helpful in relieving symptoms of rheumatoid arthritis and age-related macular degeneration, but for most other conditions for which Omega-3 has been studied, definitive conclusions cannot yet be reached (NIH, 2012h). An exception to this, and of particular interest to psychologists, may be in the treatment of ADHD. A recent meta-analysis including 10 trials of omega-3 fatty acids for the treatment of ADHD in children ($N = 699$) found that omega-3 fatty acid supplementation was modestly effective in the treatment of ADHD (Bloch & Qawasmi, 2011). The relative efficacy of omega-3 fatty acid supplementation was modest compared with currently available pharmacotherapies for ADHD; however, given its benign side effect profile and evidence of modest efficacy, the authors conclude that "it may be reasonable to use omega-3 fatty supplementation to augment traditional pharmacologic interventions or for families who decline other psychopharmacologic options" (Bloch & Qawasmi, 2011, p. 911).

Garlic

Garlic is the edible bulb from a plant (*Allium sativum*) in the lily family. It has been used as a medicine and a culinary seasoning and condiment for thousands of years, with evidence of its use

> found in Egyptian pyramids and ancient Greek temples. There are Biblical references to garlic. Ancient medical texts from Egypt, Greece, Rome, China and India each prescribed medical applications for garlic. In many cultures, garlic was administered to provide strength and increase work capacity for laborers. Hippocrates, the revered physician, prescribed garlic for a variety of conditions. Garlic was given to the original Olympic

athletes in Greece, as perhaps one of the earliest "performance enhancing" agents. (Rivlin, 2001, pp. 951–952)

As a dietary supplement, garlic is traditionally used for high cholesterol, heart disease, and high blood pressure, although NCCAM reports that another folk use is as a cancer prophylactic (NIH, 2012c). Garlic can be consumed raw or cooked, dried or powdered, in tablet and capsule, and in extruded oils and liquid extracts. Garlic is considered safe for most adults, aside from the infamous side effect of bad breath. Heartburn, stomach upset, and allergic reactions are less commonly reported, and these effects are more commonly found with raw garlic (NIH, 2012c). It has been reported that garlic does, however, thin the blood (reducing the ability of blood to clot) in a manner similar to aspirin, and this effect is potentially deleterious during or after surgery (Gardner et al., 2007).

A review conducted by the U.S. Agency for Healthcare Research and Quality examined the results of 37 randomized trials (all but one in adults) and found that, compared with placebo, a garlic preparation led to small, statistically significant reductions in cholesterol at 1 month and 3 months (but 6 months showed no significant reductions; Mulrow et al., 2000). Changes in low-density lipoprotein levels and triglycerides mirrored total cholesterol results; however, no significant changes in high-density lipoprotein levels were found. The review suggested that the trials show several promising, modest, short-term effects of garlic supplementation on lipid and antithrombotic factors, but the effects on clinical outcomes are not established, and effects on glucose and blood pressure are none to minimal (Mulrow et al., 2000). The authors of this review as well as NCCAM suggest that dietary intake of garlic may be associated with decreased risk of multiple cancers; however, no clinical trials have supported this as yet. A recent analysis of garlic intake and cancer risk using the U.S. FDA review system found only limited evidence supported a relation between garlic consumption and reduced risk of colon, prostate, esophageal, larynx, oral, ovary, or renal cell cancers (J. Y. Kim & Kwon, 2009).

Ginger

The aromatic underground stem (rhizome) of the plant *Zingiber officinale*, known in Western culture as ginger, has been used for cooking and medicinal purposes for thousands of years in multiple countries and cultures (Langner, Greifenberg, & Gruenwald, 1998). In China, ginger has been used to help digestion and treat upset stomach, diarrhea, and nausea for more than 2,000 years (Shukla & Singh, 2007). Ginger has also been used to help with arthritis, colic, diarrhea, heart conditions, the common cold, flulike symptoms, headaches, and painful menstruation (NIH, 2012c). Ginger is currently being used as a folk or traditional remedy for postsurgery nausea; nausea caused by motion, chemotherapy, and pregnancy; rheumatoid arthritis; osteoarthritis; and joint and muscle pain.

Ginger can be consumed raw or cooked, dried or powdered, in tablet and capsule, and in extruded oils and liquid extracts. Ginger is considered safe when taken in small doses with the few reported side effects being gas, bloating, heartburn, and nausea (most often associated with powdered ginger; NIH, 2012d). The research on the medical application of ginger has shown significant reductions of nausea (secondary to pregnancy, motion sickness, and surgery), osteoarthritis, and a few preliminary studies that suggests ginger lowers cholesterol and can prevent blood clotting (University of Maryland Medical Center, 2013a).

An example of the recent work being performed using ginger is found in a double-blind multicenter study of ginger for nausea in chemotherapy patients (Ryan et al., 2012). In this study, 744 cancer patients were randomly assigned to four arms: (a) placebo, (b) 0.5 g ginger, (c) 1.0 g ginger, or (d) 1.5 g ginger (Ryan et al., 2012). Primary outcomes were nausea occurrence and severity assessed at baseline and during the next two cycles of chemotherapy. The ginger and placebo were delivered in capsules twice daily for 6 days, beginning 3 days before the first day of chemotherapy. Mixed model analyses demonstrated that all doses of ginger significantly reduced acute nausea severity compared with placebo on Day 1 of chemotherapy, with the 0.5-g and 1.0-g ginger groups showing the largest reduction. The authors concluded from this study that ginger supplementation is a significant aid in the reduction of acute chemotherapy-induced nausea in adult cancer patients (University of Maryland Medical Center, 2013a).

Ginkgo biloba

One of the oldest living tree species, Ginkgo biloba has been used both for its fruit, (considered a tonic, although odiferous) and for the medical benefits of its leaves in China for more than 1,000 years (Pang, Pan, & He, 1996). The Ginkgo biloba's life can span 2,000 to 4,000 years and the tree can grow to a height of 120 feet. Ginkgos are often planted in urban streets in the United States because they are extremely hardy—a ginkgo survived the blast at Hiroshima (Pang et al., 1996). Although the seeds, fruit, and leaves of the ginkgo have been used in TCM, it is the standardized Ginkgo biloba extract (BGE) taken from the leaves that has been most often used in modern research (University of Maryland Medical Center, 2013a). Ginkgo biloba is taken in capsules, tablets, and teas and is an ingredient in some skin products. The reported side effects of gingko have been headache, nausea, gastrointestinal upset, diarrhea, dizziness, or allergic skin reaction, with other more severe allergic reactions occasionally reported (NIH, 2012e).

Additionally, NCCAM reports that ginkgo may increase bleeding risk and also cautions that raw ginkgo seeds contain a large amount of ginkgotoxin, a compound that can cause seizures (NIH, 2012e) Taken from the leaves, BGE appears to be safe when used orally and appropriately.

NCCAM reports that ginkgo has been studied for a variety of conditions, including Alzheimer's disease, other forms of dementia, memory impairment, intermittent claudication (pain or weakness of the legs), sexual dysfunction secondary to antidepressants, insulin resistance, and tinnitus, with dementia being the most widely researched (NIH, 2012e). The research on Alzheimer's disease is mixed; a NCCAM-funded study of more than 3,000 volunteers aged 75 and older who took 240 mg of ginkgo daily and were followed for 6 years resulted in data showing ginkgo to be ineffective (DeKosky et al., 2008). These results conflict with a 2009 meta-analysis including nine trials of ginkgo biloba, (specifically the well-publicized product EGb-761) which concluded that ginkgo significantly improved symptoms (Weinmann, Roll, Schwarzbach, Vauth, & Willich, 2010). Smaller studies of ginkgo for memory enhancement have shown significant results, although even these results are mixed. A National Institute on Aging study ($N = 200$ healthy adults aged over 60) found that ginkgo taken for 6 weeks did not improve memory (NIH, 2012e). The current evidence for ginkgo improving symptoms of intermittent claudication is mixed, and despite several positive early studies, further research is required to establish clinical efficacy.

In a recent study, and potentially of special interest to psychologists, Ginkgo biloba was investigated for the improvement of cognitive impairments secondary to electroconvulsive treatment for depression (Nikfarjam, Goudarzi, Heidari, & Parvin, 2012). In this trial, 81 hospitalized patients diagnosed with major depression who were to undergo bilateral electroconvulsive treatment were randomized to receive Ginkgo biloba or placebo. The primary outcomes were measures of depression and cognition status. The study results showed that mean scores in cognitive and depression tests before and after electroconvulsive treatment showed significant differences in both groups with the Ginkgo biloba showing significantly superior cognitive status and milder depression. The authors suggested that these results show Ginkgo biloba may improve cognitive and depression status.

Ginseng

Asian ginseng (Panax ginseng) is native to China and Korea and has been used in various systems of medicine for many centuries (Ernst, 2010). Asian ginseng has been taken to boost overall health, boost the immune system, increase a sense of well-being and stamina, improve mental and physical performance, treat erectile dysfunction, treat hepatitis C, treat symptoms related to menopause, lower blood sugar, and lower blood pressure (NIH, 2012a). The active chemical components thought to be responsible for the herb's medicinal properties are called ginsenosides and have been the subject of substantial empirical scrutiny (Sievenpiper, Arnason, Leiter, & Vuksan, 2004). Dried ginseng root is taken in tablets, capsules, extracts, teas, and creams. Ginseng, at recommended doses, is believed safe for most people, with the most common side effects reported to be headaches, poor sleep, and gastrointestinal problems. It should be noted that Asian ginseng may lower blood sugar levels; therefore, people with diabetes should be cautioned, particularly if they are using medication or herbs (e.g., bitter melon, fenugreek) that are also believed to lower blood sugar (NIH, 2012a).

In a recent review of ginseng in Korean literature, a broad body of research was examined, including 30 randomized, clinical trials (Choi, Kim, Choi, & Lee, 2013). In this review, nine randomized controlled trials (RCTs) assessed the effects of ginseng on exercise capacity, cognitive performance, somatic symptoms, quality of life, and sleeping in healthy persons. Six RCTs tested ginseng compared with placebo for erectile dysfunction, and another four studies evaluated the effects of ginseng against no treatment for gastric and colon cancer. Two RCTs compared the effect of red ginseng on diabetes mellitus with no treatment or placebo, and the other nine RCTs assessed the effects of ginseng compared with placebo or no treatment on various conditions. Although the literature was generally supportive, the authors concluded that the quality of the RCTs were generally poor, and thus no confident estimate of effect can be made from the studies in aggregate (Choi et al., 2013).

American ginseng (*Panax quinquefolius*) is said to have differing therapeutic properties from its Asian counterpart and is "thought to increase sex drive, memory, and learning; decrease aging; and possess both digestion-regulating and liver-protective activities in the rat" (Vuksan et al., 2000, p. 1009). There are few clinical studies of American ginseng. A preliminary short-term clinical study of 10 diabetic subjects and nine nondiabetic subjects randomized to 3 g of American ginseng or placebo showing significant effects toward diabetes mellitus by attenuating postprandial glycemia (insulin demand) in diabetic as well as nondiabetic subjects (Vuksan et al., 2000). In another pilot trial, American ginseng was evaluated for its effects on cancer-related fatigue as well as its toxicity (Barton et al., 2010). In this trial, 299 adults with cancer were randomized in a double-blind manner to receive American ginseng in doses of 750, 1,000, or 2,000 mg/day or placebo given in twice daily dosing over 8 weeks. The results of this study were nonsignificant trends in favor of the 1,000- and 2,000-mg/day doses of American ginseng with no significant differences in any measured toxicities between any of the arms of the study. The authors concluded that there appears to be some activity and tolerable toxicity at 1,000 to 2,000 mg/day doses of American ginseng with regard to cancer-related fatigue and suggested that further study of American ginseng is warranted.

Kava

Kava (aka Kava kava) is a member of the pepper family (*piper methysticum*) native to the islands of the South Pacific (NIH, 2012f). Kava has been used as a ceremonial drink, to fight fatigue, to fall asleep, to treat asthma and urinary infections, as a numbing agent, and recently to treat anxiety, insomnia, and menopausal symptoms. The root and rhizome of kava as well as the leaves have been used to prepare beverages, extracts, capsules, tablets, and topical solutions. Kava has received some empirical support for its role as an anxiolytic; a 2003 Cochrane Review of 12 randomized trials showed a small but significant effect size versus placebo in reducing anxiety (Pittler, Max, & Ernst, 2003). However, the U.S. FDA has issued a warning that using kava supplements has been linked to a risk of severe liver damage, and further NIH-funded studies on kava were suspended (NIH, 2012f). Kava has been reported to cause liver damage, including hepatitis, and potentially fatal liver failure (Teschke & Schulze, 2010). Furthermore, kava has been associated with several cases of dystonia (abnormal muscle spasm or involuntary muscle movements) and scaly, yellowed skin (after long-term and/or heavy use); kava may also interact with several drugs, including drugs used for Parkinson's disease. Although kava is not recommended for use and psychologists are urged to caution any patients who report its use, some clients may be using it, or considering its use, so being aware of these risks is important.

Peppermint

Peppermint (*Mentha piperita*), a perennial flowering hybrid of spearmint and water mint plants, is commercially cultivated in the United States and Europe (World Health Organization, 2002). Peppermint leaves can be used fresh, dried, in topical and edible essential oils, and in capsule and liquid forms (NIH, 2012g). Peppermint is widely used as a flavoring, but it is also used as a remedy for nausea, indigestion, cold symptoms, headaches, muscle and nerve pain, stomach problems, and irritable bowel syndrome (IBS). Peppermint oil appears to be safe for most adults when used in small doses. Possible side effects include allergic reactions and heartburn (NIH, 2012i).

Irritable Bowel Syndrome

A meta-analysis of eight RCTs and five placebo-controlled double-blind trials of enteric-coated peppermint oil capsules collectively suggested that peppermint oil could be efficacious for symptom relief in irritable bowel syndrome (IBS; Pittler & Ernst, 1998). In a recent randomized, double-blind, placebo-controlled study of 90 outpatients with IBS, subjects took one capsule of enteric-coated, delayed-release peppermint oil or placebo three times daily for 8 weeks (Merat et al., 2010). Subjects' symptoms and quality of life were evaluated after the 1st, 4th, and 8th weeks. Results of the study showed that the severity of abdominal pain was significantly reduced in the peppermint oil group compared with placebo control, and there was a significantly greater number of subjects free from abdominal pain or discomfort at Week 8 compared with the control group (14 subjects in the peppermint oil group vs. 6 in the control group were pain-free).

Tension Headaches

The topical application of peppermint oil is reported to produce a lasting cooling effect on the skin, caused by a steric alteration of the calcium channels of the cold-receptors (Göbel, Schmidt, Dworschak, Stolze, & Heuss, 1995). It has also been reported that peppermint oil induces a significant increase of the skin blood flow of the forehead after local application, measured by laser Doppler (Göbel et al., 1995). On the basis of this information, two small trials of peppermint oil preparations have been completed to examine peppermint oil for reducing symptoms of tension headaches. The first trial investigated the analgesic effect of the topical application of peppermint, ethanol and eucalyptus oils to the forehead and temples of 32 subjects in a double-blind, placebo-controlled, randomized crossover design (Göbel, Schmidt, & Soyka, 1994). The results of this trial revealed a statistically significant analgesic effect compared with placebo with a reduction in sensitivity to headache produced by a combination of peppermint oil and ethanol.

A second RCT then compared the efficacy of topically applied peppermint oil with that of acetaminophen in 41 adult subjects (Göbel, Fresenius, Heinze, Dworschak, & Soyka, 1996). In this randomized, placebo-controlled, double-blind crossover study, a liquid test preparation containing 10 g of peppermint oil and ethanol (90%), and 500 mg acetaminophen were compared with a corresponding placebo (a placebo control of 90% ethanol sans peppermint and a placebo tablet, respectively). The study included the analysis of 164 headache attacks, with each attack treated with the application of two capsules of the oral medication (1,000 mg of acetaminophen or placebo) and the cutaneous application of the oil preparation (peppermint oil or placebo solution). The oil was spread across the forehead and temples, and this was repeated after 15 and 30 minutes. Outcomes were assessed by headache diary assessed after 15, 30, 45, and 60 minutes. Results showed that, compared with the placebo, 10% peppermint oil in ethanol solution significantly reduced clinical headache intensity after 15 minutes, and this significant reduction of pain intensity continued over the 1-hour observation period. Acetaminophen was also found to be significantly more effective than placebo, but there was no significant difference between the efficacy of the acetaminophen and the peppermint oil. The simultaneous application of 1,000 mg of acetaminophen and the peppermint oil had an additive effect that was not significant. The subjects in the study reported no adverse events. Although the results of these two trials cannot be considered conclusive, the positive outcomes and lack of reported adverse events or side effects are encouraging. The application of peppermint oil in treating tension headaches shows promise, and additional study is warranted.

Soy

Soy (*Glycine max*) is a species of legume native to East Asia with archaeological evidence to support its use and domestication from 8,600 to 9,000 years ago in China and 7,000 years ago in Japan (G. Lee, Crawford, Liu, Sasaki, & Chen, 2011). Soy is unique among plant foods because it is high in protein, and it has been used as both a food source and for its purported medicinal properties. Besides its nutritional benefits, soy contains isoflavones, which is a phytoestrogen, a chemical that acts like the hormone estrogen (NIH, 2012h). Soy can be cooked and eaten, used to make tofu, soy milk, and other foods. It is also sold as a dietary supplement in tablet and capsule forms. Soy is sometimes used as an additive in various processed foods. Medicinally, it is believed to improve menopausal symptoms, osteoporosis, memory problems, high blood pressure, high cholesterol levels, breast cancer, and prostate cancer (NIH, 2012h). Soy is considered generally safe when used as a food or when taken for short periods as a dietary supplement, although minor stomach and bowel problems and allergic reactions (in rare cases) are possible. Though soy is one of the eight most common food allergies, actually only about 0.4% of children have a soy allergy, thus indicating that it is rare (Savage, Kaeding, Matsui, & Wood, 2010). The safety of long-term use of soy isoflavones is unknown; there is mixed evidence regarding an increased risk of endometrial hyperplasia (a thickening of the lining of the uterus that can lead to cancer), and there has been question (but no good evidence to date) into soy's possible role in breast cancer (Sirtori, 2001).

Soy isoflavones have been investigated for their ability to reduce menopausal symptoms. Clinical studies have shown that women who take soy may have fewer hot flashes, but the results are inconsistent (NIH, 2012j). A meta-analysis performed in 2006 reported on 11 trials of soy isoflavones compared with placebo (H. D. Nelson et al., 2006). Their analysis revealed that three trials (two rated as fair and one as poor) showed reduced hot-flash frequency compared with placebo, three trials (rated as fair) found no difference from placebo, hot-flash severity improved significantly compared with placebo in three trials, and five trials (four of which in women with breast cancer) found no difference in severity scores. The authors of the meta-analysis concluded that the contradictory evidence does not support soy isoflavone's benefit in relieving hot flashes. Research into soy is ongoing, with NCCAM supporting additional studies of soy in cardiovascular disease and breast cancer and on menopause-related symptoms and bone loss (NIH, 2012h).

St. John's Wort

St. John's wort (*Hypericum perforatum*), a plant with yellow flowers, has a history of medicinal use back to ancient times. It was administered as a remedy by the Roman military doctor Proscurides as early as the first century C.E. (Poldinger, 2000). It is said that the name *St. John's wort* was coined by the early Christians, who named the plant after their beloved John the Baptist because the brightly colored flowers usually reveal themselves on or before June 24, which is celebrated as his birthday (NIH, 2012i). Historically, St. John's wort has been used to treat mental disorders, nerve pain, and malaria; it is used as a sedative and as a balm for wounds, burns, and insect bites. Today, St. John's wort is used as an herbal remedy for depression, anxiety, and sleep disorders (NIH, 2011h). It can been taken in teas, tablets, capsules, concentrated extracts, and topical preparations. Researchers believe that the mechanism of action may lie in the active components of hypericin and pseudohypericin, found in both the leaves and flowers of the plant. St. John's wort extract has been demonstrated to have an inhibitory effect on the neuronal uptake of serotonin, noradrenaline, dopamine, gamma-aminobutyric acid, and l-glutamate (Müller, 2003). St. John's wort has been reported to affect the metabolism of many drugs and can cause serious side effects. For example, St. John's wort can affect serotonin-targeting antidepressants; its use in combination with certain antidepressants can lead to a potentially life-threatening increase in serotonin levels (a condition called *serotonin syndrome*), which can create symptoms that range from tremor and diarrhea to serious confusion, muscle stiffness, body temperature changes, and potentially death (Mannel, 2004; NIH, 2012k). Additionally, there is concern that St. John's wort may interfere with getting pregnant, aggravate symptoms of ADHD, increase risk of psychosis in people with schizophrenia, and aggravate dementia in people with Alzheimer's disease, although additional research is necessary (University of Maryland Medical Center, 2013b).

Depression

St. John's wort has been predominately studied for its use in easing symptoms of depression. A 2000 Cochrane Review of 37 trials, including 26 comparisons with placebo and 14 comparisons with synthetic standard antidepressants showed marked heterogeneity; however, the authors concluded that several specific extracts of St. John's wort may be effective for treating mild to moderate depression, although the authors did note that the data are not fully convincing (Linde, Mulrow, Berner, & Egger, 2000). A subsequent 2008 Cochrane Review evaluated St. John's wort in the treatment of major depression (Linde, Berner Michael, & Kriston, 2008). In this review, 29 trials ($N = 5,489$) including 18 comparisons with placebo and 17 comparisons with standard antidepressant medications were analyzed. Although the results of the placebo-controlled trials showed marked heterogeneity, as the previous review had, the authors were still able to conclude that St. John's wort showed significant effects. Nine larger trials showed a combined response rate ratio (defined as the proportion of improved patients in the treatment group divided by the proportion of improved patients in the control group) for St. John's wort extracts (*Hypericum*) compared with placebo of 1.28 and nine small trials of 1.87. The authors' conclusions from this review suggest that St. John's wort extracts were superior to placebo in patients with major depression and similarly effective as standard antidepressants with fewer side effects.

Premenstrual Syndrome

In a recent trial, St. John's wort was investigated for its efficacy in treating symptoms associated with premenstrual syndrome (PMS; Canning et al., 2010). In this randomized, double-blind, placebo-controlled crossover study, 36 women ages 18 to 45 years with regular menstrual cycles (25–35 days) prospectively diagnosed with mild PMS underwent a two-cycle placebo run-in phase. They were then randomly assigned to receive *Hypericum perforatum* tablets 900 mg/day (standardized to 0.18% hypericin, 3.38% hyperforin) or identical placebo tablets for two menstrual cycles. After a placebo-treated washout cycle, the women crossed over to receive placebo or *Hypericum perforatum* for two additional cycles. The results of this study revealed statistically superior improvements in physical and behavioral symptoms of PMS, with no significance revealed compared with placebo for mood and pain-related PMS. Markers of immune functioning and weekly report of anxiety, depression, aggression, and impulsivity were not significant compared with placebo. The authors concluded that daily treatment with *Hypericum perforatum* was more effective than placebo treatment for the most common physical and behavioral symptoms associated with PMS, but the beneficial effects are unlikely to be a result of change in proinflammatory cytokine levels.

CONTRAINDICATIONS AND RISKS

It should again be noted that herbal remedies (dietary supplements) are regulated as a subgroup of foods, not as medications, and manufacturers are not required to prove their safety and effectiveness before marketing them to consumers. Great care should be taken when considering the use of dietary supplements. Although some may seem benign and some may result in positive health gains, others may actually be dangerous and should only be used under the direct supervision of one's physician. Often consumers view certain dietary supplements as "natural" and thus safe, but many dietary supplements can be harmful, may cause serious side effects, and can even be deadly. Thus, psychologists must be knowledgeable about both the potential benefits and potential risks of dietary supplements that are currently available to consumers.

The FDA provides its "Dietary Supplement Alerts and Safety Information" at http://www.fda.gov/Food/DietarySupplements/Alerts/default.htm. Examples of alerts on this website include the following:

- Colloidal silver—dietary supplements containing silver may cause permanent discoloration of the skin and mucous membranes.
- Kava—products containing kava may be associated with hepatic (liver) toxicity.
- Ephedra—the FDA has advised that ephedra products may cause side effects including gastrointestinal distress, blood pressure changes, headache, seizures, stroke, and even death.

Mechanick et al. (2003) reported additional FDA alerts for the following products: Herbal fen-phen may have an amphetamine-like effect on the heart and central nervous system, and the FDA considered it an unapproved drug. Plantain, which has been marketed for use as a laxative, is reported to cause myocardial infarctions. The herb Sleeping Buddha, which has been marketed for the treatment of insomnia, has been shown to result in fetal damage.

Deng et al. (2009, p. 105) stated, "Herbs may attenuate or lessen the effect of a drug either by direct action on its target or by altering its pharmacokinetics," requiring all herbal supplements taken with medications to be used with caution and under the supervision of one's physician.

An additional complication that results from how dietary supplements are regulated is that specific dietary supplement products may vary in strength and effect both between and within manufacturers. A range of other substances included in the manufacturing of dietary supplements may cause adverse reactions. According to the NIH (2011e, para. 7), "an herbal supplement may contain dozens of compounds and its active ingredients may not be known." It is also important to point out that dietary supplements are not intended to be a replacement for a healthy, well-rounded diet but as supplements to one's diet. Consumers are referred to the Dietary Guidelines for Americans (http://health.gov/dietaryguidelines) for the federal government's most current guidelines for a healthy diet. Some substances are not absorbed by the body as easily if ingested in the form of a supplement and are better included as part of one's diet in the foods one eats.

Dietary supplements are not intended to be a replacement for needed medical treatment for certain diseases and health conditions. Psychologists will want to monitor their clients' use of dietary supplements to ensure that this use is evidence-based and not in place of medically necessary treatment. Some clients may find prescription medications expensive, with some not covered by their health insurance, and the use of certain dietary supplements as an alternative may seem attractive to them. Other clients may be drawn to claims of "natural" substances and prefer them over prescription medications, perhaps risking serious health consequences either from discontinuation of needed medical treatment or use of an inappropriate supplement.

TIPS FOR PRACTITIONERS

- Biologically based therapies such as herbal medicine or botanicals should not be used as a substitute for conventional care.
- Patients who wish to try a biologically based therapy such as an herbal or dietary supplement should seek clearance from a medical professional to ensure that the treatment will not interfere with their current treatment regimen—some herbs and dietary supplements have been shown to have dangerous interactions with some medications.
- Practitioners should ask their patients if they are using, or are considering using, any biologically based therapies, such as herbal remedies or dietary supplements.
- Practitioners should become aware of the empirical research on the efficacy, risks, and side effects of the most commonly used biologically based practices and disseminate this information to patients who may be using or considering them.

INTEGRATION WITH PSYCHOLOGICAL PRACTICE

Psychologists should not make recommendations for the use of dietary supplements. Rather, our role is in educating interested clients about the potential risks and benefits of dietary supplements and inquiring about clients' use of dietary supplements. As necessary, we may then refer them back to their primary care physicians. For example, a client's treatment for depression may include the use of an antidepressant medication prescribed by his or her physician in addition to the ongoing psychotherapy provided by the psychologist. A psychologist who asks this client about the use of all other substances—prescription, over-the-counter, or other—may learn that he or she has also been taking St. John's wort with the goal of enhancing the treatment of depression. Such a client should immediately be referred back to the prescribing physician for medical monitoring and intervention based on the known effects of St. John's wort on antidepressant medications.

Although many dietary supplements are generally known to have beneficial effects, psychologists may not know each client's complete medical history or his or her entire dietary supplement, other substance, and medical treatment regimen; thus, decisions about the use of dietary supplements should not be made in isolation. As has been stated, dietary supplements may interact with other substances clients may be taking, both through their diet and in the form of other substances. Clients may have sensitivities or allergies to certain substances and may even experience life-threatening side effects to others. It is therefore recommended that the use of all dietary supplements be monitored by clients' physicians. Although psychologists may not be able to require clients to meet with their physician, we can make clear recommendations for clients to do so, provide guidance about the relative benefits and potential risks associated with dietary supplement use, and document all such discussions and recommendations. Psychologists should also closely monitor their clients' functioning, being alert for possible adverse effects from dietary supplements. With our client's consent, we should share information about their use of supplements and any effects observed (positive or negative) to their physicians. It is also important to note that many individuals are not aware of the FDA's limited role in regulating dietary supplements, often assuming that they are safe and effective if they are allowed to be sold in the United States (Dodge & Kaufman, 2007). This finding further highlights the importance of psychologists actively inquiring about each client's use of dietary supplements and of educating clients about their safe and effective use, including any associated risks.

ADDITIONAL RESOURCES

1. Center for Food Safety and Applied Nutrition (CFSAN)— CFSAN is the FDA division that oversees product labeling and safety for dietary supplements, foods, and cosmetics. It provides useful information on how to safely and effectively

use dietary supplements and posts related safety alerts. It also offers a number of online resources relevant to the use of dietary supplements. One relevant resource on its website is "Tips for the Savvy Supplement User: Making Informed Decisions and Evaluating Information." The CFSAN website can be accessed at http://www.fda.gov/AboutFDA/CentersOffices/CFSAN.

2. Dietary Supplements Labels Database—This database, compiled by the National Library of Medicine, offers information on more than 6,000 brands of dietary supplements. The goal of this database is to allow consumers to compare different brands of the same dietary supplement. Information is also provided on structure and function claims made by the manufacturers of these products. The website includes information on product recalls and links to research on the active ingredients of the many products. The labels database may be accessed at http://www.dsld.nlm.nih.gov/dsld.

3. Herbs at a Glance—This website is provided by NCCAM and offers an extensive listing of the commonly used herbals. For each, information is provided on what the herb is, what it is commonly used for, how it is taken, what scientific support there is for its use, side effects and cautions, references for the information provided, and links to resources that provide additional information on that herb. Information on approximately 45 herbs is provided. The website may be accessed at http://nccam.nih.gov/health/herbsataglance.htm.

4. NCCAM Portal Page on Dietary and Herbal Supplements—This is the home page of the National Center for Complementary and Alternative Medicine of the National Institutes of Health. This website is an excellent resource for consumers and professionals alike, providing a wide range of information about dietary supplements to include links to safety information, research on their use and effectiveness, and even resources in Spanish. The site may be accessed at http://nccam.nih.gov/health/supplements/.

5. Office of Dietary Supplements (ODS)—The website of the ODS of the NIH provides extensive information about dietary supplements, including a list of each known dietary supplement and links to resources about them. Additionally, extensive information is provided about the safe use of dietary supplements. This site may be accessed at http://www.ods.od.nih.gov. Those with questions about dietary supplements may submit them by e-mail directly to ods@nih.gov.

6. International Bibliographic Information on Dietary Supplements (IBIDS)—IBIDS, a subset of PubMed, is a joint project of NIH's National Library of Medicine and the ODS. It provides a means to search online for peer-reviewed journal articles in the PubMed database relevant to dietary supplements. It can be accessed at http://ods.od.nih.gov/Health_Information/IBIDS.aspx.
7. U.S. Food and Drug Administration—The FDA is the government agency that oversees the safety of foods, medicines, dietary supplements, cosmetics, and medical devices. Its website provides information on product recalls, general safety information, product labeling, and regulation of dietary supplements and provides guidelines and information on clinical trials relevant to a wide range of products under its purview. Its website may be accessed at http://fda.gov. Additionally, the FDA may be contacted by telephone toll-free in the U.S. at 1-888-463-6332.

12

AROMATHERAPY

Aromatherapy is the use of essential oils extracted from plants for the promotion of physical and psychological well-being (Herz, 2009). Proponents of aromatherapy believe that various plant-based aromas have the ability to influence mood, behavior, and spiritual well-being by stimulation of the olfactory or somatic senses (Segen, 1998; Tisserand, 1988). Aromatherapy can be used as a single treatment or in combination with other complementary and alternative (CAM) modalities such as massage or acupuncture. In addition, it can be used in conjunction with traditional medical treatments to increase a sense of well-being.

http://dx.doi.org/10.1037/14435-013
Complementary and Alternative Medicine for Psychologists: An Essential Resource, by J. E. Barnett, A. J. Shale, G. Elkins, and W. Fisher

DEFINITIONS

There are three main types of aromatherapy: clinical, holistic, and aesthetic (Metcalfe, 1989). *Clinical aromatherapy* is "the use of essential oils for therapeutic purposes with benefits that may include relief of stress, anxiety, insomnia and reduced perception of pain" (Chalifour & Champagne, 2008, p. 1). *Holistic aromatherapy* is a mind–body approach in which the whole person is considered with the main goal of improving overall quality of life and bringing the body back into homeostasis, as opposed to curing one specific symptom (Metcalfe, 1989). *Aesthetic aromatherapy* is nonclinical and refers to the use of oils and scents to create a pleasant environment in one's home or place of work. Aesthetic aromatherapy is often used by beauticians for skin care as they incorporate "essences in treatment oils, creams and lotions" to promote comfort and relaxation (Metcalfe, 1989, p. 3).

HISTORY

The field of aromatherapy began thousands of years ago with ancient civilizations in China, India, and Egypt using essential oils as physical and psychological treatment modalities (National Cancer Institute, 2010). It is often associated with the whole medical systems of Traditional Chinese Medicine or Ayurveda (Cristina, 2004). Although historians' opinions vary, the Chinese were likely among the first to use aromatherapy (in approximately 2,000 BCE) as they often burned incense for comfort. Additionally, they used the herbs for "teas, ingestion, and inhalation to affect balance" (d'Angelo, 2002, p. 73). The ancient Egyptians "developed an elaborate system of herbology" that had both medicinal and aesthetic purposes (d'Angelo, 2002, p. 73).

Our modern perception of aromatherapy began in the early 20th century when the word *aromatherapie* was coined by French chemist René-Maurice Gattefossé in his book *L'Aromatherapy*, first published in 1937. During the late 1920s, Gattefossé discovered the powers of essential oils after an explosion left his hand badly burned. He accidentally soaked the burn in lavender oil and quickly noticed that the oil could help with pain management (National Cancer Institute, 2010). Despite that publication, Westernized aromatherapy did not garner a great deal of attention until Jean Valnet published his book *The Practice of Aromatherapy* in 1982, at which time the practice became more well known in Great Britain and the United States (National Cancer Institute, 2010).

Despite its long history, many people continue to think of aromatherapy as more of a beauty treatment than a method of healing (Price & Price, 1999).

With the recent interest in CAM, the field of aromatherapy has increasingly gained acceptance in the United States, Canada, England, France, and Germany (National Cancer Institute, 2010) as a therapeutic intervention. Aromatherapy is also easily administered, and the side effects appear to be minimal (Louis & Kowalski, 2002; Price & Price, 1999).

COMMON USES

Research has examined whether various essential oils can be used to treat different symptoms. For example, lavender has been studied in treating high blood pressure, agitation, insomnia, pain, and mood, among other things (Brooker, Snape, Johnson, & Ward, 1997; C. Holmes et al., 2002; Hur et al., 2007; Lewith, Godfrey, & Prescott, 2005; Lin, Chan, Ng, & Lam 2007; Louis & Kowalski, 2002; M. Moss, Cook, Wesnes, & Duckett 2003). Other oils such as rose, jasmine, almond, marjoram, bergamot, ylang ylang, and chamomile have also been studied, although less extensively, for the treatment of similar symptom sets (M. Cooke, Holzhauser, Jones, Davis, & Finucane, 2007; Fowler, 2006; S. H. Han et al., 2006; Hur et al., 2007; Kunstler, Greenblatt, & Moreno, 2004).

TECHNIQUE

Aromatherapy can be performed in various settings; patients may choose to apply aromatherapy themselves or seek guidance and the supervised administration of aromatherapy from a physician or a registered aromatherapist (Aromatherapy Registration Council [ARC], 2011). As aromatherapy has become increasingly popular, various books and articles have been published regarding how to use essential oils safely (e.g., La Torre, 2003; Robins, 1999). These resources may provide patients with guidance for the safe application of aromatherapy in the hope of preventing potential negative side effects (ARC, 2011).

The process of aromatherapy involves using essential oils, or volatile liquid(s), extracted from various plant parts by steam distillation (Cristina, 2004). The oils are termed *essential* because they are essential to a plant's survival and are said to be volatile because they evaporate in the air (d'Angelo, 2002). The liquid can come from the leaves, seeds, flowers, wood, or other parts of plants and are thought to provide healing power through ingestion, inhalation (e.g., diffuser, humidifier, vapor inhalation), or skin absorption—often in conjunction with massage therapy (Cristina, 2004; Price & Price, 1999).

MECHANISM OF ACTION

There is currently no established mechanism of action that adequately explains the process of aromatherapy. Proponents of aromatherapy debate whether the effects of essential oils are largely pharmacological or psychological. Some proponents of the pharmacological effects of aromatherapy have posited that aromatherapy heals as "individual constituents reach the blood, cross the blood–brain barrier and enter the CNS [central nervous system] following . . . administration" (Herz, 2009, p. 263). Some studies have suggested that oils used for sedative purposes (e.g., lavender) appear to act by slowing the activity of the central nervous system (CNS), whereas stimulant oils (e.g., jasmine and rosemary) appear to increase CNS activity (Herz, 2009; Perry & Perry, 2006). Essential oils are made of a variety of chemical components (e.g., monoterpenes, sesquiterpenes, sesquiterpenols, diterpenols, aldehydes, ketones, esters, oxides, phenols, ethers, acids, coumarins, lactones), and researchers have suggested that these components must all work together for the oil to provide the desired effect (Cristina, 2004). Practitioners of aromatherapy suggest that effects of the oils may differ depending on the route of administration because the chemical components may be metabolized at different rates before they are circulated throughout the body (Perry & Perry, 2006). Thus, it is unclear which method of administration is the most effective (e.g., ingestion, inhalation, or skin absorption).

However, proponents of the psychological effects of aromatherapy argue that a client's olfactory receptors may communicate with the amygdala and hippocampus as a means to stimulate memories and emotions in the brain (University of Maryland Medical Center, 2011). Studies have found that inhaling a scent can, at times, elicit a memory as well as regulate feelings, emotions, and the autonomic response (Cristina, 2004; Herz, 2009). Thus, proponents of aromatherapy suggest that certain aromas may be associated with emotional states and aid in healing (Herz, 2009). Additionally, other psychological factors, such as belief and expectation, may influence the effects of essential oils (Herz, 2009). Researchers examining the placebo effects of odors have concluded that the effects of the scents on physiological functions (heart rate and skin conductance) and mood were secondary to the meaning and expectation surrounding the effect of the aroma (Campenni, Crawley, & Meier, 2004; Howard & Hughes, 2008; Knasko, 1995). Thus, the effects of aromatherapy may be entirely due to expectations rather than the chemical components of the oils. Ultimately, it is unclear how and why aromatherapy may work, and further research is needed to determine the mechanism of action that adequately explains the psychological and physiological effects of essential oils.

RELEVANT RESEARCH

To date, the effects of aromatherapy have been examined in relation to anxiety, depression, pain, hypertension, and health concerns such as agitation associated with dementia, among other issues (B. Cooke & Ernst, 2000; Hur, Lee, Kim, & Ernst, 2012; Langley, Geiger, & Gartlehner, 2008; M. S. Lee, Choi, Posadzki, & Ernst, 2012; Y. L. Lee, Wu, Tsang, Leung, & Cheung, 2011; Nguyen & Paton, 2008). Although there remains a dearth of information regarding the efficacy of aromatherapy, growing interest in this modality may be attributed to its cost-effectiveness and lack of negative side effects (Herz, 2009). CAM treatments like aromatherapy attempt to promote overall well-being in patients rather than target reduction of a single symptom (Metcalfe, 1989). Although aromatherapy may be linked to psychological and physiological changes that may promote general well-being within patients, additional research will need to replicate the findings from these studies to generalize findings. Table 12.1 provides an evaluation of the scope and quality of the research and provides author recommendations based on the available evidence.

Anxiety

Aromatherapy has been associated with feelings of relaxation and calm; thus, studies have recently examined aromatherapy's anxiolytic effects. A systematic review by Y. L. Lee, Wu, et al. (2011) reviewed the effects of aromatherapy on anxiety symptoms across 16 randomized controlled trials (RCTs). Although the meta-analysis indicated positive results for the anxiolytic effects of aromatherapy, the study cautioned against the overall conclusions that could be drawn from these findings. Most of the studies examined in the meta-analysis investigated anxiety as a secondary symptom to another disorder (i.e., cancer, dementia, etc.). Additionally, the anxiety symptoms within the studies varied widely, studies varied in the means of aromatherapy administration (e.g., with massage, type of essential oil), and the sizes of samples varied widely as well. Although the outcomes from the 16 studies reviewed suggest positive evidence for the efficacy of aromatherapy in anxiety reduction, the results should be applied with caution, and further research is needed to support the claims proposed within the inconclusive literature. The results from other studies in the literature similarly support the inconclusive nature of these studies (Lehrner, Marwinski, Lehr, Johren, & Deecke, 2005; Louis & Kowalski, 2002).

Depression

Aromatherapy has often been used for stress reduction and mood enhancement. Yim, Ng, Tsang, and Leung (2009) reviewed the effects of

TABLE 12.1
Aromatherapy Summary Table

Symptom	Studies[a]	Sample	GRADE[b]	Evaluation
Anxiety	1 meta-analysis	Generalized anxiety disorder patients; mothers in labor; laboratory-induced stress; dementia patients; postpartum mothers; nursing students; patients waiting for dental procedures; palliative care patients; women waiting for surgical abortion; cancer patients	2B	Weak recommendation, moderate-quality evidence
Dementia	3 meta-analyses	Patients with dementia and Alzheimer's disease	2B	Weak recommendation, moderate-quality evidence
Depression	1 meta-analysis	Cancer patients with depression; patients with depression with psychotic features; patients with mild depression; first-time mothers	2B	Weak recommendation, moderate-quality evidence
Hypertension	1 meta-analysis	Patients with hypertension	2B	Weak recommendation, moderate-quality evidence
Insomnia	1 single-blind pilot study, 1 nonrandomized trial	Insomnia patients evaluated by the PSQI; faculty and staff members at the University of Miami Medical School	2C	Weak recommendation, low-quality evidence
Pain relief	1 meta-analysis	Cancer patients; stroke patients; patients receiving gastrointestinal endoscopy; radiotherapy patients; female college students with dysmenorrhea	2B	Weak recommendation, moderate-quality evidence

Note. PSQI = Pittsburgh Sleep Quality Index; GRADE = Grading of Recommendations, Assessment, Development and Evaluation.
[a]Citations available in text or references. Studies are representative; table should not be considered a comprehensive review of all available literature.
[b]Data from the GRADE Working Group. Available at http://www.gradeworkinggroup.org/intro.htm.

aromatherapy on depressive symptoms across six studies. The studies consisted of two RCTs, three non-RCTs, and two quasi-experimental studies. Various essential oils were used in each of the studies (lavender, chamomile, sweet orange, etc.). Although the meta-analysis showed positive results for the reduction of depressive symptoms, the study noted that previous literature had a dearth of RCTs to examine aromatherapy and depression. Additionally, almost all studies examined aromatherapy massage rather than aromatherapy alone; hence, it is unclear whether the results are due to the effects of essential oils or somatosensory-tactile stimulation (Yim et al., 2009). Ultimately, Yim et al. argued that aromatherapy may be used as a complementary and alternative therapy but that more RCTs are needed to determine its efficacy as a viable treatment option. The results from other studies similarly support the inconclusive results of aromatherapy on depressive symptoms (Itai et al., 2000; Moss et al., 2003).

Pain Relief

Aromatherapy has often been used in nursing and health care settings as a complementary treatment method. Langley et al. (2008) reviewed the effects of aromatherapy on pain reduction across 10 RCTs, examining a wide range of pain symptoms (radiotherapy, dysmenorrheal gastrointestinal endoscopy, stroke patients, cancer patients, etc.). Inconclusive results were found for the efficacy of aromatherapy on pain relief due to small sample sizes, lack of blinding, and the various types of pain analyzed. Additionally, J. T. Kim et al. (2006) examined the impact that lavender oil has on postoperative pain and did not find a difference in the pain levels of those who had lavender oil given through their oxygen facemask versus those who received only oxygen. Interestingly, they did find that those exposed to the lavender reported feeling more in control of their pain. However, these reports were subjective, and it is hard quantify the results (J. T. Kim et al., 2006). These studies suggest that further research needs to be conducted to determine the effectiveness of aromatherapy on pain relief.

Hypertension

A systematic review by Hur et al. (2012) reviewed the effects of aromatherapy on hypertension across five studies, one RCT and four nonrandomized controlled clinical trials (CCTs). The primary outcome variables were systolic blood pressure and diastolic blood pressure. Three CCTs and the one RCT reported favorable outcomes for aromatherapy versus no treatment or placebo control, whereas one CCT reported no significant findings (Hur et al., 2012). The risk of bias was determined for each study using the Cochrane

Collaboration classification, and the study found that all four of the CCTs were subject to bias. Additionally, the studies were all of questionable quality due to lack of blinding and "incomplete outcome measures" (Hur et al., 2012, p. 40). Although four of the five studies show positive effects regarding aromatherapy on hypertension, the poor quality of the studies examined in the meta-analysis suggests that adequate research does not exist, and the use of aromatherapy for treatment of hypertension should be approached with caution.

Insomnia

In the general population, individuals have begun to associate lavender with feelings of relaxation and calm. For example, lavender has been studied as a form of treatment for insomnia. A single-blinded, randomized pilot study ($N = 10$) showed that lavender oil led to better sleep, based on scores of the Pittsburgh Sleep Quality Index (Buysse, Reynolds, Monk, Berman, & Kupfer, 1989), than the use of almond oil (Lewith et al., 2005). Diego et al. (1998) examined electroencephalograph measurements as a measurement of essential oils' effects on insomnia and relaxation. The study assessed 40 individuals' brainwaves after administering a stimulant aroma (rosemary) and a relaxing aroma (lavender) and showed that the presence of lavender led to a significant increase in beta power, which leads to more drowsiness (Diego et al., 1998). Although neither study included a control group, these early findings suggest aromatherapy's positive effects on inducing sleep in insomnia patients. Ultimately, additional RCTs are needed to determine the efficacy of lavender's effect on sleep.

CONTRAINDICATIONS AND RISKS

Despite the fact that aromatherapy has recently grown in popularity, there are still various drawbacks and contraindications that both users and clinicians should consider. First and foremost, many of the oils used can be toxic if not applied in the appropriate manner or dosage (d'Angelo, 2002). In addition, there are certain compounds, such as bitter fennel, buchu, mugwort, star anise, thuja, wintergreen, and wormwood, that should never be used in aromatherapy because of their toxicity (d'Angelo, 2002, p. 78). Because of the risk associated with toxic compounds in oils, it is important to recognize that if an oil is labeled as anything other than *pure essential oil*, it is unlikely to be a pure essence (Metcalfe, 1989). Additionally, when using the oils, a patients' eyes should be shut or an alternative method used to ensure that the oil does not enter the eyes (Metcalfe, 1989).

Overexposure to sunlight, oxygen, or heat can affect the oils and their potency (Metcalfe, 1989). Thus, it is best to keep oils in a dry, cool, dark place. The doses of the oils also need to be carefully determined and monitored (Metcalfe, 1989, p. 13). As with many forms of medication, side effects can vary from person to person, and it is recommended that a small area of skin be tested with the oil before beginning a full course of treatment.

Certain populations should take specific precautions when using aromatherapy. First, women who are pregnant need to be cautious, especially when using emmenagogic essences such as camphor, caraway, cedarwood, chamomile, clary sage, cypress, jasmine, juniper, lavender, marjoram, nutmeg, peppermint, rose, and rosemary, which can lead to an increase in estrogen and thus may lead to menstrual bleeding (Ericksen, 1994). Second, one must dilute essential oils if they will be used with children or babies because they often have sensitive skin and are more likely to rub their eyes or lick their fingers (Metcalfe, 1989). Precautions should be taken when using oils in relation to open wounds, diabetes, rashes, neurological disorders, high blood pressure, and epilepsy (Cristina, 2004). Clients should be counseled to consult a physician or a registered aromatherapist before beginning an aromatherapy regimen to ensure they are using the oils appropriately. Although the risks of aromatherapy are relatively unknown and its use may be benign, further research should examine the possible risk factors regarding the use of essential oils to prevent negative outcomes for patients.

TIPS FOR PRACTITIONERS

- The most common uses for aromatherapy include anxiety, depression, pain relief, hypertension, and insomnia.
- Aromatherapy is often used in conjunction with other CAM therapies (e.g., massage therapy).
- Although no state or federal accrediting board exists, it is important to seek out trained aromatherapy professionals. The National Association for Holistic Aromatherapy (NAHA) may be a good resource and can be accessed online at http://www.NAHA.org.
- Risks regarding the toxicity and intended use of essential oils must be examined before aromatherapy treatments are recommended.
- There is no known mechanism of action for aromatherapy; however, evidence suggests that it may be an affordable therapeutic CAM option.

INTEGRATION WITH PSYCHOLOGICAL PRACTICE

Psychologists considering the use of aromatherapy in their practice have an ethical obligation to do so in a competent manner. It is the responsibility of the provider to ensure that adequate training has been obtained and that the provider understands the risks associated with the use of various essential oils. Although aromatherapy can be used in diffusers in health care offices, hospitals, or other treatment settings, it is important to obtain informed consent from patients before using it.

Currently, there is no standard set of aromatherapist certification procedures in the United States, but a variety of courses offer certification in the area. There are also specific guidelines laid out by various states that outline the restrictions and limitations for practice. NAHA was founded in 1990 with the main purposes of raising the standards of practicing aromatherapy (NAHA, 1997) and increasing public awareness. NAHA has posted a set of ethical standards regarding the practice of aromatherapy online at http://www.naha.org/membership/code-of-ethics. Their code of ethics includes standard ethical practices regarding informed consent, confidentiality, and competence but also has points specifically related to aromatherapy. These pertain to the hygiene and cleanliness of an office as well as not diagnosing in any manner unless permitted through separate licensure (NAHA, 2013b).

At present, an individual can become a registered aromatherapist after passing the examination offered by ARC. However, the examination can only be taken after a year of education in a program that is in compliance with NAHA guidelines (Aromatherapy Registration Council, 2011). The course must have a "minimum of 200 hours of specific aromatherapy education including anatomy and physiology . . . and basic pathology." The NAHA website has a list of approved schools at http://www.naha.org/education/approved-schools (NAHA, 2013a, para. 3). Additionally, there are growing opportunities to earn continuing education units in aromatherapy, although these are not required for certification because of lack of standardization in the United States.

Finally, psychologists considering integration of aromatherapy into their practices should understand the perceptions of aromatherapy among patients and other health care providers as well as its appropriate uses, possible side effects, and interactions with other treatments. There is evidence that some health care providers have either a negative or neutral perception of aromatherapy. M. M. Cohen, Penman, Pirotta, and Da Costa (2005) surveyed 2,000 general practitioners in Australia and obtained an overall response rate of 33.2%. It appeared that those who responded to their survey ($n = 636$) had an overall positive view of CAM, although they felt that certain modalities were more effective or useful than others. Considering aromatherapy, most felt that it was "relatively safe yet also relatively ineffective, with less than

20% of respondents finding them [aromatherapy] either potentially harmful or potentially effective" (M. M. Cohen et al., 2005, p. 998). Additionally, only 15% reported that they would consider using aromatherapy on themselves, and only 3% said that they would use it in their practice (M. M. Cohen et al., 2005, p. 1000). Also, it is noteworthy that nearly one quarter of the respondents (24%) stated they would "strongly discourage" the use of aromatherapy by their patients (M. M. Cohen et al., 2005, p. 1000). Whether this is due to a lack of education, research, or various other factors is unclear, but it appears that, at least in this sample of practitioners, there is not a tremendous amount of support for the prescription of aromatherapy. Although this study was not done in the United States and we cannot generalize the results to all health professionals, the results highlight the fact that additional education and research on aromatherapy are necessary.

ADDITIONAL RESOURCES

1. National Association for Holistic Aromatherapy (NAHA)—NAHA is a nonprofit organization looking to increasing public knowledge and awareness of aromatherapy. Its website offers a variety of information related to the history of aromatherapy, up-to-date information on safety and precautions, and a list of schools that offer programs in aromatherapy certification. NAHA can be accessed online at http://www.NAHA.org

2. National Cancer Institute Website—The institute's website has answers to common questions related to aromatherapy. Specifically, it discusses the history, purpose, administration, as well as side effects and risks. Additionally, there is information about various clinical trials that are being conducted. Detailed information can be found at http://www.cancer.gov/cancertopics/pdq/cam/aromatherapy/patient

3. Price, S., & Price, L. (2007). *Aromatherapy for health professionals* (3rd ed.). New York, NY: Churchill Livingstone—This text provides useful information on aromatherapy for health professionals. The book is divided into four sections: essential oil science, the foundations of practice, aromatherapy in context, and policy and practice. It is an excellent resource for psychologists seeking to enhance their knowledge of aromatherapy.

4. University of Maryland Medical Center Website—This site provides an overview of aromatherapy, as well as descriptions and disclaimers regarding the use of aromatherapy in health care settings. The article can be found at http://www.umm.edu/altmed/articles/aromatherapy-000347.htm

IV

MANIPULATIVE AND BODY-BASED PRACTICES

13

CHIROPRACTIC

Chiropractors provide "non-invasive care promoting science-based approaches to a variety of ailments" (American Chiropractic Association [ACA], 2011b, para. 4). The main treatments that chiropractors perform are called *spinal manipulations*, also known as *adjustments*, which work to "restore joint mobility by manually applying a controlled force into joints that have become hypomobile—or restricted in their movement—as a result of a tissue injury " (ACA, 2011c, para. 3). According to the 2007 National Health Interview Survey (NHIS), approximately 8% of adults and 3% of children reported using chiropractic or manipulation therapy in the previous 12 months. When put into actual numbers, the percentages equate to about 18 million adults and 2 million children (NIH, 2011c).

http://dx.doi.org/10.1037/14435-014

Complementary and Alternative Medicine for Psychologists: An Essential Resource, by J. E. Barnett, A. J. Shale, G. Elkins, and W. Fisher

DEFINITIONS

Chiropractic has been defined as "a health care approach that focuses on the relationship between the body's structure—mainly the spine—and its functioning" (NIH, 2011c, para. 1). It is said to be a treatment that works to establish the body's homeostasis and emphasizes the importance of structural integrity in proper physiological functioning, particularly in regard to removing impingements on the nervous system by manipulating the spine (Kuusisto, 2009a). *Chiropractic* comes from the Greek words *cheir*, which means "hand" and *praxis*, meaning "to practice," together meaning *hands-on therapy* (NIH, 2011c). With that, the goal of chiropractic is to use the hands to realign the spine so that the body can better heal itself.

HISTORY

The history of chiropractic dates back to 2700 B.C.E. in both China and Greece, where writings mentioning spinal manipulations have been found (ACA, 2011b). Hippocrates is also said to have written about the powerful relationship between spinal alignment and overall well-being (ACA, 2011c). Modern chiropractic is attributed to the work of Daniel David Palmer, who in 1887 claimed that he was capable of curing without using traditional medicine; he was a "spiritual and magnetic healer" who took a "drugless approach" to treating illness (Moore, 1993, p. 4). The actual birthdate of modern chiropractic is said to be September 18, 1895, when Palmer adjusted the spine of a deaf custodial worker, Harvey Lillard, and purportedly restored Lillard's hearing (Ernst, 2008). Palmer's adjustment, or spinal manipulation, is not something that he claimed to create; rather, Palmer took credit for being the first to "use specific contacts as short-leverage points for making more specific spinal 'adjustments'" (Kuusisto, 2009b, para. 3). One year after treating Mr. Lillard, Palmer opened the first chiropractic school (DeVocht, 2006). The popularity of chiropractic was relatively immediate, and more than 80 chiropractic schools had been founded in the United States by the mid-1920s. However, the establishment of the chiropractic profession and its popularity were not without conflict. Chiropractic practitioners were criticized by both allopaths (for what were deemed to be pseudoscientific practices) and osteopaths (for "bastardizing" their profession; Ernst, 2008). The conflict between medical and chiropractic professionals escalated in 1990 when the U.S. Supreme Court upheld a 1987 decision that found the medical establishment guilty of conspiring against the chiropractic profession (Kaptchuk & Eisenberg, 1998). It was this decision that would lead to internal conflict among chiropractors—that is, defining the scope of chiropractic care (Ernst, 2008).

Today the debate continues over whether practitioners should hold fast to Palmer's original ideas, that vertebral subluxation, a condition resulting from spinal nerve impingement, is the source of all illness (Freeman & Lawlis, 2001) or whether chiropractic should be viewed as a set of varied modalities, including spinal manipulation (Institute for Alternative Futures, 2005), that can be effectively incorporated with many other treatments, such as traditional medicine (Ernst, 2008).

COMMON USES

Chiropractic care is most often sought out for treatment of low back pain, acute and chronic pain, and headaches. However, chiropractors are also frequently seen for ear infections and other conditions, such as disorders of the digestive (e.g., irritable bowel syndrome), respiratory (e.g., asthma), cardiovascular (e.g., hypertension), and reproductive (e.g., dysmenorrheal) systems (K. Barnett, McLachlan, Hulbert, & Kassak, 1997; Ernst, 2008). In addition, more recent investigations have examined the use of chiropractic care in the treatment of psychological issues such as anxiety and phobias, attention-deficit/hyperactivity disorder (ADHD), and nocturnal enuresis. Although the use of chiropractic services is relatively widespread, chiropractic care is sought out for a number of uses, including musculoskeletal and non-musculoskeletal conditions alike. Nonetheless, there is some debate about the legitimacy of the profession (Institute for Alternative Futures, 2005).

TECHNIQUE

The scope of techniques that chiropractors use is wide ranging. For example, Keating (1992) found that there may be as many as 864 variations of practice just among chiropractors who believe that subluxation is the root of all illness, with differences lying in practitioners' views of disease as well as the adjustment techniques that they use. However, despite variation in technique, commonality remains in chiropractors' focus on correcting spinal nerve impingement. The main treatments that chiropractors perform and the treatments that we focus on in this chapter are spinal manipulations, or adjustments. The primary characteristic of the manipulation is "a thrust—a brief, sudden, and carefully administered 'impulsion' that is given at the end of the normal passive range of movement" (ACA, 1999, as cited in Ernst, 2003, p. 417). It is this dynamic thrust, which can be of low or high velocity, that sets manipulation apart from other manual therapy forms. Most commonly, chiropractors use a high-velocity, low-amplitude thrust. Although this type of manipulation is performed by other practitioners, it is used by chiropractors more than any other group of professionals.

MECHANISM OF ACTION

Chiropractic is based on the idea that for the body to work properly, the nervous system must maintain a high level of functioning (Chiropractors Association of Australia [CAA], 2010; Curl, 1994). Palmer believed that diseases were caused by "restrictions or perversions of nerve force" and that if the restriction resulted from a subluxation, then an adjustment could and should allow for "the nerve force to return to equilibrium," thus leading to symptom reduction (Curl, 1994, p. 23). This idea is based on the premise that the functioning of the nervous system can be impaired if the 24 moving bones that make up the spinal column are out of place or have lost their normal range of motion (CAA, 2010). Thus, the adjustment works to restore normal joint mobility, which in turn affects the nervous system as a whole and ideally resolves physical symptoms.

Although manipulation is the most common technique used by chiropractors, the active agent in chiropractic care remains in question (Hawk et al., 2002). Because of this, some have noted that manipulation may not be the specific component of chiropractic care responsible for patients' improvement, but rather that improvement may result from the entirety of the chiropractic encounter (Coulehan, 1985; Oths, 1994), which, like other health care modalities and therapies, undoubtedly encompasses variables known to influence placebo effects, such as practitioner warmth, and variables influencing expectancy (Kirsch, 1997). Until researchers investigating chiropractic care perfect the art of the randomized, placebo-controlled trial, the mechanism of action within this CAM modality will remain a mystery.

RELEVANT RESEARCH

Despite the popularity and widespread use of chiropractic, its legitimacy has been questioned, particularly in relation to the general lack of sound science that consistently demonstrates favorable, significant outcomes equivalent to or greater than those of standard treatments or other CAM modalities (Ernst, 2008). Additionally, the history of chiropractic research has been criticized as being biased in the interest of establishing, rather than testing the effectiveness of, chiropractic treatments (Keating,

Green, & Johnson, 1995), and researchers have noted that many trials that set the groundwork for the growing popularity of spinal manipulations were of low quality (Ernst & Harkness, 2001). Furthermore, some still argue that research in the field continues to be confounded by bias (Ernst, 2008).

Several explanations for the lack of high-quality research have been offered. Some have noted the challenge in creating shams and placebos to evaluate body-based therapies, citing several relevant problems: (a) difficulties arising from the lack of a known entity responsible for chiropractic's effects; (b) the use of individualized, rather than standardized, procedures; and (c) difficulty in parsing out effects of components that may be shared by the placebo and active treatments (Hawk et al., 2005). Others have focused on clinicians' insufficient experience and training to conduct clinical research (Sawyer, Haas, Nelson, & Elkington, 1997). Also, although the number of studies of chiropractic's effects is on the rise and the quality of rigorous research is increasing (e.g. Hardy & Pollard, 2006; Rubinstein, Terwee, Assendelft, de Boer, & van Tulder, 2012; Rubinstein, van Middelkoop, Assendelft, de Boer, & van Tulder, 2011), research specifically investigating chiropractic manipulation (rather than broader research examining spinal manipulation of any type) is still relatively limited.

The purpose of this section of the chapter is not to provide a systematic review of the entire body of literature investigating chiropractic's effects. Rather, it is to give an overview of findings from the best available research that may have relevance for psychological practitioners. Notably, although chiropractic treatment is used for a number of musculoskeletal disorders (e.g., Bronfort et al., 2001; McHardy et al., 2008), the broad array of these conditions for which chiropractic is used is beyond the scope of this chapter. The majority of persons seeking chiropractic care do so to address low-back pain (Meeker & Haldeman, 2002), which is reflected in this review. In addition, because spinal manipulation is not exclusive of chiropractic, only trials that have specifically examined chiropractic spinal manipulation or spinal manipulation conducted by chiropractors are included. Trials in which the effects of such manipulation could not be parsed out from other treatment modalities are not included. Finally, although chiropractic treatment commonly consists of more than spinal manipulation, the overwhelming majority of research examining chiropractic's effects does so through evaluation of spinal manipulative therapy. Thus, the presentation of research in this chapter coincides with that body of research relevant to chiropractic manipulation. Table 13.1 provides an evaluation of the scope and quality of the research as well as author recommendations based on the available evidence.

TABLE 13.1
Chiropractic Summary Table

Symptom	Studies[a]	Sample	GRADE[b]	Evaluation
Acute LBP	2 RCTs	Adults with acute LBP	2B	Weak recommendation, moderate-quality evidence
Chronic LBP	3 RCTs	Adults with LBP lasting 6 weeks or longer	2B	Weak recommendation, moderate-quality evidence
Mixed chronic and acute LBP	6 RCTs	Adults with LBP persisting for greater than 7 days	2B	Weak recommendation, moderate-quality evidence
Phobia	1 RCT	20 community college students	2C	Weak recommendation, low-quality evidence
Headaches	6 RCTs	Adults with migraines, tension headaches, or cervicogenic headaches	2B	Weak recommendation, moderate-quality evidence
ADHD	2 case studies	Two 5-year-old boys	2C	Weak recommendation, low-quality evidence
PNE	1 case series, 1 RCT	Children suffering from PNE	2C	Weak recommendation, low-quality evidence

Note. ADHD = attention-deficit/hyperactivity disorder; LBP = low-back pain; PNE = primary nocturnal enuresis; RCT = randomized controlled trial; GRADE = Grading of Recommendations, Assessment, Development and Evaluation.
[a]Citations available in text or references. Studies are representative; table should not be considered a comprehensive review of all available literature.
[b]Data from the GRADE Working Group. Available at http://www.gradeworkinggroup.org/intro.htm.

Low-Back Pain—Acute

At any given time, 31 million Americans experience low-back pain, and each year, Americans spend more than $50 billion in the treatment of back pain, including chiropractic care (American Chiropractic Association, 2013). At least two randomized controlled trials (RCTs) with adequate methodology have investigated the effects of chiropractic spinal manipulation in the treatment of acute low-back pain (Godfrey, Morgan, & Schatzker, 1984; Santilli, Beghi, & Finucci, 2006), and outcomes of these investigations have been mixed. In a double blind RCT, Santilli, Beghi, and Finucci (2006) compared the short- and long-term effects of chiropractic manipulation with those of simulated manipulation in the treatment of 102 ambulatory persons experiencing acute back pain and sciatica with disc protrusion. All participants received 5-minute sessions, 5 days weekly, for a maximum of 20 sessions or until pain relief was achieved, whichever came sooner. In the active treatment group, sessions consisted of an examination, soft tissue work, and spinal manipulation. Participants randomized to the control condition received soft tissue work without manipulation. Results indicated that persons who received chiropractic care compared with those who received simulated manipulation were more likely to become pain free, have more pain-free days, experience fewer days with moderate or severe pain, and report less local or radiating pain using visual analogue pain scales. The authors concluded that active manipulations are superior to simulated manipulations in addressing acute back pain and sciatica with disc protrusion. Although these results are encouraging, psychologists are cautioned to avoid generalizing the results until additional research further supports these findings.

Low-Back Pain—Chronic

Up to 75% of people suffering from back pain experience continuing symptoms even a year after onset (Bronfort et al., 2011). Several RCTs of acceptable quality have examined the effects of chiropractic in the treatment of chronic low back pain (e.g., Bronfort, 2011; Bronfort et al., 1996; Triano, McGregor, Hondras, & Brennan, 1995).

For example, Bronfort and colleagues (2011) randomized 301 participants ranging in age from 18 to 65 with chronic primary low-back pain that had persisted for 6 or more weeks to (a) 20 one-hour sessions of supervised, intensive, exercise therapy (SET) consisting of dynamic trunk strengthening and abdominal exercises; (b) one to two weekly sessions of short-lever, low-amplitude, high-velocity spinal manipulative therapy performed by experienced chiropractors; or (c) a simple home exercise program and advice presented in two 1-hour appointments with encouragement for daily practice. At end point and 52-week follow-up, patient-rated pain did not differ among groups; however, patients assigned to SET expressed significantly more satisfaction with treatment and demonstrated significantly greater trunk muscle endurance than those persons randomized to chiropractic manipulation or home exercise. The authors concluded that patients who completed the supervised exercise program fared significantly better than those randomized to chiropractic care or home exercise and advice in terms of treatment satisfaction and trunk strength and endurance but not in terms of pain intensity. These findings suggest that chiropractic may not be the most effective treatment for chronic low-back pain, and psychologists are urged to use caution in making recommendations.

Low-Back Pain—Mixed Acute and Chronic

A number of RCTs with relatively sound methodology have also been conducted on mixed chronic and acute back pain (e.g., Cherkin et al., 1998; Hawk et al., 2005; Hsieh et al., 2002). Cherkin and colleagues (1998) randomized 321 adults who had experienced low-back pain for more than 7 days after a primary care visit to a course of chiropractic care, physical therapy, or receipt of an educational booklet. Patients randomized to chiropractic care or physical therapy received 1 month of care; session number was determined by practitioners but could not exceed nine sessions. At 4 weeks, outcomes indicated patients assigned to chiropractic care were significantly less bothered by their symptoms than those who received an educational booklet, but they fared similarly to those who received physical therapy. Additionally, all three groups experienced similar levels of dysfunction associated with low-back pain even up to 1 year following treatment. It is noteworthy that significantly more patients who received chiropractic care or physical therapy regarded their care highly compared with those who received the education booklet.

Headaches

A number of investigators have evaluated chiropractic care in the treatment of headaches (e.g., C. F. Nelson et al., 1998; Tuchin, Pollard, & Bonello, 2000; Vernon, Jansz, Goldsmith, & McDermaid, 2009). Like much of the research comprising the chiropractic literature, methodologies and outcomes of these trials have been mixed.

Vernon et al. (2009) conducted a small ($N = 19$), randomized, placebo-controlled trial comparing the effects of chiropractic and medical care in the treatment of persons experiencing tension headaches at least 10 days each month. After a 4-week baseline period in which patients recorded their headache frequency in a diary, patients were randomized to a 14-week regimen of cervical manipulation plus amitriptyline, cervical manipulation plus placebo amitriptyline, sham manipulation plus amitriptyline, or sham manipulation plus placebo amitriptyline. Results indicated that although neither chiropractic nor medical treatment alone yielded significant effects, the combined effects were both statistically and clinically significant. The trial was unfortunately stopped early due to problems with recruitment and had obvious limitations such as small sample size, but it nonetheless demonstrates a number of methodological strengths that should be highlighted, such as blinding of participants and assessors, use of an appropriate randomization strategy, allocation concealment, accounting for dropouts, and reporting of baseline differences between groups and adjusting statistical analyses accordingly. Additionally, this investigation is the first to successfully use sham cervical manipulation in a tension headache trial. These findings suggest that chiropractic may not be the most effective treatment for tension headaches, and psychologists are urged to use caution in recommendation.

Phobia

One small RCT investigated the use of chiropractic care in addressing phobia (Peterson, 1997). Eighteen community college student volunteers who met diagnostic criteria for a simple phobia as outlined by the *Diagnostic and Statistical Manual of Mental Disorders* (3rd ed., text revision; American Psychiatric Association, 1987) were randomized to receive chiropractic or sham manipulation. Subjects were blinded to treatment assignment. Following randomization, subjects' pulse rates were taken by a registered nurse who was also blinded to treatment allocation. Participants were subsequently shown a picture of the object of their phobias and asked to consider the phobic object for approximately 20 seconds before their pulse was taken a second time. They then rated their emotional discomfort associated with the stimulus using a visual analogue scale.

Results indicated that participants randomized to chiropractic adjustment experienced a significant decrease in emotional arousal from pre- to postintervention and reported significantly less emotional arousal after presentation of the phobogenic stimulus than those randomized to the sham. Although both groups demonstrated decreases in pulse rate after treatment, between group differences did not reach statistical significance. The authors concluded that the results are potentially promising and warrant further study. This study possesses several noteworthy strengths, such as randomization of subjects, use of a placebo control, blinding of subjects and assessor, and use of a physiological measure in combination with self-report. However, the study also suffers from methodological weaknesses that deserve mention, particularly the use of a nonempirical method to evaluate whether each participant's emotional distress actually resulted from viewing the purported phobogenic stimulus. Additional research with valid measures, such as the use of objective measures of phobia symptoms, is warranted.

Attention-Deficit/Hyperactivity Disorder

It is estimated that approximately 9% of children ages 3 to 17 have ADHD (Muir, 2012). Although traditional treatment typically comprises pharmacological and behavioral interventions, the use of CAM in the treatment of ADHD is on the rise (Muir, 2012). Our review of the literature identified two case studies investigating the use of chiropractic care in the treatment of ADHD (Bastecki, Harrison, & Haas, 2004; Muir, 2012). Bastecki et al.

(2004) examined the effects of chiropractic care in the treatment of a 5-year-old boy diagnosed with ADHD who had undergone 3 years of unsuccessful treatment with pharmacological agents, including Ritalin, Adderall, and Haldol. Throughout the course of chiropractic treatment, the child's mother reported a variety of positive changes, including overall improved behavior and reduced facial tics. After 27 treatments, the child no longer met diagnostic criteria for ADHD, and his physician discontinued his prescription of Ritalin, which he had been taking for the previous 3 years. Additionally, imaging conducted before and after chiropractic treatment demonstrated a significant change in the child's spinal configuration. The authors concluded that chiropractic adjustment resulted in improved spinal function, leading to symptom reduction.

Strengths of this study include the use of imaging in evaluation of outcomes. However, the study could be improved through the use of objective measures of ADHD symptoms as well as validated behavioral rating scales, including parent and teacher reports. Furthermore, the authors did not report on posttreatment follow-up, so it is unknown whether treatment effects were maintained. Additionally, although imagery demonstrated physiological changes associated with adjustment and a corresponding reduction in symptoms, there are no current data to suggest that altering spinal physiology results in behavior change, and it should be acknowledged that the outcomes of this study could be the result of a number of factors in the treatment milieu. Finally, although outcomes of this study are positive, they are limited and not generalizable beyond the current situation. Additional research with rigorous methodology is merited.

Nocturnal Enuresis

Our review resulted in one case series (van Poecke & Cunliffe, 2009) and one RCT (Reed, Beavers, Reddy, & Kern, 1994) examining the use of chiropractic care in the treatment of primary nocturnal enuresis (PNE). Reed and colleagues (1994) randomly assigned 46 nocturnal enuretic children to chiropractic treatment or sham. Participants randomized to chiropractic care ($n = 31$) received high-velocity manual spinal manipulations, whereas subjects randomized to the sham ($n = 15$) received placebo adjustments. Following 10 weeks of active treatment or sham adjustments, participants were monitored over the course of a 2-week nontreatment period. The primary outcome measure was the number of wet nights participants had during this time of observation. Results demonstrated that the participants randomized to active chiropractic care but not to sham had significantly fewer wet nights following treatment. Additionally, 25% of the children randomized to chiropractic treatment experienced at least a 50% decrease in bed-wetting. However, the change in wet nights in the treatment group was not significantly greater than that in the control, even though outcomes demonstrated virtually no change in number of wet nights among participants randomized to the sham. The authors concluded that the results of the study "strongly suggest" that chiropractic care may be a viable treatment option for PNE and that the conduct of a larger RCT is merited (van Poecke & Cunliffe, 2009, p. 679).

One strength of this study is the use of the sham control. However, the study has a number of methodological issues that could be improved in future investigations. For example, the discrepancy between subject numbers in each group calls into question the randomization procedure used. Additionally, the authors did not mention an intention-to-treat analysis, and they do not account for how the large percentage of subjects who dropped out of the study (19.3%). Furthermore, the authors relied on multiple t tests for their statistical analyses, potentially inflating error and the possibility of biased outcomes (Côté & Mierau, 1995).

CONTRAINDICATIONS AND RISKS

In general, spinal manipulation is considered safe if properly performed by a practitioner with appropriate training and licensure. Most often, side effects are minor and include such phenomena as temporary, localized discomfort, headache, and lethargy (NIH, 2011a). According to the ACA, chiropractic is "one of the safest drug-free, non-invasive therapies available for the treatment of neuromusculoskeletal complaints" (ACA, 2011a, para. 4). However, although the risk of serious complications, such as a stroke or cauda equina syndrome (a condition resulting from compression of nerves in the lower part of the spinal cord that can lead to pain, weakness, and loss of sensation in the lower extremities), is low (NIH, 2011b), they nonetheless merit consideration.

In 2007, Ernst conducted a systematic review of adverse effects of spinal manipulation, resulting in 32 case reports as well as several case series and case control studies. Findings indicated that 30% to 61% of all patients experience mild adverse effects, and of serious adverse events, vertebral artery dissections were the most common. In such cases, if the vertebral artery is fragile, rotating the neck may lead to a tear in the inner artery wall or a vertebral artery dissection. Such an injury can result in a blood clot, which could then travel and lodge in an artery of the brain, eventually leading to a stroke (Haneline, Croft, & Frishberg, 2003). Notably, however, such an injury is rare. The actual reported likelihood that a chiropractor will have a client who had "an arterial dissection following cervical manipulation is approximately 1:8.06 million office visits, 1:5.85 million cervical manipulations,

1:1430 chiropractic practice years and 1:48 chiropractic practice careers" (Haldeman, Carey, Townsend, & Papadopoulos, 2001, p. 905). Other serious events reported by Ernst (2007) that have been associated with spinal manipulative therapy include dural tears, internal carotid dissection, bone fractures, and vertebral disc prolapse. Notably, many of these reports were from case studies and case series, and again, such incidents are rare.

There are other factors to consider when determining if chiropractic is a safe and potentially beneficial option for a client. The Mayo Clinic (2009) recommended that individuals do not seek chiropractic care if (a) they have osteoporosis or other symptoms of nerve damage; (b) they have had previous spinal surgery, unless cleared by their spinal surgeon; or (c) if fever, chills, or other symptoms that may indicate a more serious condition accompany their pain.

TIPS FOR PRACTITIONERS

- If patients are interested in seeking out chiropractic care, encourage them to familiarize themselves with the potential risks, benefits, and costs of treatment.
- Clinicians should also encourage patients who are interested in chiropractic treatment to seek out a medical evaluation to rule out potential contraindications (e.g., osteoporosis) to treatment before starting chiropractic care.
- Clinicians can also encourage patients who are considering chiropractic care to consider several treatment options before making a treatment decision.

INTEGRATION WITH PSYCHOLOGICAL PRACTICE

Chiropractic is one area of CAM that requires a particular advanced degree; to obtain licensure and practice chiropractic, a clinician must obtain a doctor of chiropractic (DC) degree from a college or university that is accredited through the Council on Chiropractic Education (CCE; NIH, 2011c). The CCE provides a list of accredited programs that is available at http://www.cce-usa.org/Accredited_Doctor_Chiro.html. Chiropractic training involves 4,200 hours of classroom, laboratory, and clinical instruction and usually takes about 3.5 years. With the education that is required to obtain licensure, psychologists will likely make referrals to chiropractors based on the symptoms that clients may present as opposed to seeking further schooling for the additional degree to provide chiropractic treatment themselves. However, even if a psychologist were to obtain the appropriate certification, it would not be appropriate to serve in this dual role because of boundary issues related to touch and the degree of physical contact that is required during chiropractic.

Psychologists need to recognize when it is appropriate to make a referral to a chiropractor. To tailor the referral to the individual, it is also important to understand licensure, qualifications, and the various approaches that chiropractors can use. Additionally, psychologists should understand that many symptoms that may lead one to seek chiropractic care can be treated by other CAM or traditional modalities. Thus, it is important to consider a patient's previous medical history in the referral process. Finally, as always, a client's preferences for treatment must be factored into to the decision-making process.

If patients are interested in seeking out chiropractic care, psychologists can also help them in their choice of providers by providing a list of guiding questions to ask a potential health care provider. The following list offers some suggestions, but more specific questions may be necessary depending on a client's symptoms and the goals of treatment:

- What are your qualifications?
- Do you practice a specialty that is related to my condition?
- Do you commonly treat my condition?
- What type of diagnostic testing is needed?
- How can chiropractic care help me?
- How many times a week must I come for an adjustment?
- How long does each session last?
- Will I need care from other health care professionals? (Spinasanta, 2010, para. 3)

Additional questions to ask include the following:

- How long do you anticipate treatment lasting, and how many adjustments will I need?
- Will I need additional follow-up appointments after this treatment ends? If so, how many are typical?
- What results and benefits can I anticipate from this treatment?
- What are the potential risks of treatment, and what potential side effects may occur?
- What research support is present for the treatment being proposed?

ADDITIONAL RESOURCES

1. Frequently Asked Questions About Chiropractic—The American Chiropractic Association has compiled a list of Frequently Asked Questions with regard to chiropractic. Topics include conditions

treated with chiropractic, how to select a chiropractor, insurance information, and information about what chiropractic entails, among others. This information can be accessed at http://www. acatoday.org/level3_css.cfm?T1ID=13&T2ID=61&T3ID=152.

2. The Council on Chiropractic Education—The council is responsible for accrediting programs that offer the doctor of chiropractic degree and works to ensure that all programs are upholding the established set of standards. Their website (http://www.cce-usa. org) offers a variety of resources, such as publications and links to additional chiropractic resources. There is also a list of accredited programs at http://www.cce-usa.org/Accredited_Doctor_ Chiro.html.

3. Haldeman, S. (2005). *Principles and practice of chiropractic* (3rd ed.). York, PA: McGraw-Hill.—This resource provides information on the history of chiropractic as well as some basic research on the efficacy of chiropractic in reducing specific symptoms. It is broken down into five introductory sections: chiropractic principles, chiropractic theory, the clinical examination, specific treatment methods, and management of specific disorders.

4. Licensed Chiropractor Locator—This resource enables you or your clients to search for licensed chiropractors. Chiropractors can be searched for by name or by location. The Licensed Chiropractor Locator may be accessed online at http://www.chiropractic. org/doctorfinder.

5. International Chiropractic Association: State Statutes Governing Chiropractic—This site has information on U.S. state laws, definitions and scope of practice of chiropractic by state. This information is particularly important because each state has its own rules and regulations with regard to chiropractic. See http://www. chiropractic.org/index.php?p=legislation/state_statutes.

14

MASSAGE THERAPY

Within complementary and alternative medicine (CAM), massage therapy falls under the general category of manipulative and body-based practices. Eisenberg et al. (1998) reported that the use of massage therapy increased by 36% between 1990 and 1997 in the United States, with between $4 billion and $6 billion spent on it by consumers each year. More recently, the 2007 National Health Interview Survey reported that more than 18 million adults and more than 700,000 children in the United States had used massage therapy in 2006 (P. M. Barnes, Bloom, & Nahin, 2008). Data provided by the American Massage Therapy Association (AMTA) in its 2009 annual consumer survey indicate that approximately 22% of adults received at least one massage in the previous year, and approximately 34% of adults received a massage in the previous 5 years (AMTA, 2010b). The AMTA also reported that of the individuals who have received at least one massage in the

http://dx.doi.org/10.1037/14435-015
Complementary and Alternative Medicine for Psychologists: An Essential Resource, by J. E. Barnett, A. J. Shale, G. Elkins, and W. Fisher

past 5 years, approximately 21% reported doing so to promote general health and wellness and approximately 19% of adults report having used massage therapy at least once for pain relief (AMTA, 2010b).

DEFINITIONS

Massage therapy is defined as the "manipulation of soft tissue by trained therapists for therapeutic purposes" (Field, 1998, p. 1270). It is described as involving "pressing, rubbing, and moving muscles and other soft tissues of the body, primarily by using the hands and fingers. The aim is to increase the flow of blood and oxygen to the massaged area" (National Institutes of Health [NIH], 2011e, para. 19). The AMTA (2010c) defined massage therapy as "a profession in which the practitioner applies manual techniques, and may apply adjunctive therapies, with the intention of positively affecting the health and well-being of the patient" (para. 1).

HISTORY

The use of massage as a therapeutic modality has a long and extensive history. Early reports of its use as a therapeutic medium are recorded in writings from more than 2,000 years ago and in the Chinese, Japanese, Egyptian, Roman, Greek, and Hindu cultures (Moyer, Rounds, & Hannum, 2004). Rich (2010), citing Calvert (2002), reported that "the ancient Greeks and Romans employed massage, known as anatripsis. Hippocrates (460–377 B.C.E.) and especially Galen (131–201 C.E.), who wrote about it extensively, both described its benefits" (p. 326). Furthermore, Hippocrates was described as defining the practice of medicine as "the art of rubbing" in 400 B.C.E. (Field, 1998, p. 1270). Rich (2010) reported that the word *massage* originates either from the Arabic word for *to touch* or *to press* or from the Greek word for *to knead*. Although the exact origin of the word remains unclear, it is known, as stated earlier, that massage has an extensive history in numerous cultures around the world. In fact, Rich (2010) reports evidence of massage being practiced in Southeast Asia in the 12th century and in Central America in pre-Columbian times.

The use of massage was an accepted component of mainstream medical practice in the United States during the 19th and early 20th centuries (Rich, 2010) but lost favor as the medical establishment increasingly focused on burgeoning medical technologies and the increased use of pharmaceuticals in medical treatment. With these shifts in medical practice, massage therapy became less a part of mainstream medical practice and was relegated to the general category of folk remedies and practices. Yet in recent decades, along with other CAM modalities, massage therapy has experienced a resurgence as the public has increasingly looked outside of mainstream medicine for alternatives in the promotion and maintenance of health (Eisenberg et al., 1993). As more and more individuals have become dissatisfied with the limitations of Western medicine and as an increasing portion of the population has become interested in alternative therapies, massage therapy has gained increased acceptance as a valuable health promotion and treatment modality (Rich, 2010).

COMMON USES

Massage therapy is most often used as a means of reducing stress, decreasing pain, and promoting relaxation. It is described as a practice that people use "for a variety of health-related purposes, including to relieve pain, rehabilitate sports injuries, reduce stress, increase relaxation, address anxiety and depression, and aid general well-being" (NIH, 2011e, para. 19). In fact, in 2009, 86% of American adults surveyed reported believing that massage can be effective in reducing pain, and 85% reported believing that massage can enhance their overall health and wellness (AMTA, 2010a). In 2007, 22% of adults in the United States had used massage at least once in the preceding five years to manage stress or promote relaxation. This figure increased to 32% of the population in 2009 (AMTA, 2010b). With regard to the public's attitude about and openness toward massage for these purposes, in 2007, 38% of adults reported considering the use of massage to manage stress or promote relaxation; this figure increased to 49% in 2009 (AMTA, 2010b).

In addition to the promotion of overall health and wellness, stress reduction, and relaxation, massage therapy may be used to treat a number of medical conditions and ailments, including anxiety, depression, and pain (Rich 2010). It is also used to promote growth and development in preterm and full-term infants (Field, 1998, 2006), to treat immune disorders and improve immune function in patients with HIV and breast cancer (Field, 2006; Field, Hernandez-Reif, Diego, Feijo, Vera, & Gil, 2004), and to improve neuromuscular function in patients with cerebral palsy and Parkinson's disease (Diego, Field, & Hernandez-Reif, 2002; Field, 2006), among others.

TECHNIQUE

Although there are many variants of massage, four main types of massage therapy have been most extensively studied and are the most widely accepted: Swedish, deep tissue, sports, and trigger point massage (see Table 14.1).

TABLE 14.1
Four Common Types of Massage Therapy

Swedish	Massage encompassing long strokes, kneading, deep circular movements, vibration, and tapping
Deep tissue	Application of soft tissue techniques that allow deeper access to the fascia and muscular layers of the body
Sports	Massage designed to help prevent athletic injury, keep the body flexible, and aid in recovery
Trigger point	Technique that focuses on myofascial trigger points—muscle "knots" that are painful when pressed and can cause symptoms elsewhere in the body

Swedish Massage

Swedish massage is the most frequently practiced type of massage in the United States today (Massage Therapy Benefits, 2010). It is a full-body massage that involves the use of "a combination of long strokes, kneading motion, and friction on the layers of muscle just beneath the skin. . . . Swedish massage is used to improve circulation, promote relaxation, improve flexibility, and rid the tissues of waste products" (Duke Center for Integrative Medicine [DCIM], 2006, p. 469). It is also described as having the goal of relaxing and energizing the recipient (AMTA, 2010e). A Swedish massage provided to an individual seated in a chair is known as *seated massage*. This variant provides massage to an individual's upper body, typically the neck, shoulders, and upper back while the recipient is fully clothed with the goal of relaxation and removing stress and tension from these muscles.

Deep Tissue Massage

Deep tissue massage, as its name implies, is a technique that "reaches the deep layers of muscle tissue to release tension. Slow strokes and deep finger pressure are applied to areas of muscle in the body that are tense" and "Deep Tissue Massage is often used to relieve low back pain and to loosen tight muscles" (DCIM, 2006, p. 469).

Sports Massage

Sports massage uses the techniques of both Swedish massage and deep tissue massage but applies them to athletes "to relieve pain from an injury or to restore or maintain mobility" (DCIM, 2006, p. 469).

Additionally, sports massage is intended to help prevent injuries by promoting flexibility in addition to aiding in the healing of injuries by athletes (AMTA, 2010e).

Trigger Point Massage

Trigger point massage involves identifying specific areas of tension and focusing massage to those areas. It is a deep tissue massage that is designed to stretch and release fascia (tight connective tissue), including trigger points, using manual pressure. Sometimes tools called T-bars or L-bars are used to apply pressure and relieve pain (DCIM, 2006). The goal of trigger point massage is to release tension in the fascia and muscles.

GENERAL TECHNIQUES OF MASSAGE THERAPY

During massage sessions, an unscented massage lotion may be used as a skin lubricant. Clients are usually instructed to lie down (on their side, face down, or face up), or they may sit in a prone position. Usually there is not conversation during the massage session, and the client often has his or her eyes closed. Massage typically involves hands-on and skin-to-skin manipulation of the soft tissue of the body using specific movements and strokes. Massage therapy sessions typically range from 15 to 90 minutes. Table 14.2 lists some of the most common strokes used in massage therapy.

Massage methods typically involve deviations from the following basic strokes and techniques.

TABLE 14.2
Common Strokes Used in Various Types of Massage Therapy

Effleurage	Rhythmic, long, firm, and gliding stroke molded to the shape of the skin
Kneading	Slow circular stroke aimed at compression of the soft tissue against underlying bone
Petrissage	Rolling, squeezing, and kneading movements of the finger and thumb done slowly, taking care not to drag uncomfortably on the skin
Frictions	Strokes using the finger tips to deliver penetrating pressure in which tendons and ligaments are treated with light pressure
Tapotement	Percussive massage technique in which the skin is struck to increase vasodilation and accelerate healing
Vibrations and shaking	Strokes that provide an energetic vibration of the tissue; vibrations are delivered by the therapist intentionally trembling his or her hands while applying pressure

Effleurage

This technique involves slow, rhythmic, stroking hand movements and frequently begins and ends a treatment session. The gradual compression reduces muscle tone and induces a general state of relaxation that relieves muscle spasm and prepares the patient for more vigorous treatment.

Kneading

The technique of *kneading* involves slow, circular, compression of soft tissue against underlying bone. Contact is continuous, and the greatest pressure is applied as the hands move proximally. Kneading reduces swelling and helps resolve inflammation. Vigorous kneading decreases muscle spasm and can stretch tissues shortened by injury.

Petrissage

A more forceful technique, *petrissage* involves skin rolling that can only be applied to fleshy regions of the body. In a continuous circular motion, a fold of skin, subcutaneous tissue, and muscle is squeezed, lifted and folded against the underlying tissues. With each cycle, the hands progress to a new area, taking care not to drag uncomfortably on the skin. Petrissage is particularly useful for stretching contracted or adherent fibrous tissue and will relieve muscle spasm.

Friction

Involving accurately delivered penetrating pressure, *friction* is a technique applied through the fingertips. The finger pressure is mainly circular or oblique to the alignment of the underlying structures with minimal lateral movement. Frictions are aimed directly at the site of damage. Tendons and ligaments are treated under slight tensions, whereas muscles are best manipulated in a relaxed position, thus avoiding excessive damage to the muscle cells. The firm pressure needed for frictions is transmitted through the index finger reinforced by the middle finger.

Tapotement

A percussive massage technique, *tapotement* is a vigorous application to vibrate tissues, trigger cutaneous reflexes, and cause vasodilation. Several techniques exist, an example being clapping, in which a therapist cups the hands and strikes to patient's skin with the concave surface of the palm. This technique increases muscle tone and disperses retained interstitial fluid from injury, reducing inflammation.

Vibrations and Shaking

A more energetic type of massage, vibrations are delivered by trembling both hands while they are held firmly in contact with the skin. Unlike effleurage, this method compresses swollen tissue and can reduce swelling with reduced risk of spreading infection from affected areas (Goats, 1994).

MECHANISM OF ACTION

A number of theories exist that attempt to explain the underlying mechanisms of action of massage therapy, and some support for each of these theories exists. In a meta-analysis of 25 studies of the physiologic correlates of massage therapy, Moraska, Pollini, Boulanger, Brooks, and Teitlebaum (2010) found significant decreases in physiologic correlates of stress—namely, salivary cortisol and heart rate, immediately after single-session massage therapy treatments. Increases in the hormone cortisone is associated with stress. Moraska et al. (2010) explained that "chronic stress will perpetually increase hypothalamic-pituitary-adrenocortical activity causing cortisol production to become elevated beyond normal levels" (p. 412). These authors described heart rate and blood pressure increases as "physiological manifestations of the sympathetic nervous system's response to stressful events" (p. 515). They found decreases in both heart rate and blood pressure in a number of studies after a single massage therapy treatment session. Some studies did not find a reduction in blood pressure after a single treatment session, but others have demonstrated significant change after multiple sessions (e.g., Hernandez-Reif et al., 2000; Olney, 2005). Although some variability of results is seen across studies, many studies used different inclusion criteria, and massage therapy outcomes were studied differently across many studies. However, the proposal that massage therapy has a significant impact on physiologic stress responses within the body by promoting a parasympathetic response has general support in the literature as assessed in the meta-analyses of 62 studies by Moraska et al. (2010) and by Moyer et al. (2004).

An alternative theory of the underlying mechanisms of action of massage therapy is that it "provides stimuli that interfere with pain consistent with gate control theory" (Moyer et al., 2004, p. 14). However, in the studies these authors analyzed, support for this theory was not consistently found. The absence of a significant reduction in pain immediately after massage therapy sessions does not lend support to this theory. Massage therapy was found to bring about significant reductions in state anxiety, trait anxiety, and depression. These reductions may be the result of changes in "body chemistry" (e.g., serotonin, endorphins) that occur in response to massage therapy treatments (p. 14). Field, Diego, and Hernandez-Reif (2006) found that medical patients who underwent massage therapy treatments exhibited significant decreases in cortisol levels and significant increases in serotonin and dopamine. Alternatively, because repeated massage therapy treatments are shown to bring about significant reductions in pain, Moyer et al. (2004) proposed that these effects are achieved as a result of "the mechanical promotion of circulation and breakdown of adhesions, or from improved sleep promoted by the treatment" (p. 14).

An additional hypothesis suggested by Moyer et al. (2004) is that massage therapy helps to promote pain reduction over time by enhancing restorative sleep. Although clear evidence of long-term pain reduction as a result of massage therapy is not found, it is possible that individuals who receive ongoing massages may experience reduced stress and tension and may be more relaxed in general, thus assisting them to experience better sleep over time. This in turn may help with the reduction of experienced pain.

Moyer et al. (2004) also proposed the novel theory that massage therapy achieves its effects in a manner similar to psychotherapy when viewed from a common factors approach. They suggested that factors such as the individual's positive expectations of the massage therapy treatment; the massage therapist's warmth, positive regard toward the patient, and positive expectations of the treatment; and the "interpersonal contact and communication that take place during treatment" (p. 15) are more likely to bring about the benefits of massage therapy than any specific treatment techniques used. In essence, these authors propose a nonspecific mechanism of action of massage therapy in contrast to the specific causes of action proposed earlier. For example, in a study of caregivers of dying relatives who each received nine massages, recipients reported experiencing the massages as comforting and that they experienced feelings of being cared for and "peace of mind" (Cronfalk, Strang, & Ternestedt, 2009). This study highlights the nonspecific effects of massage therapy that individuals may experience.

RELEVANT RESEARCH

A significant body of research exists that examines the effectiveness of massage therapy in treating a wide range of issues and ailments. Massage therapy has been shown to be effective in treating back pain (Field, 1998; Tsao, 2007), burn pain (Morien, Garrison, & Smith, 2008), cancer-related pain (Field, 2006; Wilkinson, 1995), immune function (Rich, 2002), depression in anorexic and bulimic adolescents (Field, 2000), depression in children with diabetes (Yates, 2004), and other conditions including fibromyalgia, multiple sclerosis, and hypertension (Moyer et al., 2004); it is also useful in hospice care (Kozak et al., 2008–2009). Although not adequately studied at the present time, massage therapy may have different effects based on the training, skill, and effectiveness of the massage therapist. Table 14.3 provides an evaluation of the scope and quality of the research and provides author recommendations based on the available evidence. To provide the psychologist with a better understanding of the empirical basis of massage, a few selected studies and meta-analyses were chosen by relevance and are presented here by symptom(s).

Multiple Symptoms

Moyer, Rounds, and Hannum (2004) conducted a meta-analysis of 37 studies of massage therapy. Variables examined in these studies included state anxiety, negative mood, immediate assessment of pain, cortisol levels, blood pressure, heart rate, trait anxiety, depression, and delayed assessment of pain. Participants in these studies included pregnant women, surgery patients, healthy adults, patients with spinal cord injuries, HIV+ adolescents, fibromyalgia patients, multiple sclerosis patients, back-pain patients, hypertensive adults, and others. The analysis conducted by these authors supported "the general conclusion that [massage therapy] is effective" (p. 12). More specifically, they found that the typical participant in these studies experienced a significant reduction in state anxiety. Additionally, massage therapy was found to reduce blood pressure and heart rate more effectively than the other treatments to which it was compared. However, this meta-analysis did not yield significant results on the ability of massage therapy to reduce pain or negative mood immediately after treatment. Yet a significant effect on the delayed assessment of pain was found across these studies of massage therapy effectiveness. The largest effects following conclusion of a massage therapy treatment protocol were found in a decrease in anxiety and depression. Neither length of treatment sessions nor type of massage therapy treatment offered were found to have a significant impact on outcome, and the age and gender of participants also had no effect.

Low-Back Pain

A systematic review of 13 RCTs of the effects of massage therapy on nonspecific low-back pain was conducted by Furlan, Imamura, Dryden, and Irvin (2008). Differences were seen between the studies such that some compared massage therapy with sham treatments, some compared it with other CAM treatments, and not all studies examined the same type of massage (e.g., Swedish, deep tissue). Results indicate general support for massage therapy overall as a treatment for nonspecific low-back pain and that it is at least as effective as a number of widely available and used treatments for this

TABLE 14.3
Massage Therapy Summary Table

Symptom	Studies[a]	Sample	GRADE[b]	Evaluation
Anxiety	1 meta-analysis (37 studies), multiple symptom variables	Pregnant women, surgery patients, healthy adults, spinal cord patients, HIV+ adolescents, fibromyalgia patients, multiple sclerosis patients	1B	Strong recommendation, moderate-quality evidence
Depression	2 meta-analyses (37 and 17 studies)	Pregnant women, surgery patients, healthy adults, spinal cord patients, HIV+ adolescents, fibromyalgia patients, multiple sclerosis patients; adult and adolescent depressed patients	1B	Strong recommendation, moderate-quality evidence
Stress	1 meta-analysis (25 studies)	Predominately adult females	1B	Strong recommendation, moderate-quality evidence
Low-back pain	1 systematic review (13 RCTs)	Low-back pain patients	2B	Weak recommendation, moderate-quality evidence
Neck pain	1 RCT	Chronic neck-pain patients	2C	Weak recommendation, weak-quality of evidence

Note. RCT = randomized controlled trial: GRADE = Grading of Recommendations, Assessment, Development and Evaluation.
[a]Citations available in text or references. Studies are representative; table should not be considered a comprehensive review of all available literature.
[b]Data from the GRADE Working Group. Available at http://www.gradeworkinggroup.org/intro.htm.

condition. Additionally, results indicate that massage therapy combined with exercise and education may prove more effective than massage therapy alone for most individuals. Additional studies that demonstrated reductions in low-back pain include those by Field (1998) and Preyde (2000). It is interesting to note that, consistent with the results reported by Furlan et al. (2008), the latter found that patients who received massage therapy along with exercise and posture education showed the greatest reductions in pain.

Neck Pain

Massage therapy has also been studied for its effectiveness in treating neck pain. Sherman, Cherkin, Hawkes, Miglioretti, and Deyo (2009) conducted an RCT of the effects of massage therapy in 64 patients with chronic neck pain. Patients in the control group read a self-care book, whereas patients in the treatment group received 10 massage therapy sessions over 10 weeks with follow-up conducted at 4, 10, and 26 weeks. Individuals receiving the massage therapy treatments reported significant decreases in dysfunction and symptoms at 4 weeks after treatment, but differences between the treatment and control groups decreased at subsequent follow-ups. Although these results suggest that massage therapy is a generally effective treatment for chronic neck pain, more understanding on dosing effects is needed. It is currently not clear what the optimal length of treatment is and whether follow-up or booster sessions of massage therapy are needed to help patients maintain the gains achieved from treatment.

Immune Functioning

Massage therapy has also been shown to have an effect on immune system functioning. Studies have shown that massage therapy leads to increases in natural killer cells in patients with Stage I and II breast cancer and in HIV+ adolescents along with improved immune system functioning in children with leukemia (Field, 2000, 2006). Furthermore, in a study of Swedish massage versus a light touch control condition, Rapaport, Schettler, and Bresee (2010) studied 54 participants who were randomized to condition. In this trial, a single-session of Swedish massage was examined with serial measurement performed to examine oxytocin, arginine-vasopressin, adrenal corticotropic hormone, cortisol, circulating phenotypic lymphocyte markers and mitogen-stimulated cytokine levels. Compared with light touch, massage therapy caused a large effect size decrease in arginine-vasopressin, and small effect size decrease in cortisol. Massage significantly increased the number of circulating lymphocytes, CD 56+ lymphocytes, CD4+ lymphocytes, and CD+ lymphocytes. Mitogen-stimulated levels of interleukin (IL)-1fl, IL-2, IL-4, IL-5, IL-6, IL-10, IL-13 and interferon-γ significantly decreased for subjects receiving massage therapy versus light touch.

In a subsequent study of the same population, participants were further randomized to one of four intervention groups, (a) Swedish massage once each week for 5 weeks, (b) Swedish massage twice each week for 5 weeks, (c) light touch control condition once each week for 5 weeks, or (d) light touch control condition twice each week for 5 weeks (Rapaport, Schettler, & Bresee, 2012). Forty-five participants completed the study protocol, with eight participants dropping out for reasons unrelated to the intervention. In examining the same markers as in the single-session study, results showed that massage stimulated a sustained pattern of increased circulating phenotypic lymphocyte markers and decrease mitogen-stimulated cytokine production, similar to the single-session study results, while having a minimal effect on hypothalamic-pituitary-adrenal function. Twice-weekly massage produced a different response pattern with increased production of pro-inflammatory cytokines. The results of the existent literature on the effect of massage therapy on immune functioning suggest that the intervention has a significant effect on markers of immune functioning both in single-session and sustained over multiple sessions; however, confirmatory studies in larger samples and further examination of potential covariates are needed.

Depression

Massage therapy's efficacy in the alleviation of symptoms of depression has had considerable scientific inquiry; however, the evidence is mixed. A systematic review conducted in 2007 examined the extant literature and found, from the four RCTs that met the authors' inclusion criteria, that the aggregate results did not provide sufficient data and analyses to suggest that massage therapy may be an effective treatment for depression (Coelho, Boddy, & Ernst, 2007). In contrast, a meta-analysis of RCTs of massage therapy in depressed people conducted in 2008 examined 17 studies ($N = 786$ participants) that met the authors' criteria for inclusion (Hou, Chiang, Hsu, Chiu, & Yen, 2010). The results of these analyses rated the RCTs of moderate quality but showed that all of the studies showed significant effectiveness in the treatment group compared with control, suggesting that massage therapy is associated with the alleviation of depressive symptoms.

In a recent trial of massage therapy to reduce symptoms of depression in subjects with HIV disease, subjects were randomized, nonblinded, into one of three parallel groups to receive Swedish massage or to one of two control groups, touch or no intervention, for 8 weeks (Poland et al., 2013). In this trial, which included subjects at least 16 years of age, HIV-seropositive, with a diagnosis of major depressive disorders, approximately 40% of whom were currently taking antidepressants, 54 subjects were randomized, 50 completed at least 1 week (intent-to-treat analyses completed), with 37 completing the study. The Swedish massage and touch subjects visited the massage therapist for 1 hour, twice each week, the touch group having a therapist place hands on the subject with slight pressure, but no massage, in a uniform distribution in the same pattern used for the massage subjects. The primary outcome measure was the Hamilton Rating Scale for Depression score (Hamilton, 1967), with a secondary outcome measure being the Beck Depression Inventory (Beck, Ward, Mendelson, Mock, & Erbaugh, 1961). Results showed that in both the intent-to-treat and study-completers analyses, massage significantly reduced the severity of depression beginning at Week 4 and continuing at Weeks 6 and 8 compared with no intervention and touch. The results of this study and others suggest that massage therapy may be an effective method for reducing symptoms of depression; however, further rigorous RCTs are required before this intervention can be considered evidence based.

Stress

In a comprehensive review of 25 studies of the physiologic correlates of massage therapy, Moraska, Pollini, Boulanger, Brooks, and Teitlebaum (2010) found significant decreases in physiologic correlates of stress, namely salivary cortisol and heart rate, immediately after single-session massage therapy treatments. Moraska et al. (2010) explained that "chronic stress will perpetually increase hypothalamic-pituitary-adrenocortical activity causing cortisol production to become elevated beyond normal levels" (p. 412) and described heart rate and blood pressure increases as "physiological manifestations of the sympathetic nervous system's response to stressful events" (p. 515). They found decreases in both heart rate and blood pressure in a number of studies following a single massage therapy treatment session. Although some studies did not find a reduction in blood pressure after a single-treatment session, others demonstrated significant change following multiple sessions (e.g., Hernandez-Reif et al., 2000; Olney, 2005). Although some variability of results is seen across studies, many studies used different inclusion criteria, and massage therapy outcomes were studied differently. Yet the proposal that massage therapy has a significant impact on physiologic stress responses within the body by promoting a parasympathetic response has general support in the literature as assessed in the meta-analyses of 62 studies by Moraska et al. (2010) and by Moyer et al. (2004).

CONTRAINDICATIONS AND RISKS

Massage therapy is widely reported to be generally safe, with only minimal risks associated with its use. Few side effects are reported from massage therapy, and of those reported, none are severe and they are likely to be temporary. Possible side effects include "temporary pain or discomfort, bruising, swelling, and a sensitivity or allergy to massage oils" (NIH, 2011b, para. 20). The NCCAM (NIH, 2011b, para. 21) cautioned the following:

- Vigorous massage should be avoided by people with bleeding disorders or low blood platelet counts and by people taking blood-thinning medications such as warfarin.
- Massage should not be done in any area of the body with blood clots, fractures, open or healing wounds, skin infections, or weakened bones (e.g., from osteoporosis or cancer) or where there has been a recent surgery.
- Although massage therapy appears to be generally safe for patients with cancer, they should consult their oncologist before having a massage that involves deep or intense pressure. Any direct pressure over a tumor usually is discouraged.
- Pregnant women should consult their health care provider before using massage therapy.

Overall, it appears best that patients consult with their primary care physician before using massage therapy if they have any underlying health issues or concerns. Additionally, because massage therapy has not been proven as an effective treatment for all diseases or health conditions, it is not intended to be the sole form of treatment that many patients receive. For example, although massage therapy aids in enhancing immune system function in patients with cancer and in individuals who are HIV-positive, it is not suggested that massage therapy be the only form of treatment for these individuals. Again, consultation with one's primary care physician or a medical specialist is recommended, and massage therapy should be used as an important and helpful adjunct to more conventional medical treatments.

Individuals with histories of physical assault or sexual abuse and those with certain psychiatric diagnoses that place them vulnerable to boundary incursions may not be well suited to treatment with massage therapy. The intimate nature of massage therapy and the role of physical touch may prove too stressful for some individuals. Examples may include individuals with borderline personality disorder and psychotic disorders.

TIPS FOR PRACTITIONERS

- If patients are interested in seeking out massage, encourage them to familiarize themselves with the potential risks, benefits, and costs of treatment.

- Clinicians should also encourage patients who are interested in massage to seek out a medical evaluation to rule out potential contraindications (e.g., osteoporosis) to treatment before starting care.
- Clinicians should encourage patients to educate themselves on the current credentialing standards for massage therapists where they live and to seek out an appropriately trained and certified therapist.

INTEGRATION WITH PSYCHOLOGICAL PRACTICE

Available data indicate increased acceptance of massage therapy by health professionals in the United States. It is reported that 39 million adults discussed the use of massage therapy with their medical or health professional in 2009, and 35% of these health care professionals, including physicians, nurses, chiropractors, and physical therapists, recommended the use of massage therapy as an adjunct to medical care (AMTA, 2010b). Additionally, massage therapy is increasingly accepted as an important aspect of health care in hospitals. The number of hospitals in the United States that include CAM as part of their treatment programs increased from 7.7% in 1998 to 37.3% in 2007; massage therapy is offered in 70.7% of hospitals who offer CAM treatments to patients (AMTA, 2010b).

As can be seen from the review of relevant research, the use of massage has been studied for its effectiveness in treating a number of symptoms that present to psychologists, such as anxiety, depression, stress, and pain. Therefore, it may be relevant in some instances for psychologists to consider integration of massage therapy into some patients' treatment. However, this integration must be done by referral to a qualified massage therapist. Even if a psychologist is trained in massage therapy, there are significant boundary issues because touch is required, and it would be inappropriate for psychologists to provide this type of therapeutic touch in the context of psychotherapy. Authors such as J. E. Barnett, Lazarus, Vasquez, Morehead-Slaughter, and Johnson (2007) and D. Smith and Fitzpatrick (1995) have made it clear that although nonsexual touch may at times constitute appropriate boundary crossings in psychotherapy (e.g., a handshake in greeting, a hug of a grieving patient), the intimate and extended physical contact inherent in massage therapy would most likely be seen as an inappropriate and potentially harmful boundary violation for a psychologist.

Also, before considering referring patients for massage therapy, psychologists must possess knowledge of massage therapy and its uses and limitations. In their survey of 202 American Psychological Association members,

Bassman and Uellendahl (2003) found that only 10% of those surveyed viewed themselves as possessing expert or good knowledge of massage therapy and other body-work treatment modalities. Psychologists who plan to consider massage therapy for their clients should develop familiarity with current research on massage therapy by reading relevant journals and participation in massage therapy-related continuing education activities, as well as possibly through personal experience with massage therapy as a client. As noted earlier, before referring patients for massage therapy, they should be screened by their primary care physician or other medical professional for any preexisting medical conditions that might preclude the appropriateness of participating in massage therapy. Additionally, patients should also be screened for preexisting history or psychiatric diagnoses that might make treatment with massage therapy contraindicated.

At present, more than 1,500 schools offer training in massage therapy throughout the United States and Canada; 42 states and provinces as well as the District of Columbia regulate the practice of massage therapy through licensure. Licensure requires graduation from a training program, passing a national examination of knowledge of massage therapy, and participation in ongoing continuing education activities. Although not all jurisdictions require licensure for the practice of massage therapy, a national certification credential is available that many massage therapists obtain. The AMTA is the nation's largest professional organization, representing the needs and interests of massage therapists. The AMTA currently has approximately 46,000 professional members (AMTA, 2010d). Of these, 92% reported offering Swedish massage, 76% reported offering deep tissue massage, and 49% reported offering sports massage, among other forms not discussed in this chapter (AMTA, 2010d). Professional members of the AMTA must demonstrate competence in massage therapy through one of the following: graduation from a massage therapy school requiring at least 500 hours of in-class instruction, licensure in one's state or province, or certification by the National Certification Board for Therapeutic Massage and Bodywork (NCBTMB; AMTA, 2010g).

The NCBTMB also sets standards for education, knowledge, and experience, and administers a knowledge-based examination on massage therapy. Those who meet all these criteria and successfully pass the examination are authorized to use the initials NCBTMB after their name (AMTA, 2010f). Massage therapists who are NCBTMB-certified are required to adhere to the organization's Standards of Practice and its Code of Ethics. In addition to meeting ongoing continuing education requirements to maintain certification, these massage therapists must undergo a recertification process every 4 years to demonstrate their continued competence, knowledge, skills, and ethical practice.

A psychologist may recommend that a patient seek out massage therapy, but it would likely be more helpful to the patient if the psychologist recommended specific massage therapists to contact. It is therefore important that psychologists be familiar with licensing and credentialing procedures and statuses in their jurisdiction and be able to make informed referrals to massage therapists. Just as psychologists specialize in clinical work with different patients and presenting problems, massage therapists likewise may have areas of specialization and expertise. Additionally, as has been previously highlighted, massage therapists may practice different types of massage therapy (e.g., Swedish massage, deep tissue massage, sports massage, seated massage, and others). Being knowledgeable about each of these factors will assist psychologists in making appropriate referrals by pairing patients' needs with the massage therapist's skills and expertise.

Rich (2010) provided a set of questions that can be asked of massage therapists that can be helpful in determining the appropriateness of each individual massage therapist for particular patients. These include

> basic questions regarding training, certification, and insurance, and more specific questions regarding draping and clothing and planned responses to possible patient emotional reactions, such as crying. Additional questions may be directed at learning what massage therapy techniques will be used. (Rich, 2010, p. 326)

With each patient's written and verbal permission, it may also be helpful to coordinate treatment with the massage therapist and to share relevant information about the patient to help ensure an optimal treatment experience. Psychologists can also monitor each patient's progress and response to massage therapy during ongoing psychotherapy sessions and then provide feedback to the massage therapist as is needed. Overall, a coordinated treatment approach is likely to be best for patients.

ADDITIONAL RESOURCES

1. American Massage Therapy Association (AMTA)—The AMTA is the nation's largest professional organization of massage therapists. It is a nonprofit organization that focuses on advancing the art, science, and practice of massage therapy through education, advocacy, support, dissemination of research, and the development of professional standards. The AMTA website has resources for further education and referrals, and may be accessed at http://www.amtamassage.org/index.html.

2. National Certification Board for Therapeutic Massage & Bodywork (NCBTMB)—The NCBTMB is a private, nonprofit credentialing organization that certifies massage therapists and bodywork practitioners on behalf of the profession through credentials reviews and examinations. NCBTMB certification is currently recognized or referenced in statutes in 39 states and the District of Columbia. The NCBTMB website may be accessed at http://www.ncbtmb.org.

3. American Organization for Bodywork Therapies of Asia (AOBTA)—The AOBTA is an independent, nonprofit organization that provides education and training, networking opportunities, and support to practitioners of Eastern approaches to health and wellness through the promotion of Asian Bodywork Therapies. The AOBTA website may be accessed at http://www.aobta.org.

4. Massage Therapy Body of Knowledge (MTBOK)—The MTBOK Project comprises representatives from several massage therapy–related professional associations and the Federation of State Massage Therapy Boards. It creates a continually updated set of competencies and standards for the massage therapy profession. The MTBOK website has information for the public about massage therapy and resources for those who practice massage and may be accessed at http://www.mtbok.org.

15

DANCE MOVEMENT THERAPY

Dance movement therapy (DMT) is founded on the underlying premise that the mind and body are inherently intertwined—that a person's psychological and physiological health cannot be separated (Stanton, 1991). With appreciation of this connection, DMT seeks to evaluate and address cognitive, emotional, and physical problems through a multimodal approach, combining articulation of individual expression, attention to one's own body, and movement. In DMT, movement is produced through a process of focusing on one's body, and attuning to internal feelings, imagery, and impulses (Crane-Okada et al., 2012). The product of this process, movement, is considered a manifestation of developmental stage, cognitive operations, affective state, personality, and unconscious process, and it is seen as a method through which psychological processes that may be unreachable through verbal means can be accessed.

http://dx.doi.org/10.1037/14435-016
Complementary and Alternative Medicine for Psychologists: An Essential Resource, by J. E. Barnett, A. J. Shale, G. Elkins, and W. Fisher

DEFINITIONS

DMT is "a creative arts therapy [that] is rooted in the expressive nature of dance itself" (Allied Health Profession, 2005, para. 1). Although its primary mode of action is through movement, DMT is not physiotherapy or occupational therapy (Payne, 1992); rather, it is "the psychotherapeutic use of movement and dance founded on the principle of motion and emotion being inextricably entwined," (Payne, 2006, p. xv). It is also important to distinguish DMT from partner dances, which are characterized in part by adjustment to another's movement. These dances, although potentially therapeutic for some healthy individuals or for couples, can also be challenging or frustrating and therefore counter-therapeutic (Kiepe, Stöckigt, & Keil, 2012).

HISTORY

The practice of DMT as a formal treatment began in the United States in the 1940s (Bartenieff, 1972), and its origins relate to late-19th-century changes in the art of dance, particularly the idea that dance could be used to communicate and express emotion. The development of dance as a formal therapy is often most attributed to Marian Chace, a trained dancer and choreographer influenced by Harry Stack Sullivan who believed that dance could be a unique outlet for people who were struggling to express themselves in more traditional ways. From her initial work in a psychiatric hospital, conducting group sessions in which spontaneous movement was used to assist in meeting individual and group goals, Chace began to see ways in which movement could be used to communicate with her patients, and the language of DMT was born. Around the mid-1960s, a new wave of dance movement therapists began to develop formal, professional training standards and university graduate programs, and in 1966, Chace helped to create the American Dance Therapy Association (ADTA), which grew from an initial 73 members to more than 1,200 members in 2000 (Cruz, 2002). The purpose of ADTA is to "establish, maintain, and support the highest standards of professional identity and competence among dance and movement therapists by promoting education, training, practice, and research" (ADTA, 2013b, para. 2).

TECHNIQUE

Although the exact structure of DMT can vary depending on the therapy format (e.g., group, family, individual, couple) and patient characteristics (e.g., age, physical capabilities, diagnosis; Stanton, 1991), movement serves as the primary interventional tool in DMT (Cruz, 2006). In general, therapists who practice DMT integrate movement as a nonverbal form of communication within a foundation of psychodynamic and growth-oriented psychotherapy theories. However, DMT therapists do not operate according to a theory specific to the use of movement within psychotherapy (Cruz, 2002).

In practice, the therapist frequently begins a session by observing a client's movement and imitating it in such a way as to represent the unique features of what the therapist observes within the patient's movement (Cruz, 2006; Stanton, 1991). Sessions continue in this manner with the therapist building on the client's movement in various ways (e.g., use of different parts of the body). The therapist provides a potential explanation of the meaning motivating the movements and then encourages experimentation with other movement. This method facilitates elaboration on the underlying processes of the patient's initial movement. Methods can vary depending on the particular patient population and format of therapy. For example, following an initial verbal discussion in a DMT group, each member may be asked to produce a movement, to which the rest of the group can respond with more movement influenced by personal association or imagery.

To help the members connect the movements with the group's psychological functioning, the therapist comments on shared themes of members' movement or verbal responses to the movement. This may involve structured improvisation and the use of associations, images, or choreographic and symbolic themes to create or expand on the group members' initial movements. At the end of the session, group members conclude the session with a verbal discussion in which they try to interpret the meaning of their movement, both personally and as a group. Movement evolves as clients improve over the course of treatment; thus, movement can be seen as a window into a client's relationship with himself or herself or with others (Stanton, 1991).

MECHANISM OF ACTION

Within DMT, dance and movement are seen as integral to assessment, intervention, and outcome evaluation as well as the therapeutic relationship (Payne, 1992). Additionally, the therapeutic relationship is used to support the client's movements in such a way that new, more adaptive movements and accompanying positive emotive and interpersonal changes are developed (Waller et al., 2004). The therapist's role is to analyze the patient's movements to ascertain the underlying conscious or unconscious processes that inspire them (Stanton, 1991). Although DMT therapists use traditional forms of clinical assessment to gather diagnostic and other important information, assessment practice in DMT, regardless of the specific methods, includes observing elements of clients' movement (e.g., posture and the incorporation of various body parts) as they develop and change. This evaluation of, and focus on, movement distinguishes DMT from other therapies. Observation and movement analysis also serve as an outcome indicator, and, like other psychotherapies, assessment in DMT is an ongoing process that is influenced by factors such as the context and purpose of the session (Cruz, 2006).

The most common systematic method of assessment within DMT is Laban movement analysis (S. O. Cohen & Walco, 1999), which was developed out of the theory, observation techniques, and notation system designed by dancer Rudolf Laban. Laban movement analysis is distinguished by its focus on both the qualitative aspects and the active features of the movement. With the assumption that movement and dance provide a window into an individual's intra- and interpersonal functioning, the Laban system is valued for offering a systematic method of describing observed movement without getting caught up in particular movement tasks (S. O. Cohen & Walco, 1999; Cruz, 2002).

COMMON USES

Since its inception, the uses of DMT have grown to encompass a wide array of psychological and physiological issues. DMT has been used to address anxiety (Brooks & Stark, 1989), body image (Meekums, Vaverniece, Majore-Dusele, & Rasnacs, 2012; Sandel et al., 2005); depression (Brooks & Stark, 1989; Jeong et al., 2005), fatigue (Dibbell-Hope, 2000), and quality of life (Bräuninger, 2012; Sandel et al., 2005). The populations with which DMT therapists work have also grown since its beginnings. DMT therapists have worked with a wide range of populations, including women with breast cancer (Dibbell-Hope, 2000), children with medical illnesses (e.g., S. O. Cohen & Walco, 1999), persons grappling with stress (Bräuninger, 2012), obese women (Meekums, 2010), and psychiatric inpatients (Stanton-Jones, 1992).

RELEVANT RESEARCH

Despite the increased use of DMT, well-designed research into DMT's effectiveness and efficacy is lacking. Although effectiveness studies have been conducted, most frequently the case study has served as the research method of choice (Ritter & Low, 1996). Several persons have proposed reasons for this lack of well-designed research studies. Some (e.g., Cruz, 2002) have suggested that the training focus of those practicing DMT—to develop professional practitioners—has resulted in this research shortage. Meekums (2010) noted that early efforts of DMT therapists to perform research occurred at a time when one could attain a research degree in a setting where qualitative research was well regarded. Others have pointed out problems with the application of empirical methods to dance or other art therapies.

Practically speaking, DMT researchers face significant challenges in attempting to create a study in accord with the gold standard of research, the double-blind, placebo-controlled, randomized clinical trial (RCT). For example, DMT researchers are challenged to accrue enough participants for an RCT, and the double-blind design is difficult to achieve in this modality. Therefore, most randomized DMT trials rely on either "no treatment" or "wait-list controls."

Thus, research in DMT continues to be hampered by its lack of adequately powered, randomized, well-controlled trials. Most of the available literature comprises case studies, quasi-experimental designs, or RCTs with inadequate sample sizes. Table 15.1 provides an evaluation of the scope and quality of the research and provides author recommendations based on the available evidence. Several representative studies from the table are discussed in this section.

Psychological Distress

A number of researchers have investigated the use of DMT in the treatment of psychological distress (Bräuninger, 2012; Jeong et al., 2005; Meekums et al., 2012) and the associated constructs of depression (Jeong et al., 2005) and anxiety (Brooks & Stark, 1989). Although many of these studies still suffer from various limitations (e.g., small sample sizes, no treatment controls) and outcomes demonstrate mixed results, some DMT researchers have made significant strides in study design in recent times. For example, Jeong et al. (2005) randomized 40 adolescent girls with mild depression to group DMT ($n = 20$) or to no-treatment control ($n = 20$). Following thrice-weekly treatment for 12 weeks, participants randomized to the DMT condition demonstrated significant decreases in psychological distress, as well as increases in plasma serotonin, and decreases in dopamine compared with no-treatment controls. Jeong and colleagues (2005) suggested that DMT may beneficially modulate these neurohormones, stabilizing the sympathetic nervous system, thereby producing beneficial outcomes in persons with mild depression. Although the study was limited by a relatively small sample size and a no treatment control, the researchers' findings provide potential promise for the conduct of future large-scale clinical trials.

Quality of Life

Several RCTs (e.g., Bräuninger, 2012; Crane-Okada et al., 2012; Sandel et al., 2005) and one quasi-randomized controlled trial (Dibbell-Hope, 2000)

TABLE 15.1
Dance Therapy Summary Table

Symptom	Studies[a]	Sample	GRADE[b]	Evaluation
Psychological Distress	2 RCTs, 1 controlled pilot	Adolescent girls (mean age 16); obese women with emotional eating	2B	Weak recommendation, moderate-quality evidence
Depression	2 RCTs, 1 controlled pilot	Adolescent girls; males and females aged 21–66; adolescents with mild depression; psychiatric patients with depression	2B	Weak recommendation, moderate-quality evidence
Anxiety	1 RCT, 2 controlled pilots	Undergraduate students; trade students	2B	Weak recommendation, moderate-quality evidence
Quality of life	3 RCTs; 1 quasi-RCT	Patients with breast cancer, breast cancer survivors, persons suffering from stress	2B	Weak recommendation, moderate-quality evidence
Body image	3 RCT	Obese women with emotional eating; women with breast cancer	2B	Weak recommendation, moderate-quality evidence
Psychological adjustment	1 quasi-RCT, 1 controlled pilot	Male and female patients with cancer, female patients with breast cancer	2B	Weak recommendation, moderate-quality evidence

Note. RCT = randomized controlled trial; GRADE = Grading of Recommendations, Assessment, Development and Evaluation.
[a]Citations available in text or references. Studies are representative; table should not be considered a comprehensive review of all available literature.
[b]Data from the GRADE Working Group. Available at http://www.gradeworkinggroup.org/intro.htm.

investigating the effects of DMT on quality of life in a variety of populations (e.g., patients with cancer, persons suffering from stress) have reported positive outcomes. However, outcomes have been limited by small sample sizes (e.g., Crane-Okada et al., 2012; Sandel et al., 2005). Notably, however, in a multisite, mixed-methods investigation, Bräuninger (2012) randomly assigned 162 participants suffering from stress into one of 12 DMT groups or one of nine wait-list control groups. Patients in the treatment group underwent weekly DMT sessions for a period of 10 weeks, while the control remained inactive and received no treatment. At the study end point, participants in the treatment group demonstrated significant improvement in the psychological, social relations, global value, physical health, and general life domains of the World Health Organization Quality of Life Questionnaire 100 (WHOQOL 100; Power et al., 1998). Participants in the treatment group fared significantly better than those assigned to the wait list in the areas of physical health, psychological, social life, and one item evaluating "general life." At 6-month follow-up, data from treatment group participants indicated significant improvement in the psychological, spirituality, and general life domains, and scores indicated that treatment group participants continued to experience significantly greater quality of life in the psychological domain and the "general life" item of the WHOQOL. Although findings are in no way conclusive, because generalizations cannot be made from an individual trial, and further investigation is needed, the quality and outcomes of Bräuninger's (2012) trial do provide hope for the potential of DMT to address issues of quality of life.

Body Image

Several studies (e.g., Dibbell-Hope, 2000; Meekums et al., 2012; Sandel et al., 2005) have investigated the use of DMT in body image and self-esteem. Although most of these studies suffer from the methodological shortcomings previously described, at least one trial shows methodological improvements in sample size. Meekums and colleagues (2012) investigated the effects of DMT in 92 obese females who were classified as emotional eaters and attempting to lose weight. Participants were assigned to three groups: (a) women ($n = 24$) who were not physically active were assigned to 10 twice-weekly DMT sessions, (b) those who were already completing physical activity ($n = 28$) remained physically active but did not complete DMT classes, or (c) no-treatment control. Using a repeated-measures design, outcomes demonstrated significant reductions in psychological distress, distress related to body image, and improved self-esteem compared with controls. Additionally, emotional eating was reduced in the exercise and DMT group. However, despite methodological improvements, this study has obvious limitations, such as the lack of random assignment; the lack of a structured, manualized group exercise control; and the absence of posttreatment follow-up. Clearly, further research is warranted.

Psychological Adjustment

The use of DMT has also been investigated as a potential therapy to address psychological adjustment in persons with cancer (Cohen & Walco, 1999; Dibbell-Hope, 2000). Cohen and Walco (1999) outlined the use of DMT as an adjunct to cancer treatment in children and adolescents and proposed that DMT had the potential to address a variety of issues that arise during the disease process and associated treatment period. For example, they discussed that DMT can be used to aide in psychological adjustment when factors associated with major medical illnesses and invasive medical treatments disrupt normal behavioral processes and the accomplishment of developmental milestones. Cohen and Walco proposed that, even in infancy, DMT can be used to positively influence psychological adaptation through behaviors that influence "perception, level of integration, and awareness of outside events in the environment" (p. 37).

CONTRAINDICATIONS AND RISKS

Risks associated with DMT appear minimal. However, given that dance is a form of exercise, clients should be encouraged to discuss DMT with their physician, particularly if they "have a chronic condition such as arthritis or heart disease" (Geffen, 2010, para. 7) before beginning a movement program. Similarly, clients with conditions related to pain or discomfort of the joints or muscles should consult with their physician regarding the appropriateness of DMT because physical injury may outweigh positive psychological change.

Additionally, it is important to recognize that DMT may prove to be emotionally difficult for some clients because they may be suddenly confronted with emotions they had previously pushed out of their awareness. Therefore, it is important that clients truly understand the nature of DMT when considering it as a treatment option. Furthermore, not all clients will be comfortable using their body as a part of therapy; DMT requires an open mind because clients will be asked to move relatively freely.

Finally, although DMT is not generally associated with serious risk or contraindications, as with any therapy, one must consider the cost versus the potential benefit. Given that DMT has such a small evidence base, persons considering dance therapy must also consider whether its cost is justifiable, given that the therapy is not well established by sound science.

TIPS FOR PRACTITIONERS

- Cost for DMT varies a great deal, and it is not covered by most medical insurance.
- Common uses of DMT are for quality of life, body image, or psychological distress.
- There is limited well-designed empirical research on DMT.
- When suggesting DMT as a treatment option, ensure clients fully understand the nature of DMT and what they can expect during sessions.

INTEGRATION WITH PSYCHOLOGICAL PRACTICE

To practice DMT, one should obtain certification at a graduate program that meets the requirements established by ADTA (2013b, para. 1). A list of accredited programs can be found at the ADTA website. Beginning-level dance therapists hold a master's degree and have gained at least 700 hours of supervised clinical experience. Advanced dance therapists also hold a master's degree, but they have completed 3,640 hours of supervised clinical experience (ADTA, 2013b). The DMT certification board awards certifications, and licenses are provided specific to each state (ADTA, 2013a).

DMT is a useful technique in that it can be practiced in variety of settings, including psychological rehabilitation, nursing facilities, and day-care centers, and it can be integrated with health promotion programs (Xia & Grant, 2009). Although psychologists can become certified in DMT, it is the case that except in limited circumstances (e.g., some forms of group therapy), it is best for psychologists to make a referral to a dance and movement therapist because it may prove difficult, or even embarrassing, for some clients to use DMT with their psychotherapist. Psychologists should usually not directly incorporate DMT into their work because of boundary issues, dual relationships, and ethical concerns. As always, clinicians should carefully consider the individual needs of their patients to make an appropriate referral.

ADDITIONAL RESOURCES

1. American Dance Therapy Association (ADTA)—The ADTA was founded in 1966 in support of DMT. Their website has links to information regarding conferences, certification, and finding a therapist, as well as recent articles and information about DMT that have been in the news. Their website can be found at http://www.adta.org.

2. International Dance Therapist Lookup—One valuable resource provided by the ADTA is its International Dance Therapist Lookup. This resource allows for clients to search by state, or by country if international, for a registered dance and movement therapist. See http://www.adta.org/Find_a_DMT.

3. *American Journal of Dance Therapy*—The *American Journal of Dance Therapy* is the official journal of the ADTA. It has been in production since 1977 and serves as a resource for keeping current with the ever-changing literature. It may be accessed at http://www.springer.com/psychology/journal/10465.

4. Sandel, S. L., Chaiklin, S., & Lohn, A. (Eds.). (1993). *Foundations of dance/movement therapy: The life and work of Marian Chace*. Washington, DC: American Dance Therapy Association—This book includes a biography of Marian Chace, one of DMTs most well-known contributors to this modality. Additionally, there are numerous chapters included in the book, written by dance and movement therapists, that build on the work of Chace.

V

ENERGY MEDICINE AND WHOLE MEDICAL SYSTEMS

16

REIKI

As a complementary and alternative medicine (CAM), Reiki (pronounced RAY-kee) is categorized as an *energy medicine* or biofield therapy by the National Center for Complementary and Alternative Medicine (NCCAM). Reiki practitioners help their patients' healing response by placing and positioning their hands held slightly above or lightly touching a patient's body (National Institutes of Health [NIH], 2011f). In doing this, the practitioner is thought to be passing a concentrated energy or "life force" through his or her own body, into the body of the patient as the patient enters a state of deep relaxation. This allows the body's natural energy to flow freely, facilitating healing and well-being. An interesting characteristic of Reiki is that it is assumed to be beneficial to both the practitioner and the patient because there is no depletion of energy but mutual enhancement as a higher energy is channeled through the practitioner's body, filling him or her as well

http://dx.doi.org/10.1037/14435-017
Complementary and Alternative Medicine for Psychologists: An Essential Resource, by J. E. Barnett, A. J. Shale, G. Elkins, and W. Fisher

as the patient with "Reiki energy" (Plodek, 2009). A special background or natural talent is not needed to practice Reiki, and historically it was practiced individually as a form of self-care (NIH, 2011f). Reiki, in and of itself, should not be considered a healing method but a medium that enhances the patient's natural healing process with universal life force, which is guided by a higher power (Plodek, 2009).

DEFINITIONS

Described as "a meditative state in which a practitioner channels Reiki energy from a universal source to another human being," Reiki is the derivative of two Japanese words: *Rei* which translates in the West as "universal," or "present everywhere"; and *Ki* (or *Chi* in Chinese) meaning "the vital life force or universal energy [that] permeates all life forms" (p. 13, Lübeck, Rand, & Petter, 2001). Practitioners operate under the assumption that if an individual's Ki is flowing unobstructed through the body, one's experience will be of wellness, balance, and harmony. However, if one's Ki is sluggish or blocked entirely, there will be disharmony, resulting in disease or life imbalance. Rather than practicing a "healing modality," it should be understood that Reiki practitioners see their role as an intermediary to prompt the natural healing process by channeling universal energy so that it can be used by the patient (Plodek, 2009).

HISTORY

Reiki's history is believed to date back at least 2,000 years and although the exact origins are not known, it is purportedly referenced in the Sanskrit Sutras of Tibet. The more recent rebirth of this practice is attributed to Mikao Usui (1865–1926) in the early 1900s. As a Japanese businessman and Tendai Buddhist, Usui spent many years searching to enhance his knowledge of healing methods and was using a form of qigong as he worked with the poor in Kyoto, Japan (Ringdahl & Halcon, 2006). During this time, Usui found a text referring to a different energy healing technique, although that text reportedly did not describe how to become a master in it. In an attempt to gain understanding, Usui began a fast. During this time, he meditated to receive a deeper understanding, and on the 21st day, he experienced a profound transformation when, during his meditation, he received a vision of the healing method that became known as Reiki (Plodek, 2009).

With this knowledge, Usui began to practice Reiki on the poor living in Kyoto. He also trained others in the art of Reiki and encouraged them to maintain a peaceful overall demeanor, using five principles for guidance:

Just for today, do not anger.
Just for today, do not worry.
Be humble.
Be honest in your work.
Be compassionate to yourself and others. (Miles & True, 2003, p. 63)

Over time, Usui trained 16 masters, with the best-known being Chujiru Hayashi, a former naval officer. In 1930, Usui died, and Hayashi became responsible for continuing to train new Reiki masters. During this time, Hayashi opened the Shin No Machi healing clinic in Tokyo, which led to him meeting and training Madame Takata, a Reiki patient who later became a Reiki master. Madame Takata is credited for introducing Reiki to Europe and the Americas (Plodek, 2009; Ringdahl & Halcon, 2006). Currently, there has been a rebirth and expansion of the use of Reiki; there are reportedly an estimated 50,000 Reiki masters and 1 million Reiki practitioners worldwide (Ringdahl & Halcon, 2006).

COMMON USES

Although research involving Reiki as an energy healing therapy has not been extensive, NCCAM is currently funding various research projects examining its underlying mechanisms and efficacy related to a variety of symptoms (NIH, 2011f). Reiki has most often been used in cases involving memory loss, stress, anxiety, depression, and pain. It is also being used with growing frequency among cancer patients, hospice, and HIV/AIDS programs (Ringdahl & Halcon, 2006).

TECHNIQUE

Touch therapy that is believed to pass healing from or through one person to another is not new. These energy-healing techniques, especially Reiki, are rapidly becoming more widely used, most often by nursing staff (Snyder & Lindquist, 2010).

Preparation for a Reiki session actually begins before the patient arrives and involves the practitioner's self-assessment of his or her worthiness to channel Reiki. This involves various aspects of life, including meditation, maintaining life harmony, abstinence from drugs and alcohol, and any issue, such as anger or illness, that may interfere with the practitioner's full presence. This is believed to be vital as the practitioner prepares to act as a medium, or channel for the healing energy. The actual Reiki therapy may vary based on the practitioner's level of training and practice (Plodek, 2009; Ringdahl & Halcon, 2006).

The patient is given a brief overview of the process and is then asked to lie down or sit comfortably; he or she may remain fully clothed. A typical Reiki session begins with the practitioner encouraging the patient to relax and focus inward, letting go of preconceived expectancies and conscious control. If physical contact is an issue or concern for a patient, then the practitioner may choose to position his hands up to four inches above the body (Plodek, 2009). The process continues as the practitioner places his or her hands on the patient, using eight hand positions on the front of the patient and four positions on the back. The hands are held in position for 3 to 5 minutes. These classic positions allow Reiki energy to flow freely into all of the body organs and systems. Although these positions send Reiki energy to the arms and legs, additional hand positions have been added and are sometimes used on the patient's arms, hands, legs, and especially the feet, which have energy fields corresponding to the entire body. The additional hand positions are usually held for only 1 or 2 minutes (Quest, 2009).

MECHANISM OF ACTION

Although not linked to medicine, there are various physics models, including bioelectromagnetism and quantum physics, that have aspects that may be related to the concepts of Reiki. These models are consistent with Asian scripture as they propose that within our world, there are subtle vibrations that may play a role in our well-being (Miles & True, 2003).

Bioelectric Body

With the knowledge that our world does not exist simply within the boundaries of what we can see and touch, research and innovation have brought us to a place where our brainwaves, categorized as alpha, beta, theta, and delta, can be measured. *Alpha waves* are the midrange frequencies that are associated with relaxation and dissociation (Plodek, 2009). During a Reiki healing session, the practitioner and the patient are purported to experience a synchronization of the alpha waves, such that the frequency is shared by both (Zimmerman, 1990).

Radiant Energy

Energy traveling as electromagnetic waves is referred to as *radiant energy* in the field of physics. History indicates that religious and spiritual philosophies also share in the belief and power of radiant energy. Within religions such as Christianity, Hinduism, Islam, and Buddhism lies the belief that an individual's thoughts can radiate into his or her surroundings and spread love, peace, and even healing (Plodek, 2009). Research has shown that when individuals were randomly assigned into pairs and sat facing one another, not touching, with eyes closed, there was synchronization between the brain and cardiac rhythms of the two (Russek & Schwartz, 1996).

With no clear, agreed-on theory of the mechanism that explains how it works, Reiki is sometimes criticized because of the belief that healing methods cannot be claimed as effective without an identifiable mechanism of action (Miles & True, 2003). Further research is needed to identify any existent mechanisms of action and provide empirical support for the use of Reiki.

RELEVANT RESEARCH

For the past few years, a growing body of research has been presented that evaluates the effects and feasibility of Reiki as a technique that may promote comfort and well-being among patients with cancer (Catlin & Taylor-Ford, 2011); improve quality of life and immune functioning among healthy populations (Bowden, Goddard, & Gruzelier, 2010); and provide treatment for depression, anxiety, stress, fatigue, and pain (Anderson & Taylor, 2012; Baldwin, Wagers, & Schwartz, 2008; Beard, et al., 2011; Olson, Hanson, & Michaud, 2003; Tsang, Carlson, & Olson, 2007). Although findings of the current body of research in Reiki appear to be largely exploratory, Tsang, Carlson, and Olson (2007) suggested that Reiki has recognized potential. Table 16.1 provides an evaluation of the scope and quality of the research and provides author recommendations based on the available evidence.

Quality of Life and Well-Being

In an attempt to assess the effects of Reiki on overall health and well-being, Bowden, Goddard, and Gruzelier (2010) sampled healthy undergraduate psychology students to explore whether the students who received Reiki with or without hypnosis indicated an improved sense of health and well-being compared with a no-Reiki group. The research design consisted of three hypnotic and relaxation groups with imagery suggestions of (a) healthy immune functioning, (b) an animated scenario of healthy immune functioning, and (c) deep relaxation (designed to control for possible beneficial effects of hypnosis; Bowden, Goddard, & Gruzelier, 2010). These three groups were then subdivided into Reiki or no-Reiki groups, with six participants in each group. In the Reiki groups, a Level II Usui Reiki practitioner was positioned

TABLE 16.1
Reiki Therapy Summary Table

Symptom	Studies[a]	Sample	Grade[b]	Evaluation
Quality of life and well-being	2 RCTs	Healthy undergraduate psychology students, oncology patients receiving chemotherapy	2B	Weak recommendation, moderate-quality evidence
Depression and anxiety	2 RCTs	Healthy undergraduate students, cancer patients undergoing chemotherapy	1B	Strong recommendation, moderate-quality evidence
Cancer-related symptoms	2 RCTs, 1 pilot crossover	Cancer patients	1B	Strong recommendation, moderate-quality evidence
Animal studies	1 RCT	Laboratory rats subjected to distress	1B	Strong recommendation, moderate-quality evidence

Note. RCT = randomized controlled trial; GRADE = Grading of Recommendations, Assessment, Development and Evaluation.
[a]Citations available in text or references. Studies are representative; table should not be considered a comprehensive review of all available literature.
[b]Data from the GRADE Working Group. Available at http://www.gradeworkinggroup.org/intro.htm.

behind the participant and channeled noncontact Reiki. Each participant attended ten 30-minute treatment sessions. Depression, anxiety, stress, sleep quality, and illness symptoms were assessed at before Session 1 and after Session 10.

Improvements in self-reports of stress, anxiety, and depression were seen in participants from both groups as a whole. However, Reiki participants' scores improved significantly more than the no-Reiki group on self-reports of illness symptoms. Shortcomings of this trial were that it has a small sample size and the research therapist in all groups was the same Reiki practitioner; therefore, there was no blinding. It should be noted that this study was limited by the fact that the researcher also acted as the therapist, which increases the risk of bias, however, the researchers did have blinded co-experimenters deliver the measures. It is also possible that there may have been unintentional bias resulting in physical or verbal cues. Reiki showed an advantage in health improvement as shown by the reduction in symptoms of illness as indicated by scores on the Illness Symptoms Questionnaire, a simple 20-item questionnaire (ISQ). This 20-item questionnaire assesses the presence of illness symptoms (fever, chills, general malaise, loss of appetite, muscle ache, cough, headache, skin rash, dizziness, shortness in breath/difficulty in breathing, phlegm, night sweat, diarrhea, runny nose, nausea, vomiting, abdominal pain, cold sores, painful lymph nodes). Participants stated how many days in the previous 2 weeks each symptom had been experienced. The absence of a symptom corresponded to a score of 0, a symptom present for 1–2 days corresponded to a score of 1, a symptom present for 3–4 days warranted a score of 2, a symptom experienced for 4–6 days received a score of 3, and a symptom present for 7–14 days corresponded to a score of 4. The severity score of each symptom was then summed to form a Total Illness score for each participant. The trend of improved health in the Reiki group contrasted with the symptoms of the No-Reiki group whose total Illness Symptoms Questionnaire scores showed a significant increase in symptoms. In a randomized clinical trial, Catlin and Taylor-Ford (2011) investigated the use of Reiki therapy to improve quality of life and enhance well-being among 189 patients undergoing chemotherapy. This randomized study compared three groups: standard care, Reiki, and sham Reiki. Standard care was identified as the time spent in the chemotherapy infusion clinic with no planned activities during infusion, allowing the patient to choose his or her preferred activity. The sham Reiki was delivered by a therapist who did not believe in Reiki healing and simply placed her hands on the patients' bodies in a specific order. The Reiki group received Reiki from a trained and experienced Reiki practitioner.

Although there was no reported change in well-being and comfort levels among the standard care group, there was statistical significance in the differences among both the Reiki and sham Reiki groups. A limitation is that the research was conducted in only one medical clinic with a specific population.

Depression and Anxiety

Research has identified depression and anxiety related to medical conditions as a major concern when working toward patient recovery (Shore, 2004). In an attempt to determine the efficacy of Reiki for depression and anxiety, Bowden, Goddard, and Gruzelier (2011) examined its impact on 40 university students, half of whom reported "high mood" (high depression, anxiety, or both) and the other half reported "low mood," (low depression, anxiety, or both). The participants were blindly randomized by coin toss to subgroups that received either noncontact Reiki delivered by a Reiki master or no Reiki. An additional measure to ensure the participants were blinded to their treatment was having all participants wear headphones, through which they listened to a 25-minute recording of a guided relaxation induction, and blindfolds to control for shadows that may have been cast during the delivery of the noncontact Reiki hand positioning. Pre- and postintervention self-report measures were used to look at mood, sleep, and illness symptoms. Participants were seen for six 30-minutes sessions, and data were also collected at a 5-week follow-up.

Findings of this study indicated significant improvement in depression, anxiety, and stress scores from baseline to follow-up among the Reiki plus high-mood participants. Additionally, a reduction in tension and an increase in calmness for both Reiki and control groups was found; however, no effect was reported for tiredness in either group. A greater improvement in energy level was reported among the participants in the control group. However, a weakness of this study is the absence of a method to effectively control for the placebo effect. There continues to be a need for further controlled research on the efficacy of Reiki, especially as it relates to specific processes, both biological and psychological (Bowden et al., 2011).

Before the studies by Bowden et al. (2011), long-term effects of Reiki were researched in a study by Shore (2004) in which 45 participants reporting symptoms of stress and depression were randomized to one of three groups: (a) touch Reiki ($n = 13$), (b) distance (nontouch) Reiki ($n = 16$), and (c) placebo Reiki ($n = 16$). The participants were seen for 1 to 1.5 hours per week for 6 weeks by researchers in near identical settings. The Reiki practitioners were either at Level 2 or Master Level of training and performed touch Reiki and distance Reiki according to a protocol in which the practitioners were instructed to use the same hand positions and procedures. The touch Reiki group received a full session of hands-on Reiki, whereas the participants in the nontouch Reiki group received distance Reiki from practitioners in a distant location, sometimes miles away. The placebo group mirrored that of the distance Reiki group; however, no Reiki was transmitted by a Reiki practitioner.

There were no significant differences among the groups for the pretests, and posttest indicated no significant difference between the two treatment groups (Touch Reiki and Distance Reiki), however, there was a significant difference in stress measures between the treatment groups and the placebo group. Similar results were also found for depression and hopelessness. The participants returned to complete the measures at a 1-year follow-up, and the significant differences on all three measures were maintained posttreatment. These results indicate that Reiki can be used effectively for patients experiencing depression and anxiety. It is further suggested that the positive results from this treatment may have a long-term effect (Shore, 2004).

Cancer-Related Symptoms

Men who are diagnosed with prostate cancer have been identified as a population that experiences high levels of anxiety and depression in relation not only to their cancer but also risks associated with treatments, such as sexual dysfunction and urinary problems. Beard et al. (2011) conducted a pilot RCT that examined the use of two CAM therapies, Reiki and relaxation response therapy (RRT) among men undergoing radiotherapy for prostate cancer. The researchers randomized 54 men into one of three groups (18 per group): Reiki, RRT, and wait-list control. Measures were taken to assess stress, anxiety, and depression. Patients were undergoing external-beam radiation therapy five times a week for 8 consecutive weeks. Reiki sessions were scheduled 2 days a week usually before the external-beam radiation therapy treatment. RRT sessions were scheduled 1 day a week but included instructions to practice the relaxation and to engage in journaling daily.

Although the results suggested that RRT and Reiki may be helpful among prostate cancer patients suffering from anxiety and/or depression, significance was found only among the RRT group for anxiety. In regard to depression, although there was no overall significant change among the participants, there were seven (divided evenly among the three groups) who were identified as "depressed" at baseline, and a significant decrease was reported among these participants.

The strengths of this study are study design, choice of well-validated outcome measures, and participant adherence and retention. A limitation is the relatively small sample size and limited diversity among the participants (predominately well-educated Caucasian men).

Cancer patients experience a number of problems that include pain, insomnia, cognitive dysfunction, fatigue, stress, depression, and anxiety (Catlin & Taylor-Ford, 2011; Olson et al., 2003; Tsang, Carlson, & Olson, 2007). Using an analgesic such as an opioid can have a wide variety of side effects, and therefore many patients and physicians are searching for alternatives to pain management (Olson et al., 2003). In recent research, Reiki has been studied as a viable treatment for these cancer-related symptoms.

With the objective of reducing opioid needs and relieving pain, Olson et al. (2003) began a series of research trials designed to examine the effectiveness of Reiki in reducing pain. In a pilot study, Reiki was administered to 20 participants experiencing pain for various reasons. Pre- and posttreatment measures of pain were taken using visual analogue and Likert scales. Findings were significant for a reduction in pain among this population (Olson & Hanson, 1997).

A more recent Phase II trial was conducted among patients with advanced cancer. Participants were randomly assigned to an opiate management plan plus rest or an opiate management plan plus Reiki. Physiological measures of blood pressure and pulse were taken, quality of life was assessed, and a VAS to rate pain was completed four times daily. Participants also kept track of their daily analgesic use and any other actions they were taking in an effort to reduce pain. Twenty-four participants were randomized into either the non-Reiki control group, in which participants rested for 1.5 hours an hour after their afternoon dose of analgesic on Days 1 and 4, or the Reiki treatment group, which received Reiki during that time.

A significant reduction in the participants' self-reports of pain and a significant drop in diastolic blood pressure and pulse were reported among the Reiki group compared with the control group on both Days 1 and 4. Additionally, there was significant improvement in the psychological aspect of their quality of life when comparing Day 1 to Day 7 in the Reiki group compared with no change in the control group. As expected, due to the short length of the study, there was no reported reduction in analgesic medications because patients are often told to continue taking their medications, even if they feel better, unless that directive is changed by their physician (Olson et al., 2003).

In a pilot crossover trial, Tsang and colleagues (2007) examined the use of Reiki among 16 cancer patients suffering from cancer-related fatigue (CRF), a chronic condition commonly reported by patients regardless of the type of cancer or treatment. The sustained exhaustion characteristic of CRF is not relieved by rest. In an effort to assess fatigue scores and quality of life before and after Reiki sessions compared with rest sessions, this pilot study was designed so that every participant was treated with both conditions, Reiki and resting control, but in random order. The Reiki group received five consecutive sessions of Reiki, followed by a 7-day washout, then two more Reiki sessions. The resting control group rested for approximately 45 minutes each day for 5 days, followed by 7 washout days of no scheduled resting time. After a 2-week waiting period, each participant crossed over to the other group. A measure to assess fatigue was completed pre- and postsession in both groups. Results from this study indicate a statistical significance in the reduction of fatigue among the Reiki participants from before the first treatment to after the seventh treatment. There were no significant changes among participants in the rest control group, which seems to contradict some previous research suggesting that rest is at least moderately effective in reducing CRF. This does seem to support the theory that rest plus an energy restorative intervention may help to improve and regulate energy levels (Cella, Peterman, Passik, Jacobsen, & Breitbart, 1998).

Some weaknesses of this study are (a) the absence of an active control condition; (b) small sample size; (c) the brevity of the washout period; and (d) the presence of uncontrollable variables, most involving ongoing medical care among the participants. Despite the limitations of this study, the information gathered may prove to be valuable in future research involving CRF. For patients already struggling with limited energy and the stressors of cancer and treatments, the passive nature of Reiki appears to be helpful.

Nonhuman Studies

In another trial to determine the effects of Reiki on stress, Baldwin, Wagers, and Schwartz (2008) used Reiki to reduce the heart rates and blood pressures in laboratory rats. Rats who were exposed to 90-dB white noise for 15 minutes had increased heart rates and blood pressure. With this information, six male rats were used, half of which were implanted with PhysioTel C50-PXT telemetry transmitters while the other half were not, serving only as cage mates to the implanted rats. The transmitter provided information regarding the rats' heart rates, blood pressure, and heart-rate variability; this information was recorded 15 minutes before the delivery of the white noise. On Days 1 through 3, the rats were monitored for the 15 minutes before the 30 minutes of 90-dB white noise. On the 4th through 8th days, immediately after the initial 15-minute period, the rats received 15 minutes of Reiki, followed by 30 minutes of exposure to the white noise.

The rats were then given a 2-week rest period, and the 8-day process was repeated, with the change being that sham Reiki was used by two students who were not trained in Reiki but were instructed to imitate the physical hand movements of the Reiki practitioners.

Those randomized to Reiki showed significant reduction in heart rate during a period of noise-induced stress by 5.8%—from 293 beats per minute to 276. Strengths of this study are that it had tightly controlled conditions (diet, environment, interaction), eliminating preconceived expectations encountered among human subjects; Reiki was compared with a sham Reiki; and the measure was a physiological, objective one. The only apparent weakness identified by the researchers was the small sample size. However, these findings do lend support to the claim that Reiki may be useful as a method of stress relief, thus minimizing cardiac stress and protecting the heart (Baldwin, Wagers, & Schwartz, 2008).

CONTRAINDICATIONS AND RISKS

The NCCAM stated that "no serious side effects have been reported" with Reiki, but there are a few factors that patients and clinicians should be aware of (NIH, 2011f, para. 6). One thing to consider is the fact that when in this deep state of relaxation, some patients may experience a release of emotions that can be thought of as frightening or uncomfortable (Ringdahl & Halcon, 2006). Additionally, it is possible that some patients will be uncomfortable with being touched, so assessing comfort levels and determining if it is appropriate to refer the patient to a Reiki practitioner will help to ensure the highest quality of care (Ringdahl & Halcon, 2006). Psychologists are cautioned from providing Reiki to their patients as the practice of Reiki can violate ethical boundaries in regards to touch. If psychologists believe that their patients can benefit from Reiki, they are urged to provide their clients with the resources for selecting an appropriately trained practitioner, but to inform their clients that to date, no nationally recognized certification for Reiki currently exists. It is also important to recognize that Reiki should not replace traditional care. Rather, it is a method that is often used as a complementary modality alongside mainstream medicine.

Currently, it is believed that Reiki is safe to use with both pregnant women and children. With regard to children, it is helpful if they are old enough to understand what is taking place. Reiki has been used to cope with anxiety and sleep issues in pregnant women, and it has also been shown to have a positive impact on the process of childbirth (International Center for Reiki Training, 2011).

TIPS FOR PRACTITIONERS

- Reiki sessions typically cost from $45 to $75 and are not covered by most insurance plans.
- The most common uses for Reiki are in the treatment of stress and anxiety and the promotion of well-being.
- Reiki research has recently seen a growing acceptance among cancer patients for treatment of cancer-related conditions, such as pain, fatigue, anxiety, and stress.
- Risks and side effects are minimal.
- Licensure is not required to practice Reiki, so careful research into a practitioner's background and training is important.

INTEGRATION WITH PSYCHOLOGICAL PRACTICE

Although limited, research suggests that Reiki may be of benefit when used as a complementary modality alongside other techniques and therapies. However, one must be cautious when learning and using Reiki because the parameters of appropriate training are not clearly defined and may lead to ethical and legal problems (Plodek, 2009).

As psychologists are generally not recommended to practice Reiki themselves with their own clients, they should familiarize themselves about current training standards in order to refer clients to a qualified Reiki practitioner. Additionally, it might be helpful for psychologists who are interested in Reiki to themselves experience a Reiki session in order to provide a frame of reference that may be useful as feelings and possible effects of the intervention. To develop a complete understanding of the mechanisms of Reiki, it is highly recommended that clinicians educate themselves on the technique and take at least the beginning level of instruction and/or participate as a patient in a Reiki session (NIH, 2011f). These experiences will provide a greater understanding of the treatment and how it is relatable to the patient's overall treatment. It will also provide the clinician with a frame of reference that may be useful as feelings and possible effects of the intervention are discussed. Additionally, it helps to better determine which patients would be most appropriate for treatment as one better understands its nature and the potential impact of Reiki (LaTorre, 2005).

Training in Reiki occurs in three phases, with all three phases required. The first and second phases take about 2 days and involve learning the foundations of Reiki, its history and utilization, and the actual hand positions that are used (LaTorre, 2005; NIH, 2011f). Phase I training provides basic hand positions and a history of Reiki. In Phase II training, the Reiki student is taught about the symbols that are believed to allow energy to transfer between two individuals (Ringdahl & Halcon, 2006). The Mastery Level, or Phase III level of training, takes many years and involves shadowing a Reiki master; it is only at this level that one may teach others how to use Reiki (Ringdahl & Halcon, 2006). There are numerous Reiki certification agencies and training programs available; however, at this time, there is no nationally recognized certification agency, and the training offered by the many diverse programs appears to differ substantially. When referring a client to a Reiki practitioner, psychologists are advised to gather as much information about their credentials and training and what that training entailed as possible.

It may be appropriate to integrate Reiki into specific instances of psychotherapy, specifically if a patient presents with a medical illness in addition to the clinically relevant problem, because Reiki may allow them to relieve some of those symptoms as well. With that, it is of the utmost importance to take a detailed medical and psychiatric history and potentially confer with a patient's treating physician to understand if it is appropriate to use Reiki. However, even if a clinician is competent to perform Reiki, because there is physical contact and hand placement on the body, a boundary violation would likely occur if used by psychotherapists themselves on their psychotherapy patients. Thus, it is always advisable to make a referral, as opposed to serving in both roles. Another factor to consider is cost to the client. Although a typical Reiki session is not particularly expensive, it is often not covered as a reimbursable expense by traditional health insurance plans. Discussing fees and payment issues with patients at the outset will help them make educated decisions.

ADDITIONAL RESOURCES

1. NCCAM's website on Reiki—NCCAM provides an abundance of information on a variety of CAM modalities. With regard to Reiki, it describes the history, uses, safety concerns, and licensure and certification requirements, as well as information regarding research that the NCCAM is currently funding. The NCCAM site on Reiki can be found at http://nccam.nih.gov/health/reiki/introduction.htm.

2. The International Center for Reiki Training Website—The center is a professional organization that was established for Reiki professionals. The organization holds its members to an ethics code as well as a variety of standards of practice. To join the International Center for Reiki Training, practitioners must be Reiki masters; however, all are welcome to access the materials available on the website at http://www.reiki.org.

3. Global Healing Network through Reiki.org—This network is provided through the International Center for Reiki Training and allows for all Reiki practitioners, regardless of their level of training, to communicate, interact, and share information. The Global Healing Network may be accessed online at http://www.reiki.org/GlobalHealing/GlobalHealingHomepage.html.

17

AYURVEDA

Ayurveda is a whole-medical system that endeavors to restore the innate harmony of the individual by placing equal emphasis on the balance of the mind, body, and spirit (Sharma, 2011). With its beginnings in India, Ayurveda is believed to have originated as long as 10,000 years ago (National Institutes of Health, 2013a; Sharma, 2011; Synovitz & Larson, 2012). A number of herbs, extracts, roots, and plants are used in Ayurveda, and it continues to be widely practiced in India today (Satow, Kumar, Burke, & Inciardi, 2008). However, research on this medical system is relatively new when considered alongside how long Ayurvedic medicine has been in existence. Though Ayurvedic medicine has shown potential benefits to holistic improvements in spiritual and physical health, criticism centers around the fact that, to date, there is very little scientific basis to the specific treatments for the eradication of disease (Narayanasamy & Narayanasamy, 2006). Ayurveda is

http://dx.doi.org/10.1037/14435-018
Complementary and Alternative Medicine for Psychologists: An Essential Resource, by J. E. Barnett, A. J. Shale, G. Elkins, and W. Fisher

a whole-medicine system; however, it is considered a complementary and alternative medicine (CAM) to biomedical systems in most countries (Satow et al., 2008).

DEFINITIONS

The word *Ayurveda*, meaning *knowledge of life*, is a Sanskrit word derived from two root words, *Ayus*, which translates to mean "life cycle" and *vid*, which means "knowledge" (Narayanasamy & Narayanasamy, 2006). Ayurveda bases its creed on the premise that humans live in harmony with the universe. According to Ayurvedic tradition, within the universe, all material creation, including humans, is believed to be made up of five elements—space, air, fire, water, and earth—and all existence came from the *One*. These elements are symbolic in nature; *air* signifies the kinetic force of motion, *fire* denotes heat and light, *water* is the force that binds things together, and *earth* and *space* represent the physical environment and spatial concepts. The other central concept in Ayurvedic medicine is the *dosha*. Interaction of the five elements within an individual is believed to manifest in the body as three basic constitutions, or *doshas*: (1) *vata*, (2) *pitta*, and (3) *kapha* (Narayanasamy & Narayanasamy, 2006; Synovitz & Larson, 2012). Collectively, the three doshas are referred to as an individual's *tridosha*, in which one dosha most often predominates. The *tridosha* structures the individuality of humans for all functions of the body and mind, from basic emotions, such as anger, joy, and fear, to more subtle sentiments, such as empathy and compassion (Williamson, 2006).

HISTORY

To understand the history of Ayurveda, one must have some knowledge of Hinduism, one of the oldest religions of the world. Hinduism has no documented beginning, no human founder, and in fact, predates recorded history. The scriptures of Hinduism are the four *Vedas*, which translates to *eternal truths*. In this text, God is worshipped as natural elements such as wind, fire, water, and earth. From the four Vedas, eight original texts were derived, and of these texts, Ayurveda is found in the *Caraka Samhita*, which defines the Indian healing method as it concerns medical diagnosis and treatment. Here, the function of the mind is described as having three roles: (1) to provide direction for the senses, (2) to maintain self-control, and (3) to govern reasoning and deliberation. This combination suggests a holistic view of life that includes spiritual, physical, ethical, and social aspects of health and disease (Juthani, 2001).

During the 18th century, much of India fell under British rule, and Western allopathic medicine was introduced to the Indian people. However, at the same time, the Court of Directors in London encouraged its doctors to learn more about the value of Ayurvedic medicine (Jeffery, 1988). As a result, the Native Medical School was founded in 1822 in Calcutta, where 20 students were enrolled and taught both Ayurveda and allopathic medicine in a special degree program. One of the results of this combination of medical systems is that Ayurvedic practitioners recognized that to impart the practice of Ayurveda to other parts of the world, it would be necessary to include certain aspects of Western medicine within Ayurvedic practice (Langford, 2002; Leslie, 1976).

COMMON USES

Ayurveda is growing more popular in Western and European countries (Wiese & Oster, 2010). With the increased immigration of Indians and others from nearby regions, Ayurveda-derived teas and herbal supplements have been introduced as treatments for psychological problems such as depression, anxiety, schizophrenia, and memory loss (Sharma, Chandola, Singh, & Sasisht, 2007). However, it should be noted that as a whole-medicine system Ayurveda has been applied to many medical problems. A review of the uses of Ayurveda identified 166 species of plants used in 11 disease categories: antimicrobial; antimutagens; cardiovascular; dermatology; diabetes mellitus; gastrointestinal; liver dysfunction; nervous system; pain and inflammation; renal, blood, immune system; and other (Khan & Balick, 2001). Although it is acknowledged that research on Ayurveda has lacked rigor in terms of randomization, adequacy of controls, sample size, and methodology, this review indicates the range of potential applications of Ayurveda.

TECHNIQUE

Ayurvedic medical practice involves completing an assessment and diagnosis on which treatment is prescribed. Initially, a patient's dosha is determined by completing a questionnaire or answering a series of questions, asked by the Ayurveda physician. Additionally, a family history is taken, and then the physician uses a systematic analysis to determine diagnosis. This is done using physical diagnostic techniques on the pulse, tongue (size, shape, surface, margins, and color), and facial features (wrinkle patterns, eyelids, eyes, nose, and lips). Specific characteristics are noted as significant in determining the source of illness or *imbalance*. For example, pale tongue and lips indicate anemia; drooping upper eyelids indicate a sense of insecurity, fear, or lack of confidence (*vata* imbalance); and horizontal wrinkles on the forehead suggest that the patient suffers from anxiety (Frank & Stollberg, 2002; Synovitz & Larson, 2012).

Once a diagnosis is made, the individualized and comprehensive treatment plan focuses on maintaining the patient's balanced dosha constitution, or tridosha, then "healing" any imbalance (Synovitz & Larson, 2012). This treatment plan follows the general guideline that includes (a) *shodhanam* (cleansing), (b) *shamanam* (balancing), (c) *pathya vyavastha* (prescription of diet and activity), (d) *nidan parivarjan* (avoidance of disease-causing and aggravating factors), (e) *rasayana* (rejuvenation), and *satvajaya* (mental hygiene, yoga, meditation).

MECHANISM OF ACTION

Although the mechanisms of action are not known, contemporary Ayurvedic theory contends that a healthy metabolic system, good diet and digestion, and healthy excretion are necessary for health and well-being (Synovitz & Larson, 2012). Ayurveda involves the use of plants and herbs but can also include yoga and meditation (Glaser, 1988). Most Western biomedical theories of how the body functions are described within the scope of biochemistry and the core principle of Ayurvedic medicine can be found in the ancient Vedic writings. The *Veda* emphasizes the idea of a "unified field of pure, nonmaterial intelligence and consciousness whose modes of vibration manifest as the material universe" (Sharma, 2011, p. 498). A central belief of Ayurvedic medicine is that disease is a result of the loss of connection to one's unified field, which is believed to be the innermost core of one's being and experience, and that healing comes about when the connection is restored (Sharma, 2011).

RELEVANT RESEARCH

Although preliminary research has been done on Ayurveda, some of which is described in this section, much more stringent research is needed to validate the therapeutic efficacy of pharmacology used in Ayurveda (Sharma et al., 2007). A large number of herbs, extracts, roots, and plants are used in Ayurveda, and in some cases, there is supportive evidence (Howes & Houghton, 2003). Overall, the relevant research is still evolving in regard to identifying the actual risks and benefits. Table 17.1 provides an evaluation of the scope and quality of the research and provides author recommendations based on the available evidence.

TABLE 17.1
Ayurveda Summary Table

Symptom	Studies[a]	Sample	GRADE[b]	Evaluation
Depression	1 animal study	Rats	2C	Weak recommendation, low-quality evidence
Anxiety	2 pilot studies, 1 RCT	Adults suffering from anxiety and generalized anxiety disorder	2C	Weak recommendation, low-quality evidence
Memory and cognitive function	3 animal studies, 2 RCTs	Rats, healthy adults	2B	Weak recommendation, moderate-quality evidence
Schizophrenia	Cochrane Review: 3 RCTs	Schizophrenia patients	2C	Weak recommendation, low-quality evidence

Note. RCT = randomized controlled trial; GRADE = Grading of Recommendations, Assessment, Development and Evaluation.
[a]Citations available in text or references. Studies are representative; table should not be considered a comprehensive review of all available literature.
[b]Data from the GRADE Working Group. Available at http://www.gradeworkinggroup.org/intro.htm.

Depression

Curcuma longa is known as a *rasayana* herb, which means it is used to counteract the aging process. Westerners know this herb as turmeric, and it is often used in food preparation. In a research trial by Yu, Kong, and Chen (2002), C. *longa* was administered to rats at doses ranging from 140 to 560 mg/kg for 14 days. After a series of mobility tests on the rats, it was determined that the effects of the dose at 560 mg/kg were more effective than that of fluoxetine, an antidepressant. At 140 mg/kg, significant inhibition of the monoamine oxidase (MAO) A activity was noted. However, when a dose of the extract at 560 mg/kg was given, the results indicated observable MAO B inhibitory activity, whereas only a tendency in the inhibition of MAO A and B activity were observed when fluoxetine was given. These results suggest that C. *Longa* has specific antidepressant effects and the activity of this herb, when used for depression, may be mediated in part through MAO A inhibition (Yu et al., 2002).

Anxiety

In the Ayurvedic system, it is believed that anxiety is a condition that is most common in old age because of an imbalance, specifically an elevation, of a person's *Vata*. A pilot study investigating the effects of the *Brahmi* herbal formulation on seven patients suffering from anxiety was conducted (Sharma et al., 2007). The Brahmi herbal formulation was administered at a dose of 5 grams three times a day for 2 months. The results indicated that anxious mood, tension, depressed mood, and insomnia were significantly alleviated. Additionally, there was significant improvement noted in intellectual cognition. In another pilot study, *Abhyanga*, the classic Ayurvedic oil massage, was researched to determine its effects on anxiety (Basler, 2011). Twenty participants (10 women and 10 men) were selected and received a traditional Ayurvedic *Abhyanga* treatment, providing assessment response pre- and posttreatment. In addition, heart rate and blood pressure were recorded pre- and posttreatment. The results indicated a significant improvement in the subjective reports of stress, with greater improvement among the women. There was also a reduction in heart rate posttreatment; however, there were no significant changes in the BP recordings.

In a more recent randomized control study, patients diagnosed with generalized anxiety disorder were recruited to evaluate the effect of *Manasamitra Vataka*, a formula of up to 73 herbal ingredients, alone and *Manasamitra Vataka* plus *Shirodhara*, a therapeutic technique that involves gently pouring liquids over the forehead compared with the allopathic medication clonazepam. Results indicated that *Manasamitra Vataka* was effective in reducing the severity of anxiety and daytime sleepiness and increasing self-reported quality of life to same degree as the pharmaceutical group. The treatments were well tolerated and no adverse effects were reported (Tubaki et al., 2012). The results of this trial, although promising, should be taken with caution because comparative studies are typically viewed more favorably when the effect size of the experimental condition exceeds the benefits of comparative therapies (in this case, pharmacotherapy). Additional study, including cost–benefit analysis and a study of side effects and possible interactions of these agents is needed.

Memory and Cognitive Function

Some of the Ayurveda preparations studied for use in improving memory and cognitive function are *Celastrus paniculatus* (Warrier, Nambiar, & Ramankutty, 1995), *Centella asiatica* (Manyam, 1999), *B. monnieri* (also known as Brahmi; Roodenrys et al., 2002; Singh & Dhawan, 1982; Singh et al., 1988; Stough et al., 2001), and *Emblica officinalis* (Vasudevan & Parle, 2007).

In animal studies using the seeds and seed oil from *C. paniculatus*, an enhanced stimulation of the intellect and improved memory was found (Warrier et al., 1995). When the seed oil was administered orally to rats, decreased levels of noradrenaline, dopamine, and 5-hydroxytryptamine were observed in the brain. These findings correlated with improvements in learning and memory processing (Nalini, Karanth, Rao, & Aroot, 1995). Research using the extract of *C. asiatica* found it to have a sedating, tranquilizing effect on rats, which might suggest that it may be appropriate in the treatment of some of the accompanying symptoms of Alzheimer's disease, such as depression and anxiety (Veerendra Kumar & Gupta, 2002). Findings from two animal studies by Singh and Dhawan (1982) and Singh, Rastogi, Srimal, & Dhawan (1988) found that *B. monnieri* appeared to improve flight reaction time and indicated a significant effect on mental retention capacity in rats.

Two double-blind, placebo-controlled, randomized human studies found mixed results for the use of *B. monnieri* in humans. In one, 46 healthy participants were randomly placed into one of two groups, the *B. monnieri* group or placebo control group, and each participant was given a bottle containing a 12-week supply of capsules that looked identical. Participants were instructed to take two capsules per day for 12 weeks. Findings relative to the improvement of memory and cognitive functioning suggest that there was improvement in verbal learning rate and information processing (Stough et al., 2001).

In contrast, another study failed to show a benefit for *B. monnieri*. In this study, 76 participants were randomized to take either *B. monnieri* or a placebo preparation. Participants were tested at three points using various memory and recall tests: baseline, end of trial, and 3-month postbaseline. Results showed no significant effect of using Brahmi in measures of memory (short term or working), retrieval of information from long-term memory, or attention. Additionally, no significance was found among subjective measures of psychological state (i.e., depression, anxiety, and stress; Roodenrys et al., 2002). These contradictory findings indicate that further research is needed to better understand the appropriate uses of these preparations for improving memory and cognitive function.

Schizophrenia

A review of three studies using Ayurvedic medicine for schizophrenia was done by the Cochrane Collaboration. Each study compared Ayurvedic treatments with chlorpromazine, an antipsychotic drug. It was noted that all of the trials were conducted in India and that they were all of short duration. The authors noted that this review's primary outcome was "change in global state and no data were available on this broad, clinically meaningful, outcome" (Agarwal, Abhijnhan, & Raviraj, 2007, p. 9). On the basis of this review, the authors concluded that while Ayurvedic medication may provide slight improvement over placebo, there is no evidence of improvement that it is better than the use of chlorpromazine, and in fact, there were reports of unwanted gastrointestinal effects. In the use of Ayurvedic treatments, it was determined that possible real effects do exist in the short term and treatments may be useful as an adjunct to allopathic treatment (Agarwal et al., 2007).

CONTRAINDICATIONS AND RISKS

The major risk factor in Ayurvedic practice is that many of the prescriptions of herbal medicines have been found to contain lead, mercury, and arsenic (Synovitz & Larson, 2012). These potential toxicities occur because many of the ingredients have not been methodically researched in the United States or India. In the United States, Ayurvedic medications are regulated as dietary supplements, so there is no requirement or standard in place to ensure safety and efficacy, as there is for conventional allopathic medicines. The Centers for Disease Control and Prevention has reported cases of lead poisoning that were connected to the use of Ayurvedic medications.

Herbs, minerals, and metals used in Ayurvedic herbal medicinal plants have been associated with lead toxicity and poisonous conditions including developmental delay (Moore & Adler, 2000), congenital paralysis and sensorineural deafness (Tait, Vora, James, Fitzgerald, & Pester, 2002), and status epilepticus (Centers for Disease Control and Prevention, 2004). In 2004, Saper, Kales, et al. reported at least 55 cases of heavy metal intoxication associated with Ayurvedic herbal medicinal plants in adults and children in the United States and abroad. These authors later reported that one fifth of Internet purchases of both U.S.- and Indian-manufactured Ayurvedic medicines contain detectable lead, mercury, or arsenic (Saper et al., 2008).

TIPS FOR PRACTITIONERS

- Patients considering Ayurveda should be referred to their primary physician before beginning an Ayurvedic treatment or medicine.
- Women who are pregnant or nursing and parents considering the use of Ayurvedic medicine for children should be cautioned regarding the potential for toxicities associated with some Ayurvedic preparations.
- Practitioners should be knowledgeable of scientific studies and risks and benefits of Ayurveda to advise their patients.

INTEGRATION WITH PSYCHOLOGICAL PRACTICE

To advise clients, psychologists should be knowledgeable about the training required to practice Ayurveda and about the relevant research. Ayurveda may be of benefit to some patients, but there are significant cautions, as noted earlier. Ayurveda is a whole-medical system and extensive training is required for competent practice.

To become a licensed Ayurvedic physician in India, one must complete training at a state-approved school (Satow et al., 2008). The National Ayurvedic Medical Association (NAMA) set up educational standards in the United States in 2004. Although there is no established or widely accepted certification or licensure requirement for the practice of Ayurvedic medicine in the United States, there are schools that provide extensive training. These programs vary from correspondence programs to internships and may take as little as 12 weekends to 18 months of full-time course study (Synovitz & Larson, 2012). NAMA provides information about training and was established to "preserve, protect, improve and promote the philosophy, knowledge, science and practice of Ayurveda for the benefit of humanity" (NAMA, 2013, para. 3).

ADDITIONAL RESOURCES

1. The National Center for Complementary and Alternative Medicine's (NCCAM)—The NCCAM web page on Ayurveda provides an abundance of information on a variety of CAM modalities. With regard to Ayurveda, it offers history, uses, safety concerns, licensure and certification requirements, and information regarding research that the NCCAM is currently funding. The NCCAM site on Ayurveda can be found at http://nccam.nih.gov/health/Ayurveda.
2. National Ayurvedic Medical Association (NAMA)—NAMA, established in 1998, is a volunteer organization with the primary goal of supporting Ayurvedic education and professional practice. Annual NAMA conferences have been held since 2003 and provide a forum where developing professionals may increase knowledge and understanding of this healing system. The NAMA website may be accessed at http://www.ayurvedanama.org.
3. Alternative Medicine Foundation (AMF)—The AMF provides a wide range of information including the history and principles of Ayurveda, as well as a listing of training and research facilities, treatment centers, and additional web resources. This website can be accessed at http://www.amfoundation.org/ayurveda.htm.

REFERENCES

Abbot, N. C. (2000). Healing as a therapy for human disease: A systematic review. *The Journal of Alternative and Complementary Medicine, 6,* 159–169. doi:10.1089/acm.2000.6.159

Abrahamsen, R., Baad-Hansen, L., & Svensson, P. (2008). Hypnosis in the management of persistent idiopathic orofacial pain—clinical and psychosocial findings. *Pain, 136,* 44–52. doi:10.1016/j.pain.2007.06.013

Abrahamsen, R., Dietz, M., Lodahl, S., Roepstorff, A., Zachariae, R., Ostergaard, L., & Svensson, P. (2010). Effect of hypnotic pain modulation on brain activity in patients with temporomandibular disorder pain. *Pain, 151,* 825–833. doi:10.1016/j.pain.2010.09.020

Accreditation Commission for Acupuncture and Oriental Medicine. (2010). *Accredited and candidate schools.* Retrieved from http://www.acaom.org/accdtd_cndtdschls.htm

Agarwal, V., Abhijnhan, A., & Raviraj, P. (2007). Ayurvedic medicine for schizophrenia. *Cochrane Database of Systematic Reviews, 4,* CD006867. doi:10.1002/14651858.CD006867

Alexander, C. N., Langer, E. J., Newman, R. I., Chandler, H. M., & Davies, J. L. (1989). Transcendental meditation, mindfulness, and longevity: An experimental study with the elderly. *Journal of Personality and Social Psychology, 57* (6), 950–964.

Alexander, C. N., Robinson, P., & Rainforth, M. (1994). Treating and preventing alcohol, nicotine, and drug abuse through transcendental meditation: A review and statistical meta-analysis. *Alcoholism Treatment Quarterly, 11,* 13–88.

Alimi, D., Rubino, C., Pichard-Leandri, E., Fermand-Brule, S., Dubreuil-Lemaire, M., & Hill, C. (2003). Analgesic effect of auricular acupuncture for cancer pain: A randomized, blinded controlled trial. *Journal of Clinical Oncology, 21,* 4120–4126. doi:10.1200/JCO.2003.09.011

Allied Health Profession. (2005). *Dance/movement therapy.* Retrieved from http://www.healthpronet.org/ahp_month/04_05.html

Allison, D. B., & Faith, M. S. (1996). Hypnosis as an adjunct to cognitive-behavioral psychotherapy for obesity: A meta-analytic reappraisal. *Journal of Consulting and Clinical Psychology, 64,* 513–516. doi:10.1037/0022-006X.64.3.513

American Cancer Society. (2011). *Music therapy.* Retrieved from http://www.cancer.org/treatment/treatmentsandsideeffects/complementaryandalternativemedicine/mindbodyandspirit/music-therapy

American Chiropractic Association. (2011a). *Frequently asked questions.* Retrieved from http://www.acatoday.org/level3_css.cfm?T1ID=13&T2ID=61&T3ID=152

American Chiropractic Association. (2011b). *History of chiropractic care.* Retrieved from http://www.acatoday.org/level3_css.cfm?T1ID=13&T2ID=61&T3ID=149

American Chiropractic Association. (2011c). *What is chiropractic?* Retrieved from http://www.acatoday.org/level2_css.cfm?T1ID=13&T2ID=61

American Chiropractic Association. (2013). *Basic Pain Facts and Statistics*. Retrieved from http://www.acatoday.org/level2_css.cfm?T1ID=13&T2ID=68

American Dance Therapy Association. (2013a). *Dance Therapy Certification Board*. Retrieved from http://www.adta.org/DMTCB

American Dance Therapy Association. (2013b). *Mission & purpose*. Retrieved from http://www.adta.org/Mission_&_Purpose

American Massage Therapy Association. (2010a). *2009 consumer survey fact sheet*. Retrieved from http://www.amtamassage.org/research/Consumer-Survey-Fact-Sheets.html

American Massage Therapy Association. (2010b). *2010 massage therapy industry fact sheet*. Retrieved from http://www.amtamassage.org/articles/2/PressRelease/detail/2146#6

American Massage Therapy Association. (2010c). *AMTA definition of massage therapy*. Retrieved from http://www.amtamassage.org/infocenter/economic_industry-fact-sheet.html

American Massage Therapy Association. (2010d). *AMTA member demographics*. Retrieved from http://www.amtamassage.org/uploads/cms/documents/AMTA demographics03.pdf

American Massage Therapy Association. (2010e). *Choosing a type of massage*. Retrieved from http://www.amtamassage.org/findamassage/massage_type.html

American Massage Therapy Association. (2010f). *Credentials for the massage therapy profession*. Retrieved from http://www.amtamassage.org/findamassage/credential.html#2

American Massage Therapy Association. (2010g). *Membership and benefits*. Retrieved from http://www.amtamassage.org/membership/Benefits/professional.html

American Massage Therapy Association. (2013). *Consumer survey fact sheet*. Retrieved from http://www.amtamassage.org/research/Consumer-Survey-Fact-Sheets.html

American Music Therapy Association. (2011a). *About the American Music Therapy Association*. Retrieved from http://www.musictherapy.org/about

American Music Therapy Association. (2011b). *What is the profession of music therapy?* Retrieved from http://www.musictherapy.org/about/requirements

American Psychiatric Association. (1987). *Diagnostic and statistical manual of mental disorders* (3rd ed., text rev.). Washington, DC: Author.

American Psychiatric Association. (1994). *Diagnostic and statistical manual of mental disorders* (4th ed.). Washington, DC: Author.

American Psychological Association. (2010). *Ethical principles of psychologists and code of conduct (2002; amended June 1, 2010)*. Retrieved from http://www.apa.org/ethics/code/index.aspx

American Psychological Association Presidential Task Force. (2006). Evidence-based practice in psychology. *American Psychologist, 61*, 271–285. doi:10.1037/0003-066X.61.4.271

American Society of Clinical Hypnosis. (2010). *Certification referral.* Retrieved from http://www.asch.net/Public/CertificationInformation/Requirements CertificationinClinicalHypnosis/tabid/157/Default.aspx

American Society of Colon and Rectal Surgeons. (2013). What is Irritable Bowel Syndrome. Retrieved from http://www.fascrs.org/patients/conditions/irritable_bowel_syndrome/

Amsterdam, J. D., Li, Y., Soeller, I., Rockwell, K., Mao, J. J., & Shults, J. (2009). A randomized, double-blind, placebo-controlled trial of oral *Matricaria recutita* (chamomile) extract therapy of generalized anxiety disorder. *Journal of Clinical Psychopharmacology, 29*, 378. doi:10.1097/JCP.0b013e3181ac935c

Anandayoga.org. (2011). *What is Ananda yoga?* Retrieved from http://www.ananda yoga.org/whatis/about_what_is.htm

Anderson, J. G., & Taylor, A. G. (2012). Biofield therapies and cancer pain. *Clinical Journal of Oncology Nursing, 16*, 43–48. doi:10.1188/12.CJON.43-48

Andersson, G. (2008). Chronic pain and praying to a higher power: Useful or useless? *Journal of Religion and Health, 47*, 176–187. doi:10.1007/s10943-007-9148-8

Anusarayoga.com. (2011). *About Anusara yoga.* Retrieved from http://www.anusara.com/index.php?option=com_content&view=article&id=68&Itemid=77

Arias, A. J., Steinberg, K., Banga, A., & Trestman, R. L. (2006). Systematic review of the efficacy of meditation techniques as treatments for medical illness. *The Journal of Alternative and Complementary Medicine, 12*, 817–832. doi:10.1089/acm.2006.12.817

Arndorfer, R. E., & Allen, K. D. (2001). Extending the efficacy of a thermal biofeedback treatment package to the management of tension-type headaches in children. *Headache, 41*, 183–192. doi:10.1046/j.1526-4610.2001.111006183.x

Arns, M., de Ridder, S., Strehl, U., Breteler, M., & Coenen, A. (2009). Efficacy of neurofeedback treatment in ADHD: The effects of inattention, impulsivity, and hyperactivity: A meta-analysis. *Clinical EEG and Neuroscience, 40*, 180–189. doi:10.1177/155005940904000311

Aromatherapy Registration Council. (2011). Minimum Standards of Eligibility. Retrieved from http://aromatherapycouncil.org/?page_id=218

Ashida, S., & Heaney, C. A. (2008). Differential associations of social support and social connectedness with structural features of social networks and the health status of older adults. *Journal of Aging and Health, 20*, 872–893. doi:10.1177/0898264308324626

Ashtanga.com. (2011). *Ashtanga yoga background.* Retrieved from http://ashtanga.com/html/background.html

Askay, S. W., Patterson, D. R., Jensen, M. P., & Sharar, S. R. (2007). A randomized controlled trial of hypnosis for burn wound care. *Rehabilitation Psychology, 52*, 247–253. doi:10.1037/0090-5550.52.3.247

Association for Applied Psychophysiology and Biofeedback. (2008). *About AAPB*. Retrieved from http://www.aapb.org/i4a/pages/index.cfm?pageid=3285

Astin, J. A. (1998). Why patients use alternative medicine. *JAMA, 279*, 1548–1553. doi:10.1001/jama.279.19.1548

Astin, J. A., Harkness, E., & Ernst, E. (2000). The efficacy of "distant healing": A systematic review of randomized trials. *Annals of Internal Medicine, 132*, 903–910. doi:10.7326/0003-4819-132-11-200006060-00009

Avila, D., & Nummela, R. (1977). Transcendental meditation: A psychological interpretation. *Journal of Clinical Psychology, 33*(3), 842–844.

Babu, A. S., Mathew, E., Danda, D., & Prakash, H. (2007). Management of patients with fibromyalgia using biofeedback: A randomized control trial. *Indian Journal of Medical Sciences, 61*, 455–461. doi:10.4103/0019-5359.33710

Baer, R. A. (2006). *Mindfulness-based treatment approaches: Clinician's guide to evidence base and applications*. San Diego, CA: Elsevier Academic Press.

Baldwin, A. L., Wagers, C., & Schwartz, G. E. (2008). Reiki improves heart rate homeostasis in laboratory rats. *The Journal of Alternative and Complementary Medicine, 14*, 417–422. doi:10.1089/acm.2007.0753

Banerjee, B., Vadiraj, H., Ram, A., Rao, R., Jayapal, M., Gopinath, K., . . . Hande, M. P. (2007). Effects of an integrated yoga program in modulating psychological stress and radiation-induced genotoxic stress in breast cancer patients undergoing radiotherapy. *Integrative Cancer Therapies, 6*, 242–250. doi:10.1177/1534735407306214

Barnes, J., Dong, C. Y., McRobbie, H., Walker, N., Mehta, M., & Stead, L. F. (2010). Hypnotherapy for smoking cessation. *Cochrane Database of Systematic Reviews, 10*, CD001008. Retrieved from http://onlinelibrary.wiley.com/doi/10.1002/14651858.CD001008.pub2/abstract

Barnes, L. L. (2005). American acupuncture and efficacy: Meanings and their points of insertion. *Medical Anthropology Quarterly, 19*, 239–266. doi:10.1525/maq.2005.19.3.239

Barnes, P. M., Bloom, B., & Nahin, R. (2008). Complementary and alternative medicine use among adults and children: United States, 2007. *National Health Statistics Report, 12*, 1–23. Atlanta, GA: Centers for Disease Control and Prevention.

Barnes, P. M., Powell-Griner, E., McFann, K., & Nahin, R. L. (2004). Complementary and alternative medicine use among adults: United States, 2002. In *Seminars in Integrative Medicine* (Vol. 2, pp. 54–71). Hyattsville, MD: Division of Health Interview Statistics, National Center for Health Statistics. doi:10.1016/j.sigm.2004.07.003

Barnett, J. E., Behnke, S., Rosenthal, S., & Koocher, G. (2007). In case of ethical dilemma, break glass: Commentary on ethical decision making in practice. *Professional Psychology: Research and Practice, 38*, 7–12. doi:10.1037/0735-7028.38.1.7

Barnett, J. E., & Johnson, W. B. (2008). *Ethics desk reference for psychologists.* Washington, DC: American Psychological Association.

Barnett, J. E., Lazarus, A. A., Vasquez, M. J. T., Moorehead-Slaughter, O., & Johnson, W. B. (2007). Boundary issues and multiple relationships: Fantasy and reality. *Professional Psychology: Research and Practice, 38*, 401–410. doi:10.1037/0735-7028.38.4.401

Barnett, J. E., & Shale, A. J. (2012). The integration of complementary and alternative medicine (CAM) into the practice of psychology: A vision for the future. *Professional Psychology: Research and Practice, 43*, 576–585. doi:10.1037/a0028919

Barnett, J. E., Wise, E., Johnson-Greene, D., & Bucky, S. (2007). Informed consent: Too much of a good thing or not enough? *Professional Psychology, Research and Practice, 38*, 179–186. doi:10.1037/0735-7028.38.2.179

Barnett, K., McLachlan, C., Hulbert, J., & Kassak, K. (1997). Working together in rural South Dakota: Integrating medical and chiropractic primary care. *Journal of Manipulative and Physiological Therapeutics, 20*, 577–582.

Bartenieff, I. (1972, Fall/Winter). Dance therapy: A new profession or a rediscovery of an ancient role of the dance? *Dance Scope, 6*–18.

Barton, D. L., Soori, G. S., Bauer, B. A., Sloan, J. A., Johnson, P. A., Figueras, C., . . . Atherton, P. J. (2010). Pilot study of Panax quinquefolius (American ginseng) to improve cancer-related fatigue: A randomized, double-blind, dose-finding evaluation: NCCTG trial N03CA. *Supportive Care in Cancer, 18*, 179–187. doi:10.1007/s00520-009-0642-2

Basler, A. J. (2011). Pilot study investigating the effects of Ayurvedic Abhyanga massage on subject stress experience. *The Journal of Alternative and Complementary Medicine, 17*, 435–440. doi:10.1089/acm.2010.0281

Basmajian, J. V. (1963). Control and training of individual motor units. *Science, 141*, 440–441. doi:10.1126/science.141.3579.440

Basmajian, J. V. (1989). *Biofeedback—Principles and practice for clinicians* (3rd ed.). Baltimore, MD: Williams & Wilkins.

Bassman, L. E., & Uellendahl, G. (2003). Complementary/alternative medicine: Ethical, professional, and practical challenges for psychologists. *Professional Psychology: Research and Practice, 34*, 264–270. doi:10.1037/0735-7028.34.3.264

Bastecki, A. V., Harrison, D. E., & Haas, J. W. (2004). Cervical kyphosis is a possible link to attention deficit/hyperactivity disorder. *Journal of Manipulative and Physiological Therapeutics, 27*, e14. doi:10.1016/j.jmpt.2004.08.007

Beard, C., Stason, W. B., Wang, Q., Manola, J., Dean-Clower, E., Dusek, J. A., & Benson, H. (2011). Effects of complementary therapies on clinical outcomes in patients being treated with radiation therapy for prostate cancer. *Cancer, 117*, 96–102. doi:10.1002/cncr.25291

Beck, A. T., Ward, C. H., Mendelson, M., Mock, J., & Erbaugh, J. (1961). An inventory for measuring depression. *Archives of General Psychiatry, 4*, 561–571. doi:10.1001/archpsyc.1961.01710120031004

Belleggia, G., & Birbaumer, N. (2001). Treatment of phantom limb pain with combined EMG and thermal biofeedback: A case report. *Applied Psychophysiology and Biofeedback, 26*, 141–146. doi:10.1023/A:1011391223713

Ben-Eliyahu, S. (2003). The promotion of tumor metastasis by surgery and stress: Immunological basis and implications for psychoneuroimmunology. *Brain, Behavior, and Immunity, 17*, S27–36. doi:10.1016/S0889-1591(02)00063-6

Benor, D. (1990). Survey of spiritual healing research. *Complementary Medical Research, 4*, 9–33.

Bensimon, M., Amir, D., & Wolf, Y. (2008). Drumming through trauma: Music therapy with posttraumatic soldiers. *The Arts in Psychotherapy, 35*, 34–48. doi:10.1016/j.aip.2007.09.002

Benson, H. (1975). *The relaxation response*. New York, NY: HarperCollins.

Benson, H. (1984). The faith factor. *American Health, 5*, 50–53.

Benson, H., Dusek, J. A., Sherwood, J. B., Lam, P., Bethea, C. F., Carpenter, W., . . . Hibberd, P. L. (2006). Study of therapeutic effects of intercessory prayer (STEP) in cardiac bypass patients: A multicenter randomized trial of uncertainty and certainty intercessory prayer. *American Heart Journal, 151*, 934–942. doi:10.1016/j.ahj.2005.05.028

Bent, S. (2008). Herbal medicine in the United States: Review of efficacy, safety, and regulation. *Journal of General Internal Medicine, 23*, 854–859. doi:10.1007/s11606-008-0632-y

Bent, S., & Ko, R. (2004). Commonly used herbal medicines in the United States: A review. *The American Journal of Medicine, 116*, 478–485. doi:10.1016/j.amjmed.2003.10.036

Bernardy, K., Fuber, N., Klose, P., & Hauser, W. (2011). Efficacy of hypnosis/guided imagery in fibromyalgia syndrome—a systematic review and meta-analysis of controlled trials. *BMC Musculoskeletal Disorders, 12*, 133. doi:10.1186/1471-2474-12-133

Bier, I. D., Wilson, J., Studt, P., & Shakleton, M. (2002). Auricular acupuncture, education, and smoking cessation: A randomized, sham-controlled trial. *American Journal of Public Health, 92*, 1642–1647. doi:10.2105/AJPH.92.10.1642

Bikramyoga.com. (2011a). *About Bikram yoga*. Retrieved from http://www.bikramyoga.com/BikramYoga/about_bikram_yoga.php

Bikramyoga.com. (2011b). *Bikram yoga FAQs*. Retrieved from http://www.bikramyoga.com/BikramYoga/FAQ.php

Biley, F. C. (2000). The effects on patient well-being of music listening as a nursing intervention: A review of the literature. *Journal of Clinical Nursing, 9*, 668–677. doi:10.1046/j.1365-2702.2000.00392.x

Biofeedback Certification International Alliance. (2011a). *Home*. Retrieved from http://www.bcia.org/i4a/pages/index.cfm?pageid=1

Biofeedback Certification International Alliance. (2011b). *Overview of clinical entry-level neurofeedback certification*. Retrieved from http://www.bcia.org/i4a/pages/index.cfm?pageid=3435

Bishop, S. R. (2002). What do we really know about mindfulness-based stress reduction? *Psychosomatic Medicine, 64*, 71–83.

Bksiyengar.com. (2011). *B. K. S. Iyengar yoga: Our Guruji.* Retrieved from http://bksiyengar.com/modules/Guruji/guru.htm

Blanchard, E. B., & Epstein, L. H. (1978). *A biofeedback primer.* Reading, PA: Addison-Wesley.

Bloch, M. H., & Qawasmi, A. (2011). Omega-3 fatty acid supplementation for the treatment of children with attention-deficit/hyperactivity disorder symptomatology: Systematic review and meta-analysis. *Journal of the American Academy of Child & Adolescent Psychiatry, 50*, 991–1000. doi:10.1016/j.jaac.2011.06.008

Boelens, P. A., Reeves, R. R., Replogle, W. H., & Koenig, H. G. (2009). A randomized trial of the effect of prayer on depression and anxiety. *International Journal of Psychiatry in Medicine, 39*, 377–392. doi:10.2190/PM.39.4.c

Boelens, P. A., Reeves, R. R., Replogle, W. H., & Koenig, H. G. (2012). The effect of prayer on depression and anxiety: Maintenance of positive influence one year after prayer intervention. *International Journal of Psychiatry in Medicine, 43*, 85–98. doi:10.2190/PM.43.1.f

Borchers, A. T., Keen, C. L., Stern, J. S., & Gershwin, M. E. (2000). Inflammation and Native American medicine: The role of botanicals. *The American Journal of Clinical Nutrition, 72*, 339–347.

Bourgeois, P., Chales, G., Dehais, J., Delcambre, B., Kuntz, J.-L., & Rozenberg, S. (1998). Efficacy and tolerability of chondroitin sulfate 1200 mg/day vs chondroitin sulfate 3× 400 mg/day vs placebo. *Osteoarthritis and Cartilage, 6*, 25–30. doi:10.1016/S1063-4584(98)80008-3

Bowden, D., Goddard, L., & Gruzelier, J. (2010). A randomised controlled single-blind trial of the effects of Reiki and positive imagery on well-being and salivary cortisol. *Brain Research Bulletin, 81*, 66–72. doi:10.1016/j.brainresbull.2009.10.002

Bowden, D., Goddard, L., & Gruzelier, J. (2011). A randomised controlled single-blind trial of the efficacy of Reiki at benefiting mood and well-being. *Evidence-Based Complementary and Alternative Medicine, 2011*, 1–8. doi:10.1155/2011/381862

Boyer College of Music and Dance at Temple University. (2011). *What is music therapy?* Retrieved from http://www.temple.edu/musictherapy/home/program/faq.htm#a

Bräuninger, I. (2012). Dance movement therapy group intervention in stress treatment: A randomized controlled trial (RCT). *The Arts in Psychotherapy, 39*, 443–450. doi:10.1016/j.aip.2012.07.002

Breslin, M. J., & Lewis, C. A. (2008). Theoretical models of the nature of prayer and health: A review. *Mental Health, Religion & Culture, 11*, 9–21. doi:10.1080/13674670701491449

Brinkhaus, B., Witt, C. M., Jena, S., Bockelbrink, A., Ortiz, M., & Willich, S. N. (2011). Integration of complementary and alternative medicine into medical schools in Austria, Germany and Switzerland—results of a cross-sectional study. *Wiener Medizinische Wochenschrift, 161,* 32–43. doi:10.1007/s10354-010-0834-x

Bronfort, G., Evans, R., Nelson, B., Aker, P. D., Goldsmith, C. H., & Vernon, H. (2001). A randomized clinical trial of exercise and spinal manipulation for patients with chronic neck pain. *Spine, 26,* 788–797. doi:10.1097/00007632-200104010-00020

Bronfort, G., Goldsmith, C. H., Nelson, C. F., Boline, P. D., & Anderson, A. V. (1996). Trunk exercise combined with spinal manipulative or NSAID therapy for chronic low back pain: A randomized, observer-blinded clinical trial. *Journal of Manipulative and Physiological Therapeutics, 19,* 570–582.

Bronfort, G., Maiers, M. J., Evans, R. L., Schulz, C. A., Bracha, Y., Svendsen, K. H., . . . Transfeldt, E. E. (2011). Supervised exercise, spinal manipulation, and home exercise for chronic low back pain: A randomized clinical trial. *The Spine Journal, 11,* 585–598. doi:10.1016/j.spinee.2011.01.036

Brooker, D. J. R., Snape, M., Johnson, E., & Ward, D. (1997). Single case evaluation of the effects of aromatherapy and massage on disturbed behaviour in severe dementia. *British Journal of Clinical Psychology, 36,* 287–296. doi:10.1111/j.2044-8260.1997.tb01415.x

Brooks, D., & Stark, A. (1989). The effect of dance/movement therapy on affect: A pilot study. *American Journal of Dance Therapy, 11,* 101–112. doi:10.1007/BF00843774

Brown, D. P., & Fromm, E. (1987). *Hypnosis and behavioral medicine.* Hillsdale, NJ: Erlbaum.

Bruscia, K. E. (1998). *Defining music therapy.* New Braunfels, TX: Barcelona.

Burke, A., Upchurch, D. M., Dye, C., & Chyu, L. (2006). Acupuncture use in the United States: Findings from the National Health Interview Survey. *The Journal of Alternative and Complementary Medicine, 12,* 639–648. doi:10.1089/acm.2006.12.639

Burkett, V. S., Cummins, J. M., Dickson, R. M., & Skolnick, M. (2005). An open clinical trial utilizing real-time EEG operant conditioning as an adjunctive therapy in the treatment of crack cocaine dependence. *Journal of Neurotherapy, 9,* 27–47. doi:10.1300/J184v09n02_03

Buysse, D. J., Reynolds, C. F., Monk, T. H., Berman, S. R., & Kupfer, D. J. (1989). The Pittsburgh Sleep Quality Index (PSQI): A new instrument for psychiatric research and practice. *Psychiatry Research, 28,* 193–213. doi:10.1016/0165-1781(89)90047-4

Cahn, B. R., Delorme, A., & Polich, J. (2013). Event-related delta, theta, alpha and gamma correlates to auditory oddball processing during Vipassana meditation. *Social Cognitive and Affective Neuroscience, 8,* 100–111. doi:10.1093/scan/nss060

Campenni, C. E., Crawley, E. J., & Meier, M. E. (2004). Role of suggestion in odor induced mood change. *Psychological Reports, 94,* 1127–1136.

Campos, M. P., Hassan, B. J., Riechelmann, R., & Del Giglio, A. (2011). Cancer–related fatigue: A practical review. *Annals of Oncology, 22*, 1273–1279. doi: 10.1093/annonc/mdq458

Canning, S., Waterman, M., Orsi, N., Ayres, J., Simpson, N., & Dye, L. (2010). The efficacy of Hypericum perforatum (St John's Wort) for the treatment of premenstrual syndrome. *CNS Drugs, 24*, 207–225. doi:10.2165/11530120-000000000-00000

Cao, H., Pan, X., Li, H., & Liu, J. (2009). Acupuncture for treatment of insomnia: A systematic review of randomized controlled trials. *The Journal of Alternative and Complementary Medicine, 15*, 1171–1186. doi:10.1089/acm.2009.0041

Capasso, L. (1998). 5300 years ago, the Ice Man used natural laxatives and antibiotics. *The Lancet, 352*, 1864. doi:10.1016/S0140-6736(05)79939-6

Cardeña, E., Svensson, C., & Hejdström, F. (2013). Hypnotic tape intervention ameliorates stress: A randomized, control study. *International Journal of Clinical and Experimental Hypnosis, 61*, 125–145. doi:10.1080/00207144.2013.753820

Carei, T. R., Fyfe-Johnson, A. L., Breuner, C. C., & Brown, M. A. (2010). Randomized controlled clinical trial of yoga in the treatment of eating disorders. *Journal of Adolescent Health, 46*, 346–351. doi:10.1016/j.jadohealth.2009.08.007

Carmody, J., & Baer, R. A. (2008). Relationships between mindfulness practice and levels of mindfulness, medical and psychological symptoms and well-being in amindfulness-based stress reduction program. *Journal of Behavioral Medicine, 31*, 23–33. doi:10.1007/s10865-007-9130-7

Carmody, J., & Baer, R. A. (2009). How long does a mindfulness-based stress reduction program need to be? A review of class contact hours and effect sizes for psychological distress. *Journal of Clinical Psychology, 65*, 627–638. doi:10.1002/jclp.20555

Carmody, J., Baer, R. A., Lykins, E. L. B., & Olendzki, N. (2009). An empirical study of the mechanisms of mindfulness in a mindfulness-based stress reduction program. *Journal of Clinical Psychology, 65*, 613–626. doi:10.1002/jclp.20579

Carr, C., D'Ardenne, P., Sloboda, A., Scott, C., Wang, D., & Priebe, S. (2012). Group music therapy for patients with persistent post-traumatic stress disorder-an exploratory randomized controlled trial with mixed methods evaluation. *Psychology and Psychotherapy: Theory, Research, and Practice, 85*, 179–202. doi:10.1111/j.2044-8341.2011.02026.x

Carroll, S. (1993). Spirituality and purpose in life in alcoholism recovery. *Journal of Studies on Alcohol and Drugs, 54*, 297.

Carson, J. W., Carson, K. M., Jones, K. D., Bennett, R. M., Wright, C. L., & Mist, S. D. (2010). A pilot randomized controlled trial of the Yoga of Awareness program in the management of fibromyalgia. *Pain, 151*, 530–539. doi:10.1016/j.pain.2010.08.020

Catlin, A., & Taylor-Ford, R. L. (2011). Investigation of standard care versus sham Reiki placebo versus actual Reiki therapy to enhance comfort and well-being in a chemotherapy infusion center. *Oncology Nursing Forum, 38,* E212–E220. doi:10.1188/11.ONF.E212-E220

Cella, D., Peterman, A., Passik, S., Jacobsen, P., & Breitbart, W. (1998). Progress toward guidelines for the management of fatigue. *Oncology, 12,* 369–377.

Center for Spirituality and Healing. (2009). *Taking charge of your health & well-being: Prayer.* Retrieved from http://www.takingcharge.csh.umn.edu/explore-healing-practices/prayer

Centers for Disease Control and Prevention. (2004). Lead poisoning associated with use of Ayurvedic medications—five states, 2000–2003. *MMWR: Morbidity and Mortality Weekly Report, 53,* 582–584.

Cepeda, M. S., Carr, D. B., Lau, J., & Alvarez, H. (2006). Music for pain relief. *Cochrane Database Syst Rev, 2*(2).

Certification Board for Music Therapists. (2011). *CBMT examination.* Retrieved from http://www.cbmt.org/examination

Chalifour, M., & Champagne, T. (2008) *Aromatherapy.* Retrieved from http://www.ot-innovations.com/content/view/35/46/

Chambless, D. L., & Ollendick, T. H. (2001). Empirically supported psychological interventions: Controversies and evidence. *Annual Review of Psychology, 52*(1), 685–716.

Chapman, R. J. (1996). Spirituality in the treatment of alcoholism: A worldview approach. *Counseling and Values, 41,* 39–50. doi:10.1002/j.2161-007X.1996.tb00861.x

Cheek, D. B. (1994). *Hypnosis: The application of ideomotor techniques.* Boston, MA: Allyn and Bacon.

Chen, M. L., Lin, L. C., Wu, S. C., & Lin, J. G. (1999). The effectiveness of the acupressure in improving the quality of sleep of institutionalized residents. *Journal of Gerontology. Series A, Biological Sciences and Medical Sciences, 54,* M389–394.

Chen, Z. J., Guo, Y. P., & Wu, Z. C. (2008). Observation of the therapeutic of acupuncture at pain points on cancer points. *Chinese Acupuncture & Moxibustion, 28,* 251–253.

Cheng, J., Wang, G., Xiao, L., Wang, H., & Wang, X. (2009). Electro-acupuncture versus sham electro-acupuncture for auditory hallucinations in patients with schizophrenia: A randomized controlled trial. *Clinical Rehabilitation, 23,* 579–588. doi:10.1177/0269215508096172

Cheng, K. J. (2009). Neuroanatomical basis of acupuncture treatment for some common illnesses. *Acupuncture in Medicine, 27,* 61–64. doi:10.1136/aim.2009.000455

Cherkin, D. C., Deyo, R. A., Battié, M., Street, J., & Barlow, W. (1998). A comparison of physical therapy, chiropractic manipulation, and provision of an educational booklet for the treatment of patients with low back pain. *The New England Journal of Medicine, 339,* 1021–1029. doi:10.1056/NEJM19981 0083391502

Chiesa, A., & Serretti, A. (2009). Mindfulness-based stress reduction for stress management in healthy people: A review and meta-analysis. *The Journal of Alternative and Complementary Medicine, 15*, 593–600. doi:10.1089/acm. 2008.0495

Chiesa, A., & Serretti, A. (2010). A systematic review of neurobiological and clinical features of mindfulness meditations. *Psychological Medicine: A Journal of Research in Psychiatry and the Allied Sciences, 40*, 1239–1252. doi:10.1017/S0033291709991747

Chiropractors Association of Australia. (2010). *How does chiropractic work?* Retrieved from http://www.chiropractors.asn.au/index.php?option=com_k2&view=item &layout=item&id=144&Itemid=262

Choi, J., Kim, T.-H., Choi, T.-Y., & Lee, M. S. (2013). Ginseng for health care: A systematic review of randomized controlled trials in Korean literature. *PLoS ONE, 8*, e59978. doi:10.1371/journal.pone.0059978

Clark, M., Isaacks-Downton, G., Wells, N., Redlin-Frazier, S., Eck, C., Hepworth, J. T., . . . Chakravarthy, B. (2006). Use of preferred music to reduce emotional distress and symptom activity during radiation therapy. *Journal of Music Therapy, 43*, 247–265.

Clauson, K. A., Santamarina, M. L., & Rutledge, J. C. (2008). Clinically relevant safety issues associated with St. John's wort product labels. *BMC complementary and alternative medicine, 8*(1), 42.

Cochrane, G., & Friesen, J. (1986). Hypnotherapy in weight loss treatment. *Journal of Consulting and Clinical Psychology, 54*, 489–492. doi:10.1037/0022-006X. 54.4.489

Cohen, M. M., Penman, S., Pirotta, M., & Da Costa, C. (2005). The integration of complementary therapies in Australian general practice: Results of a national survey. *The Journal of Alternative and Complementary Medicine, 11*, 995–1004. doi:10.1089/acm.2005.11.995

Cohen, S. O., & Walco, G. A. (1999). Dance/movement therapy for children and adolescents with cancer. *Cancer Practice, 7*, 34–42. doi:10.1046/j.1523-5394. 1999.07105.x

Collipp, P. J. (1969). The efficacy of prayer: A triple-blind study. *Medical Times, 97*, 201–204.

Complementary and Alternative Medicine. (2011). *Acupuncture and pain: Applying modern science to an ancient practice.* Retrieved from http://nccam.nih.gov/news/newsletter/2010_february/acu.htm

Cook, C. C. (2004). Addiction and spirituality. *Addiction, 99*, 539–551. doi:10.1111/j.1360-0443.2004.00715.x

Cooke, B., & Ernst, E. (2000). Aromatherapy: A systematic review. *The British Journal of General Practice, 50*, 493–496.

Cooke, M., Holzhauser, K., Jones, M., Davis, C., & Finucane, J. (2007). The effect of aromatherapy massage with music on the stress and anxiety levels of emergency nurses: Comparison between summer and winter. *Journal of Clinical Nursing, 16,* 1695–1703. doi:10.1111/j.1365-2702.2007.01709.x

Cooper, Z., & Fairburn, C. (1987). The Eating Disorder Examination: A semi-structured interview for the assessment of the specific psychopathology of eating disorders. *International Journal of Eating Disorders, 6,* 1–8. doi:10.1002/1098-108X(198701)6:1{1::AID-EAT2260060102}3.0.CO;2-9

Côté, P., & Mierau, D. (1995). Chiropractic management of primary nocturnal enuresis. *Journal of Manipulative and Physiological Therapeutics, 18,* 184–190.

Cottone, R. R., & Claus, R. E. (2000). Ethical decision-making models: A review of the literature. *Journal of Counseling & Development, 78,* 275–283. doi:10.1002/j.1556-6676.2000.tb01908.x

Coulehan, J. L. (1985). Chiropractic and the clinical art. *Social Science & Medicine, 21,* 383–390. doi:10.1016/0277-9536(85)90218-7

Cox, P. A., & Balick, M. J. (1994). The ethnobotanical approach to drug discovery. *Scientific American, 270,* 82–87. doi:10.1038/scientificamerican0694-82

Cramer, H., Lauche, R., Klose, P., Langhorst, J., & Dobos, G. (2013). Yoga for schizophrenia: A systematic review and meta-analysis. *BMC Psychiatry, 13,* 32. doi:10.1186/1471-244X-13-32

Crane, F. L. (2001). Biochemical functions of coenzyme Q10. *Journal of the American College of Nutrition, 20,* 591–598. doi:10.1080/07315724.2001.10719063

Crane-Okada, R., Kiger, H., Anderson, N. L., Carroll-Johnson, R. M., Sugerman, F., Shapiro, S. L., & Wyman-McGinty, W. (2012). Participant perceptions of a mindful movement program for older women with breast cancer: Focus group results. *Cancer Nursing, 35,* E1–10. doi:10.1097/NCC.0b013e31822539c5

Crasilneck, H. B., & Hall, J. A. (1985). *Clinical hypnosis: Principles and applications* (pp. 245–246). New York, NY: Grune & Stratton.

Crawford, H. J., Gur, R. C., Skolnick, B., Gur, R. E., & Benson, D. M. (1993). Effects of hypnosis on regional cerebral blood flow during ischemic pain with and without suggested hypnotic analgesia. *International Journal of Psychophysiology, 15,* 181–195. doi:10.1016/0167-8760(93)90002-7

Cristina, E. D. (2004). Understanding true aromatherapy: Understanding essential oils. *Home Health Care Management & Practice, 16,* 474–479. doi:10.1177/1084822304265851

Cronfalk, B. S., Strang, P., & Ternestedt, B. M. (2009). Inner power, physical strength and existential well-being in daily life: Relatives' experiences of received soft tissue massage in palliative home care. *Journal of Clinical Nursing, 18,* 2225–2233. doi:10.1111/j.1365-2702.2008.02517.x

Cruz, R. F. (2002). Perspectives on the profession of dance/movement therapy: Past, present and future. *Bulletin of Psychology and the Arts, 2,* 74–78.

Cruz, R. F. (2006). Assessment in dance/movement therapy. In S. Brooke (Ed.), *Creative arts therapies manual: A guide to the history, theoretical approaches, assessment, and work with special populations of art, play, dance, music, drama, and poetry therapies* (pp. 133–142). Springfield, IL: Charles C Thomas.

Curl, D. D. (1994). *Chiropractic approach to head pain*. Baltimore, MD: Williams & Wilkins.

Dang, W., & Yang, J. (1998). Clinical study on acupuncture treatment of stomach carcinoma pain. *Journal of Traditional Chinese Medicine, 18*, 31–38.

d'Angelo, R. (2002). Aromatherapy. In S. Shannon (Ed.), *Handbook of complementary and alternative therapies in mental health* (pp. 71–92). San Diego, CA: Academic Press. doi:10.1016/B978-012638281-5/50005-X

DeKosky, S. T., Williamson, J. D., Fitzpatrick, A. L., Kronmal, R. A., Ives, D. G., Saxton, J. A., . . . Fried, L. P. (2008). Ginkgo biloba for prevention of dementia. *JAMA, 300*, 2253–2262. doi:10.1001/jama.2008.683

Deng, G., Chan, Y., Sjoberg, D., Vickers, A., Yeung, S., Kris, M., . . . Cassileth, B. (2013). Acupuncture for the treatment of post-chemotherapy chronic fatigue: A randomized, blinded, sham-controlled trial. *Supportive Care in Cancer, 21*, 1735–1741. doi:10.1007/s00520-013-1720-z

Deng, G. E., Frankel, M., Cohen, L., Cassileth, B., Abrams, D., Capodice, J., . . . Sagar, S. (2009). Evidence-based clinical practice guidelines for integrative oncology: Complementary therapies and botanicals. *Journal of the Society for Integrative Oncology, 7*, 85–120.

DeVocht, J. W. (2006). History and overview of theories and methods of chiropractic: A counterpoint. *Clinical Orthopaedics and Related Research, 444*, 243–249. doi:10.1097/01.blo.0000203460.89887.8d

Dhond, R. P., Kettner, N., & Napadow, V. (2007). Neuroimaging acupuncture's effects in the brain. *The Journal of Alternative and Complementary Medicine, 13*, 603–616. doi:10.1089/acm.2007.7040

Dibbell-Hope, S. (2000). The use of dance/movement therapy in psychological adaptation to breast cancer. *The Arts in Psychotherapy, 27*, 51–68. doi:10.1016/S0197-4556(99)00032-5

Diego, M. A., Field, T., & Hernandez-Reif, M. (2002). Spinal cord patients benefit from massage therapy. *International Journal of Neuroscience, 112*, 133–142. doi:10.1080/00207450212023

Diego, M. A., Jones, N. A., Field, T., Hernandez-Reif, M., Schanberg, S., Kuhn, C., . . . Galamaga, M. (1998). Aromatherapy positively affects mood, EEG patterns of alertness and math computations. *International Journal of Neuroscience, 96*, 217–224. doi:10.3109/00207459808986469

Dietz, B. M., & Bolton, J. L. (2011). Biological reactive intermediates (BRIs) formed from botanical dietary supplements. *Chemico-Biological Interactions, 192*, 72–80.

Dinges, D. F., Whitehouse, W. G., Orne, E. C., Bloom, P. B., Carlin, M. M., Bauer, N. K., . . . Orne, M. T. (1997). Self-hypnosis training as an adjunctive treatment in the management of pain associated with sickle cell disease. *International Journal of Clinical and Experimental Hypnosis, 45*, 417–432. doi:10.1080/00207149708416141

Dinsmoor, R. S. (2006, June). *Biofeedback*. Retrieved from http://www.diabetesselfmanagement.com/articles/diabetes-definitions/biofeedback

Dittman, M. (2004). Alternative health care gains steam. *Monitor on Psychology, 35,* 42–45.

Dodge, T., & Kaufman, A. (2007). What makes consumers think dietary supplements are safe and effective? The role of disclaimers and FDA approval. *Health Psychology, 26,* 513–517.

Duke Center for Integrative Medicine. (2006). *The Duke encyclopedia of new medicine: Conventional & alternative medicine for all ages.* London, England: Rodale Books International.

Ehrlich, S. D. (2009). *Biofeedback.* Retrieved from http://www.umm.edu/altmed/articles/biofeedback-000349.htm

Eich, H., Agelink, M. W., Lehmann, E., Lemmer, W., & Kliesser, E. (2000). Acupuncture in patients with minor depression or generalized anxiety disorder: Results of an experimental study. *Fortschritte der Neurologie-Psychiatrie, 68,* 137–144.

Eisenberg, D. M., Davis, R. B., Ettner, S. L., Appel, S., Wilkey, S., Van Rompay, M., & Kessler, R. C. (1998). Trends in alternative medicine use in the United States, 1990–1997. *JAMA, 280,* 1569–1575. doi:10.1001/jama.280.18.1569

Eisenberg, D. M., Kessler, R. C., Foster, C., Norlock, F. E., Calkins, D. R., & Delbanco, T. L. (1993). Unconventional medicine in the United States: Prevalence, costs, and patterns of use. *The New England Journal of Medicine, 328,* 246–252. doi:10.1056/NEJM199301283280406

Elkins, G., Marcus, J., Bates, J., Rajab, H. M., & Cook, T. (2006). Intensive hypnotherapy for smoking cessation: A prospective study. *International Journal of Clinical and Experimental Hypnosis, 54,* 303–315. doi:10.1080/0020714 0600689512

Elkins, G., Marcus, J., Rajab, M. H., & Durgam, S. (2005). Complementary and alternative therapy use by psychotherapy clients. *Psychotherapy: Theory, Research, Practice, Training, 42,* 232–235. doi:10.1037/0033-3204.42.2.232

Elkins, G., Marcus, J., Stearns, V., Perfect, M., Rajab, M. H., Ruud, C., . . . Keith, T. (2008). Randomized trial of a hypnosis intervention for treatment of hot flashes among breast cancer survivors. *Journal of Clinical Oncology, 26,* 5022–5026. doi:10.1200/JCO.2008.16.6389

Elkins, G., & Perfect, M. (2008). Hypnosis for health-compromising behaviors. In M. Nash & A. Barnier (Eds.), *The Oxford handbook of hypnosis: Theory, research and practice* (pp. 569–592). New York, NY: Oxford University Press. doi:10.1093/oxfordhb/9780198570097.013.0023

Elkins, G., Sliwinski, J., Bowers, J., & Encarnacion, E. (2013). Feasibility of clinical hypnosis for the treatment of Parkinson's disease: A case study. *International Journal of Clinical and Experimental Hypnosis, 61,* 172–182. doi:10.1080/002071 44.2013.753829

Elkins, G. R. (2013). *Hypnotic relaxation therapy: Principles and applications.* New York, NY: Springer.

Elkins, G. R., & Hammond, D. C. (1998). Standards of training in clinical hypnosis: Preparing professionals for the 21st century. *American Journal of Clinical Hypnosis, 41,* 55–64. doi:10.1080/00029157.1998.10404185

Elkins, G. R., & Rajab, M. H. (2004). Clinical hypnosis for smoking cessation: Preliminary results of a three-session intervention. *International Journal of Clinical and Experimental Hypnosis, 52,* 73–81. doi:10.1076/iceh.52.1.73.23921

Ellis, R. J., & Thayer, J. F. (2010). Music and autonomic nervous system dysfunction. *Music Perception, 27,* 317–326. doi:10.1525/mp.2010.27.4.317

Emmerson, G., & Trexler, G. (1999). An hypnotic intervention for migraine control. *Australian Journal of Clinical & Experimental Hypnosis, 27,* 54–61.

Eppley, K. R., Abrams, A. I., & Shear, J. (1989). Differential effects of relaxation techniques on trait anxiety: A meta-analysis. *Journal of Clinical Psychology, 45*(6), 957–974.

Ergil, K., & Ergil, M. (2010). Acupuncture. In M. S. Micozzi (Ed.), *Fundamentals of complementary and alternative medicine* (4th ed., pp. 403–437). St. Louis, MO: Saunders Elsevier.

Ericksen, M. (1994). *Aromatherapy for childbearing.* Retrieved from http://www.gentlebirth.org/archives/aromathr.html

Erkkilä, J., Punkanen, M., Fachner, J., Ala-Ruona, E., Pontio, I., Tervaniemi, M., . . . Gold, C. (2011). Individual music therapy for depression: Randomized controlled trial. *The British Journal of Psychiatry, 199,* 132–139. doi:10.1192/bjp.bp.110.085431

Ernst, E. (2003). Chiropractic spinal manipulation for neck pain: A systematic review. *The Journal of Pain, 4,* 417–421. doi:10.1067/S1526-5900(03)00735-1

Ernst, E. (2007). Adverse effects of spinal manipulation: A systematic review. *Journal of the Royal Society of Medicine, 100,* 330–338. doi:10.1258/jrsm.100.7.330

Ernst, E. (2008). Chiropractic: A critical evaluation. *Journal of Pain and Symptom Management, 35,* 544–562. doi:10.1016/j.jpainsymman.2007.07.004

Ernst, E. (2010). *Panax ginseng:* An overview of the clinical evidence. *Journal of Ginseng Research, 34,* 259–263. doi:10.5142/jgr.2010.34.4.259

Ernst, E., & Harkness, E. (2001). Spinal manipulation: A systematic review of sham-controlled, double-blind, randomized clinical trials. *Journal of Pain and Symptom Management, 22,* 879–889. doi:10.1016/S0885-3924(01)00337-2

Ernst, E., & White, A. R. (2001). Prospective studies of the safety of acupuncture: a systematic review. *The American Journal of Medicine, 110,* 481–485.

Esterlis, I., Cosgrove, K. P., Batis, J. C., Bois, F., Kloczynski, T. A., Stiklus, S. M., . . . Staley, J. K. (2009). GABAA-benzodiazepine receptor availability in smokers and nonsmokers: Relationship to subsyndromal anxiety and depression. *Synapse, 63,* 1089–1099. doi:10.1002/syn.20688

Evans, D. (2002). The effectiveness of music as an intervention for hospital patients: A systematic review. *Journal of Advanced Nursing, 37,* 8–18. doi:10.1046/j.1365-2648.2002.02052.x

Everett, J. J., Patterson, D. R., Burns, G. L., Montgomery, B., & Heimbach, D. (1993). Adjunctive interventions for burn pain control: Comparison of hypnosis and ativan: The 1993 Clinical Research Award. *The Journal of Burn Care & Rehabilitation, 14*, 676–683. doi:10.1097/00004630-199311000-00014

Ezra, Y., Gotkine, M., Goldman, S., Adahan, H. M., & Ben-Hur, T. (2012). Hypnotic relaxation vs amitriptyline for tension-type headache: Let the patient choose. *Headache, 52*, 785–791. doi:10.1111/j.1526-4610.2011.02055.x

Fang, C. Y., Reibel, D. K., Longacre, M. L., Rosenzweig, S., Campbell, D. E., & Douglas, S. D. (2010). Enhanced psychosocial well-being following participation in a mindfulness-based stress reduction program is associated with increased natural killer cell activity. *The Journal of Alternative and Complementary Medicine, 16*, 531–538. doi:10.1089/acm.2009.0018

Faymonville, M. E., Mambourg, P. H., Joris, J., Vrijens, B., Fissette, J., Albert, A., & Lamy, M. (1997). Psychological approaches during conscious sedation. Hypnosis versus stress reducing strategies: A prospective randomized study. *Pain, 73*, 361–367. doi:10.1016/S0304-3959(97)00122-X

Fehring, R. J., Miller, J. F., & Shaw, C. (1997). Spiritual well-being, religiousness, hope, depression, and other mood states in elderly people coping with cancer. *Oncology Nursing Forum, 24*, 663–671.

Field, T. (1998). Massage therapy effects. *American Psychologist, 53*, 1270–1281. doi:10.1037/0003-066X.53.12.1270

Field, T. (2000). *Touch therapy.* New York, NY: Churchill Livingston.

Field, T. (2006). *Massage therapy research.* New York, NY: Elsevier.

Field, T., Diego, M., & Hernandez-Reif, M. (2006). Prenatal depression effects on the fetus and the newborn: A review. *Infant Behavior & Development, 29*, 445–455. doi:10.1016/j.infbeh.2006.03.003

Field, T., Hernandez-Reif, M., Diego, M., Feijo, L., Vera, Y., & Gil, K. (2004). Massage therapy by parents improves early growth and development. *Infant Behavior and Development, 27*, 435–442.

Field, T. M. (2008). *Complementary and alternative therapies research.* Washington, DC: American Psychological Association.

Fischer-Terworth, C. (2010). *Psychological therapies in dementia: Evaluation of a TEACCH-based music therapy intervention* (Doctoral dissertation, University of Hamburg). Saarbrücken, Germany: Südwestdeutscher Verlag für Hochschulschriften.

Fischer-Terworth, C., & Probst, P. (2011). Evaluation of a TEACCH- and music therapy-based intervention in mild to moderate dementia. *Geriatric Psychology, 24*, 93–101. doi:10.1024/1662-9647/a000037

Forbes, A., MacAuley, S., & Chiotakakou-Faliakou, E. (2000). Hypnotherapy and therapeutic audiotape: effective in previously unsuccessfully treated irritable bowel syndrome? *International Journal of Colorectal Disease, 15*, 328–334.

Foster, R. (1992). *Prayer: Finding the heart's true home.* New York, NY: HarperCollins.

Fowler, N. A. (2006). Aromatherapy, used as an integrative tool for crisis management by adolescents in a residential treatment center. *Journal of Child and Adolescent Psychiatric Nursing, 19*, 69–76. doi:10.1111/j.1744-6171.2006.00048.x

Frank, R., & Stollberg, G. (2002). Ayurvedic patients in Germany. *Anthropology & Medicine, 9*, 223–244. doi:10.1080/13648470216332

Freedman, R. R., Ianni, P., & Wenig, P. (1985). Behavioral treatment of Raynaud's disease: Long-term follow-up. *Journal of Consulting and Clinical Psychology, 53*, 136. doi:10.1037/0022-006X.53.1.136

Freedman, R. R., Sabharwal, S. G., Ianni, P., Desai, N., Wenig, P., & Mayes, M. (1988). Nonneural beta-adrenergic vasodilating mechanism in temperature biofeedback. *Psychosomatic Medicine, 50*, 394–401.

Freeman, L. W., & Lawlis, G. F. (2001). *Mosby's complementary and alternative medicine—A research based approach.* St. Louis, MO: Mosby.

Furlan, A. D., Imamura, M., Dryden, T., & Irvin, E. (2008). Massage for low-back pain. *Cochrane Database of Systematic Reviews, 4.* Retrieved from http://onlinelibrary. wiley.com/doi/10.1002/14651858.CD001929.pub2/abstract

Galili, O., Shaoul, R., & Mogilner, J. (2009). Treatment of chronic recurrent abdominal pain: Laparoscopy or hypnosis? *Journal of Laparoendoscopic & Advanced Surgical Techniques. Part A., 19*, 93–96. doi:10.1089/lap.2008.0059

Galton, F. (1872). Statistical inquiries into the efficacy of prayer. *Fortnightly Review, 12*, 125–135.

Gardner, C. D., Lawson, L. D., Block, E., Chatterjee, L. M., Kiazand, A., Balise, R. R., & Kraemer, H. C. (2007). Effect of raw garlic vs commercial garlic supplements on plasma lipid concentrations in adults with moderate hypercholesterolemia: A randomized clinical trial. *Archives of Internal Medicine, 167*, 346–353. doi:10.1001/archinte.167.4.346

Gay, M. C., Philippot, P., & Luminet, O. (2002). Differential effectiveness of psychological interventions for reducing osteoarthritis pain: A comparison of Erikson [correction of Erickson] hypnosis and Jacobson relaxation. *European Journal of Pain, 6*, 1–16. doi:10.1053/eujp.2001.0263

Geffen, J. R. (2010). *Dance therapy.* Retrieved from http://www.caring4cancer.com/ go/cancer/wellbeing/complementary-alternative/dance-therapy.htm

Geffen, J. R. (2011). *Music therapy.* Retrieved from http://www.caring4cancer.com/ go/cancer/wellbeing/complementary-alternative/music-therapy.htm

Ginandes, C. S., & Rosenthal, D. I. (1999). Using hypnosis to accelerate the healing of bone fractures: A randomized controlled pilot study. *Alternative Therapies in Health and Medicine, 5*, 67–75.

Glaser, J. L. (1988). Maharishi Ayurveda: An introduction to recent research. *Modern Science and Vedic Science, 2*, 88–108.

Glasziou, P., Vandenbroucke, J. P., & Chalmers, I. (2004). Assessing the quality of research. *BMJ, 328*, 39–41. doi:10.1136/bmj.328.7430.39

Glover, F. S. (1961). Use of hypnosis for weight reduction in a group of nurses. *The American Journal of Clinical Hypnosis, 3*, 250–251. doi:10.1080/00029157.1961.10401851

Glynn, T. J., & Manley, M. (1993). *How to help your patients stop smoking: A National Cancer Institute manual for physicians* (Issues 90-3064). Bethesda, MD: Smoking and Tobacco Control Program. Division of Cancer Prevention and Control, National Cancer Institute, U.S. Department of Health and Human Services, Public Health Service, National Institutes of Health.

Goats, G. C. (1994). Massage—the scientific basis of an ancient art: Part 1. The techniques. *British Journal of Sports Medicine, 28*, 149–152.

Gobel, B. H., Beck, S. L., & O'Leary, C. (2006). Nursing-sensitive patient outcomes: The development of the Putting Evidence Into Practice resources for nursing practice. *Clinical Journal of Oncology Nursing, 10*, 621–624. doi:10.1188/06.CJON.621-624

Göbel, H., Fresenius, J., Heinze, A., Dworschak, M., & Soyka, D. (1996). Effectiveness of Oleum menthae piperitae and paracetamol in therapy of headache of the tension type. *Der Nervenarzt, 67*, 672–681.

Göbel, H., Schmidt, G., Dworschak, M., Stolze, H., & Heuss, D. (1995). Essential plant oils and headache mechanisms. *Phytomedicine, 2*, 93–102. doi:10.1016/S0944-7113(11)80053-X

Göbel, H., Schmidt, G., & Soyka, D. (1994). Effect of peppermint and eucalyptus oil preparations on neurophysiological and experimental algesimetric headache parameters. *Cephalalgia, 14*, 228–234. doi:10.1046/j.1468-2982.1994.014003228.x

Godfrey, C. M., Morgan, P. P., & Schatzker, J. (1984). A randomized trial of manipulation for low-back pain in a medical setting. *Spine, 9*, 301–304. doi:10.1097/00007632-198404000-00015

Gold, C., Solli, H. P., Krüger, V., & Lie, S. A. (2009). Dose–response relationship in music therapy for people with serious mental disorders: Systematic review and meta-analysis. *Clinical Psychology Review, 29*, 193–207.

Goldin, P. R., & Gross, J. J. (2010). Effects of mindfulness-based stress reduction (MBSR) on emotion regulation in social anxiety disorder. *Emotion, 10*, 83–91. doi:10.1037/a0018441

Grant, J. A., Courtemanche, J., & Rainville, P. (2011). A non-elaborative mental stance and decoupling of executive and pain-related cortices predicts low pain sensitivity in Zen meditators. *Pain, 152*, 150–156. doi:10.1016/j.pain.2010.10.006

Gravitz, M. A., & Gerton, M. I. (1984). Origins of the term hypnotism prior to Braid. *American Journal of Clinical Hypnosis, 27*, 107–110. doi:10.1080/00029157.1984.10402865

Green, J. P., Barabasz, A. F., Barrett, D., & Montgomery, G. H. (2005). Forging ahead: The 2003 APA Division 30 definition of hypnosis. *International Journal of Clinical and Experimental Hypnosis, 53*, 259–264. doi:10.1080/00207140590961321

Griggs, B., & Van der Zee, B. (1997). *Green pharmacy: The history and evolution of Western herbal medicine*. Rochester, VT: Inner Traditions/Bear.

Grøndahl, J. R., & Rosvold, E. O. (2008). Hypnosis as a treatment of chronic widespread pain in general practice: A randomized controlled pilot trial. *BMC Musculoskeletal Disorders, 9*, 1–7. doi:10.1186/1471-2474-9-124

Grossman, P., Niemann, L., Schmidt, S., & Walach, H. (2004). Mindfulness-based stress reduction and health benefits: A metaanalysis. *Journal of Psychosomatic Research, 57*, 35–43. doi:10.1016/S0022-3999(03)00573-7

Guétin, S. G., Ginies, P., Siou, D. K., Picot, M. C., Pommie, C., Guldner, E., . . . Touchon, J. (2012). The effects of music intervention in the management of chronic pain: A single-blind, randomized controlled trial. *The Clinical Journal of Pain, 28*, 329–337. doi:10.1097/AJP.0b013e31822be973

Guyatt, G. H., Oxman, A. D., Vist, G. E., Kunz, R., Falck-Ytter, Y., Alonso-Coello, P., & Schünemann, H. J. (2008). GRADE: An emerging consensus on rating quality of evidence and strength of recommendations. *BMJ, 336*, 924–926. doi:10.1136/bmj.39489.470347.AD

Haake, M., Müller, H. H., Schade-Brittinger, C., Basler, H. D., Schafer, H., Maier, C., . . . Molsberger, A. (2007). German Acupuncture Trials (GERAC) for chronic low back pain: randomized, multicenter, blinded, parallel-group trial with 3 groups. *Archives of Internal Medicine, 167*, 1892–1898. doi:10.1001/Archinte.167.17.1892

Haldeman, S. (2005). *Principles and practice of chiropractic* (3rd ed.). York, PA: McGraw-Hill.

Haldeman, S., Carey, P., Townsend, M., & Papadopoulos, C. (2001). Arterial dissections following cervical manipulation: The chiropractic experience. *Canadian Medical Association Journal, 165*, 905–906. Retrieved from http://www.cmaj.ca/cgi/reprint/165/7/905

Haller, C. A., Benowitz, N. L., & Jacob III, P. (2005). Hemodynamic effects of ephedra-free weight-loss supplements in humans. *The American Journal of Medicine, 118*, 998–1003.

Hamilton, M. (1959). The assessment of anxiety state by rating. *British Journal of Medical Psychology, 32*, 50–55. doi:10.1111/j.2044-8341.1959.tb00467.x

Hamilton, M. (1960). A rating scale for depression. *Journal of Neurology, Neurosurgery, & Psychiatry, 23*, 56–62. doi:10.1136/jnnp.23.1.56

Hamilton, M. (1967). Development of a rating scale for primary depressive illness. *British Journal of Clinical Psychology, 6*, 278–296.

Hammond, D. C. (2005). Neurofeedback treatment of depression and anxiety. *Journal of Adult Development, 12*, 131–137. doi:10.1007/s10804-005-7029-5

Hammond, D. C. (2007). Review of the efficacy of clinical hypnosis with headaches and migraines. *International Journal of Clinical and Experimental Hypnosis, 55*, 207–219. doi:10.1080/00207140601177921

Hammond, D. C., & Elkins, G. R. (1994). *Standards of training in clinical hypnosis*. Des Plaines, IL: American Society of Clinical Hypnosis Press.

Han, J. S., & Terenius, L. (1982). Neurochemical basis of acupuncture analgesia. *Annual Review of Pharmacology and Toxicology, 22*, 193–220. doi:10.1146/annurev.pa.22.040182.001205

Han, P., Kwan, M., Chen, D., Yusoff, S. Z., Chionh, H. L., Goh, J., & Yap, P. (2010). A controlled naturalistic study on a weekly music therapy and activity program on disruptive and depressive behaviors in dementia. *Dementia and Geriatric Cognitive Disorders, 30*, 540–546. doi:10.1159/000321668

Han, S. H., Hur, M., Buckle, J., Choi, J., & Lee, M. S. (2006). Effect of aromatherapy on symptoms of dysmenorrhea in college students: A randomized placebo-controlled clinical trial. *The Journal of Alternative and Complementary Medicine, 12*, 535–541. doi:10.1089/acm.2006.12.535

Haneline, M. T., Croft, A. C., & Frishberg, B. M. (2003). Association of internal carotid artery dissection and chiropractic manipulation. *The Neurologist, 9*, 35–44. doi:10.1097/01.nrl.0000038583.58012.10

Harden, R. N., Houle, T. T., Green, S., Remble, T. A., Weinland, S. R., Colio, S., . . . Kuiken, T. (2005). Biofeedback in the treatment of phantom limb pain: A time-series analysis. *Applied Psychophysiology and Biofeedback, 30*, 83–93. doi:10.1007/s10484-005-2177-8

Hardy, K., & Pollard, H. (2006). The organisation of the stress response, and its relevance to chiropractors: A commentary. *Chiropractic & Osteopathy, 14*, 1–13. doi:10.1186/1746-1340-14-25

Harris, W. S., Gowda, M., Kolb, J. W., Strychacz, C. P., Vacek, J. L., Jones, P. G., . . . McCallister, B. D. (1999). A randomized, controlled trial of the effects of remote, intercessory prayer on outcomes in patients admitted to the coronary care unit. *Archives of Internal Medicine, 159*, 2273–2278. doi:10.1001/archinte.159.19.2273

Hassett, A. L., Radvanski, D. C., Vaschillo, E. G., Vaschillo, B., Sigal, L. H., Karavidas, M. K., & Lehrer, P. M. (2007). A pilot study of the efficacy of heart rate variability (HRV) biofeedback in patients with fibromyalgia. *Applied Psychophysiology and Biofeedback, 32*, 1–10. doi:10.1007/s10484-006-9028-0

Hatch, J. P., Fisher, J. G., & Rugh, J. D. (Eds.). (1987). *Biofeedback: Studies in clinical efficacy*. New York, NY: Plenum Press.

Hathaway, L., Scott, S. Y., & Garver, S. A. (2004). Assessing religious/spiritual functioning: A neglected domain in clinical practice? *Professional Psychology: Research and Practice, 35*, 97–104. doi:10.1037/0735-7028.35.1.97

Hawk, C., Long, C. R., Reiter, R., Davis, C. S., Cambron, J. A., & Evans, R. (2002). Issues in planning a placebo-controlled trial of manual methods: Results of a pilot study. *The Journal of Alternative and Complementary Medicine, 8*, 21–32. doi:10.1089/107555302753507159

Hawk, C., Long, C. R., Rowell, R. M., Gudavalli, M. R., & Jedlicka, J. (2005). A randomized trial investigating a chiropractic manual placebo: A novel design using standardized forces in the delivery of active and control treatments. *The Journal of Alternative and Complementary Medicine, 11,* 109–117. doi:10.1089/acm.2005.11.109

Hawkins, R. S., & Hart, A D. (2003). The use of thermal biofeedback in the treatment of pain associated with endometriosis: Preliminary findings. *Applied Psychophysiology and Biofeedback, 28,* 279–289. doi:10.1023/A:1027378825194

Hayashi, N., Tanabe, Y., Nakagawa, S., Noguchi, M., Iwata, C., Koubuchi, Y., . . . Koike, I. (2002). Effects of group music therapy on in patients with chronic psychoses: A controlled study. *Psychiatry Clinical Neuroscience, 56,* 187–193.

Hayes, S. C., Strosahl, K. D., & Wilson, K. G. (1999). *Acceptance and commitment therapy: An experiential approach to behavior change.* New York, NY: Guilford Press.

Henderson, L., Yue, Q. Y., Bergquist, C., Gerden, B., & Arlett, P. (2002). St John's wort (*Hypericum perforatum*): Drug interactions and clinical outcomes. *British Journal of Clinical Pharmacology, 54,* 349–356. doi:10.1046/j.1365-2125.2002.01683.x

Herbal Medicines Advisory Committee (2008). *Public health risk with herbal medicines: An overview.* United Kingdom Medicines and Healthcare Products Regulatory Agency. Retrieved from http://www.mhra.gov.uk/home/groups/es-herbal/documents/websiteresources/con023163.pdf

Hernandez-Reif, M., Field, T., Krasnegor, J., Theakston, H., Hossain, Z., & Burman, I. (2000). High blood pressure and associated symptoms were reduced by massage therapy. *Journal of Bodywork and Movement Therapies, 4,* 31–38. doi:10.1054/jbmt.1999.0129

Herz, R. S. (2009). Aromatherapy facts and fictions: A scientific analysis of olfactory effects on mood, physiology and behavior. *The International Journal of Neuroscience, 119,* 263–290. doi:10.1080/00207450802333953

Hofmann, S. G., Grossman, P., & Hinton, D. E. (2011). Loving-kindness and compassion meditation: Potential for psychological interventions. *Clinical Psychology Review, 31,* 1126–1132. doi:10.1016/j.cpr.2011.07.003

Holmes, C., Hopkins, V., Hensford, C., MacLaughlin, V., Wilkinson, D., & Rosenvinge, H. (2002). Lavender oil as a treatment for agitated behaviour in severe dementia: A placebo controlled study. *International Journal of Geriatric Psychiatry, 17,* 305–308. doi:10.1002/gps.593

Holmes, D. (2012). Music therapy's breakthrough act. *Lancet Neurology, 11,* 486–487. doi:10.1016/S1474-4422(12)70126-6

Holroyd, J. (1980). Hypnosis treatment for smoking: An evaluative review. *International Journal of Clinical and Experimental Hypnosis, 28,* 341–357. doi:10.1080/00207148008409863

Hölzel, B. K., Carmody, J., Vangel, M., Congleton, C., Yerramsetti, S. M., Gard, T., & Lazar, S. W. (2011). Mindfulness practice leads to increases in regional brain gray matter density. *Psychiatry Research, 191,* 36–43. doi:10.1016/j.pscychresns.2010.08.006

Hou, W. H., Chiang, P. T., Hsu, T. Y., Chiu, S. Y., & Yen, Y. C. (2010). Treatment effects of massage therapy in depressed people: a meta-analysis. *The Journal of Clinical Psychiatry, 71,* 894–901.

Howard, S., & Hughes, B. M. (2008). Expectancies, not aroma, explain impact of lavender aromatherapy on psychophysiological indices of relaxation in young healthy women. *British Journal of Health Psychology, 13,* 603–617. doi:10.1348/ 135910707X238734

Howes, M.-J. R., & Houghton, P. J. (2003). Plants used in Chinese and Indian traditional medicine for improvement of memory and cognitive function. *Pharmacology, Biochemistry and Behavior, 75,* 513–527. doi:10.1016/S0091- 3057(03)00128-X

Hsieh, C. Y. J., Adams, A. H., Tobis, J., Hong, C. Z., Danielson, C., Platt, K., . . . Rubel, A. (2002). Effectiveness of four conservative treatments for subacute low back pain: A randomized clinical trial. *Spine, 27,* 1142–1148. doi:10.1097/00007632-200206010-00003

Huang, L. S., Wang, D. L., Wang, C. W., Hu, Y. P., Zhou, J. W., & Li, N. (2009). The needle-rolling therapy for treatment of non-organic chronic insomnia in 90 cases. *Journal of Traditional Chinese Medicine, 29,* 19–23. doi:10.1016/ S0254-6272(09)60025-X

Hur, M. H., Lee, M. S., Kim, C., & Ernst, E. (2012). Aromatherapy for treatment of hypertension: A systematic review. *Journal of Evaluation in Clinical Practice, 18,* 37–41. doi:10.1111/j.1365-2753.2010.01521.x

Hur, M. H., Oh, H., Lee, M. S., Kim, C., Choi, A. N., & Shin, G. R. (2007). Effects of aromatherapy massage on blood pressure and lipid profile in Korean climacteric women. *International Journal of Neuroscience, 117,* 1281–1287. doi:10.1080/00207450600936650

Institute for Alternative Futures. (2005). *The future of chiropractic revisited: 2005–2015.* Retrieved from http://www.altfutures.com/future-chiropractic-revisited-2005-2015

International Center for Reiki Training. (2011). *Reiki, questions and answers.* Retrieved from http://www.reiki.org/FAQ/Questions&Answers.html

International Encyclopedia of Rehabilitation. (2010). *Alternative therapy: TCM therapies.* Retrieved from http://cirrie.buffalo.edu/encyclopedia/en/article/325

International Society for Neurofeedback and Research (2011). *The mission of ISNR.* Retrieved from http://www.isnr.org/about-isnr/our_mission.cfm

Itai, T., Amayasu, H., Kuribayashi, M., Kawamura, N., Okada, M., Momose, A., . . . Kaneko, S. (2000). Psychological effects of aromatherapy on chronic hemodialysis patients. *Psychiatry and Clinical Neurosciences, 54,* 393–397. doi:10.1046/j.1440-1819.2000.00727.x

Iyengar-yoga.com. (2011). *What is Iyengar yoga?* Retrieved from http://www.iyengar-yoga.com/iyengaryoga

Jacknow, D. S., Tschann, J. M., Link, M. P., & Boyce, W. T. (1994). Hypnosis in the prevention of chemotherapy-related nausea and vomiting in children: A prospective study. *Journal of Developmental and Behavioral Pediatrics, 15,* 258–264. doi:10.1097/00004703-199408000-00007

Jacobs, B., & Gundling, K. (2009). *American College of Physicians evidence-based guide to complementary and alternative medicine.* Washington, DC: American College of Physicians.

Jacobsen, P. B., Hann, D. M., Azzarello, L. M., Horton, J., Balducci, L., & Lyman, G. H. (1999). Fatigue in women receiving adjunct chemotherapy for breast cancer: Characteristics, course, and correlate. *Journal of Pain and Symptom Management, 18,* 233–242. doi:10.1016/S0885-3924(99)00082-2

Jacobson, A. M., Manschreck, T. C., & Silverberg, E. (1979). Behavioral treatment for Raynaud's disease: A comparative study with long-term follow-up. *The American Journal of Psychiatry, 136,* 844–846.

Javnbakht, M., Hejazi Kenari, R., & Ghasemi, M. (2009). Effects of yoga on depression and anxiety of women. *Complementary Therapies in Clinical Practice, 15,* 102–104. doi:10.1016/j.ctcp.2009.01.003

Jeffery, R. (1988). *The politics of health in India.* Berkeley: University of California Press.

Jensen, M. P., Barber, J., Hanley, M. A., Engel, J. M., Romano, J. M., Cardenas, D. D., . . . Patterson, D. R. (2008). Long-term outcome of hypnotic-analgesia treatment for chronic pain in persons with disabilities. *International Journal of Clinical and Experimental Hypnosis, 56,* 156–169. doi:10.1080/0020714 0701849486

Jensen, M. P., Barber, J., Romano, J. M., Hanley, M. A., Raichle, K. A., Molton, I. R., . . . Patterson, D. R. (2009a). Effects of self-hypnosis training and EMG biofeedback relaxation training on chronic pain in persons with spinal-cord injury. *International Journal of Clinical and Experimental Hypnosis, 57,* 239–268. doi:10.1080/00207140902881007

Jensen, M. P., Barber, J., Romano, J. M., Molton, I. R., Raichle, K. A., Osborne, T. L., . . . Patterson, D. R. (2009b). A comparison of self-hypnosis versus progressive muscle relaxation in patients with multiple sclerosis and chronic pain. *International Journal of Clinical and Experimental Hypnosis, 57,* 198–221. doi:10.1080/00207140802665476

Jeong, Y. J., Hong, S. C., Lee, M. S., Park, M. C., Kim, Y. K., & Suh, C. M. (2005). Dance movement therapy improves emotional responses and modulates neurohormones in adolescents with mild depression. *International Journal of Neuroscience, 115,* 1711–1720. doi:10.1080/00207450590958574

John, P. J., Sharma, N., Sharma, C. M., & Kankane, A. (2007). Effectiveness of yoga therapy in the treatment of migraine without aura: A randomized controlled trial. *Headache: The Journal of Head and Face Pain, 47,* 654–661. doi:10.1111/j.1526-4610.2007.00789.x

Jones, H., Cooper, P., Miller, V., Brooks, N., & Whorwell, P. J. (2006). Treatment of non-cardiac chest pain: A controlled trial of hypnotherapy. *Gut, 55,* 1403–1408. doi:10.1136/gut.2005.086694

Jones, J., & Saad, L. (2011). Gallup poll social series: Values and beliefs. *USA Today/Gallup poll*. Retrieved from http://www.gallup.com/poll/File/147890/Belief_in_God_110603%20.pdf

Juthani, N. V. (2001). Psychiatric treatment of Hindus. *International Review of Psychiatry, 13*, 125–130. doi:10.1080/09540260125005

Kabat-Zinn, J. (1982). An outpatient program in behavioral medicine for chronic pain patients based on the practice of mindfulness meditation: Theoretical considerations and preliminary results. *General Hospital Psychiatry, 4*, 33–47. doi:10.1016/0163-8343(82)90026-3

Kabat-Zinn, J. (1990). *Full catastrophe living: Using the wisdom of your body and mind to face stress, pain, and illness*. New York, NY: Dell.

Kabat-Zinn, J. (1994). *Wherever you go, there you are*. New York: Hyperion.

Kabat-Zinn, J. (2003a). Mindfulness-based interventions in context: Past, present, and future. *Clinical Psychology: Science and Practice, 10*, 144–156. doi:10.1093/clipsy.bpg016

Kabat-Zinn, J. (2003b). Mindfulness-based stress reduction (MBSR). *Constructivism in the Human Sciences, 8*(2), 73–107.

Kabat-Zinn, J. (2005). *Full catastrophe living: Using the wisdom of your body and mind to face stress, pain, and illness: Fifteenth anniversary edition*. New York, NY: Delta Trade Paperback/Bantam Dell.

Kaplan, M. (1996). Ambushed by spirituality. *Time Magazine, 24*, 62–64.

Kaptchuk, T. J. (2002). Acupuncture: Theory, efficacy, and practice. *Annals of Internal Medicine, 136*, 374–383. doi:10.7326/0003-4819-136-5-200203050-00010

Kaptchuk, T. J., & Eisenberg, D. M. (1998). Chiropractic: Origins, controversies, and contributions. *Archives of Internal Medicine, 158*, 2215–2224. doi:10.1001/archinte.158.20.2215

Kaptchuk, T. J., Stason, W. B., Davis, R. B., Legedza, A. R., Schnyer, R. N., Kerr, C. E., . . . Goldman, R. H. (2006). Sham device v. inert pill: Randomised controlled trial of two placebo treatments. *BMJ, 332*, 391–397. doi:10.1136/bmj.38726.603310.55

Karagozoglu, S., Tekyasar, F., & Yilmaz, F. A. (2013). Effects of music therapy and guided visual imagery on chemotherapy-induced anxiety and nausea-vomiting. *Journal of Clinical Nursing, 22*, 39–50. doi:10.1111/jocn.12030

Karavidas, M. K., Lehrer, P. M., Vaschillo, E., Vaschillo, B., Marin, H., Buyske, S., . . . Hassett, A. (2007). Preliminary results of an open label study of heart rate variability biofeedback for the treatment of major depression. *Applied Psychophysiology and Biofeedback, 32*, 19–30. doi:10.1007/s10484-006-9029-z

Karavidas, M. K., Tsai, P., Yucha, C., McGrady, A., & Lehrer, P. M. (2006). Thermal biofeedback for primary Raynaud's phenomenon: A review of the literature. *Applied Psychophysiology and Biofeedback, 31*, 203–216. doi:10.1007/s10484-006-9018-2

Katz, J. B. (2000). Music therapy: Some possibilities in the Indian Tradition. In P. Horden (Ed.), *Music as medicine: The history of music therapy since antiquity* (pp. 84–102). Brookfield, VT: Ashgate.

Kay, S. R., Opler, L. A., & Fiszbein, A. (1987). *Positive and Negative Syndrome Scale (PANSS) rating manual.* San Rafael, CA: Social Behavioral Sciences Document.

Keating, J. C., Jr. (1992). Shades of straight: Diversity among the purists. *Journal of Manipulative and Physiological Therapeutics, 15,* 203–209.

Keating, J. C., Jr., Green, B. N., & Johnson, C. D. (1995). "Research" and "science" in the first half of the chiropractic century. *Journal of Manipulative and Physiological Therapeutics, 18,* 357–378.

Keefe, F. J., Surwit, R. S., & Pilon, R. N. (1980). Biofeedback, autogenic training, and progressive relaxation in the treatment of Raynaud's disease: A comparative study. *Journal of Applied Behavior Analysis, 13,* 3–11. doi:10.1901/jaba.1980.13-3

Kendler, K. S., Gardner, C. O., & Prescott, C. A. (1997). Religion, psychopathy, and substance abuse and abuse: A multimeasure, genetic-epidemiologic study. *The American Journal of Psychology, 154,* 322–329.

Kerns, R. D., Turk, D. C., & Rudy, T. E. (1985). The West Haven Yale multidimensional pain inventory (WHYMPI). *Pain, 23,* 345–356. doi:10.1016/0304-3959(85)90004-1

Kessler, R. C., Soukup, J., Davis, R. B., Foster, D. F., Wilkey, S. A., Van Rompay, M. M., & Eisenberg, D. M. (2001). The use of complementary and alternative therapies to treat anxiety and depression in the United States. *The American Journal of Psychiatry, 158,* 289–294. doi:10.1176/appi.ajp.158.2.289

Khalsa, S. B. S., Shorter, S. M., Cope, S., Wyshak, G., & Sklar, E. (2009). Yoga ameliorates performance anxiety and mood disturbance in young professional musicians. *Applied Psychophysiology and Biofeedback, 34,* 279–289. doi:10.1007/s10484-009-9103-4

Khan, S., & Balick, M. (2001). Therapeutic plants of Ayurveda: A review of selected clinical and other studies for 166 species. *Journal of Complementary and Alternative Medicine, 7,* 405–515. doi:10.1089/10755530152639729

Kiecolt-Glaser, J. K., McGuire, L., Robles, T. F., & Glaser, R. (2002). Psychoneuroimmunology: Psychological influences on immune function and health. *Journal of Consulting and Clinical Psychology, 70,* 537–547. doi:10.1037/0022-006X.70.3.537

Kiepe, M. S., Stöckigt, B., & Keil, T. (2012). Effects of dance therapy and ballroom dances on physical and mental illnesses: A systematic review. *The Arts in Psychotherapy, 39,* 404–411. doi:10.1016/j.aip.2012.06.001

Kim, J. T., Wajda, M., Cuff, G., Serota, D., Schlame, M., Axelrod, D. M., . . . Bekker, A. Y. (2006). Evaluation of aromatherapy in treating postoperative pain: Pilot study. *Pain Practice, 6,* 273–277. doi:10.1111/j.1533-2500.2006.00095.x

Kim, J. Y., & Kwon, O. (2009). Garlic intake and cancer risk: An analysis using the Food and Drug Administration's evidence-based review system for the scientific evaluation of health claims. *The American Journal of Clinical Nutrition*, *89*, 257–264. doi:10.3945/ajcn.2008.26142

Kim, Y. S., Lee, S. H., Jung, W. S., Park, S. U., Ko, C. N., Cho, K. H., Bae, H. S. (2004). Intradermal acupuncture on *Shen-men* and *Nei-kuan* acupoints in patients with insomnia after stroke. *The American Journal of Chinese Medicine*, *32*, 771–778. doi:10.1142/S0192415X04002399

King, D. E., & Bushwick, B. (1994). Beliefs and attitudes of hospital inpatients about faith healing and prayer. *The Journal of Family Practice*, *39*, 349–352.

Kirsch, I. (1991). The social learning theory of hypnosis. In S. J. Lynn & J. W. Rhue (Eds.), *Theories of hypnosis: Current models and perspectives* (pp. 439–465). New York, NY: Guilford Press.

Kirsch, I. (1996). Hypnotic enhancement of cognitive-behavioral weight loss treatments: Another meta-reanalysis. *Journal of Consulting and Clinical Psychology*, *64*, 517–519. doi:10.1037/0022-006X.64.3.517

Kirsch, I. (1997). Specifying nonspecifics: Psychological mechanisms of placebo effects. In A. Harrington (Ed.), *The placebo effect: An interdisciplinary exploration* (pp. 166–186). Boston, MA: First Harvard University Press.

Kirsch, I., Montgomery, G., & Sapirstein, G. (1995). Hypnosis as an adjunct to cognitive–behavioral psychotherapy: A meta-analysis. *Journal of Consulting and Clinical Psychology*, *63*, 214–220. doi:10.1037/0022-006X.63.2.214

Knapp, S. J., & VandeCreek, L. D. (2012). *Practical ethics for psychologists: A positive approach* (2nd ed.). Washington, DC: American Psychological Association.

Knasko, S. C. (1995). Pleasant odors and congruency: Effects on approach behavior. *Chemical Senses*, *20*, 479–487. doi:10.1093/chemse/20.5.479

Knaudt, P. R., Connor, K. M., Weisler, R. H., Churchill, L. E., & Davidson, J. R. (1999). Alternative therapy use by psychiatric outpatients. *Journal of Nervous and Mental Disease*, *187*, 692–695. doi:10.1097/00005053-199911000-00007

Koenig, H. G. (2009). Research on religion, spirituality, and mental health: A review. *Canadian Journal of Psychiatry*, *54*, 283–291.

Koenig, H. G., McCullough, M., & Larson, D. (2000). *Handbook of religion and health*. New York, NY: Oxford University Press.

Kohen, D. P. (2010). Long-term follow-up of self-hypnosis training for recurrent headaches: What the children say. *International Journal of Clinical and Experimental Hypnosis*, *58*, 417–432. doi:10.1080/00207144.2010.499342

Kohlmann, T., & Raspe, H. (1996). Hannover Functional Questionnaire in ambulatory diagnosis of functional disability caused by backache. *Die Rehabilitation*, *35*, I–VIII.

Kopp-Hoolihan, L. (2001). Prophylactic and therapeutic uses of probiotics: A review. *Journal of the American Dietetic Association*, *101*, 229–238. doi:10.1016/S0002-8223(01)00060-8

Koszycki, D., Benger, M., Shlik, J., & Bradwejn, J. (2007). Randomized trial of a meditation-based stress reduction program and cognitive behavior therapy in generalized social anxiety disorder. *Behaviour Research and Therapy, 45,* 2518–2526. doi:10.1016/j.brat.2007.04.011

Kozak, L. E., Kayes, L., McCarty, R., Walkinshaw, C., Congdon, S., Kleinberger, J., . . . Standish, L. J. (2008–2009). Use of complementary and alternative medicine (CAM) by Washington State hospices. *American Journal of Hospice & Palliative Medicine, 25,* 463–468. doi:10.1177/1049909108322292

Kroger, W. (1977). *Clinical and experimental hypnosis* (2nd ed.). Philadelphia, PA: Lippincott.

Kunstler, R., Greenblatt, F., & Moreno, N. (2004). Aromatherapy and hand massage: Therapeutic recreation interventions for pain management. *Therapeutic Recreation Journal, 38,* 133–147.

Kuusisto, L. (2009a). *What are the basic concepts?* Retrieved from http://www.takingcharge.csh.umn.edu/explore-healing-practices/chiropractic/what-are-basic-concepts

Kuusisto, L. (2009b). *Where does chiropractic come from?* Retrieved from http://www.takingcharge.csh.umn.edu/explore-healing-practices/chiropractic/where-does-it-come

Ladd, K. L., & Spilka, B. (2002). Inward, outward, and upward: Cognitive aspects of prayer. *Journal for the Scientific Study of Religion, 41,* 475–484. doi:10.1111/1468-5906.00131

Ladd, K. L., & Spilka, B. (2006). Inward, outward, upward: Scale reliability, and validation. *Journal for the Scientific Study of Religion, 45,* 233–251. doi:10.1111/j.1468-5906.2006.00303.x

Laird, B., Colvin, L., & Fallon, M. (2008). Management of cancer pain: Basic principles and neuropathic cancer pain. *European Journal of Cancer, 44,* 1078–1082. doi:10.1016/j.ejca.2008.03.022

Laird, S. P., Snyder, C. R., Rapoff, M. A., & Green, S. (2004). Measuring private prayer: Development, validation, and clinical application of the multidimensional prayer inventory. *International Journal for the Psychology of Religion, 14,* 251–272. doi:10.1207/s15327582ijpr1404_2

Lambe, R., Osier, C., & Franks, P. (1986). A randomized controlled trial of hypnotherapy for smoking cessation. *The Journal of Family Practice, 22,* 61–65.

Lane, J. D., Seskevich, J. E., & Peiper, C. F. (2007). Brief meditation training can improve perceived stress and negative mood. *Alternative Therapies in Health and Medicine, 13,* 38–44.

Lang, E. V., Benotsch, E. G., Fick, L. J., Lutgendorf, S., Berbaum, M. L., Berbaum, K. S., . . . Spiegel, D. (2000). Adjunctive non-pharmacological analgesia for invasive medical procedures: A randomised trial. *The Lancet, 355,* 1486–1490. doi:10.1016/S0140-6736(00)02162-0

Lang, E. V., Berbaum, K. S., Faintuch, S., Hatsiopoulou, O., Halsey, N., Li, X., . . . Baum, J. (2006). Adjunctive self-hypnotic relaxation for outpatient medical procedures: A prospective randomized trial with women undergoing large core breast biopsy. *Pain, 126,* 155–164. doi:10.1016/j.pain.2006.06.035

Lang, E. V., Berbaum, K. S., Pauker, S. G., Faintuch, S., Salazar, G. M., Lutgendorf, S., . . . Spiegel, D. (2008). Beneficial effects of hypnosis and adverse effects of empathic attention during percutaneous tumor treatment: When being nice does not suffice. *Journal of Vascular and Interventional Radiology, 19,* 897–905. doi:10.1016/j.jvir.2008.01.027

Lang, E. V., Joyce, J. S., Spiegel, D., Hamilton, D., & Lee, K. K. (1996). Self-hypnotic relaxation during interventional radiological procedures: Effects of pain perception and intravenous drug use. *International Journal of Clinical and Experimental Hypnosis, 44,* 106–119. doi:10.1080/00207149608416074

Langford, M. J. (2002). *Fluent bodies: Remedies for postcolonial imbalance.* Durham, NC: Duke University Press.

Langley, T., Geiger, W., & Gartlehner, G. (2008). *Aromatherapy for pain relief and psychological problems. Systematic review* (Decision Support Document 16). Retrieved from http://eprints.hta.lbg.ac.at/765/1/DSD_16.pdf

Langner, E., Greifenberg, S., & Gruenwald, J. (1998). Ginger: History and use. *Advances in Therapy, 15,* 25–44.

Lansky, M. (2009). Forgiveness as the working through of splitting. *Psychoanalytic Inquiry, 29,* 374–385. doi:10.1080/07351690903032090

Lao, L. (1996). Safety issues in acupuncture. *The Journal of Alternative and Complementary Medicine, 2,* 27–31. doi:10.1089/acm.1996.2.27

LaTorre, M. A. (2002). Spirituality and psychotherapy: An important combination. *Perspectives in Psychiatric Care, 38,* 108–110. doi:10.1111/j.1744-6163.2002.tb00664.x

LaTorre, M. A. (2003). Aromatherapy and the use of scents in psychotherapy. *Perspectives in Psychiatric Care, 39,* 35. doi:10.1111/j.1744-6163.2003.tb00672.x

LaTorre, M. A. (2005). The use of Reiki in psychotherapy. *Perspectives in Psychiatric Care, 41,* 184–187. doi:10.1111/j.1744-6163.2005.00035.x

Lazar, S. W., Bush, G., Gollub, R. L., Fricchione, G. L., Khalsa, G., & Benson, H. (2000). Functional brain mapping of the relaxation response and meditation. *Neuroreport, 11,* 1581–1585. doi:10.1097/00001756-200005150-00041

Ledesma, D., & Kumano, H. (2009). Mindfulness-based stress reduction and cancer: A meta-analysis. *Psycho-Oncology, 18,* 571–579. doi:10.1002/pon.1400

Lee, G. A., Crawford, G. W., Liu, L., Sasaki, Y., & Chen, X. (2011). Archaeological soybean *Glycine max* in East Asia: Does size matter? *PLoS ONE, 6,* e26720. Retrieved from http://www.plosone.org/article/info%3Adoi%2F10.1371%2Fjournal.pone.0026720.

Lee, M. S., Choi, J., Posadzki, P., & Ernst, E. (2012). Aromatherapy for health care: An overview of systematic reviews. *Maturitas, 71,* 257–260. doi:10.1016/j.maturitas.2011.12.018

Lee, M. S., Shin, B. C., Ronan, P., & Ernst, E. (2009). Acupuncture for schizophrenia: A systematic review and meta-analysis. *International Journal of Clinical Practice, 63,* 1622–1633. doi:10.1111/j.1742-1241.2009.02167.x

Lee, S. W., Mancuso, C. A., & Charlson, M. E. (2004). Prospective study of new participants in a community-based mind–body training program. *Journal of General Internal Medicine, 19,* 760–765. doi:10.1111/j.1525-1497.2004.30011.x

Lee, Y. L., Wu, Y., Tsang, H. W., Leung, A. Y., & Cheung, W. M. (2011). A systematic review on the anxiolytic effects of aromatherapy in people with anxiety symptoms. *The Journal of Alternative and Complementary Medicine, 17,* 101–108. doi:10.1089/acm.2009.0277

Lehrner, J., Marwinski, G., Lehr, S., Johren, P., & Deecke, L. (2005). Ambient odors of orange and lavender reduce anxiety and improve mood in a dental office. *Physiology & Behavior, 86,* 92–95. doi:10.1016/j.physbeh.2005.06.031

Leslie, C. (1976). The ambiguities of medical revivalism in modern India. In L. Charles (Ed.), *Asian medical systems: A comparative study* (pp. 356–367). Berkeley, CA: University of California Press.

Levetin, E., & McMahon, K. (1996). *Plants and society.* New York, NY: McGraw-Hill.

Levine, E. G., Aviv, C., Yoo, G., Ewing, C., & Au, A. (2009). The benefits of prayer on mood and well-being of breast cancer survivors. *Supportive Care in Cancer, 17,* 295–306. doi:10.1007/s00520-008-0482-5

Lewith, G. T., Godfrey, A. D., & Prescott, P. (2005). A single-blinded, randomized pilot study evaluating the aroma of lavandula augustifolia as a treatment for mild insomnia. *The Journal of Alternative and Complementary Medicine, 11,* 631–637. doi:10.1089/acm.2005.11.631

Lin, M. F., Hsieh, Y. J., Hsu, Y. Y., Fetzer, S., & Hsu, M. C. (2011). A randomized controlled trial of the effect of music therapy and verbal relaxation on chemotherapy-induced anxiety. *Journal of Clinical Nursing, 20,* 988–999. doi:10.1111/j.1365-2702.2010.03525.x

Lin, P. W., Chan, W., Ng, B. F., & Lam, L. C. (2007). Efficacy of aromatherapy (*Lavandula angustifolia*) as an intervention for agitated behaviours in Chinese older persons with dementia: A cross-over randomized trial. *International Journal of Geriatric Psychiatry, 22,* 405–410. doi:10.1002/gps.1688

Linde, K., Berner, M. M., & Kriston, L. (2008). St John's wort for major depression. *Cochrane Database of Systematic Reviews, 4,* CD000448. Retrieved from http://onlinelibrary.wiley.com/doi/10.1002/14651858.CD000448.pub3/abstract

Linde, K., & Mulrow, C. (2000). St John's wort for depression. *The Cochrane Database of Systematic Reviews, 2,* CD000448.

Linehan, M. M. (1993). *Cognitive-behavioral treatment of borderline personality disorder.* New York, NY: Guilford Press.

Liossi, C., & Hatira, P. (1999). Clinical hypnosis versus cognitive behavioral training for pain management with pediatric cancer patients undergoing bone marrow aspirations. *International Journal of Clinical and Experimental Hypnosis, 47,* 104–116. doi:10.1080/00207149908410025

Liossi, C., White, P., & Hatira, P. (2009). A randomized clinical trial of a brief hypnosis intervention to control venepuncture-related pain of paediatric cancer patients. *Pain, 142,* 255–263. doi:10.1016/j.pain.2009.01.017

Livergood, N. D. (2011). *Brain, mind, and altered states of consciousness.* Retrieved from http://www.hermes-press.com/altstates.htm

Louis, M., & Kowalski, S. D. (2002). Use of aromatherapy with hospice patients to decrease pain, anxiety, and depression and to promote an increased sense of well-being. *American Journal of Hospice & Palliative Care, 19,* 381–386. doi:10.1177/104990910201900607

Lübeck, W., Rand, L., & Petter, F. (2001). *The spirit of Reiki: The complete handbook of the Reiki system: From tradition to the present: Fundamental, lines of transmission, original writings, mastery, symbols, treatments, Reiki as a spiritual path in life, and much more.* Twin Lakes, WI: Lotus Press.

Lund, I., & Lundeberg, T. (2006). Are minimal, superficial or sham acupuncture procedures acceptable as inert placebo controls? *Acupuncture in Medicine, 24,* 13–15. doi:10.1136/aim.24.1.13

Lykins, E. L. B., & Baer, R. A. (2009). Psychological functioning in a sample of long-term practitioners of mindfulness meditation. *Journal of Cognitive Psychotherapy, 23,* 226–241. doi:10.1891/0889-8391.23.3.226

Lynn, S. J., & Kirsch, I. (2006). Depression. In *Essentials of clinical hypnosis: An evidence-based approach.* Washington, DC: American Psychological Association.

Lynn, S. J., Kirsch, I., Barabasz, A., Cardena, E., & Patterson, D. (2000). Hypnosis as an empirically supported clinical intervention: The state of the evidence and a look to the future. *International Journal of Clinical and Experimental Hypnosis, 48,* 239–259. doi:10.1080/00207140008410050

Lynn, S. J., & Shindler, K. (2002). The role of hypnotizability assessment in treatment. *American Journal of Clinical Hypnosis, 44,* 185–197. doi:10.1080/00029157.2002.10403479

Ma, S. H., & Teasdale, J. D. (2004). Mindfulness-based cognitive therapy for depression: Replication and exploration of differential relapse prevention effects. *Journal of Consulting and Clinical Psychology, 72*(1), 31–40.

MacHovec, F. (1988). Hypnosis complications, risk factors, and prevention. *American Journal of Clinical Hypnosis, 31,* 40–49. doi:10.1080/00029157.1988.10402766

MacHovec, F. J. (2012). *Hypnosis complications.* Bloomington, IN: iUniverse.

Manicavasagar, V., Parker, G., & Perich, T. (2011). Mindfulness-based cognitive therapy vs cognitive behaviour therapy as a treatment for non-melancholic depression. *Journal of Affective Disorders, 130,* 138–144.

Manicavasagar, V., Perich, T., & Parker, G. (2012). Cognitive predictors of change in cognitive behaviour therapy and mindfulness-based cognitive therapy for depression. *Behavioural and Cognitive Psychotherapy, 40,* 227–232. doi:10.1017/S1352465811000634

Mannel, M. (2004). Drug interactions with St John's wort. *Drug Safety, 27,* 773–797. doi:10.2165/00002018-200427110-00003

Manyam, B. V. (1999). Dementia in Ayurveda. *The Journal of Alternative and Complementary Medicine, 5,* 81–88. doi:10.1089/acm.1999.5.81

Maquet, P., Faymonville, M.-E., Degueldre, C., Delfiore, G., Franck, G., Luxen, A., & Lamy, M. (1999). Functional neuroanatomy of hypnotic state. *Biological Psychiatry, 45*, 327–333. doi:10.1016/S0006-3223(97)00546-5

Maratos, A. S., Gold, C., Wang, X., & Crawford, M. J. (2009). Music therapy for depression. *Cochrane Database of Systematic Reviews, 1*, CD004517. doi:10.1002/14651858

Marc, I., Rainville, P., Verreault, R., Vaillancourt, L., Masse, B., & Dodin, S. (2007). The use of hypnosis to improve pain management during voluntary interruption of pregnancy: An open randomized preliminary study. *Contraception, 75*, 52–58. doi:10.1016/j.contraception.2006.07.012

Martinsen, E. W., Hoffart, A., & Solberg, O. (1989). Comparing aerobic with nonaerobic forms of exercise in the treatment of clinical depression: A randomized trial. *Comprehensive Psychiatry, 30*, 324–331. doi:10.1016/0010-440X(89)90057-6

Marwick, C. (1997). Acceptance of some acupuncture applications. *JAMA, 278*, 1725–1727. doi:10.1001/jama.1997.03550210021013

Massage Therapy Benefits. (2010). *The most popular massage types.* Retrieved from http://www.massage-therapy-benefits.net/massage-types.html

Masters, K. S., Speilman, G. I., & Goodson, J. T. (2006). Are there demonstrable effects of distant intercessory prayer? A meta-analytic review. *Annals of Behavioral Medicine, 32*, 21–26. doi:10.1207/s15324796abm3201_3

Mayo Clinic. (2009). *Back pain: Will chiropractic care help?* Retrieved from http://www.mayoclinic.org/health/back-pain/SA00080

Mayo Clinic. (2010). *Book of alternative medicine* (2nd ed.). New York, NY: Time.

Mayo Clinic. (2011). *Chondroitin sulfate. Mayo Clinic health information, drugs and supplements.* Retrieved from http://www.mayoclinic.org/health/chondroitin-sulfate/NS_patient-chondroitin

Mayo Clinic. (2012). *Coenzyme Q10. Mayo Clinic health information, drugs and supplements.* Retrieved from http://www.mayoclinic.org/health/coenzyme-q10/NS_patient-coenzymeq10

Mayo Clinic (2013). *Biofeedback: Using your mind to improve your health.* Retrieved from http://www.mayoclinic.org/tests-procedures/biofeedback/basics/definition/prc-20020004

McCaffrey, A. M., Eisenberg, D. M., & Legedza, A. T. R. (2004). Prayer for health concerns: Results of a national survey on prevalence and patterns of use. *Archives of Internal Medicine, 164*, 858–862. doi:10.1001/archinte.164.8.858

McHardy, A., Hoskins, W., Pollard, H., Onley, R., & Windsham, R. (2008). Chiropractic treatment of upper extremity conditions: A systematic review. *Journal of Manipulative and Physiological Therapeutics, 31*, 146–159. doi:10.1016/j.jmpt.2007.12.004

McNeill, J. A., Sherwood, G. D., Starck, P. L., & Thompson, C. J. (1998). Assessing clinical outcomes patient satisfaction with pain management. *Journal of pain and symptom management, 16*, 29–40.

Mechanick, J. I. (2005). The rational use of dietary supplements and nutraceuticals in clinical medicine. *The Mount Sinai Journal of Medicine, 72,* 161–165.

Mechanick, J. I., Brett, E., Chausmer, A., Dickey, R., Wallach, S., & American Association of Clinical Endocrinologists. (2003). American Association of Clinical Endocrinologists medical guidelines for the clinical use of dietary supplements and nutraceuticals. *Endocrine Practice, 9,* 417–470. doi:10.4158/EP.9.5.417

Meeker, W. C., & Haldeman, S. (2002). Chiropractic: A profession at the crossroads of mainstream and alternative medicine. *Annals of Internal Medicine, 136,* 216–227. doi:10.7326/0003-4819-136-3-200202050-00010

Meekums, B. (2010). Moving towards evidence for dance movement therapy: Robin Hood in dialogue with the king. *The Arts in Psychotherapy, 37,* 35–41. doi:10.1016/j.aip.2009.10.001

Meekums, B., Vaverniece, I., Majore-Dusele, I., & Rasnacs, O. (2012). Dance movement therapy for obese women with emotional eating: A controlled pilot study. *The Arts in Psychotherapy, 39,* 126–133. doi:10.1016/j.aip.2012.02.004

Meisenhelder, J. B., & Chandler, E. N. (2000). Prayer and health outcomes in church members. *Alternative Therapies in Health and Medicine, 6,* 56–60.

Melis, P. M., Rooimans, W., Spierings, E. L., & Hoogduin, C. A. (1991). Treatment of chronic tension-type headache with hypnotherapy: A single-blind time controlled study. *Headache, 31,* 686–689. doi:10.1111/j.1526-4610.1991.hed3110686.x

Mendoza, T. R., Wang, X. S., Cleeland, C. S., Morrissey, M., Johnson, B. A., Wendt, J. K., & Huber, S. L. (1999). The rapid assessment of fatigue severity in cancer patients: Use of the Brief Fatigue Inventory. *Cancer, 85,* 1186–1196. doi:10.1002/(SICI)1097-0142(19990301)85:5{1186::AID-CNCR24}3.0.CO;2-N

Merat, S., Khalili, S., Mostajabi, P., Ghorbani, A., Ansari, R., & Malekzadeh, R. (2010). The effect of enteric-coated, delayed-release peppermint oil on irritable bowel syndrome. *Digestive Diseases and Sciences, 55,* 1385–1390. doi:10.1007/s10620-009-0854-9

Metcalfe, J. (1989). *Herbs and aromatherapy.* Exeter, England: Webb and Bower.

Michalsen, A., Jeitler, M., Brunnhuber, S., Lüdtke, R., Büssing, A., Musial, F., . . . Kessler, C. (2012). Iyengar yoga for distressed women: A 3-armed randomized controlled trial. *Evidence-Based Complementary and Alternative Medicine, 2012,* 408727. doi:10.1155/2012/408727

Mickley, J. R., Soeken, K., & Belcher, A. (1992). Spiritual well-being, religiousness, and hope among women with breast cancer. *IMAGE—Journal of Nursing Scholarship, 24,* 267–272. doi:10.1111/j.1547-5069.1992.tb00732.x

Miles, P., & True, G. (2003). Reiki—Review of a biofield therapy history, theory, practice, and research. *Alternative Therapies in Health and Medicine, 9,* 62–72. Retrieved from www.reikiinmedicine.org/pdf/alt_therapies_reiki.pdf

Miller, J. J., Fletcher, K., & Kabat-Zinn, J. (1995). Three-year follow-up and clinical implications of a mindfulness meditation-based stress reduction intervention in the treatment of anxiety disorders. *General Hospital Psychiatry, 17,* 192–200. doi:10.1016/0163-8343(95)00025-M

Miller, W. (1990). Spirituality: The silent dimension of addiction research. *Drug and Alcohol Review, 9,* 259–266. doi:10.1080/09595239000185341

Miller, W. R., & Kurtz, E. (1994). Models of alcoholism used in treatment: Contrasting AA and other perspectives with which it is often confused. *Journal of Studies in Alcohol, 55,* 159–166.

Mischoulon, D., & Fava, M. (2000). Docosahexanoic acid and ω-3 fatty acids in depression. *Psychiatric Clinics of North America, 23,* 785–794.

Mischoulon, D., & Fava, M. (2002). Role of S-adenosyl-L-methionine in the treatment of depression: a review of the evidence. *The American Journal of Clinical Nutrition, 76,* 1158S–1161S.

Moffet, H. H. (2009). Sham acupuncture may be as efficacious as true acupuncture: A systematic review of clinical trials. *The Journal of Alternative and Complementary Medicine, 15,* 213–216. doi:10.1089/acm.2008.0356

Montgomery, G. H., Bovbjerg, D. H., Schnur, J. B., David, D., Goldfarb, A., Weltz, C. R., . . . Silverstein, J. H. (2007). A randomized clinical trial of a brief hypnosis intervention to control side effects in breast surgery patients. *Journal of the National Cancer Institute, 99,* 1304–1312. doi:10.1093/jnci/djm106

Montgomery, H. A., Miller, W. R., & Tonigan, J. S. (1995). Does Alcoholics Anonymous involvement predict outcome? *Journal of Substance Abuse Treatment, 12,* 241–246. doi:10.1016/0740-5472(95)00018-Z

Moore, C., & Adler, R. (2000). Herbal vitamins: Lead toxicity and developmental delay. *Pediatrics, 106,* 600–602. doi:10.1542/peds.106.3.600

Moore, J. S. (1993). *Chiropractic in America.* Baltimore, MD: Johns Hopkins University Press.

Moore, R. D. (1990). Youthful precursors of alcohol abuse in physicians. *American Journal of Medicine, 88,* 332–336.

Moraska, A., Pollini, R. A., Boulanger, K., Brooks, M. Z., & Teitlebaum, L. (2010). Physiological adjustments to stress measures following massage therapy. *Evidence-Based Complementary and Alternative Medicine, 7,* 409–418. doi:10.1093/ecam/nen029

Morgan, K., Bartrop, R., Telfer, J., & Tennant, C. (2011). A controlled trial investigating the effect of music therapy during an acute psychotic episode. *Acta Psychiatrica Scandinavica, 124,* 363–371. doi:10.1111/j.1600-0447.2011.01739.x

Morien, A., Garrison, D., & Smith, N. K. (2008). Range of motion improves after massage in children with burns: A pilot study. *Journal of Bodywork and Movement Therapies, 12,* 67–71. doi:10.1016/j.jbmt.2007.05.003

Morley, S., Eccleston, C., & Williams, A. (1999). Systematic review and meta-analysis of randomized controlled trials of cognitive behaviour therapy and behaviour therapy for chronic pain in adults, excluding headache. *Pain, 80,* 1–13. doi:10.1016/S0304-3959(98)00255-3

Moss, D. (2002). Biofeedback. In S. Shannon (Ed.), *Handbook of complementary and alternative therapies in mental health* (pp. 135–158). San Diego, CA: Academic Press. doi:10.1016/B978-012638281-5/50008-5

Moss, M., Cook, J., Wesnes, K., & Duckett, P. (2003). Aromas of rosemary and lavender essential oils differentially affect cognition and mood in healthy adults. *International Journal of Neuroscience, 113*, 15–38. doi:10.1080/00207450390161903

Moyer, C. A., Rounds, J., & Hannum, J. W. (2004). A meta-analysis of massage therapy research. *Psychological Bulletin, 130*, 3–18. doi:10.1037/0033-2909.130.1.3

Muir, J. M. (2012). Chiropractic management of a patient with symptoms of attention-deficit/hyperactivity disorder. *Journal of Chiropractic Medicine, 11*, 221–224. doi:10.1016/j.jcm.2011.10.009

Müller, W. E. (2003). Current St. John's wort research from mode of action to clinical efficacy. *Pharmacological Research, 47*, 101–109. doi:10.1016/S1043-6618(02)00266-9

Mulrow, C., Lawrence, V., Ackermann, R., Gilbert Ramirez, G., Morbidoni, L., Aguilar, C., . . . Young, V. (2000). *Garlic: Effects on cardiovascular risks and disease, protective effects against cancer, and clinical adverse effects* (AHRQ Evidence Report/Technology Assessment Summary 20, 01-E022). Rockville, MD: Agency for Healthcare Research and Quality. Retrieved from http://text.nlm.nih.gov/ftrs/dbaccess.pl?collect=epc&dbName=garlsum

Nagy, T. E. (2005). *Ethics in plain English: An illustrative casebook for psychologists* (2nd ed.). Washington, DC: American Psychological Association.

Nalini, K., Karanth, K. S., Rao, A., & Aroot, A. R. (1995). Effects of *Celastrus paniculatus* on passive avoidance performance and biogenic amine turnover in albino rats. *Journal of Ethnopharmacology, 47*, 101–108. doi:10.1016/0378-8741(95)01264-E

Napadow, V., Kettner, N., Liu, J., Li, M., Kwong, K. K., Vangel, M., . . . Hui, K. K. S. (2007). Hypothalamus and amygdala response to acupuncture stimuli in carpal tunnel syndrome. *Pain, 130*, 254–266. doi:10.1016/j.pain.2006.12.003

Narayanasamy, A., & Narayanasamy, M. (2006). Ayurvedic medicine: An introduction for nurses. *British Journal of Nursing, 15*, 1185–1190.

Nash, M. R., & Barnier, A. J. (Eds.). (2008). *The Oxford handbook of hypnosis: Theory, research, and practice*. New York, NY: Oxford University Press.

National Association for Holistic Aromatherapy. (1997). *Our history*. Retrieved from http://www.naha.org/about/our-history

National Association for Holistic Aromatherapy. (2013a). *NAHA approved schools*. Retrieved from http://www.naha.org/education/approved-schools

National Association for Holistic Aromatherapy. (2013b). *NAHA code of ethics*. Retrieved from http://www.naha.org/membership/code-of-ethics

National Ayurvedic Medical Association. (2013). *Mission statement*. Retrieved from http://www.ayurvedanama.org/?page=about_us

National Cancer Institute. (2010). *Aromatherapy and essential oils.* Retrieved from http://www.cancer.gov/cancertopics/pdq/cam/aromatherapy/healthprofessional/page3

National Certification Commission for Acupuncture and Oriental Medicine. (2011). *About NCCAOM: A historical perspective.* Retrieved from http://www.nccaom.org/about/index.html

National Institutes of Health. (1996). Integration of behavioral and relaxation approaches into the treatment of chronic pain and insomnia. NIH Technology Assessment Panel on Integration of Behavioral and Relaxation Approaches into the Treatment of Chronic Pain and Insomnia. *JAMA, 276,* 313–318. doi:10.1001/jama.1996.03540040057033

National Institutes of Health, National Center for Complementary and Alternative Medicine. (2004). *Whole medical systems: An overview* (Backgrounder D236). Retrieved from www.fvpt.com/wholemed.pdf

National Institutes of Health, National Center for Complementary and Alternative Medicine. (2006). *Massage therapy: An introduction* (Backgrounder D327). Retrieved from http://nccam.nih.gov/health/massage/massageintroduction.htm

National Institutes of Health, National Center for Complementary and Alternative Medicine. (2007a). *Biologically based practices: An overview* (Backgrounder, D237). Retrieved from http://www.mhcinc.org/poc/view_doc.php?type=doc&id=8927&cn=15

National Institutes of Health, National Center for Complementary and Alternative Medicine. (2007b). *Chamomile. Herbs at a glance.* Retrieved from http://nccam.nih.gov/health/chamomile/ataglance.htm

National Institutes of Health, National Center for Complementary and Alternative Medicine. (2007c). *Energy medicine: An overview* (Backgrounder D235). Retrieved from http://markmaluga.com/files/Energy-Medicine-NCCAM.pdf

National Institutes of Health, National Center for Complementary and Alternative Medicine. (2008). *What is complementary and alternative medicine?* (NCCAM Pub. No. D347, updated July 2011). Retrieved from http://nccam.nih.gov/health/whatiscam

National Institutes of Health, National Center for Complementary and Alternative Medicine. (2010a). *Meditation: An introduction.* Retrieved from http://nccam.nih.gov/health/meditation/overview.htm

National Institutes of Health, National Center for Complementary and Alternative Medicine. (2010b). *Mind–body medicine practices in complementary and alternative medicine.* Retrieved from http://report.nih.gov/nihfactsheets/Pdfs/MindBodyMedicinePracticesinComplementaryandAlternativeMedicine%28NCCAM%29.pdf

National Institutes of Health, National Center for Complementary and Alternative Medicine. (2011a). *2007 statistics on CAM use in the United States: National Health Interview Survey.* Retrieved from http://nccam.nih.gov/news/camstats/2007

National Institutes of Health, National Center for Complementary and Alternative Medicine. (2011b). *Acupuncture: An introduction.* Retrieved from http://nccam. nih.gov/health/massage/massageintroduction.htm#history

National Institutes of Health, National Center for Complementary and Alternative Medicine. (2011c). *Chiropractic: An introduction.* Retrieved from http://nccam. nih.gov/health/chiropractic/introduction.htm

National Institutes of Health, National Center for Complementary and Alternative Medicine. (2011d). *Dietary and herbal supplements.* Retrieved from http://nccam. nih.gov/health/supplements

National Institutes of Health, National Center for Complementary and Alternative Medicine. (2011e). *Massage therapy: An introduction.* Retrieved from http:// nccam.nih.gov/health/massage/massageintroduction.htm

National Institutes of Health, National Center for Complementary and Alternative Medicine. (2011f). *Reiki: An introduction.* Retrieved from http://nccam.nih. gov/health/reiki/introduction.htm

National Institutes of Health, National Center for Complementary and Alternative Medicine. (2011g). *Sleep disorders and CAM: At a glance.* Retrieved from http:// nccam.nih.gov/health/sleep/ataglance.htm

National Institutes of Health, National Center for Complementary and Alternative Medicine. (2011h). *What is complementary and alternative medicine?* Retrieved from http://nccam.nih.gov/health/whatiscam/#manipulative

National Institutes of Health, National Center for Complementary and Alternative Medicine. (2011i). *Yoga for health: An introduction.* Retrieved from http://nccam. nih.gov/health/yoga/introduction.htm

National Institutes of Health, National Center for Complementary and Alternative Medicine. (2012a). *Herbs at a glance: Asian ginseng.* Retrieved from http:// nccam.nih.gov/health/asianginseng/ataglance.htm

National Institutes of Health, National Center for Complementary and Alternative Medicine. (2012b). *Herbs at a glance: Echinacea.* Retrieved from http://nccam. nih.gov/health/echinacea/ataglance.htm

National Institutes of Health, National Center for Complementary and Alternative Medicine. (2012c). *Herbs at a glance: Garlic.* Retrieved from http://nccam.nih. gov/health/garlic/ataglance.htm

National Institutes of Health, National Center for Complementary and Alternative Medicine. (2012d). *Herbs at a glance: Ginger.* Retrieved from http://nccam.nih. gov/health/ginger

National Institutes of Health, National Center for Complementary and Alternative Medicine. (2012e). *Herbs at a glance: Ginkgo biloba.* Retrieved from http:// nccam.nih.gov/health/ginkgo/ataglance.htm?nav=gsa

National Institutes of Health, National Center for Complementary and Alternative Medicine. (2012f). *Herbs at a glance: Kava.* Retrieved from http://nccam.nih. gov/health/kava

National Institutes of Health, National Center for Complementary and Alternative Medicine. (2012g). *Herbs at a glance: Peppermint oil.* Retrieved from http://nccam.nih.gov/health/peppermintoil

National Institutes of Health, National Center for Complementary and Alternative Medicine. (2012h). *Herbs at a glance: Soy.* Retrieved from http://nccam.nih.gov/health/soy/ataglance.htm

National Institutes of Health, National Center for Complementary and Alternative Medicine. (2012i). *Herbs at a glance: St. John's wort.* Retrieved from http://nccam.nih.gov/health/stjohnswort/ataglance.htm?nav=gsa

National Institutes of Health, National Center for Complementary and Alternative Medicine. (2012j). NCCAM *facts-at-a-glance and mission.* Retrieved from http://nccam.nih.gov/about/ataglance

National Institutes of Health, National Center for Complementary and Alternative Medicine. (2012k). *Omega-3 supplements: An introduction.* Retrieved from http://nccam.nih.gov/health/omega3/introduction.htm

National Institutes of Health, National Center for Complementary and Alternative Medicine. (2013a). *Ayurvedic medicine: An introduction* (Backgrounder D287). Retrieved from http://nccam.nih.gov/sites/nccam.nih.gov/files/D287_BKG.pdf?nav=gsa

National Institutes of Health, National Center for Complementary and Alternative Medicine. (2013b). *Natural Medicine Comprehensive Database—fish oil.* Retrieved from http://www.nlm.nih.gov/medlineplus/druginfo/natural/993.html

National Institutes of Health, National Center for Complementary and Alternative Medicine. (2014). NCCAM *funding: Appropriations history.* Retrieved from http://nccam.nih.gov/about/budget/appropriations.htm?nav=gsa

Nelson, C. F., Bronfort, G., Evans, R., Boline, P., Goldsmith, C., & Anderson, A. V. (1998). The efficacy of spinal manipulation, amitriptyline and the combination of both therapies for the prophylaxis of migraine headache. *Journal of Manipulative and Physiological Therapeutics, 21,* 511–519.

Nelson, H. D., Vesco, K. K., Haney, E., Fu, R., Nedrow, A., Miller, J., . . . & Humphrey, L. (2006). Nonhormonal therapies for menopausal hot flashes. *JAMA: The JAMA, 295,* 2057–2071

Nestoriuc, Y., & Martin, A. (2007). Efficacy of biofeedback for migraine: A meta-analysis. *Pain, 128,* 111–127. doi:10.1016/j.pain.2006.09.007

Nestoriuc, Y., Martin, A., Rief, W., & Andrasik, F. (2008). Biofeedback treatment for headache disorders: A comprehensive efficacy review. *Applied Psychophysiology and Biofeedback, 33,* 125–140. doi:10.1007/s10484-008-9060-3

Nestoriuc, Y., Rief, W., & Martin, A. (2008). Meta-analysis of biofeedback for tension-type headache: Efficacy, specificity, and treatment moderators. *Journal of Consulting and Clinical Psychology, 76,* 379–396. doi:10.1037/0022-006X.76.3.379

Nguyen, Q. A., & Paton, C. (2008). The use of aromatherapy to treat behavioural problems in dementia. *International Journal of Geriatric Psychiatry, 23,* 337–346. doi:10.1002/gps.1886

Ni, M. S. (1995). *The Yellow Emperor's classic of internal medicine: A new translation of the Neijing Suwen with commentary* (pp. 14–17). Boston, MA: Shambhala.

Nikfarjam, M., Goudarzi, I., Heidari, S., & Parvin, N. (2012). Effect of *Ginkgo biloba* tablets on patients with major depression treated with electroconvulsive therapy. *Journal of Mazandaran University of Medical Sciences, 22,* 62–69.

Nilsson, U. (2008). The anxiety and pain-reducing effects of music interventions: A systematic review. *AORN Journal, 87,* 780–807. doi:10.1016/j.aorn.2007.09.013

Office of Dietary Supplements, National Institutes of Health. (2011). *Botanical dietary supplements: Background information.* Retrieved from http://ods.od.nih.gov/factsheets/BotanicalBackground-HealthProfessional

Office of Dietary Supplements, National Institutes of Health. (2013). *National Institutes of Health Botanical Research Centers Program.* Retrieved from http://ods.od.nih.gov/Research/Dietary_Supplement_Research_Centers.aspx

Olness, K., MacDonald, J. T., & Uden, D. L. (1987). Comparison of self-hypnosis and propranolol in the treatment of juvenile classic migraine. *Pediatrics, 79,* 593–597.

Olney, C. M. (2005). The effect of therapeutic back massage in hypertensive persons: A preliminary study. *Biological Research for Nursing, 7,* 98–105. doi:10.1177/1099800405280827

Olson, K., & Hanson, J. (1997). Using Reiki to manage pain: A preliminary report. *Cancer Prevention and Control, 1,* 108.

Olson, K., Hanson, J., & Michaud, M. (2003). A Phase II trial of Reiki for the management of pain in advanced cancer patients. *Journal of Pain and Symptom Management, 26,* 990–997. doi:10.1016/S0885-3924(03)00334-8

Olver, I. N., & Dutney, A. (2012). A randomized, blinded study of the impact of intercessory prayer on spiritual well-being in patients with cancer. *Alternative Therapies in Health and Medicine, 18,* 18–27.

Orme-Johnson, D. W., Schneider, R. H., Son, Y. D., Nidich, S., & Cho, Z. H. (2006). Neuroimaging of meditation's effects on brain reactivity to pain. *Neuroreport, 17,* 1359–1363. doi:10.1097/01.wnr.0000233094.67289.a8

Orme-Johnson, D. W., & Walton, K. G. (1998). All approaches to preventing and reversing the effects of stress are not the same. *American Journal of Health Promotion, 12,* 297–299.

Oster, M. I. (2006). Hypnosis: History, definitions, theory, and application. In R. A. Chapman (Ed.), *The clinical use of hypnosis in cognitive behavior therapy: A practitioner's casebook* (pp. 25–44). New York, NY: Springer.

Oths, K. (1994). Communication in a chiropractic clinic: How a DC treats his patients. *Culture, Medicine and Psychiatry, 18,* 83–113. doi:10.1007/BF01384878

Paley, C., Johnson, M., Tashani, O., & Bagnall, A. (2011). Acupuncture for cancer pain in adults. *The Cochrane Database of Systematic Reviews, 1,* CD007753. doi:10.1002/14651858.CD007753.pub2

Palsson, O. S., Turner, M. J., Johnson, D. A., Burnett, C. K., & Whitehead, W. E. (2002). Hypnosis treatment for severe irritable bowel syndrome: Investigation of mechanism and effects on symptoms. *Digestive Diseases and Sciences, 47,* 2605–2614.

Pang, Z., Pan, F., & He, S. (1996). *Ginkgo biloba L.:* History, current status, and future prospects. *The Journal of Alternative and Complementary Medicine, 2,* 359–363. doi:10.1089/acm.1996.2.359

Pargament, K. I., & Krumrie, E. J. (2009). Clinical assessment of clients' spirituality. In J. D. Aten & M. M. Leach (Eds.), *Spirituality and the therapeutic process: A comprehensive resource from intake to termination* (pp. 93–120). Washington, DC: American Psychological Association. doi:10.1037/11853-005

Patterson, D. R., & Jensen, M. P. (2003). Hypnosis and clinical pain. *Psychological Bulletin, 129,* 495–521. doi:10.1037/0033-2909.129.4.495

Patterson, D. R., Wiechman, S. A., Jensen, M., & Sharar, S. R. (2006). Hypnosis delivered through immersive virtual reality for burn pain: A clinical case series. *International Journal of Clinical and Experimental Hypnosis, 54,* 130–142. doi:10.1080/00207140500528182

Paul, M., & Garg, K. (2012). The effect of heart rate variability biofeedback on performance psychology of basketball players. *Applied Psychophysiology and Biofeedback, 37,* 131–144. doi:10.1007/s10484-012-9185-2

Paul-Labrador, M., Polk, D., Dwyer, J. H., Velasquez, I., Nidich, S., Rainforth, M., . . . Bairey Merz, N. (2006). Effects of a randomized controlled trial of transcendental meditation on components of the metabolic syndrome in subjects with coronary heart disease. *Archives of Internal Medicine, 166,* 1218–1224. doi: 10.1001/archinte.166.11.1218

Payne, H. (1992). *Dance movement therapy: Theory and practice.* New York, NY: Tavistock/Routledge.

Payne, H. (Ed.) (2006). *Dance movement therapy: Theory, research and practice.* London, England: Routledge.

Pearson, J., Rademaker, R. L., & Tong, F. (2011). Evaluating the mind's eye: The metacognition of visual imagery. *Psychological Science, 22,* 1535–1542. doi:10.1177/0956797611417134

Pelletier, C. L. (2004). The effect of music on decreasing arousal due to stress: A meta-analysis. *Journal of Music Therapy, 41,* 192–214.

Peniston, E. G., & Kulkosky, P. J. (1989). Alpha theta brainwave training and beta-endorphin levels in alcoholics. *Alcoholism: Clinical and Experimental Research, 13,* 271–279. doi:10.1111/j.1530-0277.1989.tb00325.x

Peniston, E. G., & Kulkosky, P. J. (1990). Alcoholic personality and alpha-theta brainwave training. *Medical Psychotherapy: An International Journal, 3,* 37–55.

Peniston, E. G., & Kulkosky, P. J. (1991). Alpha-theta brainwave neurofeedback for Vietnam veterans with combat related post-traumatic stress disorder. *Medical Psychotherapy: An International Journal, 4,* 47–60.

Perelman, A. M., Miller, S. L., Clements, C. B., Rodriguez, A., Allen, K., & Cavanaugh, R. (2012). Meditation in a Deep South prison: A longitudinal study of the effects of Vipassana. *Journal of Offender Rehabilitation, 51,* 176–198. doi:10.1080/10509674.2011.632814

Perry, N., & Perry, E. (2006). Aromatherapy in the management of psychiatric disorders: Clinical and neuropharmacological perspectives. *CNS Drugs, 20,* 257–280. doi:10.2165/00023210-200620040-00001

Peterson, K. B. (1997). The effects of spinal manipulation on the intensity of emotional arousal in phobic subjects exposed to a threat stimulus: A randomized, controlled, double-blind clinical trial. *Journal of Manipulative and Physiological Therapeutics, 20,* 602–606.

Piderman, K. M., Schneekloth, T. D., Pankratz, V. S., Maloney, S. D., & Altchuler, S. I. (2007). Spirituality in alcoholics during treatment. *The American Journal on Addictions, 16,* 232–237.

Pilkington, K., Kirkwood, G., Rampes, H., Cummings, M., & Richardson, J. (2007). Acupuncture for anxiety and anxiety disorders—a systematic literature review. *Acupuncture in Medicine, 25,* 1–10.

Pilkington, K., Kirkwood, G., Rampes, H., & Richardson, J. (2005). Yoga for depression: The research evidence. *Journal of Affective Disorders, 89,* 13–24. doi:10.1016/j.jad.2005.08.013

Pittler, M. H., & Ernst, E. (1998). Peppermint oil for irritable bowel syndrome: A critical review and metaanalysis. *The American Journal of Gastroenterology, 93,* 1131–1135. doi:10.1016/S0002-9270(98)00224-X

Plante, T. G. (2007). Integrating spirituality and psychotherapy: Ethical issues and principles to consider. *Journal of Clinical Psychology, 63,* 891–902. doi:10.1002/jclp.20383

Plante, T. G. (2009). Religion–spirituality in the practice and science of psychology. In *Spiritual practices in psychotherapy: Thirteen tools for enhancing psychological health* (pp. 9–28). Washington, DC: American Psychological Association. doi:10.1037/11872-001

Plodek, J. (2009). Reiki: An ancient therapy in modern times. In L. Freeman (Ed.), *Mosby's complementary and alternative medicine: A research based approach* (3rd ed., pp. 533–554). St. Louis, MO: Mosby Elsevier.

Poland, R. E., Gertsik, L., Favreau, J. T., Smith, S. I., Mirocha, J. M., Rao, U., & Daar, E. S. (2013). Open-label, randomized, parallel-group controlled clinical trial of massage for treatment of depression in HIV-infected subjects. *The Journal of Alternative and Complementary Medicine, 19,* 334–340. doi:10.1089/acm.2012.0058

Poldinger, W. (2000). History of St. John's wort. *Praxis, 89,* 2102–2109.

Poloma, M. M., & Pendleton, B. F. (1991). The effects of prayer and prayer experiences on measures of general well-being. *Journal of Psychology and Theology, 19,* 71–83.

Power, M., Kuyken, W., Orley, J., Hermann, H., Shofield, H., Murphy, B., . . . Picardami, L. (1998). The World Health Organisation Quality of Life Assessment (WHOQOL)-Development and general psychometric properties. *Social Science & Medicine*, 46, 1569–1585. doi:10.1016/S0277-9536(98)00009-4

Powers, M. B., Vörding, M. B. Z., & Emmelkamp, P. M. G. (2009). Acceptance and commitment therapy: A meta-analytic review. *Psychotherapy and Psychosomatics*, 78, 73–80. doi:10.1159/000190790

Poyser, M. (2004). Healing trauma and spiritual growth: The relevance of religious education to emotionally and behaviorally disturbed children looked after by local authorities. *Support for Learning*, 19, 125–131. doi:10.1111/j.0268-2141.2004.00334.x

Preyde, M. (2000). Effectiveness of massage therapy for subacute low-back pain: A randomized controlled trial. *Canadian Medical Association Journal*, 162, 1815–1820.

Price, S., & Price, L. (1999). *Aromatherapy for health professionals* (2nd ed.). London, England: Churchill Livingstone.

Price, S., & Price, L. (Eds.). (2007). *Aromatherapy for health professionals* (3rd ed.). New York, NY: Churchill Livingstone.

Propst, L. (1996). Cognitive–behavioral therapy and the religious person. In E. P. Shafranske (Ed.), *Religion and the clinical practice of psychology* (pp. 391–407). Washington, DC: American Psychological Association. doi:10.1037/10199-014

Quest, P. (2009). *Reiki for life: The complete guide to Reiki practice for levels 1, 2 & 3: The essential guide to Reiki practice*. London, England: Piatkus Books, Ltd.

Radimer, K., Bindewald, B., Hughes, J., Ervin, B., Swanson, C., & Picciano, M. F. (2004). Dietary supplement use by US adults: Data from the National Health and Nutrition Examination Survey, 1999–2000. *American Journal of Epidemiology*, 160, 339–349. doi:10.1093/aje/kwh207

Raghavendra, R. M., Nagarathna, R., Nagendra, H. R., Gopinath, K. S., Srinath, B. S., Ravi, B. D., . . . Nalini, R. (2007). Effects of an integrated yoga programme on chemotherapy-induced nausea and emesis in breast cancer patients. *European Journal of Cancer Care*, 16, 462–474. doi:10.1111/j.1365-2354.2006.00739.x

Raglio, A., Bellelli, G., Traficante, D., Gianotti, M., Ubezio, M. C., Gentile, S., . . . Trabucchi, M. (2010). Efficacy of music therapy treatment based on cycles of sessions: A randomized controlled trial. *Aging & Mental Health*, 14, 900–904. doi:10.1080/13607861003713158

Rainforth, M. V., Schneider, R. H., Nidich, S. I., Gaylord-King, C., Salerno, J. W., & Anderson, J. W. (2007). Stress reduction programs in patients with elevated blood pressure: A systemic review and meta-analysis. *Current Hypertension Reports*, 9, 520–528. doi:10.1007/s11906-007-0094-3

Rainone, F. (2000). Acupuncture for mental health. In P. R. Muskin (Ed.), *Complementary and alternative medicine and psychiatry* (pp. 67–105). Washington, DC: American Psychiatric Press.

Rainville, P., Hofbauer, R. K., Bushnell, M. C., Duncan, G. H., & Price, D. D. (2002). Hypnosis modulates activity in brain structures involved in the regulation of consciousness. *Journal of Cognitive Neuroscience*, 14, 887–901. doi:10.1162/089892902760191117

Rainville, P., Hofbauer, R. K., Paus, T., Duncan, G. H., Bushnell, M. C., & Price, D. D. (1999). Cerebral mechanisms of hypnotic induction and suggestion. *Journal of Cognitive Neuroscience, 11*, 110–125. doi:10.1162/089892999563175

Rakhshani, A., Maharana, S., Raghuram, N., Nagendra, H., & Venkatram, P. (2010). Effects of integrated yoga on quality of life and interpersonal relationship of pregnant women. *Quality of Life Research: An International Journal of Quality of Life Aspects of Treatment, Care & Rehabilitation, 19*, 1447–1455.

Rani, K., Tiwari, S. C., Singh, U., Agrawal, G. G., & Srivastava, N. (2011). Six-month trial of Yoga Nidra in menstrual disorder patients: Effects on somatoform symptoms. *Industrial Psychiatry Journal, 20*, 97–102.

Rapaport, M. H., Schettler, P., & Bresee, C. (2010). A preliminary study of the effects of a single session of Swedish massage on hypothalamic–pituitary–adrenal and immune function in normal individuals. *The Journal of Alternative and Complementary Medicine, 16*, 1079–1088. doi:10.1089/acm.2009.0634

Rapaport, M. H., Schettler, P., & Bresee, C. (2012). A preliminary study of the effects of repeated massage on hypothalamic–pituitary–adrenal and immune function in healthy individuals: A study of mechanisms of action and dosage. *The Journal of Alternative and Complementary Medicine, 18*, 789–797. doi:10.1089/acm.2011.0071

Raynaud's Treatment Study Investigators. (2000). Comparison of sustained-release nifedipine and temperature biofeedback for treatment of primary Raynaud phenomenon. *Archives of Internal Medicine, 160*, 1101–1108. doi:10.1001/archinte.160.8.1101

Redd, W. H., Andresen, G. V., & Minagawa, R. Y. (1982). Hypnotic control of anticipatory emesis in patients receiving cancer chemotherapy. *Journal of Consulting and Clinical Psychology, 50*, 14. doi:10.1037/0022-006X.50.1.14

Reed, W. R., Beavers, S., Reddy, S. K., & Kern, G. (1994). Chiropractic management of primary nocturnal enuresis. *Journal of Manipulative and Physiological Therapeutics, 17*, 596–600.

Reston, J. (1971, July 26). *Now about my operation in Peking. New York Times*, 1, 6.

Rich, G. J. (Ed.). (2002). *Massage therapy: The evidence for practice*. New York, NY: Elsevier.

Rich, G. J. (2010). Massage therapy: Significance and relevance to professional practice. *Professional Psychology: Research and Practice, 41*, 325–332. doi:10.1037/a0020161

Richards, P. S., & Bergin, A. E. (1997). *A spiritual strategy for counseling and psychotherapy*. Washington, DC: American Psychological Association. doi:10.1037/10241-000

Richards, P. S., & Potts, R. W. (1995). Using spiritual interventions in psychotherapy: Practices, successes, failures, and ethical concerns of Mormon psychotherapists. *Professional Psychology: Research and Practice, 26*, 163–170.

Richardson, J., Smith, J. E., McCall, G., Richardson, A., Pilkington, K., & Kirsch, I. (2007). Hypnosis for nausea and vomiting in cancer chemotherapy: A systematic review of the research evidence. *European Journal of Cancer Care, 16,* 402–412. doi:10.1111/j.1365-2354.2006.00736.x

Riley, D. (2003). Hatha yoga and the treatment of illness. *Alternative Therapies in Health and Medicine, 10,* 20–21.

Riley, J. F., Ahern, D. K., & Follick, M. J. (1988). Chronic pain and functional impairment: Assessing beliefs about their relationship. *Archives of Physical Medicine and Rehabilitation, 69,* 579–582.

Ringdahl, D., & Halcon, L. L. (2006). Reiki. In M. Snyder & R. Lindquist (Eds.), *Complementary/alternative therapies in nursing* (pp. 243–269). New York, NY: Springer.

Riskin, J. D., & Frankel, F. H. (1994). A history of medical hypnosis. *Psychiatric Clinics of North America, 17,* 601–609.

Ritter, M., & Low, K. G. (1996). Effects of dance/movement therapy: A meta-analysis. *The Arts in Psychotherapy, 23,* 249–260. doi:10.1016/0197-4556(96)00027-5

Rivlin, R. S. (2001). Historical perspective on the use of garlic. *The Journal of Nutrition, 131,* 951S–954S.

Roberts, L., Ahmed, I., Hall, S., & Davison, A. (2009). Intercessory prayer for the alleviation of ill health. *Cochrane Database of Systematic Reviews, 2,* CD000368. Retrieved from http://onlinelibrary.wiley.com/doi/10.1002/14651858. CD000368.pub3/abstract

Robins, J. L. (1999). The science and art of aromatherapy. *Journal of Holistic Nursing, 17,* 5–17. doi:10.1177/089801019901700102

Rocha, K. K., Ribeiro, A., Rocha, K., Sousa, M., Albuquerque, F., Ribeiro, S., & Silva, R. (2012). Improvement in physiological and psychological parameters after 6 months of yoga practice. *Consciousness and Cognition: An International Journal, 21,* 843–850. doi:10.1016/j.concog.2012.01.014

Rodolfa, E., Bent, R., Eisman, E., Nelson, P., Rehm, L., & Ritchie, P. (2005). A cube model for competency development: Implications for psychology educators and regulators. *Professional Psychology: Research and Practice, 36,* 347–354. doi:10.1037/0735-7028.36.4.347

Roodenrys, S., Booth, D., Bulzomi, S., Phipps, A., Micallef, C., & Smoker, J. (2002). Chronic effects of Brahmi (*Bacopa monnnieri*). *Neuropsychopharmacology, 27,* 279–281. doi:10.1016/S0893-133X(01)00419-5

Rosa, L., Rosa, E., Sarner, L., & Barrett, S. (1998). A close look at therapeutic touch. *JAMA, 279,* 1005–1010. doi:10.1001/jama.279.13.1005

Rosenstiel, A. K., & Keefe, F. J. (1983). The use of coping strategies in chronic low back pain patients: Relationship to patient characteristics and current adjustment. *Pain, 17,* 33–44. doi:10.1016/0304-3959(83)90125-2

Rubinstein, S. M., Terwee, C. B., Assendelft, W. J. J., de Boer, M. R., & van Tulder, M. W. (2012). Spinal manipulative therapy for acute low-back pain. *Cochrane Database of Systematic Reviews,* Issue 9. Art. No.: CD008880. doi:10.1002/14651858.CD008880.pub2.

Rubinstein, S. M., van Middelkoop, M., Assendelft, W. J. J., de Boer, M. R., & van Tulder, M. W. (2011). Spinal manipulative therapy for chronic low-back pain. *Cochrane Database of Systematic Reviews*, Issue 2. Art. No.: CD008112. doi:10.1002/14651858.CD008112.pub2.

Rubinstein, S. M., van Middelkoop, M., Kuijpers, T., Ostelo, R., Verhagen, A. P., de Boer, M. R., . . . van Tulder, M. W. (2010). A systematic review on the effectiveness of complementary and alternative medicine for chronic non-specific low-back pain. *European Spine Journal*, 19, 1213–1228. doi:10.1007/s00586-010-1356-3

Runck, B. (1983). *What is biofeedback?* Retrieved from http://www.healthy.net/scr/article.asp?ID=451

Russek, L. G., & Schwartz, G. E. (1996). Energy cardiology: A dynamical energy systems approach for integrating conventional and alternative medicine. *Advances*, 12, 4–24.

Ryan, J. L., Heckler, C. E., Roscoe, J. A., Dakhil, S. R., Kirshner, J., Flynn, P. J., . . . Morrow, G. R. (2012). Ginger (*Zingiber officinale*) reduces acute chemotherapy-induced nausea: A URCC CCOP study of 576 patients. *Supportive Care in Cancer*, 20, 1479–1489. doi:10.1007/s00520-011-1236-3

Sanatansociety.org. (2010). *Hatha yoga*. Retrieved from http://www.sanatansociety.org/yoga_and_meditation/hatha_yoga.htm

Sandel, S. L., Judge, J. O., Landry, N., Faria, L., Ouellette, R., & Majczak, M. (2005). Dance and movement program improves quality-of-life measures in breast cancer survivors. *Cancer Nursing*, 28, 301–309. doi:10.1097/00002820-200507000-00011

Sandor, P. S., Di Clemente, L., Coppola, G., Saenger, U., Fumal, A., Magis, D., . . . Schoenen, J. (2005). Efficacy of coenzyme Q10 in migraine prophylaxis: A randomized controlled trial. *Neurology*, 64, 713–715. doi:10.1212/01.WNL.0000151975.03598.ED

Santilli, V., Beghi, E., & Finucci, S. (2006). Chiropractic manipulation in the treatment of acute back pain and sciatica with disc protrusion: A randomized double-blind clinical trial of active and simulated spinal manipulations. *The Spine Journal*, 6, 131–137. doi:10.1016/j.spinee.2005.08.001

Saper, R. B., Eisenberg, D. M., Davis, R. B., Culpepper, L., & Phillips, R. S. (2004). Prevalence and patterns of adult yoga use in the United States: Results of a national survey. *Alternative Therapies in Health and Medicine*, 10, 44–49.

Saper, R. B., Kales, S. N., Paquin, J., Burns, M. J., Eisenberg, D. M., Davis, R. B., & Phillips, R. S. (2004). Heavy metal content of ayurvedic herbal medicine products. *JAMA*, 292, 2868–2873. doi:10.1001/jama.292.23.2868

Saper, R. B., Phillips, R. S., Sehgal, A., Khouri, N., Davis, R. B., & Kales, S. N. (2008). Lead, mercury, and arsenic in US- and Indian-manufactured Ayurvedic medicines sold via the internet. *JAMA*, 300, 915–923. doi:10.1001/jama.300.8.915

Sarbin, T. R., & Coe, W. C. (1972). *Hypnosis: A social psychological analysis of influence communication*. New York, NY: Holt, Rinehart & Winston.

Satow, Y. E., Kumar, P. D., Burke, A., & Inciardi, J. F. (2008). Exploring the prevalence of Ayurveda use among Asian Indians. *The Journal of Alternative and Complementary Medicine, 14*, 1249–1253. doi:10.1089/acm.2008.0106

Savage, J. H., Kaeding, A. J., Matsui, E. C., & Wood, R. A. (2010). The natural history of soy allergy. *Journal of Allergy and Clinical Immunology, 125*, 683–686.

Sawyer, C., Haas, M., Nelson, C., & Elkington, W. (1997). Clinical research within the chiropractic profession: Status, needs and recommendations. *Journal of Manipulative and Physiological Therapeutics, 20*, 169–178.

Schachter, H., Kourad, K., Merali, Z., Lumb, A., Tran, K., & Miguelez, M. (2005). Effects of omega-3 fatty acids on mental health. *Evidence Report/Technology Assessment (Summary)*, (116), 1–11.

Scheier, M. F., & Carver, C. S. (1985). Optimism, coping, and health: Assessment and implications of generalized outcome expectancies. *Health Psychology, 4*, 219–247. doi:10.1037/0278-6133.4.3.219

Schneider, R. H., Alexander, C. N., Staggers, F., Rainforth, M., Salerno, J., Hartz, A., . . . Nidich, S. I. (2005). Long-term effects of stress reduction on mortality in persons ≥55 years of age with systemic hypertension. *The American Journal of Cardiology, 95*, 1060–1064. doi:10.1016/j.amjcard.2004.12.058

Schnoll, R. A., Harlow, L. L., & Brower, L. (2000). Spirituality, demographic and disease factors, and adjustment to cancer. *Cancer Practice, 8*, 298–304. doi:10.1046/j.1523-5394.2000.86006.x

Schwartz, M. S., & Andrasik, F. (2003). *Biofeedback: A practitioner's guide* (3rd ed.). New York, NY: Guilford Press.

Segal, Z. V., Williams, J. M. G., & Teasdale, J. D. (2002). *Mindfulness-based cognitive therapy for depression: A new approach to preventing relapse*. New York, NY: Guilford Press.

Segen, J. C. (1998). *Dictionary of alternative medicine*. Stamford, CT: Appleton and Lange.

Shapiro, S. L., Carlson, L. E., Astin, J. A., & Freedman, B. (2006). Mechanisms of mindfulness. *Journal of Clinical Psychology, 62*, 373–386. doi:10.1002/jclp.20237

Sharma, H., Chandola, H. M., Singh, G., & Sasisht, G. (2007). Utilization of Ayurveda in health care: An approach for prevention, health promotion, and treatment of disease. Part 2—Ayurveda in primary health care. *The Journal of Alternative and Complementary Medicine, 13*, 1135–1150. doi:10.1089/acm.2007.7017-B

Sharma, H. M. (2011). Contemporary Ayurveda. In M. S. Micozzi (Ed.), *Fundamentals of complementary and alternative medicine* (pp. 495–508). St. Louis, MO: Saunders Elsevier.

Shelton, R. C., Keller, M. B., Gelenberg, A., Dunner, D. L., Hirschfeld, R., Thase, M. E., . . . Halbreich, U. (2001). Effectiveness of St John's wort in major depression: A randomized controlled trial. *JAMA, 285*, 1978–1986. doi:10.1001/jama.285.15.1978

Sherman, K. J., Cherkin, D. C., Eisenberg, D. M., Erro, J., Hrbek, A., & Deyo, R. A. (2005). The practice of acupuncture: Who are the providers and what do they do? *Annals of Family Medicine, 3*, 151–158. doi:10.1370/afm.248

Sherman, K. J., Cherkin, D. C., Hawkes, R. J., Miglioretti, D. L., & Deyo, R. A. (2009). Randomized trail of therapeutic massage for chronic neck pain. *The Clinical Journal of Pain, 25*, 233–238. doi:10.1097/AJP.0b013e31818b7912

Shore, A. G. (2004). Long-term effects of energetic healing on symptoms of psychological depression and self-perceived stress. *Alternative Therapies in Health and Medicine, 10*, 42–48.

Shukla, Y., & Singh, M. (2007). Cancer preventive properties of ginger: A brief review. *Food and Chemical Toxicology, 45*, 683–690. doi:10.1016/j.fct.2006.11.002

Shults, C. W., Oakes, D., Kieburtz, K., Beal, M. F., Haas, R., Plumb, S., . . . the Parkinson Study Group. (2002). Effects of coenzyme Q10 in early Parkinson disease: Evidence of slowing of the functional decline. *Archives of Neurology, 59*, 1541. doi:10.1001/archneur.59.10.1541

Sicher, F., Targ, E., Moore, D., & Smith, H. S. (1998). A randomized double-blind study of the effect of distant healing in a population with advanced AIDS. Report of a small scale study. *The Western Journal of Medicine, 169*, 356–363.

Sievenpiper, J. L., Arnason, J. T., Leiter, L. A., & Vuksan, V. (2004). Decreasing, null and increasing effects of eight popular types of ginseng on acute postprandial glycemic indices in healthy humans: The role of ginsenosides. *Journal of the American College of Nutrition, 23*, 248–258. doi:10.1080/07315724.2004.10719368

Sigerist, H. E. (1987). *A history of medicine: II. Early Greek, Hindu, and Persian medicine* (Vol. 38). New York, NY: Oxford University Press.

Singh, H. K., & Dhawan, B. N. (1982). Effect of *Bacopa Monniera Linn.* (Brahmi) extract on avoidance responses in rat. *Journal of Ethnopharmacology, 5*, 205–214. doi:10.1016/0378-8741(82)90044-7

Singh, H. K., Rastogi, R. P., Srimal, R. C., & Dhawan, B. N. (1988). Effect of Bacosides A and B on avoidance responses in rats. *Phytotherapy Research, 2*, 70–75. doi:10.1002/ptr.2650020205

Sirtori, C. R. (2001). Risks and benefits of soy phytoestrogens in cardiovascular diseases, cancer, climacteric symptoms and osteoporosis. *Drug Safety, 24*, 665–682. doi:10.2165/00002018-200124090-00003

Sivananda, S. S. (2011). *Bhakti yoga: What is Bhakti?* Retrieved from http://www.dlshq.org/teachings/bhaktiyoga.htm

Sloan, R. P., Bagiella, E., & Powell, T. (1999). Religion, spirituality, and medicine. *The Lancet, 353*, 664–667. doi:10.1016/S0140-6736(98)07376-0

Smith, C. A., Hay, P. J., & MacPherson, H. (2010). Acupuncture for depression. *Cochrane Database of Systematic Reviews, 1*, Art. No.: CD004046. doi:10.1002/14651858.CD004046.pub3

Smith, D., & Fitzpatrick, M. (1995). Patient–psychotherapist boundary issues: An integrative review of theory and research. *Professional Psychology: Research and Practice, 26*, 499–506. doi:10.1037/0735-7028.26.5.499

Smith, J. G., & Fisher, R. (2000). The effect of remote intercessory prayer on clinical outcomes [letter]. *Archives of Internal Medicine, 160*, 1876. doi:10.1001/archinte.160.12.1876

Smith, K. R. (2011). Factors influencing the inclusion of complementary and alternative medicine (CAM) in undergraduate medical education. *BMJ Open, 1*. doi:10.1136/bmjopen-2011-000074

Snow, A., Dorfman, D., Warbet, R., Cammarata, M., Eisenman, S., Zilberfein, F., . . . Navada, S. (2012). A randomized trial of hypnosis for relief of pain and anxiety in adult cancer patients undergoing bone marrow procedures. *Journal of Psychosocial Oncology, 30*, 281–293. doi:10.1080/07347332.2012.664261

Snyder, M., & Lindquist, R. (Eds.). (2010). *Complementary and alternative therapies in nursing* (6th ed.). New York, NY: Springer.

So, K. T., & Orme-Johnson, D. W. (2001). Three randomized experiments on the holistic longitudinal effects of the Transcendental Meditation technique on cognition. *Intelligence, 29*, 419–440.

Sood, A., Ebbert, J. O., Sood, R., & Stevens, S. R. (2006). Complementary treatments for tobacco cessation: A survey. *Nicotine & Tobacco Research, 8*, 767–771. doi:10.1080/14622200601004109

Soothill, K., Morris, S. M., Harman, J. C., Thomas, C., Francis, B., & McIllmurray, M. B. (2002). Cancer and faith. Having faith-does it make a difference among patients and their informal careers? *Scandinavian Journal of Caring Sciences, 16*, 256–263. doi:10.1046/j.1471-6712.2002.00097.x

Spinasanta, S. (2010). *Questions to ask your chiropractor*. Retrieved from http://www.spineuniverse.com/treatments/chiropractic/questions-ask-your-chiropractor

Stanton, K. (1991). Dance movement therapy: An introduction. *British Journal of Occupational Therapy, 4*, 108–110.

Stanton-Jones, K. (1992). *An introduction to dance movement therapy in psychiatry*. New York, NY: Tavistock/Routledge.

Stough, C., Lloyd, J., Clarke, J., Downey, L. A., Hutchison, C. W., & Nathan, P. J. (2001). The chronic effects of an extract of *Bacopa Monniera* (Brahmi) on cognitive function in healthy human subjects. *Psychopharmacology, 156*, 481–484. doi:10.1007/s002130100815

Streeter, C. C., Whitfield, T. H., Owen, L., Rein, T., Karri, S. K., Yakhkind, A., . . . Jensen, J. E. (2010). Effects of yoga versus walking on mood, anxiety, and brain GABA levels: A randomized controlled MRS study. *The Journal of Alternative and Complementary Medicine, 16*, 1145–1152. doi:10.1089/acm.2010.0007

Surwit, R. S., Pilon, R. N., & Fenton, C. H. (1978). Behavioral treatment of Raynaud's disease. *Journal of Behavioral Medicine, 1*, 323–335. doi:10.1007/BF00846683

Swanson, K. S., Gevirtz, R. N., Brown, M., Spira, J., Guarneri, E., & Stoletniy, L. (2009). The effect of biofeedback on function in patients with heart failure. *Applied Psychophysiology and Biofeedback, 34*, 71–91. doi:10.1007/s10484-009-9077-2

Synovitz, L. B., & Larson, K. L. (2012). *Complementary and alternative medicine for health professionals: A holistic approach to consumer health*. Burlington, MA: Jones & Bartlett Learning.

Tahiri, M., Mottillo, S., Joseph, L., Pilote, L., & Eisenberg, M. J. (2012). Alternative smoking cessation aids: A meta-analysis of randomized controlled trials. *The American Journal of Medicine, 125*, 576–584. doi:10.1016/j.amjmed.2011.09.028

Tait, P. A., Vora, A., James, S., Fitzgerald, D. J., & Pester, B. A. (2002). Severe congenital lead poisoning in a preterm infant due to an herbal remedy. *The Medical Journal of Australia, 177*, 193–195.

Tan, G., Hammond, D. C., & Gurrala, J. (2005). Hypnosis and irritable bowel syndrome: A review of efficacy and mechanism of action. *American Journal of Clinical Hypnosis, 47*, 161–178. doi:10.1080/00029157.2005.10401481

Tang, W. H. (2007). Clinical observation of auricular therapy and head massage on treatment of 53 patients of insomnia. *Hunan Journal of Traditional Chinese Medicine, 31*, 23.

Targ, E. (1997). *Evaluating distant healing: A research review. Alternative Therapy Health*, 3, 74–78.

Tataryn, D. J. (2002). Paradigms of health and disease: A framework for classifying and understanding complementary and alternative medicine. *The Journal of Alternative and Complementary Medicine, 8*, 877–892. doi:10.1089/10755530260511874

Teasdale J. D., Segal Z. V., Williams J. M. G., Ridgeway V. A., Soulsby J. M., & Lau M. A. (2000). Prevention of relapse/recurrence in major depression by mindfulness-based cognitive therapy. *Journal of Consulting and Clinical Psychology, 68*, 615–623.

Tekur, P., Nagarathna, R. R., Chametcha, S. S., Hankey, A., & Nagendra, H. R. (2012). A comprehensive yoga programs improves pain, anxiety and depression in chronic low back pain patients more than exercise: An RCT. *Complementary Therapies in Medicine, 20*, 107–118. doi:10.1016/j.ctim.2011.12.009

ter Kuile, M. M., Spinhoven, P., Linssen, A. C. G., & van Houwelingen, H. C. (1996). Cognitive coping and appraisal processes in the treatment of chronic headaches. *Pain, 64*, 257–264. doi:10.1016/0304-3959(95)00135-2

Teschke, R., & Schulze, J. (2010). Risk of kava hepatotoxicity and the FDA consumer advisory. *JAMA, 304*, 2174–2175. doi:10.1001/jama.2010.1689

Thomas, J. (2011). *Biofeedback*. Retrieved from http://www.minddisorders.com/A-Br/Biofeedback.html

Thomas, K. J., MacPherson, H., Radcliffe, J., Thorpe, L., Brazier, J., Campbell, M., . . . Nicholl, J. P. (2005). Longer term clinical and economic benefits of offering acupuncture care to patients with chronic low back pain. *Health Technology Assessment, 9*, iii–iv, ix–x, 1–109. doi:10.1016/S0965-2299(99)80087-9

Thurber, M. R., Boderhamer-Davis, E., Johnson, M., Chesky, K., & Chandler, C. K. (2010). Effects of heart rate variability coherence biofeedback training and emotional management techniques to decrease music performance anxiety. *Biofeedback, 38*, 28–39. doi:10.5298/1081-5937-38.1.28

Tisserand, R. (1988). *Aromatherapy for everyone*. London, England: Penguin.

Transcendental Meditation Program. (2010a). *Maharishi Mahesh Yogi*. Retrieved from http://www.tm.org/maharishi

Transcendental Meditation Program. (2010b). *Research on meditation*. Retrieved from http://www.tm.org/research-on-meditation

Transcendental Meditation Program. (2010c). *The technique*. Retrieved from http://www.tm.org/meditation-techniques

Triano, J. J., McGregor, M., Hondras, M. A., & Brennan, P. C. (1995). Manipulative therapy versus education programs in chronic low back pain. *Spine, 20*, 948–955. doi:10.1097/00007632-199504150-00013

Tsang, K. L., Carlson, L. E., & Olson, K. (2007). Pilot crossover trial of Reiki versus rest for treating cancer-related fatigue. *Integrative Cancer Therapies, 6*, 25–35. doi:10.1177/1534735406298986

Tsao, J. C. I. (2007). Effectiveness of massage therapy for chronic, nonmalignant pain: A review. *Evidence-Based Complementary and Alternative Medicine, 4*, 165–179. doi:10.1093/ecam/nel109

Tsay, S. L., Cho, Y. C., & Chen, M. L. (2004). Acupressure and transcuteaneous electrical acupoint stimulation in improving fatigue, sleep quality, and depression in hemodialysis patients. *The American Journal of Chinese Medicine, 32*, 407–416. doi:10.1142/S0192415X04002065

Tsay, S. L., Rong, J. R., & Lin, P. F. (2003). Acupoints massage in improving the quality of sleep and quality of life in patients with end-stage renal disease [retraction in *Journal of Advanced Nursing, 67*, 923]. *Journal of Advanced Nursing, 42*, 134–142. doi:10.1046/j.1365-2648.2003.02596.x

Tubaki, B. R., Chandrashekar, C. R., Sughakar, D., Prabha, T. N. S., Lavekar, G. S., & Kutty, B. M. (2012). Clinical efficacy of *Manasamitra Vataka* (and Ayurveda medication) on generalized anxiety disorder with comorbid generalized social phobia: A randomized controlled study. *The Journal of Alternative and Complementary Medicine, 18*, 612–621. doi:10.1089/acm.2010.0778

Tuchin, P. J., Pollard, H., & Bonello, R. (2000). A randomized controlled trial of chiropractic spinal manipulative therapy for migraine. *Journal of Manipulative and Physiological Therapeutics, 23*, 91–95. doi:10.1016/S0161-4754(00)90073-3

Turk, D., Swanson, K., & Tunks, E. (2008). Psychological approaches in the treatment of chronic pain patients—When pills, scalpels, and needles are not enough. *Canadian Journal of Psychiatry, 53*, 213–223. Retrieved from http://www.ncbi.nlm.nih.gov/pubmed/18478824

University of Maryland Medical Center. (2011). *Aromatherapy: Overview*. Retrieved from http://www.umm.edu/altmed/articles/aromatherapy-000347.htm

University of Maryland Medical Center. (2013a). *St. John's wort*. Retrieved from the University of Maryland Medical Center's Complementary and Alternative Medicine Guide: http://umm.edu/health/medical/altmed/herb/st-johns-wort

University of Maryland Medical Center. (2013b). *Ginger*. Retrieved from the University of Maryland Medical Center's Complementary and Alternative Medicine Guide: http://umm.edu/health/medical/altmed/herb/ginger

Unschuld, P. U. (2003). *Huang di nei jing su wen: Nature, knowledge, imagery in an ancient Chinese medical text*. Berkley: University of California Press. doi:10.1525/california/9780520233225.001.0001

U.S. Food and Drug Administration. (1999). Food labeling: Health claims; soy protein and coronary heart disease (Health and Human Services. Final rule). *Federal Register, 64,* 57700–57733.

U.S. Food and Drug Administration. (2012). *Dietary supplements*. Retrieved from http://www.fda.gov/food/dietarysupplements/#.URKUY792QDo.email

U.S. Food and Drug Administration. (2013). *Current good manufacturing practices (CGMPs) for dietary supplements*. Retrieved from http://www.fda.gov/Food/GuidanceRegulation/CGMP/ucm079496.htm

Uslu, T., Ilhan, A., Ozcan, O., Turkoglu, D., Ersoy, A., & Celik, E. (2012). Cerebral blood flow evaluation during the hypnotic state with transcranial Doppler sonography. *International Journal of Clinical and Experimental Hypnosis, 60,* 81–87. doi:10.1080/00207144.2011.622202

Vadiraja, H. S., Raghavendra, R. M., Nagarathna, R., Nagendra, H. R., Rekha, M., Vanitha, N., . . . Kumar, V. (2009). Effects of a yoga program on cortisol rhythm and mood states in early breast cancer patients undergoing adjuvant radiotherapy: A randomized controlled trial. *Integrative Cancer Therapies, 8,* 37–46. doi:10.1177/1534735409331456

Vancampfort, D., De Hert, M., Knapen, J., Wampers, M., Demunter, H., Deckx, S., . . . Probst, M. (2011). State anxiety, psychological stress and positive well-being responses to yoga and aerobic exercise in people with schizophrenia: A pilot study. *Disability and Rehabilitation: An International Multidisciplinary Journal, 33,* 684–689. doi:10.3109/09638288.2010.509458

Vancampfort, D., Vansteelandt, K. K., Scheewe, T. T., Probst, M. M., Knapen, J. J., De Herdt, A. A., & De Hert, M. M. (2012). Yoga in schizophrenia: A systematic review of randomised controlled trials. *Acta Psychiatrica Scandinavica, 126,* 12–20. doi:10.1111/j.1600-0447.2012.01865.x

Vandenbroucke, J. P. (2001). In defense of case reports and case series. *Annals of Internal Medicine, 134,* 330–334. doi:10.7326/0003-4819-134-4-200102200-00017

van Poecke, A. J., & Cunliffe, C. (2009). Chiropractic treatment for primary nocturnal enuresis: A case series of 33 consecutive patients. *Journal of Manipulative and Physiological Therapeutics, 32,* 675–681. doi:10.1016/j.jmpt.2009.08.019

Varambally, S., Gangadhar, B. N., Thirthalli, J., Jagannathan, A., Kumar, S., Venkatasubramanian, G. G., . . . Nagendra, H. R. (2012). Therapeutic efficacy of add-on yogasana intervention in stabilized outpatient schizophrenia: Randomized controlled comparison with exercise and waitlist. *Indian Journal of Psychiatry, 54,* 227–232. doi:10.4103/0019-5545.102414

Västjäll, D., Larsson, P., & Kleiner, M. (2002). Emotion and auditory virtual environmental affect-based judgments of music reproduces with virtual reverberation times. *Cyberpsychology & Behavior, 5,* 19–32. doi:10.1089/109493102753685854

Vasudevan, M., & Parle, M. (2007). Memory enhancing activity of Anwala Churna (*Emblica officinalis* Gaertn.): An Ayruvedic preparation. *Psychology & Behavior, 91*, 46–54.

Veehof, M. M., Oskam, M. J., Schreurs, K. M., & Bohlmeijer, E. T. (2011). Acceptance-based interventions for the treatment of chronic pain: A systematic review and meta-analysis. *Pain, 152*, 533–542. doi:10.1016/j.pain.2010.11.002

Veerendra Kumar, M. H. V., & Gupta, Y. K. (2002). Effect of different extracts of *Centella asiatica* on cognition and markers of oxidative stress in rats. *Journal of Ethnopharmacology, 79*, 253–260. doi:10.1016/S0378-8741(01)00394-4

Verhoef, M. J., & Brundin-Mather, R. (2007). A national approach to teaching complementary and alternative medicine in Canadian medical schools: The CAM in UME project. *Proceedings of the Western Pharmacology Society, 50*, 168–173.

Vernon, H., Jansz, G., Goldsmith, C. H., & McDermaid, C. (2009). A randomized, placebo-controlled clinical trial of chiropractic and medical prophylactic treatment of adults with tension-type headache: Results from a stopped trial. *Journal of Manipulative and Physiological Therapeutics, 32*, 344–351. doi:10.1016/j.jmpt.2009.04.004

Vickers, A. J., Straus, D. J., Fearon, B., & Cassileth, B. R. (2004). Acupuncture for postchemotherapy fatigue: A phase II study. *Journal of Clinical Oncology, 22*, 1731–1735. doi:10.1200/JCO.2004.04.102

Visceglia, E., & Lewis, S. (2011). Yoga therapy as an adjunctive treatment for schizophrenia: A randomized, controlled pilot study. *The Journal of Alternative and Complementary Medicine, 17*, 601–607. doi:10.1089/acm.2010.0075

Von Korff, M., Ormel, J., Keefe, F. J., & Dworkin, S. F. (1992). Grading the severity of chronic pain. *Pain, 50*, 133–149.

Vuksan, V., Sievenpiper, J. L., Koo, V. Y., Francis, T., Beljan-Zdravkovic, U., Xu, Z., & Vidgen, E. (2000). American ginseng (*Panax quinquefolius L*) reduces postprandial glycemia in nondiabetic subjects and subjects with Type 2 diabetes mellitus. *Archives of Internal Medicine, 160*, 1009. doi:10.1001/archinte.160.7.1009

Wakim, J. H., Smith, S., & Guinn, C. (2010). The efficacy of music therapy. *Journal of Perianesthesia Nursing, 25*, 226–232. doi:10.1016/j.jopan.2010.05.009

Walker, S. R., Tonigan, S., Miller, W. R., Corner, S., & Kahlich, L. (1997). Intercessory prayer in the treatment of alcohol abuse and dependence: A pilot investigation. *Alternative Therapies in Health and Medicine, 3*, 79–86.

Waller, D., Dokter, D., Gersie, A., Karkou, V., Redsull, H., Sibbett, C., . . . Woodward, A. (2004). Subject benchmark statement: Healthcare programmes, Phase 2: Arts Therapy. *eResearch* (QAA 05909/04). Retrieved from http://eresearch.qmu.ac.uk/2062/1/eResearch_2062.pdf

Walton, K. G., Schneider, R. H., & Nidich, S. (2004). Review of controlled clinical research on the Transcendental Meditation program and cardiovascular disease: Risk factors, morbidity, and mortality. *Cardiology in Review, 12*(5): 262–266

Wang, H., Xiong, Q., Levkoff, S., & Yu, X. (2010). Social support, health service use and mental health among caregivers of the elderly in rural China. *Ageing International*, *35*, 72–84. doi:10.1007/s12126-009-9049-0

Wang, L. P., Zhang, X. Z., Guo, J., Liu, H. L., Zhang, Y., Liu, C. Z., . . . Li, S. S. (2011). Efficacy of acupuncture for migraine prophylaxis: A single-blinded, double-dummy, randomized controlled trial. *Pain*, *152*, 1864–1871. doi:10.1016/j.pain.2011.04.006

Wang, S. M., & Kain, Z. N. (2001). Auricular acupuncture: A potential treatment for anxiety. *Anesthesia and Analgesia*, *92*, 548–553. doi:10.1213/00000539-200102000-00049

Warrier, P. K., Nambiar, V. P. K., & Ramankutty, C. (1995). *Indian medicinal plants* (Vol. 2). New Dehli, India: Orient Longman.

Watson, J., Byars, M., McGill, P., & Kelman, A. (1993). Cytokine and prostaglandin production by monocytes of volunteers and rheumatoid arthritis patients treated with dietary supplements of blackcurrant seed oil. *British Journal of Rheumatology*, *32*, 1055–1058. doi:10.1093/rheumatology/32.12.1055

Weinmann, S., Roll, S., Schwarzbach, C., Vauth, C., & Willich, S. (2010). Effects of *Ginkgo biloba* in dementia: Systematic review and meta-analysis. *BMC Geriatrics*, *10*, 14. Retrieved from http://www.biomedcentral.com/1471-2318/10/14 doi:10.1186/1471-2318-10-14

Weinstein, E. J., & Au, P. K. (1991). Use of hypnosis before and during angioplasty. *American Journal of Clinical Hypnosis*, *34*, 29–37. doi:10.1080/00029157.1991.10402957

Weitzenhoffer, A. M., & Hilgard, E. R. (1959). *Stanford Hypnotic Susceptibility Scale, Forms A and B*. Palo Alto, CA: Consulting Psychologists Press.

Wells, R., Outhred, T., Heathers, J. A. J., Quintana, D. S., & Kemp, A. H. (2012). Matter over mind: A randomized-controlled trial of single-session biofeedback training on performance anxiety and heart rate variability in musicians. *PLoS ONE*, *7*, e46597. doi:10.1371/journal.pone.0046597

West, S., King, V., Carey, T. S., Lohr, K. N., McKoy, N., Sutton, S. F., & Lux, L. (2002). Systems to rate the strength of scientific evidence: Summary. In *AHRQ Evidence Report Summaries 47*. Rockville, MD: Agency for Healthcare Research and Quality. Retrieved from http://www.ncbi.nlm.nih.gov/books/NBK11930

West, W. (2000). *Psychotherapy and spirituality—Crossing the line between therapy and religion*. Thousand Oaks, CA: Sage.

Wetzel, M. S., Eisenberg, D. M., & Kaptchuk, T. J. (1998). Courses involving complementary and alternative medicine at US medical schools. *JAMA*, *280*, 784–787. doi:10.1001/jama.280.9.784

White, A., & Ernst, E. (2004). A brief history of acupuncture. *Rheumatology (Oxford)*, *43*, 662–663. doi:10.1093/rheumatology/keg005

Whorton, J. (2006). History of complementary and alternative medicine. In N. G. Cuellar (Ed.), *Conversations in comparative and alternative medicine* (pp. 1–8). Sudbury, MA: Jones and Bartlett.

Whorwell, P. J., Prior, A., & Faragher, E. B. (1984). Controlled trial of hypnotherapy in the treatment of severe refractory irritable-bowel syndrome. *The Lancet, 2*, 1232–1234. doi:10.1016/S0140-6736(84)92793-4

Wiese, M., & Oster, C. (2010). "Becoming accepted": The complementary and alternative medicine practitioners; Response to the uptake and practice of traditional medicine therapies by the mainstream health sector. *Health, 14*, 415–433. doi:10.1177/1363459309359718

Wilkinson, S. (1995). Aromatherapy and massage in palliative care. *International Journal of Palliative Nursing, 1*, 21–30. doi:10.1191/026921699678148345

Williams, P. D., Piamjariyakul, U., Ducey, K., Badura, J., Bolt, K. D., Olberding, K., . . . Williams, A. R. (2006). Cancer treatment, symptom monitoring, and self-care in adults: Pilot study. *Cancer Nursing, 29*, 347–355. doi:10.1097/00002820-200609000-00001

Williamson, E. (2006). Ayurveda: Introduction for pharmacists. *The Pharmaceutical Journal, 276*, 108–110.

Winkelstein, L. B. (1959). Hypnosis, diet, and weight reduction. *New York State Journal of Medicine, 59*, 1751–1756.

Winslow, L. C., & Kroll, D. J. (1998). Herbs as medicines. *Archives of Internal Medicine, 158*, 2192–2199. doi:10.1001/archinte.158.20.2192

Witt, C. M., Pach, D., Brinkhaus, B., Wruck, K., Tag, B., Mank, S., & Willich, S. N. (2009). Safety of acupuncture: Results of a prospective observational study with 229,230 patients and introduction of a medical information and consent form. *Forschende Komplementärmedizin [Research in Complementary Medicine], 16*, 91–97.

Wolsko, P. M., Eisenberg, D. M., Davis, R. B., & Phillips, R. S. (2004). Use of mind–body medical therapies: Results of a national survey. *Journal of General Internal Medicine, 19*, 43–50. doi:10.1111/j.1525-1497.2004.21019.x

Woolery, A., Myers, H., Sternlieb, B., & Zeltzer, L. (2004). A yoga intervention for young adults with elevated symptoms of depression. *Alternative Therapies in Health and Medicine, 10*, 60–63.

World Health Organization. (2002). *WHO monographs on selected medicinal plants* (Vol. 2). Geneva, Switzerland: World Health Organization.

Xia, J., & Grant, T. (2009). Dance therapy for schizophrenia. *The Cochrane Database of Systematic Reviews, (1)*, CD006868. doi:10.1002/14651858.CD006868.pub2

Xuan, Y. B., Guo, J., Wang, L. P., & Wu, X. (2007). Randomized and controlled study on the effect of acupuncture on sleep quality in the patient of primary insomnia. *Chinese Acupuncture & Moxibustion, 27*, 886–888.

Yang, C. Y., Chen, C. H., Chu, H., Chen, W. C., Lee, T. Y., Chen, S. G., & Chou, K. R. (2012). The effect of music therapy on hospitalized psychiatric patient's anxiety, finger temperature, and electroencephalography: A randomized clinical trial. *Biological Research for Nursing, 14*, 197–206. doi:10.1177/1099800411406258

Yapko, M. D. (2003). *Trancework: An introduction to the practice of clinical hypnosis.* Boston, MA: Psychology Press.

Yates, J. (2004). *A physician's guide to therapeutic massage* (3rd ed.). Toronto, Ontario, Canada: Curties-Overzet Publications.

Yim, V. W. C., Ng, A. K., Tsang, H. W., & Leung, A. Y. (2009). A review on the effects of aromatherapy for patients with depressive symptoms. *Journal of Alternative and Complementary Medicine, 15*, 187–195. doi:10.1089/acm.2008.0333

Yogayoga.com. (2011). *Kundalini yoga.* Retrieved from http://www.yogayoga.com/classes/kundalini-yoga

Yu, Z. F., Kong, L. D., & Chen, Y. (2002). Antidepressant activity of aqueous extracts of *Curcuma Longa* in mice. *Journal of Ethnopharmacology, 83*, 161–165. doi:10.1016/S0378-8741(02)00211-8

Yuan, J., Purepong, N., Kerr, D. P., Park, J., Bradburry, I., & McDonough, S. (2008). Effectiveness of acupuncture for low back pain: A systematic review. *Spine, 33*, E887–900. doi:10.1097/BRS.0b013e318186b276

Yüksel, R., Ozcan, O., & Dane, S. (2013). The effects of hypnosis on heart rate variability. *International Journal of Clinical and Experimental Hypnosis, 61*, 162–171. doi:10.1080/00207144.2013.753826

Yung, P. M., Chui-Kam, S., French, P., & Chan, T. M. (2002). A controlled trial of music and pre-operative anxiety in Chinese undergoing transurethral resection of prostate. *Journal of Advanced Nursing, 39*, 352–359.

Zeidan, F., Gordon, N. S., Merchant, J., & Goolkasian, P. (2010). The effects of brief mindfulness meditation on experimentally induced pain. *The Journal of Pain, 11*, 199–209. doi:10.1016/j.jpain.2009.07.015

Zeig, J. K. (1985). *Ericksonian psychotherapy: Clinical applications* (Vol. 2). Philadelphia, PA: Brunner-Routledge.

Zeltzer, L. K., Dolgin, M. J., LeBaron, S., & LeBaron, C. (1991). A randomized, controlled study of behavioral intervention for chemotherapy distress in children with cancer. *Pediatrics, 88*, 34–42.

Zhang, W. J., Yang, X. B., & Zhong, B. L. (2009). Combination of acupuncture and fluoxetine for depression: a randomized, double-blind, sham-controlled trial. *The Journal of Alternative and Complementary Medicine, 15*, 837–844.

Zhao, L., Guo, Y., Wang, W., & Yan, L. J. (2011). Systematic review on randomized controlled clinical trials of acupuncture therapy for neurovascular headache. *Chinese Journal of Integrative Medicine, 17*, 580–586.

Zigmond, A. S., & Snaith, R. P. (1983). The hospital and depression. *Acta Psychiatrica Scandinavica, 67*, 361–370. doi:10.1111/j.1600-0447.1983.tb09716.x

Zimmerman, J. (1990). Laying-on-of-hands healing and therapeutic touch: A testable theory. *BEMI Currents: Journal of the BioElectroMagnetics Institute, 2*, 8–17.

INDEX

Boelens, P. A., 126–127
Bone fractures, hypnosis for, 75
Botanical Research Centers Program, 157
Botanicals (herbs), 155. *See also* Herbals
    in Ayurveda, 256–258, 260
    defined, 17
    historical use of, 157
Boulanger, K., 215, 221
Boundaries, as ethical issue, 25–26
Boundaries of Competence (Standard 2.01a), 23
Bowden, D., 243–246
Boyer College of Music and Dance, Temple University, 117
Brahmi, 257–259
Braid, James, 74
Brain
    acupuncture and changes in, 136–137
    and hypnosis, 76
    meditation and changes in, 65–66
    yoga and altered chemistry of, 92
Brainwave states
    and ADHD, 56
    and depression, 54
    differentiating between, 47
    and meditation, 65
    and Reiki, 242
    and substance abuse, 55
Bräuninger, I., 233
Breast cancer
    hypnosis for, 75, 77, 79
    massage therapy for, 218
    yoga for, 96–97
Breathing
    deep, 6
    slow, 55
Bresee, C., 218, 219
Breteler, M., 56
Breuer, Josef, 74
Breuner, C. C., 99–100
Bronfort, G., 201
Brooks, M. Z., 215, 221
Brown, M. A., 99–100
Bruscia, K. E., 106
BSIs (biologically reactive intermediates), 159–160
Burke, A., 148

Burnout, hypnosis for, 77
Byars, M., 159

CAM. *See* Complementary and alternative medicine
Cancer. *See also* Chemotherapy side effects; *specific types of cancer*
    dance movement therapy for, 234
    and garlic, 167
    hypnosis for, 75
    massage therapy for, 218, 222
    spirituality and prayer for, 124–126
Cancer-related fatigue (CRF)
    acupuncture for, 139, 142–143
    herbals and biologically based practices for, 163
    Reiki for, 248
Cancer-related pain, acupuncture for, 139, 141–142
Cancer-related symptoms, Reiki for, 244, 246–248
Canning, S., 175
Cao, H., 143
Cardiac care, intercessory prayer and, 123–125
Carei, T. R., 99–100
Carlson, L. E., 64–65
Carmody, J., 65
Carr, C., 112
Carr, D. B., 113
Carson, J. W., 95
Catlin, A., 245
CBGT. *See* Cognitive behavioral group therapy
CBMT (Certification Board for Music Therapists), 106, 117
CCE (Council on Chiropractic Education), 206, 208
Celastrus paniculatus, 258
Centella asiatica, 258, 259
Center for Food Safety and Applied Nutrition (CFSAN), 178–179
Central American cultures, whole medical systems of, 19
Cepeda, M. S., 113
Certification Board for Music Therapists (CBMT), 106, 117
CFSAN (Center for Food Safety and Applied Nutrition), 178–179
Chace, Marian, 228, 236

Complementary and alternative
medicine (CAM), *continued*
number of hospitals offering, 223
psychologists' need for knowledge
of, 6–8
psychotherapy clients' use of, 7
research in. *See* Research in CAM
spending on, 9
whole medical systems, 19–20
Complementary medicine
defined, 3–4
increasing use of, 4
Confidentiality, 27–29
Consensus Statement on Acupuncture
(NIH), 135
Consultations (Standard 4.06), 25
Cooperation With Other Professionals
(Standard 3.09), 25
Cope, S., 88
Coping skills, yoga for, 94
Coping with illness, aromatherapy for, 18
Corner, S., 128
Cost of CAM, 9
Cottone, R. R., 26
Council on Chiropractic Education
(CCE), 206, 208
Cramer, H., 98
Crawford, M. J., 111
CRF. *See* Cancer-related fatigue
Cultural background (of client), 24, 28
Cummings, M., 138
Curcuma longa, 257
Cybernetics, 47

Da Costa, C., 190–191
Dance movement therapy (DMT), 19,
227–236
common uses of, 230
contraindications and risks of, 234
defined, 228
history of, 228
integration with psychological
practice, 235
mechanism of action, 229–230
research on uses of, 230–234
resources for, 235–236
technique, 228–229
tips for, 235
Danda, D., 52
Davis, W., 117

Decision-making models, 26
Deep breathing, 6
Deep tissue massage, 212
Dementia
aromatherapy for, 186
and ginkgo biloba, 169
music therapy for, 109, 113–114
Deng, G., 142–145
Deng, G. E., 176
Depression
acupuncture for, 139–141
aromatherapy for, 185–187
Ayurveda for, 257
biofeedback for, 49, 54
CAM for, 8
cognitive impairment secondary to
treatment for, 163, 169
dance movement therapy for, 232
herbals and biologically based
practices for, 164, 178
herbal supplements for, 18
massage therapy for, 18, 218,
220–221
meditation for, 67, 68
music therapy for, 109, 111–112
Reiki for, 244–247
spirituality and prayer for, 124,
126–127
St. John's wort for, 18, 175
yoga for, 93–95
De Ridder, S., 56
Deyo, R. A., 218
Dhond, R. P., 136
Dialectical behavioral therapy, 62, 71
Diego, M. A., 188
Dietary Supplement Current Good
Manufacturing Practices
(FDA), 17
Dietary Supplement Health and
Education Act of 1994, 17
Dietary supplements, 17, 153. *See also*
Herbals
CGMPs for, 154
defined, 154
regulation of, 176–177
Dietary Supplements Labels Database,
179
Diets
special, 7, 17
whole, 156

for fibromyalgia, 52–52
with hypnosis, 76
for performance anxiety, 55
Heathers, J. A. J., 55
Hejazi Kenari, R., 93
Herbal medicine
in Ayurveda, 256–258, 260
in biologically based practices,
157, 158
Herbal Medicines Advisory Committee,
158
Herbals, 17, 153–180
for anxiety and depression, 8
common uses of, 157–158
contraindications and risks of,
176–177
definitions related to, 154–156
deleterious effects of, 17–18
early use of, 15–16
fallacious notions about, 17
history of, 157
integration with psychological
practice, 177–178
mechanism of action, 158–160
research on uses of, 160–175
resources for, 178–180
technique, 158
tips for, 177
Herbs at a Glance, 179
Herz, R. S., 184
Heuss, D., 172
Hilgard, Ernest, 74
Hinduism, 254
Hippocrates, 196, 210
Hispanics, CAM use by, 5–6
Holistic aromatherapy, 182
Hölzel, B. K., 65
Homeopathic treatments, 6
Hospitalizations, CAM use and, 6
Hot flashes
hypnosis for, 75
soy for, 174
Hot yoga, 91, 100–101
HRV. See Heart rate variability
Hsieh, Y. J., 110
Hsu, M. C., 110
Hsu, Y. Y., 110
Hull, Clark, 74
Hur, M. H., 187–188

Hypertension
aromatherapy for, 186–188
meditation for, 67, 69
Hypnosis (hypnotherapy), 73–86
common uses of, 75
contraindications and risks of, 83
definitions of, 73–74
early use of, 15–16
history of, 74–75
integration with psychological
practice, 84–85
mechanism of action, 76–77
research on uses of, 77–83
resources for, 85–86
technique, 75–76
tips for, 83–84
Hypnosis and Suggestibility
(Clark Hull), 74

IBIDS (International Bibliographic
Information on Dietary
Supplements), 180
IBS. *See* Irritable bowel syndrome
IJCEH (*International Journal of
Clinical and Experimental
Hypnosis*), 86
Illness symptoms, Reiki for, 244–245
Imamura, M., 217
Immune functioning, massage therapy
and, 219–220
IN-CAM, 31
Income, CAM use and level of, 6
Informal practice (meditation), 62
Informed consent
and awareness of treatment options, 24
covered services in, 27
as ethical issue, 27–29
Informed Consent (Standard 3.10), 27
Insight Meditation Society, 72
Insomnia
acupuncture for, 139, 143–144
aromatherapy for, 186, 188
use of CAM for, 8
Instrumental conditioning, 47
Insurance. *see* Health insurance
Integration of CAM with psychological
practice, 8–10, 30. *See also under
specific modalities*
Integrity, as ethical principle, 22
Intercessory prayer, 121, 123–126, 128

Nonmaleficence, as ethical principle, 22

Nummela, R., 72

Office of Alternative Medicine (OAM), 4

Office of Dietary Supplements (ODS), 17, 154, 157, 179

Olendzki, N., 65

Ollendick, T. H., 52

Olson, K., 247–248

Olver, I. N., 126

Omega-3 fatty acids, 159, 163, 166

Oncology Nursing Society, 39

Operant conditioning, 47, 50

Osteopathic care, 6

Osteopathy, early use of, 16

Outhred, T., 55

Outward prayer, 120

Pacemakers, biofeedback and, 56

Pain. *See also specific areas of pain, e.g.*: Low-back pain
  aromatherapy for, 186, 187
  herbal supplements for, 18
  massage therapy for, 18
  meditation for, 68–69
  Reiki for, 247–248
  yoga for, 94–96

Palmer, Daniel David, 196, 198

Pan, X., 143

Pargament, K. I., 130

Parkinson's disease
  and coenzyme Q10, 165
  hypnosis for, 75

Passive music therapy, 107, 108

Patanjali, 88

Paul, M., 54–55

Paul-Labrador, M., 69

Peniston, E. G., 54

Peniston Protocol, 5

Penman, S., 190–191

Peppermint, 163, 164, 171–173

Performance anxiety, biofeedback for, 54–55

Peripheral skin temperature feedback (TEMP), 46
  for phantom limb pain, 53
  for Raynaud's disease, 53–54
  for tension-type headaches, 51

Peterson, K. B., 203

Petrissage, 213, 214

Phantom limb pain (PLP), 49, 53

Phobias, chiropractic for, 200, 203

Physical modalities, 7

Pilkington, K., 138

Pilon, R. N., 53

Pirotta, M., 190–191

Pitta, 254

Placebo effect/response. *See also* Sham conditions (in research)
  in chiropractic PNE study, 204
  and prayer, 122
  with Reiki, 246

Plantain, 176

Plante, T. G., 129

PLP (phantom limb pain), 49, 53

PNE (primary nocturnal enuresis), 200, 204–205

Poland, R. E., 220–221

Pollini, R. A., 215, 221

Posttraumatic stress disorder (PTSD)
  biofeedback for, 54
  music therapy for, 109, 112

Powers, M. B., 66, 67

Practical Ethics for Psychologists: A Positive Approach (S. J. Knapp and L. D. VandeCreek), 31

The Practice of Aromatherapy (Jean Valnet), 182

Prakash, H., 52

Prayer, 119–120. *See also* Spirituality and prayer
  defined, 120
  intercessory, 121, 123–126, 128
  inward, 120
  outward, 120
  practice of, 121–122
  upward, 120

Prebiotics, 156

Pregnancy
  acupuncture during, 138, 146
  and aromatherapy, 189
  and massage therapy, 222
  and Reiki, 260
  yoga during, 99, 100

Premenstrual syndrome, St. John's wort for, 175

Price, L., 191

Price, S., 191

RRT (relaxation response therapy),
246–247

Samaveda, 105
SAMe, 159
Sandel, S. L., 236
Santilli, V., 200–201
Saper, R. B., 260
SCEH (Society for Clinical and
Experimental Hypnosis), 85
Schettler, P., 218, 219
Schizophrenia
acupuncture for, 139, 145
Ayurveda for, 257, 259
music therapy for, 109, 114–115
yoga for, 94, 97–98
Schmidt, G., 172
Schneider, R. H., 69
Schwartz, G. E., 249
Scott Kaiser modification, 55
Seated massage, 212, 213
Serotonin syndrome, 174
Serretti, A., 67
Shaking (in massage), 213, 215
Sham conditions (in research), 36. *See
also* Placebo effect/response
in acupuncture, 141–145
in Reiki, 245, 249
Shapiro, S. L., 64–65
Sharma, C. M., 95
Sharma, H., 257–258
Sharma, N., 95
Sherman, K. J., 148, 218
Shin, B. C., 145
Shirodhara, 258
Shore, A. G., 246
Shorter, S. M., 88
Silver, colloidal, 176
Singh, U., 99
Sklar, E., 88
Sleeping Buddha (herb), 176
Sleep problems. *See also* Insomnia
herbal supplements for, 18
Reiki for, 260
Slow breathing, for performance
anxiety, 55
Slow cortical potentials feedback, for
ADHD, 56
Smith, C. A., 140–141
Smith, D., 223

Smoking cessation
and CAM use, 6
hypnosis for, 75, 78, 80–81
Society for Clinical and Experimental
Hypnosis (SCEH), 85
Society of Psychological Hypnosis,
American Psychological
Association Division 30, 85
South American cultures, whole
medical systems of, 19
Soy, 164, 173–174
Soyka, D., 172
Special diets, 7, 17
Spending on CAM, 9
Spinal cord injury, chronic pain
with, 79
Spinal manipulations, 18, 195, 198
Spiritual assessment, 130
Spirituality
defined, 120
practice of, 122
Spirituality and prayer, 119–132
common uses of, 121
contraindications and risks of,
128–129
definitions and types of, 120
history of, 120–121
integration with psychological
practice, 129–131
mechanism of action, 122–123
research on uses of, 123–128
resources for, 131–132
technique, 121–122
Spiritual modalities, use of, 7
Sports injuries, massage therapy
for, 18
Sports massage, 212–213
Srivastava, N., 99
St. John's wort, 18, 164, 174–175
Standardized training protocols,
23–24
Stanford Hypnotic Susceptibility Scales,
74–75
Steinberg, K., 69–70
Stens Corporation, 59
Sternlieb, B., 93, 95
Stolze, H., 172
Stough, C., 259
Streeter, C. C., 92
Strehl, U., 56

Vancampfort, D., 97, 98
VandeCreek, L. D., 31
Varambally, S., 97
Vasquez, M. J. T., 223
Vata, 254, 257–258
Veritable energy fields, 19
Vernon, H., 202–203
Vibrations (in massage), 213, 215
Vipassana (insight meditation), 63
Visceglia, E., 97
Vitamins, 156
Vuksan, V., 170

Wagers, C., 249
Walco, G. A., 234
Walker, S. R., 128
Wang, L. P., 144
Wang, W., 144
Wang, X., 111
Watson, J., 159
Web of Knowledge database, 34
Weight loss, hypnosis for, 75, 78, 81
Weitzenhoffer, Andre, 74
Well-being
    hypnosis for, 77
    and intercessory prayer, 126
    massage therapy for, 18
    Reiki for, 243–245
Well-established treatments, 36
Wells, R., 55
West, W., 130–131
White, A., 135
White, A. R., 147
Whites, CAM use by, 5–6
Whole diets, 156
Whole medical systems (WMS), 19–20
    Ayurveda, 20, 253–261
    in five-domain model, 16
    Traditional Chinese Medicine, 15,
        20, 148, 182
Williams, A., 52

WMS. *See* Whole medical systems
Women, CAM use by, 6
Woolery, A., 93, 95
Wound healing, hypnosis for, 75
Wu, Y., 185
Wyshak, G., 88

Yan, L. J., 144
Yang, 20, 134, 137
Yang, C. Y., 115
*The Yellow Emperor's Classics of Internal
    Medicine*, 105, 135
Yilmaz, F. A., 110–111
Yim, V. W. C., 185, 187
Yin, 20, 134, 137
Yoga, 87–104
    in Ayurveda, 256
    common uses of, 89
    contraindications and risks of,
        100–101
    defined, 88
    history of, 88–89
    integration with psychological
        practice, 101–102
    mechanism of action, 92
    research on uses of, 92–100
    resources for, 103–104
    technique, 89–92
    tips for, 101
Yoga Movement, 104
Yoga nidra, 90
Yoga Point, 104
Yoga Resource Center, 103
The Yoga Sutras (Patanjali), 88
Yoga Vidya Gurukul, 104
Yu, Z. F., 257
Yucha, C., 53

Zeltzer, L., 93, 95
Zen meditation, brain changes from, 66
Zhao, L., 144

ABOUT THE AUTHORS

Jeffrey E. Barnett, PsyD, is a professor and the associate chair of the Department of Psychology at Loyola University Maryland. He also is a licensed psychologist in private practice, Board Certified by the American Board of Professional Psychology, and a Distinguished Practitioner of the National Academies of Practice. He has published and presented extensively on ethics, legal, and professional practice issues for psychologists and other mental health professionals. Among other awards, he received the 2009 American Psychological Association (APA) Award for Distinguished Contributions to the Independent Practice of Psychology and the 2011 APA Outstanding Ethics Educator Award.

Allison J. Shale, PsyD, is a postdoctoral fellow at *ANDRUS*, a community mental health clinic in While Plains, New York, where she works primarily with children, adolescents, and families. She has published and presented at professional conferences on the ethical and effective integration of various complementary and alternative medicine modalities into clinical practice for mental health professionals. Her other areas of interest include clinical child/pediatric psychology and ethical issues in practice.

Gary Elkins, PhD, is a professor and director of the Doctoral Program in Clinical Psychology at Baylor University. He is also the director of the Mind–Body Medicine Research Laboratory at Baylor, where he leads a team of graduate students, postdoctoral fellows, and clinical staff. In 2012, he received the Complementary and Alternative Medicine Research Investigator Award from the Society of Behavioral Medicine. Dr. Elkins is the president-elect of the Society for Psychological Hypnosis (APA Division 30) and the author of three books and over 75 articles in the areas of clinical psychology, health, and hypnosis.

William Fisher, PhD, is the author of over a dozen journal articles and book chapters. His research interests include health psychology, with a particular interest in women's health. He has presented his work at professional conferences nationally and internationally and is a recipient of the Texas Psychological Foundation's Alexander Psychobiology/Psychophysiology Award.